Courtesy of the British Museum

GARDEN SCENE

From a manuscript of the *Roman de la Rose,* Flemish illumination.   Chaucer's first long poem is a translation of the *Roman.*

PREFACE

You will find in these pages no formal lists of "works," few references to minor authors, and but little biography. I believe that the function of an Introduction to English Literature is to interest the student in the content and spirit of great books and in their relation to their times and to one another. To re-create in some measure — especially in the earlier chapters — the historical and social background; to describe as simply as possible the movements of literature— the flux of moods and modes; to forego inclusiveness for the sake of amplitude; to justify praise or blame by ample quotation; to share enthusiasms; to write, not didactically, but in the spirit of friendly talk—that is what I have aimed at. I cannot hope that I have always hit the mark. But after many years of teaching, I find my pedagogical notions reduced to a very simple *credo:* that the only thing that really matters is to persuade the student to go on a voyage of discovery for himself with his own aroused curiosity at the helm.

I am under great obligation to my wife, and to Mr. Joseph Fisher of the department of English of the University of Alberta, for reading the proof and for many helpful suggestions; for suggestions no less helpful, to Professors R. K. Gordon of the department of English and W. N. Alexander and W. G. Hardy of the department of Classics, of the University of Alberta; and to Miss Olive I. Carter of The Macmillan Company for coöperation remarkably efficient, cordial — and patient!

E. K. B.

ACKNOWLEDGMENTS

The author and publisher wish to acknowledge their indebtedness for use of copyrighted material to the following:

For "The Janeites," from *Debits and Credits*, copyright 1924 by Rudyard Kipling, and reprinted by permission of Messrs. A. P. Watt & Son, agents, and of Doubleday, Doran and Company, Inc., publishers, New York, owners of the American copyright. For use of this material we are also indebted to Macmillan & Company, Ltd., London, owners of the British copyright, and to The Oxford University Press, of Canada, owners of the Canadian copyright.

For "Mandalay," "M'Andrew's Hymn," and "Recessional," from *Rudyard Kipling's Verse: Inclusive Edition, 1885–1926*, copyright 1919 by Rudyard Kipling, and reprinted by permission of Messrs. A. P. Watt & Son, agents, and of Doubleday, Doran and Company, Inc., New York, owners of the American copyright. For use of this material we are also indebted to Messrs. Methuen & Company, London, owners of the British copyright, and to The Oxford University Press, of Canada, owners of the Canadian copyright.

For selection from J. R. Clark Hall's translation of *Beowulf*, Cambridge University Press, London.

For selections by Thomas Hardy, "Nature's Questioning," "The Darkling Thrush," "The Oxen," "Lines to an Unborn Pauper Child," "Waiting Both," "Paying Calls," "Voices from Things Growing in a Churchyard," and "Weathers," from *Collected Poems of Thomas Hardy*, published by The Macmillan Company, New York, and for selections from the works of Alfred, Lord Tennyson and Matthew Arnold.

For selections from *Gawain and the Green Knight* by Jessie L. Weston, published by New Amsterdam Book Company, New York.

For selections from *The Vision of Piers the Plowman*, translated into modern prose by Kate M. Warren, published by Edward Arnold, London.

CONTENTS

THE STORY OF
ENGLISH LITERATURE

EDMUND KEMPER BROADUS
[Ph.D., Harvard]

PROFESSOR OF ENGLISH LANGUAGE AND
LITERATURE IN THE UNIVERSITY OF
ALBERTA, EDMONTON, CANADA

NEW YORK
THE MACMILLAN COMPANY
1931

· PRINTED IN THE UNITED STATES OF AMERICA ·

ILLUSTRATIONS

"The images of men's wits and knowledge remain in books, exempted from the wrong of time and capable of perpetual renovation."

Bacon, *The Advancement of Learning*

When I would know thee, Goodyere, my thought looks
Upon thy well-made choice of friends and books;
Then do I love thee, and behold thy ends
In making thy friends books, and thy books friends.

Ben Jonson, *Epigrams*

THE STORY OF ENGLISH LITERATURE

THE STORY OF
ENGLISH LITERATURE

I

THE BEGINNINGS OF LITERATURE IN
ENGLAND

There is nothing strange or forbidding about Literature.
It is not so much a "subject" to be studied, as a thing to
be enjoyed. We enjoy interesting talk. Nothing is more
delightful than a good story well told. If it is so well told
that every sentence is clear in itself and fits naturally into
its place; if it is so well told that the characters in it become real to us; if it is so well told that we are keen to know
how the story is coming out, and, at the end, are moved to
pleasure or sympathy or a feeling that we have lived with
the people in it, then that story is the material of literature. It will be written down — so that we may enjoy it
again. It will be printed — so that many may enjoy it.
But printing and putting it between the covers of a book
do not change it into a solemn affair invented by task-
masters. Printing it merely keeps it alive.

If, again, the good talk to which we are listening turns
upon some book which we have read, or our general ideas
about people and things, or if the talker is merely telling us
about himself, his own habits and tastes and ways of thinking — that, too, if it is well done, is the material of literature. It too will be written down and printed and read.
When we see it in print, we shall call it an Essay. But it
will not have changed or become something strange to us.

3

It will still be just as natural, just as much a part of us, as if the talker-writer were there in person talking it over with us.

Even poetry itself, which may seem to us a kind of word-puzzle to be laboriously "worked out" in school, is after all only a special sort of good talk. The words will be arranged in ordered groups or lines, sometimes but not always of even length. In some poems there will be rhymes or renewals of the same vowel sound to bind the lines together and make music to the ear. But poetry does not have to rhyme. All that it really needs to make it different from prose is, first, a sort of *measure* — a *flow* of sound which, though it varies from line to line, yet renews itself in such a way that the ear welcomes it and expects its return; and second, in its subject matter, what we call Imagination — the power of the teller to make us see beauty or truth or grace or joy which we could not see for ourselves. We do not readily think of this as just a special sort of good talk, because we are so accustomed to seeing the lines of poetry all arranged and blocked off on the printed page; and yet there was a time, long before the art of printing was invented, when our ancestors were constantly *bearing* poetry without ever even writing it down — much less reading it in a book. It is with these early ancestors of ours that the story of English literature begins.

Our ancestors — we call them Anglo-Saxons — were scattered tribes, Angles and Saxons and Jutes, living along the northwestern coast of Europe from the mouth of the Rhine to the peninsula of Jutland. They spoke a language somewhat like modern Dutch. Back of their little settlements were almost impenetrable forests. In front of them was the stormy northern ocean. Much of their lives was spent on the sea in their long-oared boats, fishing or exploring or fighting. They fought with spears and swords and clubs. They protected themselves with armor and shields. When they returned from their voyages, the warriors would gather in the long frame buildings which were the centers of their tribal life, and tell stories of strange monsters that lived beneath the sea, or in the marshes and dark forests inland.

The best of these stories — perhaps mere little anecdotes to start with — would be told again and again, and, as with all good stories everywhere, would be enlarged and improved with each telling. Naturally, too, they were retold by those who could tell them best — and so each group, each Big House of warriors, came to have its own special story-teller. This story-teller was called a *scôp*, which in their language meant a Shaper or Maker of Songs. For it was in song, in a sort of chant, that these stories were told. It was true of these people, just as it is true of every people when they are only in the beginnings of civilization, that any good story seemed the better for being sung or chanted. This gave them a chance, too, to use words which might not have seemed so natural in ordinary talk, but, in song, helped to stir the imagination of the hearers. Thus the sea, so full of strange creatures, became in their songs "the seal-bath" or "the whale-path," and their long-oared boat the "sea-steed" or "the wave-house of warriors." We picture them then — these rough and hardy warriors just back from a voyage — gathered on the long wooden benches of the Big House, drinking their deep mugs of "mead," and listening by the dim light of smoking torches to the songs of the *scôp*.

These songs were their "literature"; and when, about the end of the fourth century, the Anglo-Saxons began to find their way across the sea to England, they brought with them their old habits of life, their songs of the wild country in which they had lived, their custom of gathering in the "mead-hall" of an evening to hear the *scôp* chant stories of strange adventure.

They came to Britain in little groups, a few boatloads at a time. They found a country which had already been fought over for many centuries. A people of the Celtic race had possessed it first, or at least as far back as history knows anything about it; not adventurous seafarers and fighting men like the Anglo-Saxons, but a rather dreamy and fanciful folk, who saw fairies in the British forests, and whose poets made up songs and stories about them. How long these Celts had remained in peaceful possession of the country, nobody knows; but in the first century of our era the Romans began to send expeditions into Britain. The well-trained Roman legions drove the Celts before them and for almost 400 years ruled the land and made their own civilization. They built wide roads, some of which are still trodden; they built high-walled cities, parts of whose walls still remain; they built fortifications, whose outlines may still be traced; and then they began to melt away, legion by legion, called home to defend Rome itself from invasion; and as they went, leaving fewer and fewer men to defend their cities, the Anglo-Saxon invaders came.

The Romans had been masters. To them Britain was just one of the provinces of the great Roman empire, to be ruled and used. The Anglo-Saxons were a far rougher and more uncivilized people; but they had come to stay, to make a home for themselves, not to pay tribute to some other country. Before long as they spread and multiplied, Britain became their country, Anglo-Saxon land, Angle-land, England.

We remember that they brought their old customs with

them and their stories of the country whence they came. The *scôps* still sang songs, improving on the stories with each telling, and sometimes weaving several different adventures into a long narrative. Passed on for generations by word of mouth from one *scôp* to another, these stories came at last to be written down; and one of the best of them is the poem called *Beowulf*.

Hrothgar, King of the West-Danes, is in trouble. Night after night, a terrible monster named Grendel visits Heorot, Hrothgar's mead-hall, and carries away the sleeping warriors. The young hero, Beowulf, who lives across the sea in Gothland, decides to go to Hrothgar's assistance. With fifteen companions he embarks in his long-oared vessel, his "foamy-necked floater" as the poet calls it, and sets out for Hrothgar's land. Two days' voyage brings them to the shore. In their bright armor they march up to Hrothgar's hall.

The street was stone-paven; together they went
with the path as their guide, and each war-byrnie shone,
and each bright iron ring, hard and linked by the smith
sang out in their sarks as they hied them along
on their way to the hall, in their war-harness dread.
They put up their shields, those sea-weary men,
against the house-wall, — their bucklers right hard.
Then bent they to bench, the men's byrnies rang —
their harness of war. The javelins stood,
the mariners' arms, in a heap by themselves —
ash-wood gray at the tip, for the iron-clad troop
with weapons was grave.[1]

[1] This translation, made by J. R. C. Hall (Cambridge University Press), imitates in some particulars the arrangement of Anglo-Saxon poetry. Note the interval between the two parts of the line, the frequent alliteration or recurrence through the line of the same initial letter in accented syllables, and the absence of rhyme.

The king gives them a feast; the *scôp* sings songs to entertain them; there are compliments and speeches.   Then
Beowulf and his young companions stretch out on the floor
of the hall to await the monster.   The others go to sleep, but
Beowulf watches.   Then comes Grendel.

> There streamed from his eyes
> fearful flashes, like flame to see.

He devours a sleeping warrior, biting through his "bone-
frame," drinking his blood.   He approaches the watchful
Beowulf, and a great struggle begins.   Beowulf seizes the
monster's arm.

> The fiend moved off,   the earl went too;
> the monster thought,   far off to wend,
> where'er he might   away from thence
> and gain his fen-lair, —   knew his finger's power
> was in the foeman's grip.   A sorry journey that,
> which he, the baleful fiend,   had ta'en to Heorot.

At last Grendel's arm is torn from its socket, remaining in
Beowulf's grasp.   Mortally wounded, Grendel flees to his
lair beneath the sea.

This is the end of Grendel; but now another horrid monster, Grendel's mother, begins to make away with Hrothgar's warriors.   Beowulf and his men pursue her to the "sea-
pool" in which she lives —

> The troop all sat down: then of snake-broods enow
> in the water they saw, —   sea-reptiles uncouth
> exploring the deep, —   and on the cliff-slopes
> beheld sea-monsters lie,   who as morning draws on
> often take their dread course   on the mariner's path —
> wild creatures and snakes.

Down into the pool Beowulf dives — it takes him a whole day to reach the bottom — and with a magic blade left by the giants of olden time, he hews off the monster's head. There too he finds the body of Grendel himself, and cuts off his head as well. The two heads, each so large that four men can hardly carry it, are borne to the hall, and once more Beowulf's triumph is celebrated in feasting and song.

Now at last there is peace in Hrothgar's hall. Beowulf returns to his own country, over which he rules for fifty years. And then a great fire-dragon ravages the countryside and burns the king's hall. Beowulf, an old man now, fights the dragon single-handed. The dragon is killed, but Beowulf is mortally wounded in the combat. Sorrowfully, the warriors bear the dying king to a headland, a promontory stretching out into the sea. There, when he has breathed his last, they heap a great pile of stones over his body, so high that sailors far out at sea may see and know it as "Beowulf's Mount."

There were probably many such stories told or chanted by the *scôp* to the listening warriors. Many of them, too, after being handed on by word of mouth from one generation to another, were probably committed to writing as this one was; but of these long adventure stories of very early times, *Beowulf* is the only one to be preserved. For a long time it and others like it were handed on in their original form, as stories of the ancestral land whence the Anglo-Saxons came. But as these people multiplied and spread over England, a new influence came into their lives. When the Angles and Saxons and Jutes lived in Northwestern Europe, they were pagan; but after they had been in England for a while, Christian missionaries from Rome began to come into the land. Gradually — from about the end of the sixth century onwards — the Anglo-Saxons changed their faith; and as they embraced Christianity, the tone of their literature began to alter.   The old gods — Woden, the father of the gods, Thor, the god of thunder, Freya, the mother-goddess — were forgotten; and even in a wild pagan story like *Beowulf*, passages were inserted which reflect the new belief in Christ and the newly learned story of the Bible.   Christianity too gave them new subjects for their poetry; and while, to one gathering of warriors, a *scôp* might be chanting the old story of Beowulf, another to another group would be telling the Biblical story of creation, or stirring his warlike audience with a poetic version of the overwhelming of Pharaoh's host in the Red Sea.

Meanwhile, too, a prose literature came — rather slowly — into existence.   This prose literature was chiefly associated with England's first great king — Alfred, king of the West-Saxons, who did so much to organize and to enlighten his people.   He did not write much himself; but many Latin books which would do his people good he caused to be translated into Anglo-Saxon.   To him also we owe much of the information about the Anglo-Saxons, for it was he who encouraged them to record their own doings in chronicles.

Alfred's reign, which came in the ninth century, marked the end of Anglo-Saxon power.   Gradually the scattered tribes which he had brought into unity fell apart again, and again Danes ravaged the north.   Meanwhile another and much more able people began to find their way into England.

These were the Normans.   They were really kinsmen of the Anglo-Saxons, Northmen who had at one time lived in the northwestern corner of Europe; but while the Anglo-

SCENE FROM THE DEPICTION OF THE BATTLE OF HASTINGS IN THE BAYEUX
TAPESTRY

The Bayeux Tapestry depicts the entire story of the Norman Conquest, including the arrival of Harold in Normandy (c. 1064), his taking the oath to support Duke William's claim to the English throne, Harold's coronation as King of
England, the building of the Norman fleet, the landing of the Normans at Peven-
sey, the battle of Hastings, and the death of Harold.

The original, which is 230 feet long and 20 inches wide, hangs in a room built
for it in the Public Library of Bayeux. A full-size photographic reproduction,
colored by hand, is in the Victoria and Albert Museum.

The work is generally considered to be contemporary or almost contemporary
with the events which it portrays.

SCENE FROM THE DEPICTION OF THE BATTLE

Saxons had been settling in England, these Northmen or Normen had been establishing themselves in France, in the country which, taking its name from them, came to be called Normandy. They had married French women and

OF HASTINGS IN THE BAYEUX TAPESTRY

adopted the French tongue. The blending of these hardy and warlike Northmen with the quick-minded French had produced a brilliant and powerful race, dashing in battle, gay of spirit, lovers of beauty, men of warfare and of song.

SCENE FROM THE DEPICTION OF THE BATTLE

In the first half of the eleventh century Norman knights with their glittering retinues became familiar figures in the courts of the Anglo-Saxon kings.   As the Normans grew in power under their leader Duke William, their thoughts

OF HASTINGS IN THE BAYEUX TAPESTRY

turned to conquest. In 1066 Duke William assembled a great expedition, sailed across the channel, and gave battle to the Saxon forces under King Harold at Hastings. It was a battle in which the possession of England was at stake; but it was even more than that. It was a struggle between two kinds of minds, two opposed ways of living and of thinking about life — on the one side a rugged and dogged people, content to live within their own boundaries, rough and rather grim in their mode of living and their way of thinking about things; on the other, a people ambitious, quick of mind, rich in imagination. The Anglo-Saxons grimly set their backs to Hastings hill and fought. A court minstrel led the Norman forces, tossing up his sword as he rode, and chanting the songs which the Normans loved. Probably Duke William thought only of conquest; but what he really did at Hastings was to bring into England a quality of mind which, blended with the sturdy Anglo-Saxon spirit, was to develop a great literature.

For a time, after the conquest at Hastings, this literature was wholly French. The Anglo-Saxons were a subject people. They continued to write their chronicles and their sermons in their native tongue; they spoke it among themselves; but their Norman masters paid little attention to these things. The Normans took possession of the land; built their castles and hung tapestries and paintings in them; gathered at the court of that Duke William who was now King William of England; spoke their own Norman French tongue; listened to the songs which their own minstrels sang to them or to the narrative poems which their learned clerks wrote and read aloud. Many of these songs and stories were about their own land of Normandy; but the Normans were an eager people, quick to use new things. It was not long before they discovered a rich mine of story in the country of their adoption.

We have been thinking so far of England, first as an Anglo-Saxon and then as a Norman country; but we have not forgotten that when the Anglo-Saxons came in, they found England peopled by a Celtic race. These Celts had not been destroyed; but they had been driven back into the Welsh mountains and along the western coast. A poetic and imaginative people, they had kept alive in song and story the traditions of their past; and of these traditions, the one which they cared for most was the story of a Celtic leader and king named Arthur.

There probably was a real Arthur to start with — a good fighting man who got his men together and managed for a while to stave off the attacks of the Anglo-Saxons. The Celts were few and on the whole rather cowed by their ferocious enemies; and if, as is supposed, Arthur's success gave them a good many years of peace, the feat was quite enough in itself to make his name remembered. But the Celts were what is called a myth-making people. They had a way of building up their stories and adding marvels to them, as they passed them on from generation to generation. This is what happened to the story of Arthur. First he was just a good fighting man, the leader of his tribe. Then he was a ruler, a great king of a great people, with warriors gathered round him in his great hall, and a magician, Merlin, to perform wonders in his behalf. Soon he was leading his armies abroad to conquer Europe. Then he himself became a figure of mystery, borne away at the end of his career to a magic country, whence he might come again some day to save his people. These things were not told as mere vague guesses about Arthur, mere "it-is-saids." Every story-teller, though he added details of his own invention, was as definite about it as if the whole thing had happened yesterday. Here, for example, is the way in which an English writer of a somewhat later date described the hero.

King Arthur was fifteen foote longe in the prime of his yers. His berd was somwhat flaxen, but gray in his age, and longe and very brod; his hair gray and longe, a brod full face, somewhat ruddy, a gren juell in his right eare; a thick body, well made, and a full breste; a ringe on the lyttel finger on his right hand set with rubies. He slue fifty knights with his own handes that day he was slaine. He had five thousand and more men in his last battell, and Murdred had four thousand, and all were slaine ner Glassenbury. And he was buried by Morgan le Fay in the valle of Avalen. He was buried fifteen foote depe.

This was the way in which the tale was growing when the Normans got hold of it. To them it was the material of romance, a thread on which to weave beautiful stories in verse. Their own actual life, their way of living, made a picturesque setting for these stories. These Norman conquerors lived in England as they had in Normandy under what is called the Feudal System. The ruler or king could do what he liked with all the land in his kingdom. He would give large tracts of it to his best leaders, his best fighting men, on condition that they would do military service, help him in his wars. These great lords, in turn, would parcel out their tracts to their knights, who were pledged to do military service for them. Underneath were the vassals, who worked the land and were at the beck and call of the knights. These great feudal lords built massive castles, strong against attack, in which, when there was no fighting going on, they lived luxurious lives with many servants and entertainers. But when they fought among themselves, or when the king needed them, the lord would put his armor on and take his sword and lance, and assemble his knights. They would come riding in their armor and with their swords and lances, and with their vassals, their bowmen, following them. Then they would all march together, gleaming and glittering through the forests and fields or along the highways, to the battle. Or in times of peace they would arrange tournaments, in which, as you read in Scott's _Ivanhoe_, the knights would ride full tilt against each other with their lances in rest, and the victor would be crowned by the fair ladies who watched them from the high seats round about.

It was natural for the poets who made up stories about Arthur and his followers to transform these Celtic fighting-men into just such glittering and adventurous knights as they saw around them, and to relate just such stories about them as were happening, or, in their lively imagination, could happen, in their own day.

For a while these stories were written only in Norman French, for the amusement of the court and the lords and ladies of the castles. But after a time the Anglo-Saxon language which had, so to speak, gone underground at the Conquest, began to reappear in an altered form. The cumbersome old "inflections" — alterations in the forms of words to show their relation to the rest of the sentence — began to die away. The shape of the words themselves began to change under the influence of the French, and many new words from the French came into the language. Anglo-Saxon grew into a language both simpler and richer. After a while the conquerors themselves fell into the habit of speaking this language; English was born; and by the time the Normans had lived for about two hundred years in the country, English began to take the place of French as the language of literature.

All sorts of stories in verse began now to be written in English — stories of ancient times about the siege of Troy and the wars of Alexander the Great; stories of the great French King Charlemagne and his followers — but still

12,036

the stories of King Arthur and his knights were most liked
and most often retold. A particularly interesting example
of these romances is the poem called *Sir Gawain and the
Green Knight,* composed about the middle of the fourteenth
century. It tells of a mysterious knight clad in green who
on New Year's Day rushes into Arthur's court and challenges Arthur's nephew, Gawain, to a curious experiment.
Gawain is to cut the Green Knight's head off, on condition
that the Green Knight shall return the compliment a year
later. Away goes the Knight, his head in his hands—and
only the Green Knight's forbearance saves Gawain from
paying his forfeit when next New Year's Day comes round.
The story itself cannot be fairly represented by a brief
selection; and the actual words of the poem, though easily
recognizable as English, are too different from modern
English to be readily made out; but a modernization of the
opening lines will show how the medieval poets decked the
legendary Arthur with all the trappings and usages of their
own times:

King Arthur lay at Camelot upon a Christmas-tide, with many
a gallant lord and lovely lady, and all the noble brotherhood of
the Round Table. There they held rich revels with gay talk
and jest; one while they would ride forth to joust and tourney,
and again ride back to the court to make carols; for there was
the feast holden fifteen days with all the mirth that men could
devise, song and glee, glorious to hear in the daytime, and dancing at night. Halls and chambers were crowded with noble
guests, the bravest of knights and the loveliest of ladies, and
Arthur himself was the comeliest king that ever held a court.
For all this fair folk were in their youth, the fairest and most
fortunate under heaven, and the king himself of such fame that
it were hard now to name so valiant a hero.

Now the New Year had but newly come in, and on that day
a double portion was served on the high table to all the noble

guests, and thither came the king with all his knights, when the
service in the chapel had been sung to an end. And they greeted
each other for the New Year, and gave rich gifts, the one to the
other (and they that received them were not wroth, that may
ye well believe!), and the maidens laughed and made mirth till
it was time to get them to meat. Then they washed and sat
them down to the feast in fitting rank and order, and Guinevere
the queen, gaily clad, sat on the high daïs. Silken was her seat,
with a fair canopy over her head, of rich tapestries of Tars, embroidered, and studded with costly gems; fair she was to look
upon, with her shining gray eyes, a fairer woman might no man
boast himself of having seen.

But Arthur would not eat till all were served, so full of joy
and gladness was he, even as a child; he liked not either to lie
long, or to sit long at meat, so worked upon him his young blood
and his wild brain. And another custom he had also, that came
of his nobility, that he would never eat upon an high day till he
had been advised of some knightly deed, or some strange and
marvellous tale, of his ancestors, or of arms, or of other ventures.
Or till some stranger knight should seek of him leave to joust with
one of the Round Table, that they might set their lives in jeopardy,
one against another, as fortune might favour them. Such was the
king's custom when he sat in hall at each high feast with his noble
knights, therefore on that New Year tide, he abode, fair of face, on
the throne, and made much mirth withal.[1]

But for a realization of how rich and varied these stories of
King Arthur and his court became during this period, it is
best to turn to two great collections of them made in later
times. One of these is the *Morte Darthur*, the account of the
life and death of Arthur and of the adventures of the knights
of the Round Table, made by Sir Thomas Malory. The
other is Tennyson's *Idylls of the King*. It is necessary to
bear in mind that these versions do not belong to the period

[1]This modernization — or paraphrase — is by Miss Jessie L. Weston, *Gawain and the Green Knight* (New Amsterdam Book Co., N. Y., 1900).

of which we are speaking.   Malory wrote the *Morte Darthur* in the late fifteenth century; Tennyson, the *Idylls* in the latter half of the nineteenth century.   Both Malory and Tennyson, of course, colored the stories to suit themselves and the time in which they wrote; but both followed pretty closely the plots which these Anglo-Norman and early English poets had invented.   Because the Anglo-Norman and the early English are difficult to read, it is to these two collections that you will turn.   In them you will hear of how the young Arthur found a sword imbedded in a rock and, drawing it forth when all others had failed, showed that he was destined to be King; of the magic that Merlin did; of Arthur's great hall, bravely decked with shields, where his knights gathered; of the Round Table which became a symbol of unity among the knights, pledged to work together for all good causes; of the tourneys that they fought to show their courage; of Lancelot the bravest of the knights and Galahad, the purest; of Guinevere, Arthur's Queen, and of Elaine, whose sleeve Lancelot bore as a pennon in the tournament; of how the knights went forth to find the Holy Graal, which only the pure in heart could see, and how Galahad saw it; and of how at last when the organization of the Round Table was breaking up, Arthur fought a great battle with the rebels and was sorely wounded; and of how, as he lay near to death, Arthur caused the sword Excalibur to be cast into the lake where the spirits took it to themselves again; and of how at last came three queens in a stately barge to bear the King to the mystic country of Avalon.   All of us like adventures — specially with a touch of magic.   It would be hard to find anything in modern fiction more delightful than these stories which Malory has reset in flowing prose and Tennyson in musical verse.

Following the thread of these Arthurian stories has carried us almost to the point where modern English literature — the literature which Chaucer started — may be said to begin. It must not be thought that these narratives of knightly adventure were all that the poets wrote in the period just preceding Chaucer. There were charming little poems about nature. There were long histories of England written in verse. There were religious poems in which we are told how knights devoted themselves to the service of their spiritual queen, the Virgin Mary. And when we reach the threshold of Chaucer's time we find one especially famous poem called *Piers Plowman*, attributed to William Langland, a native of Shropshire and a clerk of the Church in minor orders, in which the hero is no knight at all, but only a humble plowman who sees in a vision the way to serve God and his fellowmen. As with *Gawain and the Green Knight* the vocabulary is just different enough from modern English to be somewhat difficult to follow; but here is a prose-rendering of the opening lines:

In a summer season when the sun was warm, I clad me in clothing as a shepherd, in the habit of a hermit unholy of works, and I went far and wide through the world to hear the wonders. But on a May morning on the Malvern Hills, a marvellous thing befell me; methought it was of faery. I was outwearied with wandering, and went to rest down by a broad bank beside a burn, and as I lay there leaning, and looked in the water, it sounded so merrily that I slipped into a slumber.

Then I dreamed a marvellous dream: that I was in a wilderness, I wist not where, and as I looked on high, into the East toward the sun, I saw a tower upon a hill wonderfully wrought. There was a deep dale below, and therein a dungeon with deep and dark ditches, and dreadful to look at. A fair field full of folk I found betwixt the dale and hill, with all manner of men, the mean and the rich, working and wandering as the world requireth. Some put themselves to the plough and full seldom played. They laboured full hard in planting and in sowing, and won what wasters destroy with their gluttony. And some held to pride, and thereafter apparelled themselves and came quaintly bedecked with show of clothing.[1]

All the England of his time, the author of *Piers Plowman* sees in his vision — the rich and the poor, the oppressors and the oppressed, the hypocrites and the good folk — all needing the lesson and the example that Piers the Plowman sets them, that if they would make a better England, honest labor and serviceableness are the only way to make it.

As in the next chapter we shall see the life of fourteenth-century England through Chaucer's eyes, it will be interesting before we leave *Piers Plowman* to catch a glimpse of the life of fourteenth-century England as Langland saw it. It takes (in the trite old saying) all sorts of people to make a world. The shabby and sordid and mean people whom Langland wanted to put to shame; the varied types, the representatives of this class and of that, whom Chaucer watched with an amused eye and drew with such deft touches; Glutton guzzling in his miserable tavern; and the Knight and the Squire and the Prioress and the Monk and the rest whom, in the next chapter, we shall see gathering at the Tabard Inn: all have their place in the picture. Here, then, are some of the fourteenth-century folk who live in Langland's pages:

Now Glutton goeth to shrift, and betaketh him churchward to show his sins. But Beton the brewster bade him good-morrow, and with that asked him, Whitherward would he?

---

[1] This and the following selections are from *The Vision of Piers the Plowman,* translated into modern prose by Kate M. Warren, Edward Arnold, London.

"To Holy Church," quoth he, "to hear mass, and afterwards I will be shriven and sin no more."

"I have good ale, gossip," said she: "Glutton, wilt thou try it?"

"Hast thou at all in thy store any hot spices?"

"I have pepper and seeds of paeony," quoth she, "and a pound of garlic, and a farthing's-worth of fennel seed for fasting days."

Then goeth Glutton in and great oaths after him; Cis the shoe-maker sat on the bench, Wat the warrener and his wife also, Tim the tinker and twain of his prentices, Hick the hackneyman, and Hugh the needle-seller, Clarice of Cock Lane, and the clerk of the church, Daw the Ditcher, and a dozen others; Sir Piers of Pridie and Pernel of Flanders, a fiddle player, a ratter, a sweeper of Cheap, a ropemaker, a riding-man, and Rose the dishmaker, Godfrey of Garlickhithe and Griffin the Welshman, and many old-clothes-men; and early in the morning, with brave cheer, they gave Glutton good ale for fellowship.

Then Clement the cobbler cast off his cloak, and put it for sale at the New Fair; Hick the hackneyman threw down his hood and bade Bat the butcher be on his side. There were chapmen chosen to value these wares; whoso hath the hood should have amends for the cloak. Two rose up quickly and whispered to-gether, and apart by themselves appraised these pennyworths; and they could not in their conscience agree aright till Robin the roper arose for the truth, and named himself umpire to settle the bargain between the three, that there should be no debate. Hick the hostler had the cloak, in covenant that Clement should fill the cup, and have Hick the hostler's hood, and hold himself con-tent; and whoso first repented it should then rise up and pledge Sir Glutton in a gallon of ale. There was laughing and louring, and they cried "Let the cup go round," and so they sat till even-song, and at times they sang, till Glutton had gulped down a gallon and a gill.

He could neither step nor stand until he had his staff, and then he went like a gleeman's dog, sometimes aside, and sometimes behind, as one who layeth nets to catch fowl. And when he drew nigh the door then his eyes grew dim, and he stumbled on the threshold and fell to the ground. . . . With all the woe in the world his wife and his daughter bear him home to bed and put him therein; and after all this excess he had a fit of sloth, so that he slept Saturday and Sunday till the sun went down. Then he awoke from his slumber, and the first word he said was, "Where is the bowl?" Then his wife upbraided him for his wicked living, and also Repentance rebuked him thus: "Thou hast wrought evil in thy life, in words and works, shrive thee therefore and be ashamed thereof, and declare it with thy mouth."

"I, Glutton," said the man, "confess me guilty: that I have trespassed with my tongue I cannot tell how often; sworn 'God's soul' and 'So God and halidom help me' when there was no need, nine hundred times; and have overeaten me at supper and sometimes at dinner, so that I, Glutton, threw it up before I had gone a mile, and spilled what might be saved and spent on some hungry one; I have both eaten and drunken overdelicately on fasting days, and at one time sat so long there that I slept and ate together. For love of idle tales in taverns, and to drink the more, I dined, and hied to the meat before noon on fasting days."

"This open confession," said Repentance, "shall be for merit to thee."

And then Glutton began to weep and make great mourning for his wicked life that he had lived, and vowed to fast; "Neither for hunger nor thirst shall fish on Friday pass within me till Abstinence, my aunt, hath given me leave; and yet have I hated her all my lifetime."

II

CHAUCER AND HIS TIMES

In this chapter we are to get a glimpse of fourteenth-century England through Chaucer's eyes. What Chaucer saw — or at least what he chose to record — is by no means all the story. Between the Conquest and Chaucer's time, Saxon and Norman had been gradually blending into one fairly homogeneous people. The kings of England had gradually become, not Norman, or French, but English kings. The people had come to look upon themselves, not as belonging primarily to this or that feudal lord, but as subjects, all together, of their English king. They had made the discovery that as a people they had rights of their own and by acting together could enforce them. In the thirteenth century they had wrested from King John the bill of rights called *Magna Carta*. In the early fourteenth century the elected representatives of the people, who constituted the "parliament," and who acted with the king in making laws, were strong enough to depose King Edward II. In the last year of Chaucer's life, parliament deposed King Richard II. The political strife of which such incidents are typical does not get into Chaucer's picture. Nor does the growing unrest of the lower classes concern him. Grinding poverty, oppressive taxation, the destitution wrought by war and by the great plague called the Black Death which swept over England in 1349, the great peasant rebellion headed by Wat Tyler in 1381, do not tempt Chaucer's pen. It is to Langland's *Vision of*

Piers Plowman (1362) with its grimly realistic picture of
the selfish luxury of the rich and the wretchedness of the
poor, that you must turn for this darker side of the picture. Nor does the intense religious unrest of the time
interest Chaucer. The central figure of that unrest was
John Wyclif (1324?–1384), whose sermons and tracts
roused the people to revolt against the luxury and oppressive authority of the church, and whose translation of the
Bible (1380), made in order that the people might read
and think for themselves, stands as the first great monument of English prose. The revolt of Wyclif and his followers caused great excitement in England and laid the
foundation for the Reformation; but as far as Chaucer is
concerned it is as if it had not been.

What did interest Chaucer was human nature and the
pageant of life. His own career gave him opportunity to sample and to see. He was born about 1340 when Edward III
was on the throne. He became a page in the household
of Lionel, Duke of Clarence, second son of the king, and
learned, like the Prioress of the *Canterbury Tales*,

> to countrefete cheere
> Of court, and been estatlich of manere.

He followed King Edward to France, was captured in the
campaign of 1359, and was duly ransomed. He returned to
take a place at court and married Philippa, a lady-in-wait-
ing to the queen. He was sent on a mission to Italy in
1372. A year after the accession of King Richard II in
1377, he went to Italy again. During the later years of his
life he held the office of comptroller of the customs in the
port of London. He saw Richard deposed in 1399. He died
during the first year of the reign of Richard's successor,
Henry IV. During this long and busy public life Chaucer

THE TOWER OF LONDON

From a manuscript of poems by Charles, Duke of Orléans, Flemish illumination. Charles's ballades and rondels, many of which were written while he was a prisoner in the Tower, were much read in England in the fifteenth century.

Upon this scene Chaucer looked as he made his "rekininges" as Controller of the Customs of the port of London. He gives us a glimpse of his work and of his leisure in *The Hous of Fame*, 11, 641–660.

found time to translate or paraphrase a French poem, the *Romance of the Rose;* to retell in English verse, with extraordinary vigor and vividness, the tale of *Troilus and Criseyde,* the material for which he borrowed from Boccaccio; to compose various other narrative and lyric poems; and at length, with his powers fully ripe, to write the *Canterbury Tales* which have made his name immortal. These purport to be tales told by a group of pilgrims on their way to the shrine of St. Thomas à Becket at Canterbury. The host of the Tabard Inn (at which they assemble for the start) decides to accompany them and persuades them to beguile the journey with stories — each traveler to tell one on the way to Canterbury and one on the way back. As there are thirty in the company, this would provide for sixty stories. In fact, the Canterbury Tales number only twenty-four — just about enough to tide them over the four days' journey to the shrine. What they did there and how they entertained one another on the way back, Chaucer leaves untold. But the long "Prologue" describing the pilgrims, the twenty-four tales, and the little prologues in which Mine Host designates the storyteller and gets him going, are enough in themselves to make up a sizable library.

That indeed was a part of Chaucer's intention in writing the *Canterbury Tales.* Printing had not been invented — manuscripts were rare and precious. The medieval scholar who was fortunate enough to have access to a variety of them, tapped this rich mine, brought together stories from every quarter, and, weaving them into some plausible connection, made a compact library of them. It was what the great Italian scholar, Boccaccio, whom Chaucer admired and imitated, had done in the *Decameron,* gathering some of his material from actual life, much of it from old French *fabliaux*, and weaving it together in the form of stories, told in turn by a group of people who have retreated to a country house near Florence to escape the plague and wish to while away the tedium of the days. So Chaucer gathers stories from many old manuscripts, adds others of his own invention, and weaves them together on the thread of this pilgrimage to Canterbury, assigning each story to the pilgrim from whose lips it would most appropriately come.

But if the stories are to be appropriate, the pilgrims themselves must of course be real people, not mere pegs to hang a story on. It is in this characterization of the pilgrims, and in giving each story just the color and tone and turn that that very pilgrim and no other would give to it, that Chaucer shows his skill and takes his chief delight. And that, and the vivid picture of the life of the times which is thus created, is *our* chief delight in the *Canterbury Tales*. So vivid is the picture, so real are the people, that I think that we cannot do better than see them through Chaucer's eyes. Chaucer imagines himself as one of the pilgrims on that Canterbury journey. We, I think, may claim the same privilege, and as we proceed to join them may pick up a few general impressions on the way.

The first thing, certainly, that will strike us is that manifestations of the church, of the usages and practices of religion, are everywhere. Everywhere we shall see men and women clad in garments that mark them as belonging to some organized form of religious life. Monks, lady prioresses, nuns, priests, friars, pardoners, palmers, we shall hear them called. Even the military men, the knights clad in armor, are as likely as not to belong to some religious order, or to have just come back from a religious pilgrimage to Palestine. And when we find ourselves with a merry crowd of Chaucer's people traveling along an English highway, we shall discover that all of them — knights and merchants and millers and doctors and lawyers as well as monks and nuns and priests — are going on a religious pilgrimage. What does it mean, this religious life that is everywhere around us?

In England, as in all the countries of western Europe, there was only what we now call the Roman Catholic Church. England, like the other countries of western Europe, was divided into innumerable little "parishes," each of which had its priest. The daily life of the people centered in the big stone church, towering high over the little cottages of the parish. Everybody had helped to build it. Under the watchful eye of the priest, everybody contributed to its support and to the support of the Church at large. The priest, who thus had charge of the people of his parish, was himself under the authority of a bishop or overseer over a number of churches. The bishop in turn was under the authority of the Archbishop of Canterbury, and the Archbishop was the personal representative in England of the pope. As Roman Catholicism was also the state religion, that is, the king and his government were pledged to support and obey it, this meant that everybody in England had to do as the pope said. As the authority of the pope extended to many things which today would belong only to the state (the Church had its own law courts, for example) there were sometimes clashes between the authority of the pope and the authority of the king. It happened on the occasion of one of these quarrels between Church and State that the pope's representative, Thomas à Becket, was killed in his own cathedral of Canterbury. The people of England were so sorry for this deed that for many years they made pilgrimages to the shrine or burial place of Thomas in Canterbury Cathedral. It is on such a pilgrimage that we shall find the people going in Chaucer's *Canterbury Tales.*

But though there were occasional differences between Church and State, the close contact of the Church with the daily life of the people was never interrupted. While the parish priest stood always nearest to them, there were many other churchmen who played a part in their daily lives. Scattered about through England were buildings called monasteries, where groups of monks lived together. Many of these monastic organizations owned large estates, on which many peasants worked, and from which the monasteries derived considerable income. The word monk means "solitary" or "living alone," and the men who lived in the monasteries were supposed to be thus provided for in order that they might devote their time to religious services and religious contemplation. Many did live in this way and were full of good works for the community besides; but not a few were worldly and preferred to ride about having a jolly time. We shall meet a monk among Chaucer's pilgrims who would rather go hunting any day in the week than stay cooped up in a monastery. But worldly or pious, the monks were a very important part of the community, whether for the small farmer who paid his annual rental into their coffers, or for the sick man, rich or poor, to whom they gave lodging and medicine, or to the wayfaring knight whom they cheerfully entertained.

In addition to the occasional "monk out of his cloister," the English highways were full of friars of the "mendicant orders." These friars (the name itself means "brothers") were members of great brotherhoods which had spread all over western Europe and England. They wandered about from place to place, living on whatever people gave them, and preaching (somewhat as the Salvation Army does today) to any who would listen. Gray friars, black friars, white friars, the color of their long gowns marking the order to which they belonged, they were everywhere,— dropping in at a cottage for a meal, playing a fiddle for the village boys and girls to dance by, performing a marriage here, and listening to confession and giving absolution there. Chaucer's friar, certainly, is a merry fellow.

> Ful swetely herde he confessioun
> And plesaunt was his absolucioun;
> He was an esy man to yeve penaunce
> Ther as he wiste to han a good pitaunce;
> For unto a povre order for to yive
> Is signe that a man is well y-shrive.[1]

Priests and friars everywhere; and here and there a monk out of his cloister; and here and there, also, though perhaps not quite so frequently, a nun out of her nunnery. For there were religious orders of women, as well. The nunneries, like the monasteries, were surrounded by broad lands which pious persons had given for their support. Even more than the monks, the nuns were supposed to spend their time within their own place; but they too were sometimes worldly and liked to ride abroad. Many of them were gentlefolk who had been placed in the nunneries when they were young girls. However earnest they might be in their desire to lead a religious life, they would tire occasionally of the formal exercises and frequent prayers. Daughters of gentlefolk, they had well-to-do relatives whom they would get permission to visit when they could.

---

[1] It is easy to catch the rhythm of Chaucer's lines if we remember that final *e* is pronounced as a distinct syllable. *To yeve* and *to yive* both mean to give. *Ther as* means whenever. *To han* is to have. *Pitaunce* is the older form of pittance — a small gift. *Wiste* means knew. *Y-shrive* means shriven — purged of sin.

The prioress or head of the nunnery, especially, could find all sorts of excuses to get away; for the nunneries held large properties and she was business manager as well as overseer of the nuns. But even better than a business errand as an excuse was an occasional pilgrimage. It is true that the bishop frowned on any excursion for the nuns; but after all a pilgrimage, even if it was a bit of a picnic, was a pious journey. We shall not be surprised if we find a lady prioress and a nun or two among Chaucer's pilgrims to Canterbury.

What with prioresses and nuns and monks and priests and friars, and summoners haling delinquents before the church courts, and pardoners selling pardons "hot from Rome," we shall meet with the life of the Church at every turn. And at every turn, also, we shall encounter another phase of medieval life that it will be equally worth our while to stop to think about, before we join Chaucer's pilgrimage. These knights in chain mail, riding gayly caparisoned horses or proceeding more soberly in plain doublets rust-stained from armor recently doffed — what do they mean in the life of the time? We remember the part that the knight played in the feudal system — holding his lands in fief to his feudal lord, and ready to gather his vassals about him to do battle for his lord or for the king. We remember too that he is the central figure of the romantic literature of the time. So completely, indeed, does he fill the imagination of these story-tellers that even if they are writing about a King Arthur who lived back in the sixth century, or of some adventure of Alexander the Great in the fourth century, B.C., or of the Biblical King David,[1] they will still people their story with knights.

[1] "For David in his day dubbed knights and made them swear on their sword to serve Truth for ever."   *Piers Plowman*, Passus I.

Further, we may see, not only in the romantic stories about knights but also in such a plain and homely commentary on the life of the times as *Piers Plowman*, that it is the duty of the knight "to guard Holy Church" and that "the profession that pertaineth to knights" is to observe the truth of Christ and to "ride through the kingdoms and take trangressors [against the truth] and bind them fast."

It would seem from these things that knighthood, like the Church, touches the life of the time on many sides; and if we turn to the description which Chaucer gives us of the knight who took part in the Canterbury pilgrimage, we shall find the whole thing put in a nutshell. We discover that Chaucer's Knight has fought against the Moors and against the Turks, that he has been in Africa, in Egypt, in Russia, that he has taken part in fifteen great battles. Chaucer sums up for us in very few words the most important things in this adventurous life. The Knight was worthy "in his lordes werre"; he fought "for our feith"; he

> loved chivalrye
> Trouthe and honour, fredom and curteisye.

It was probably the king who "dubbed" our Knight[1] in reward for some brave deed. Thereafter, a knight was ready to gather his yeomen about him and lead them in "his lord's wars." But the ceremony of knighting was itself deeply religious. "In the name of God and of St. George, I make you knight," was the common formula at the dubbing; and dubbing was often accompanied by vigils and vows. Service to the feudal lord and service "for our faith" were

---

[1] That is, performed the ceremony of conferring the rank of knighthood upon him. The candidate knelt, the conferrer touched him upon the shoulder with the sword-blade. Knighthood was conferred by the king, or on occasion by a high official personage, or by the commander of an army on the field of battle.

blended. Thirty years after the Conquest, when Jerusalem, the Holy City, had been captured by the Turks, knights gathered from all over the Christian world to make the long journey to Jerusalem and recapture it for Christianity. This, the first "Crusade," as it was called, was followed by many others; and though the great Crusades had come to an end before Chaucer's day, the spirit of them still prevailed. A "worthy" knight always aspired to the two great adventures — to fight against the pagans "for the faith," and to make a pilgrimage to the Holy Sepulchre. Often, too, the knight became a member of a religious order, a fraternity of knights vowed to special forms of service for the faith.

And along with these things, the Knight "loved chivalry." Although Chaucer devotes only thirty-four lines to the description of the Knight, and spends most of them in enumerating the places where he fought, the ideal of "Chivalry" becomes abundantly clear. To protect the weak, to rescue the downfallen, to prefer the greater risk, to give the foe every advantage for the greater glory, to be unswervingly truthful and unfailingly courteous to friend and foe alike — these things our Knight practiced in his daily life, in the formal challenges of tournaments and in the helter skelter of battle. And because he had practiced these things and because he had (see how Chaucer hammers it in with negatives)

> never yet ne vileinye[1] ne sayde
> In all his lyf, unto no maner wight,[2]

he was, Chaucer says

> a verray parfit gentil knight.

---

[1] coarseness, rough or unseemly language.
[2] no kind of person.

It is often said that the poetry of chivalry — the old romantic tales of knights who spent their lives in fulfilling vows, in challenging chance-met foes, and in rescuing fair ladies — bears no resemblance to the real life of the time. It is quite true that the poets gave free rein to their imagination. It is equally true that the "hallowed accolade"[1] worked no spell to make a bad man good or an average man superhuman. Coarseness and cruelty and meanness and selfishness were at least as common in the fourteenth century as they are now. But Chaucer was a pretty shrewd observer of human nature and not given to exaggeration. He meant to make each of his characters a true representative of the class to which he belonged. Even a verray parfit gentil knight had to be convincing to the readers of his own day who knew what knights were really like. And so, even when we turn to such a modern poet as Tennyson (who dressed the Arthur stories up to suit himself), and read of how Arthur bound his knights

> To break the heathen and uphold the Christ,
> To ride abroad redressing human wrongs,
> To speak no slander, no, nor listen to it,
> To honour his own word as if his God's,

we can recall Chaucer's Knight and feel that the romance and the reality were after all not too hopelessly far apart.

But in our need to stop and think about these knights and monks and nuns and priests and friars, at once so representative of their own time and so different from our own, we have not yet found ourselves in the very midst of Chaucer's company. We remember that they are all going together on a pilgrimage to Canterbury. Feeling sure that they will make their start from London, we

---

[1] the formal stroke with the flat of the sword-blade upon the shoulder when the knight was "dubbed."

naturally "happen" there. As we wander along the "Chepe," watching the stalls crowded with buyers, the aldermen in their gowns of velvet lined with fur, the young squires in their gayly broidered coats, the women in their fine kerchiefs and scarlet stockings, their girdles barred all of silk, their white smocks "broidered all before," we hear it said that the pilgrimage will start tomorrow from the Tabard Inn in Southwark. Why not spend the night there and be all ready for the start?

We make our way down to the Thames, and through the tunnel-like passage of London Bridge, between houses that rise from the bridge piers and meet above our heads. When we come out at the south end we see hundreds of carts, hurrying back to farmhouses in Kent and Surrey, after disposing of their produce in the city. We find ourselves on High Street and there, projecting from a roomy house of timber-work, is a creaking sign, with a gaudy sleeveless cloak painted upon it. Here is the Tabard and at the door stands Host Harry Bailey

> A large man he was with eyen stepe,[1]
> A fairer burgeys[2] is ther noon in Chepe;
> Bold of his speche, and wys, and wel y-taught
> And of manhod him lakkede right naught.

At his hearty invitation we enter under an archway and find ourselves in a paved court inclosed on all four sides by the two-story frame structure of the inn. We see that there is an open gallery overlooking the court from the second story, and decide to go up, and watch for new-comers. Some one is ahead of us — a short fat man, seated on a bench, with his elbows on the gallery railing. He has a paunch as round as Harry Bailey's own, but his

[1] bright eyes.　　　　[2] burgess.

eyes, unlike mine host's, have a dreamy look as if he were repeating to himself a rhyme he "lerned longe agoon." He tells us that he is an officer of the Customs, but that the government has just granted him an assistant, a deputy, and that he is going to have a little holiday. He too is going to watch the pilgrims assemble and if they appeal to him he will join them on the pilgrimage to Canterbury. It has just dawned on us that this must be Chaucer himself, when the pilgrims begin to come in.

One — two — three — we count, and they keep coming until they have filled the courtyard. "Wel nyne and twenty," Chaucer estimates; so many, indeed, that we get only a confused impression of color-play, of many-hued gowns and doublets, jingling of bridles, babel of talk. They dismount; and hardly has the last horse been led away by the busy hostlers, before the tooting of Harry Bailey's horn summons us all to supper.

A big caldron is simmering on a fire of fagots in the open courtyard; and on an open hearth in the center of the room where the guests assemble is another steaming caldron with the smoke from its fire billowing out on all sides and rising to the rafters. Around the room are boards laid on trestles. Little boys come running in with basins and towels, and after we have laved our fingers (for we have no forks and are all going to dip our fingers into the dishes together) we take our seats back of the trestle-boards facing toward the center of the room. And then waiters bring in the big covered dishes, some already filled, some to be filled with smoking meats from the caldron — and the meal is on.

It is not an easy crowd to satisfy. There is the Summoner, for example, who loves "garleek, oynons, and eek leeks." There is the Monk —

A fat swan loved he best of any roost.

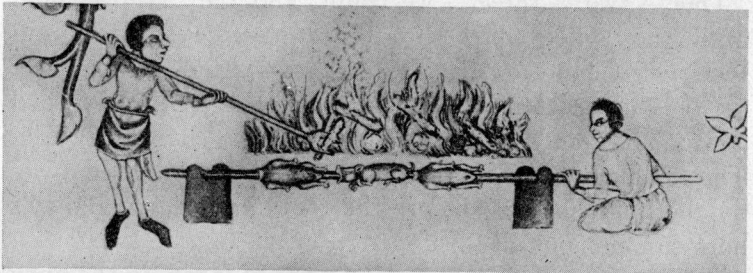

"Greet chere made our hoste us everichon,
    And to the soper sette us anon;
    And served us with vitaille at the beste."

(Scenes from the Louterell Psalter. This psalter was executed about 1340 for Sir Geoffrey Louterell, and decorated with drawings illustrating contemporary life and manners.)

There is the Prioress who has brought her little pet dogs along and wants them fed

> With rosted flesh, or milk and wastel-breed.[1]

Especially there is the Franklin who keeps his own larder at home so well supplied that

> It snewed[2] in his hous of mete and drinke
> Of alle deyntees[3] that men coude thinke,

and who could make it very unpleasant for his own cook

> but-if his sauce were
> Poynaunt and sharp, and redy al his gere.[4]

But Harry Bailey's supper, what with larded boar's head, roasted rabbit, "pestles" (legs) of pork, roasted chickens, and a "flampoynte" of chopped pork and grated cheese baked in a crust of dough, is voted by everybody

> vitaille at the beste.

And when it is added that

> Strong was the wyn, and wel to drink us leste,

there is obviously not a word of criticism to be said.

But now dinner is over, the boards are lifted, the trestles are removed, all of us pay our "rekininges"— and then mine host has an idea. Why, he says, shouldn't he leave the Tabard in his wife's hands and go with us? *She* can manage. "Why," he says,

> "whan I bete my knaves
> She bringth me forth the grete clobbed staves
> And cryeth, 'slee the dogges everichoon,[5]
> And brek hem, bothe bak and every boon;'

---

[1] cake-bread. [2] snowed. [3] dainties.
[4] utensils. [5] kill the dogs everyone.

and when I fail to suit her — 'By corpus bones,' she cries,

> 'I wol have thy knyf
> And thou shalt have my distaf and go spinne.'

She can manage the Tabard and I'll go to Canterbury with you. Besides, I've just thought of a pleasant plan. As we go, let each of us tell a story. I'll be manager, if you like, and call on each in turn. And when we get back to the Tabard, the one who has told the best story

> Shal have a supper at our aller cost [1]
> Here in this place, sitting by this post."

We are for it, one and all. But there is not much time to talk. Dusk is near and we must to bed.

It is a wonder that there should be room for all of us, and for all of the horses too; but the rooms and the stables are wide. The Prioress and her chaplain nun, and the Knight and his young son, the Squire, get the two best rooms. Through an open door, we catch a glimpse of the Knight's bed, a big four-poster affair with curtains around it, and a wooden bench about half the height of the bed itself projecting along one side. Already the Knight is seated there unlacing his doublet, and beside him is the young Squire, admiring his curled locks in a round mirror of polished steel. Fastened to the foot of the bed we notice too a "hutch" or wooden locker, where the Knight if he chooses can put his gold signet ring and the Squire his embroidered cloak for safe-keeping. Our own chamber is not so comfortable. Great bags or mattresses of straw are thrown upon the floor and blankets are spread upon them. Near us is a pilgrim who has bibbed so much ale

> That as an hors he snorteth in his sleep,

---

[1] paid for by the rest of us.

and through the thin partition we can hear the Squire singing to himself so persistently that it would seem as if he slept

> Namore than dooth a nightingale.

There are other things too that make us restless — trials which are no mystery to one of our fellow sufferers when he wakes us next morning:

> What eyleth thee to slepe by the morwe?[1]
> Hastow had fleen[2] al night?

But the night is over at last and after rubbing our eyes through a six o'clock breakfast, we are away.

It is April and the morning of English poetry.

> Whan that Aprille with his shoures sote[3]
> The droghte of Marche hath perced to the rote,[4]
> And bathed every veyne in swich licour,
> Of which vertu engendred is the flour;
> Whan Zephirus eek with his swete breeth
> Inspired hath in every holt and heeth
> The tendre croppes,[5] and the yonge sonne
> Hath in the Ram his halfe cours y-ronne,[6]
> And smale fowles[7] maken melodye,
> That slepen al the night with open ye,[8]
> (So priketh hem nature in hir corages);[9]
> Than longen folk to goon on pilgrimages
> (And palmers for to seken straunge strondes)[10]
> To ferne halwes,[11] couthe[12] in sondry londes;

---

[1] What's the matter with you that you sleep into the morning?
[2] fleas.   [3] sweet showers.   [4] root.
[5] has breathed into the tender buds in every wood and open field.
[6] The "young" (or early spring-time) sun is just passing out of the sign of the Zodiac called the Ram (Aries). In other words, it is the middle of April.
[7] birds.   [8] eye.
[9] so does Nature prick (spur) them in their hearts.
[10] foreign shores.   [11] distant shrines.   [12] known.

1   3   4   5   7   9 10 11 12 13-14 15
  2   6   8   •   •   16

CHAUCER'S CANTER-

"Painted in fresco by William Blake and by him engraved and published Octo-
as represented are: 1. Reeve. 2. Chaucer. 3. Clerk of Oxenford. 4. Cook.
10. Plowman. 11. Physician. 12. Franklin. 13-14. Two Citizens. 15. Ship-
21. Friar. 22. A Citizen. 23. Lady Abbess. 24. Nun. 25-26-27. Three

And specially, from every shires ende
Of Engelond, to Caunterbury they wende,
The holy blisful martir for to seke,[1]
That hem hath holpen, whan that they were seke.[2]

And here are the pilgrims, with Chaucer to help us see
them. We ride on ahead and then stop beside the road to
watch them pass. There is our friend the Knight who has
just landed from a long voyage and who has so recently
laid aside his chain-mail that you can still see the rust-
streaks of it on his fustian doublet. He rides soberly along,

Of his port as meke as is a mayde,

---

[1] seek.   [2] sick.

but his son, the Squire, goes caracoling. The young Squire's
locks are curled "as they were leyd in presse"[1] (perhaps
that was what he was doing when we caught a glimpse of
him last night!); his short cloak with the fashionable wide
sleeves is embroidered like any meadow with flowers white
and red. He is still singing lustily, and his head is probably
full of fancies about

Gawain with his olde curteisye

and the other knights of Arthur's court, or of wild tales of
magic rings and of miraculous horses that will carry you
flying through the air. But he is going to be as worthy a

[1] as if they had been laid in a press ("love-locks," artificially curled).

knight as his father, for all that. He has already fought in France, where a war with England has been dragging on for almost a hundred years. He sits his horse well and has already shown his prowess in tournaments. Indeed, he will make just such a knight as the poets like to write about, for he can compose songs as well as sing them and whatever feats he has done so far have been

In hope to stonden in his lady grace.[1]

And there, a pace behind the Squire, is the Knight's Yeoman, clade in cote and hood of grene. He carries a mighty bow of the sort that has been winning victories for the English at Crecy and Calais, and the arrows at his belt are tipped with peacock feathers. And as if that were not enough, he has a sword and a dagger in his belt and a buckler on his arm. It is evident that there will be no meddling with the Yeoman.

And here is our friend the Prioress, with a nun from her own house and three priests attending her. What a to-do the bishop in authority over her nunnery would make if he could see her! She oughtn't, as a matter of fact, to be here at all, and she certainly oughtn't to wear that wimple up so high as to expose her "fair forheed," for that is considered very immodest in a nun. And what of her coral beads "gauded al with grene" and her big gold brooch? But perhaps she is rather too much the fine lady to care greatly what the bishop says. It is not every prioress who has learned to speak French at a fashionable school and who knows how to assume the stateliness and fine manners of the court.

Even gayer and rather less demure is this Monk riding near at hand. His coat-sleeves have a wide border of

[1] for the sake of standing well in his lady's favor.

costly fur at the wrist. His monk's hood, thrown back and leaving his bald head shining in the sun, is fastened under his chin with a broad gold pin curiously wrought. His big boots glisten in the sun and his chestnut horse, whose bridle jingles with silver mountings, is as round and glossy as the rider. A great hunter is this Monk, a lover of hawk and hound; and if you quote to him the old saw that a monk out of his cloister is like a fish out of water — "Tut, tut!" he will say; "I hold *that* text not worth an oyster!"

And not far away in the procession are other church-men — our merry Friar, with his bell-like cloak stuffed full of pins and pretty knives to give to the womenfolk. It is to be feared that he prefers the tavern to the church, and that he is a better collector of coin than of souls; but fortunately there are good churchmen too. Over there is the Parson — a simple village priest — the real rock upon which the great structure of the Church is builded. There are many all over England like him — "rich of holy thought and work," a devoted teacher of his flock, ready to travel from one end to the other of his widely scattered parish to do a service, humble in his daily walk and yet bold to reprove wrongdoers "of heigh or lowe estat." And always

Christes lore, and his apostles twelve
He taughte, and first he folwed it himselve.

Beside him rides his brother the Plowman — just such a one as the poet who wrote *Piers Plowman* dreamed of — a hard worker and one who loves God with his whole heart and his neighbor as himself. It is a good thing that this honest priest and his plowman brother joined the pilgrimage, for otherwise we might think that there are more knaves than good people among the churchmen of Chaucer's world. But Chaucer loves a laugh, and it is the rascals who are amusing.

But here come a group that will evidently give us another side of fourteenth-century life. Yonder Weaver and his friends the Dyer and the Upholsterer and the Haberdasher and the Carpenter are

> clothed alle in o Iyveree
> Of a solempne and greet fraternitee.

That "livery," that long and wide-sleeved gown, indicates that they are members of a town-gild or union of the various merchants and craftsmen of the town. Not a general on the battlefield could wear his uniform with more pride. Their gowns are richly trimmed, and their girdles and their pouches and even the knives at their belts are all decked with silver. They carry themselves with such dignity that any one of them might be an alderman — and as for their wives, if you didn't make a low bow and address them as "My Lady," they would put you to rights in no time. Not far behind this gild-group rides a portly red-faced lady who might show the weaver a thing or two, for at cloth-making she is even more expert than the Flemings or the French. She has knocked around the world a bit and seems quite able to take care of herself. The Prioress looks askance at her, for she is a rollicking loud-voiced dame. But what a touch of color she gives, with her great broad-brimmed hat, her bright silken kerchief, her stockings of "fyn scarlet red," and her shining shoes heeled with long sharp spurs! Not far from this "Good-Wyf"[1] of Bath ride two men who, like the gild-group, are making England rich. That Merchant with his Flemish beaver hat and his long forked beard is an important figure in English life.

---

[1] a woman possessing "goods" (a property-holder).

He is a merchant of "the Staple," the powerful organization for the sale of wool. He buys his wool direct from the
sheep-shearers in the Cotswolds, where it is packed in great
bales. Then it is carted to Ipswich, to the "port of Orwell"
and thence shipped to Middelburg in the Netherlands, a
"town of the Staple," where it is woven and made into
garments and so brought home again to England. There
is no love lost between the Merchant and our friends the
Weaver and Dyer, for they do not like to admit that the
Netherlanders and the Flemings can beat them at their
own game. The Merchant's companion is the Shipman,
who looks rather uncomfortable on horseback but can ride
a ship's deck with the best of them.

> With many a tempest hadde his berd been shake,

and he is rather a tempestuous old fellow himself, who will
make you "walk the plank" if he doesn't like your ways.
But he knows every harbor from Spain to the Baltic, and
wherever he can go England's trade goes with him.

There are other prosperous men in the company, too.
There is a Miller with "a thumb of gold"— a most useful
thumb when he slyly presses the scales in weighing out
the flour. There is a Reeve or overseer who manages
a nobleman's estate so skilfully that he is now grown
richer than the nobleman himself. There is our friend the
Franklin, white-bearded and red-faced, with a gleaming
dagger and a beautiful purse of white leather hanging
from his girdle. He looks cheerful, as if Harry Bailey's
dinner had agreed with him, and he is probably thinking
of his rich farm lands, and of how, as "knight of the shire,"
he will preside over the other magistrates at the district
court.

And here, to make the tale complete, come a Lawyer

and a Doctor and a "Clerk of Oxenford." You would never guess, from the homely coat the Lawyer wears, that he is such a learned man; but indeed there is not a statute, from the days of William the Conqueror down, that he cannot explain. He is a busy man too when he is at home: and he has caught the trick so useful to men of his profession of looking even busier than he is. As for the Doctor, you should hear him rattle off the names of Æsculapius and Deiscorides and all the other ancient sages that his profession swears by. The list would seem strange to us; but even stranger would seem the Doctor's doings if we should be sick and send for him. No feeling of the pulse for him. Instead —"When were you born?" he would say. "Tell me the very day and hour." Then he would consult his chart, find out what planet was in the ascendant at the hour of your birth, tell you what your chance of recovery was according to the stars, explain to you that your body was made up of four "humors," hot, cold, moist and dry,— and prescribe accordingly. If you got better, the Doctor and the stars would share the credit. If you got worse, you could blame it on the stars.

And finally, in the long procession of the pilgrims, we spy the Clerk of Oxenford. He is not much to look at. His rough homespun coat is threadbare and he seems half-starved, but he is worth thinking about. He is a part of that great university life of the Middle Ages which flows back and forth between England and the continent — students at Oxford or Cambridge drifting over to the University of Paris, students from Paris and other continental universities drifting over to Oxford or Cambridge, seeking always men who can expound the learning of the time to them, and a chance at those precious manuscripts which are the only "books" they have. And how they

value them! This Clerk, for example (who will some day
be a priest, but for the moment thinks only of his studies)
would

> lever[1] have at his beddes heed
> Twenty bokes clad in blak or reed

than any amount of fine clothes or other luxuries.   It is this
same devoted clerk and his successors during all the five
centuries and a half that have elapsed since Chaucer's time
who have preserved the life and the learning of their times in
books for us to read. What with the invention of printing,
the Clerk's "twenty bokes" have considerably multiplied
since then — perhaps rather too much for the comfort of
most of us. But just as some of the very buildings at Oxford
in which Chaucer's Clerk lived and studied are still being
lived in and studied in by Oxford students today, just so
the Clerk's candle keeps burning, and the "twenty bokes
clad in blak or reed" are still precious to each new generation of us.

But somehow the Clerk has carried us out of his time into
our own. We have not forgotten mine host's plan that the
pilgrims should tell stories by the way. They do — just
such stories as a gentil knight or a demure prioress or a
lusty miller or a merry friar or a rascally pardoner or a
studious clerk would naturally tell. If we want to read
them we must turn to Chaucer's own pages. But for us at
the moment, as we leave the pilgrims ambling along toward
Canterbury, it suffices to realize that with Chaucer's help
we have really made the acquaintance of pretty nearly
every sort of person in fourteenth-century England; and
that, as a great critic, who wrote three hundred years after
Chaucer's day, puts it: "We have our forefathers and great-

[1] rather.

granddames all before us, as they were in Chaucer's days; their general characters are still remaining in mankind, and even in England, though they are called by other names than those of monks and friars, and canons, and lady abbesses, and nuns; for mankind is ever the same, and nothing lost out of Nature, though everything is altered."

III

ENGLISH DRAMA FROM THE MIRACLE PLAYS TO THE CLOSING OF THE THEATERS

If we had accompanied Chaucer's pilgrims to Canterbury, we might have heard the Wife of Bath telling her fellow-travelers how fond she was of going

> To vigilies and to processiouns,
> To preching eek and to thise pilgrimages,
> To pleyes of miracles and mariages.

It was in "pleyes of miracles" that the English drama had its start. If we are to see these miracle plays at their best, let us imagine ourselves in the town of Wakefield in Yorkshire on the Thursday after Trinity Sunday in (let us say) the year 1390. It is Corpus Christi Day. We shall take our stand on a street corner and watch what may befall.

In spite of the fact that it is early in the morning, a crowd is already gathered. There are few folk of high degree, mostly artisans and shopkeepers in doublet and hose, with a sprinkling of Yorkshire farmers and shepherds, in for the day. Here and there is a knight of the shire or a franklin or a long-robed friar — just such a group as we saw on the Canterbury pilgrimage — except that, pressing in with the rest, are the wives and daughters of the tradespeople, decked for a holiday, with hair coiffed high in a gilded net, with rows of big bright buttons down the front of their close-fitting bodices, and with long full skirts which they gather up in wrath when a clumsy foot imperils them. There is much laughter and chatter. But the dignified

53

mayor passes with his wand of office.   "Quiet, good people,"
he says, "the scaffolds are coming."

Down the street comes an extraordinary affair on wheels.
Built on a projecting framework are two decks or floors,
the upper exposed on all sides to the public view, the lower
inclosed as a room by rough curtains or draperies.   On the
drapery is painted a vast yawning devil-mouth, with
painted flames spouting from it.   There is evidently a trap-
door between the room and the upper stage, and, as the
wagon approaches, curiously clad figures are climbing up
and arranging themselves for some kind of performance.
One, wearing a long white robe and heavy gilt girdle, and
with a enormous "chevril" or wig of golden hair, seats
himself on an improvised throne upon the stage.   "There's
God," says one of the crowd.   "Yes," says another, "'Tis
Tim the Barker,[1] and he gets three and four pence for
playing it."   But God is about to speak and there are no
more whispers among the crowd.   It is a hush of genuine
reverence, with no sense of incongruity or absurdity in this
make-believe.

And now God proclaims

> Ego sum[2] Alpha and O,
> I am the first and last also,
> Oone God in mageste;
> Marvelose, of myght most,
> Fader, and sone, and Holy Ghost,
> One God in Trinyte.

And then God acts the processes of creation, bringing light
into the world by swinging a lighted lantern, and lift-
ing up and pretending to shape little wooden images of
birds and beasts.   As God rests from his work and, rising,
moves toward the rear of the stage, Lucifer springs upon the

---

[1] a tanner, a worker in bark.   [2] I am.

throne, and appeals to the angels to rebel against God. While the angels are hesitating, Lucifer attempts to display his powers by spreading his wings and flying; but he falls plump into hell-mouth and God returns to mold Adam out of clay and from a rib taken from Adam to make Eve.[1]

The two are duly warned —

> Here thou Adam, and Eve thi wife,
> I forbede you the tre of life;

but Adam, unwisely leaving Eve, sets out

> To se what trees that here been;

Eve eats of the forbidden tree, and God expels them from the garden.

This, then, is what the wife of Bath meant by a "pleye of miracles"! Here in Wakefield, weeks before this Corpus Christi Day, the different gilds or craft-unions of the town have got together and prepared their stage and learned the simple lines which some humble clerk wrote for them, and bought their "properties," and rehearsed their parts — and now the gild of the barkers or tanners have acted before us this first chapter of the biblical story.

But this is not all. As the "creation" moves away, another stage approaches; and this time the gild of the glovers act the killing of Abel. Next comes a ship drawn on wheels. We begin by now to realize that an orderly succession of scenes and episodes from the Bible is in prospect, and we guess at once that this is to be Noah and the Ark. "Sex hundreth yeris and od," says Noah, "have I lived in grief over the sins of the world,

> And now I wax old,
> Seke, sory, and cold."

---

[1] Among the "stage properties," listed in one of the records, is a "rybbe colleryd red."

But now God appears to him, warns him of the approaching flood and instructs him to build an ark, and when all is done, "thi wife . . .

> Take in to the,
> Thi sonnes of good fame,
> Sem, Japhet and Came,
> Take in also to hame
>   Thare wifis also thre. . . .
> Noe, to the and thi fry,
> My blyssyng graunt I:
> Ye shall wax and multiply
>   And fill the erth agane
> When all thise floodis ar past" —

Noah sets to work —

> To begyn of this tree my bonys will I bend.

He moves about, describing, with each gesture, what he is doing —

> Now my gowne will I cast, and wyrk in my cote;
> Make will I the mast —

and so on, through all the stages of hammering in the nails, making windows and doors, spreading pitch and tar — until, behold, the ark (which has been standing there all the while — but that, nobody minds) is duly finished —

> better wroght
> Then I coude haif thoght.

But when it comes to persuading his obstinate wife, things do not go so well. She enters the ark, peers about with a critical eye, remarks skeptically that she

> can not fynd
> Which is before, which is behynd,

drifts out again and opines that she doesn't think it's
going to rain anyway. "But, behold," says Noah: "The
cataract, the thunder, the lightning!" See how the

> Halles and bowers,
> Castels and towres

are dissolving in the downpour!

> Therefor, wife, have done; com into ship fast.

Still she hangs back; and when at last to escape a wetting
she rushes into the ark, Noah's patience is exhausted and
he gives her a beating. There is a terrific fracas, with words
and blows flying— until Noah's three sons separate the
combatants. Noah's wrath promptly cools —

> We will do as ye bid us; we will no more be wroth,
> Dere barnes!

He takes the helm, and they all sail comfortably on till
they spy

> The hyllis of Armonye[1]

rising from the flood.

With the passing of the ark comes a procession of other
scenes, each wagon pausing long enough before the crowd
to permit the members of the gild to whom that episode
has been intrusted to recite their lines and play their
parts. One by one, these scenes from Old Testament story
pass us by, and after these come a few scenes from the life
of Christ. One of these, in which the beauty of a supernatural moment and the homeliest realism are daringly
blended, makes us wonder if we are not sharing in the beginnings of what will some day become great drama.

It is only a quaint pageant-wagon like the rest, to be
sure; but somehow when the actors begin their parts, the

[1] Armenia. The "hyllis" are the twin peaks of Mt. Ararat.

effect of mere make-believe vanishes under the spell of the spoken word. It is night, on a bare hillside. Shepherds are lying on the ground. "Lord, how cold it is!" says one. "I am half frozen, stiff as can be, I have slept too long. And this rain, will it never stop? 'Tis a hard life, what with the taxes and the way the gentry use us. The other day came one of them to borrow my wagon and my plow. What could I do?

> I were better be hangyd
> Than oones say hym nay."

There is an answering murmur from the onlookers. It was only a few years past that the peasants, ground down by special taxes and by the oppressions of the gentry, had risen in revolt; and after they had been tricked with false promises had heard King Richard say: "Villeins you were and villeins you are. In bondage you shall remain." We saw nothing of that among Chaucer's merry pilgrims. But it was all there, underneath the bright surface of life which Chaucer pictured; and the sting of it is not lost to this crowd on the street corner as they watch the play.

But another shepherd takes up the tale. The weather is even worse than the taxes — and there's no getting away from it.

> Now in dry, now in wete,
> Now in snaw, now in slete:
> When my shone freys to my fete,
> It is not all esy.

And when I do get home, that old scold, my wife, makes it worse than out-of-doors.

But this new plaint gets scant attention from the others. Bad weather and poverty are absorbing topics.

> Was never syn noe flood sich floodys seyn;
> Wyndys and ranys so rude and stormes so keyn.

And while we are out in this, and half starved, the rich
have good food and comfortable beds —

> Sich servandys as I that swettys and swynkys,[1]
> Etys our brede full dry, and that me forthynkys:
> We ar oft weytt and wery when master-men wynkys.[2]

So drifts the talk, till a newcomer interrupts them. "'Tis
that rascal, Mak," whispers one of the shepherds. "We
had best look to our sheep." But Mak seems harmless,
and after they have exchanged a jape[3] or two they all
lie down and go to sleep.

All but Mak, who is only pretending. When the rest
are snoring, Mak jumps up, seizes a fat sheep, carries it
off to his own cottage, and slips back to lie down with the
shepherds. When they wake toward dawn, there he is
sleeping so soundly that they have to rouse him. Home
Mak goes again, innocently enough. But when the shepherds discover their loss, they suspect him none the less,
and follow him home. When Mak hears them at the door,
he slips the sheep into his wife's bed. "Don't wake the
baby," he says: and the shepherds, finding no trace of the
missing sheep, apologize and start away. "But perhaps,"
says one of them, "Mak's feelings are hurt. I'll just slip
back again and make the baby a little present." Mak
seems strangely unwilling, but the shepherd insists —

> The child will it not grefe, that lytyl day-starne.[4]
> Mak, with youre leyfe, let me gyf youre barne
>   Bot sexpence.

> *Mak.*   Nay, go way, he slepys.
> *The Shepherd.*   Me thynk he pepys.
> *Mak.*   When he wakyns he wepys;
>   I pray you go hence.

---

[1] labor.   [2] sleep.   [3] jest.   [4] day-star.

But Mak's protests are vain. They pull down the bed-clothes. "A long-nosed baby!" says the shepherd. But the shepherds are good fellows. They know that death is the penalty for sheep-stealing, and so instead of having Mak arrested, they toss him in a blanket. Then, taking the stolen sheep, they go back to their hillside and, as the dusk of another evening gathers, they fall asleep again.

In the moment's pause we fall to wondering. These shepherds are English to the core. And they are so real! Barring the mere convention of rhyme, their talk is alto-gether natural. Is this a little comedy of English peasant life that has slipped into the pageant by mistake? What on earth can it have to do with the Bible story?

But something is happening again and we turn our eyes to the stage. There is a strain of music and angels appear, singing *Gloria in Excelsis*,[1] and an angel speaks to the shepherds. "Rise, herdmen," the angel says,

> For now is (Christ) borne . . .
> God is made your friend now at this morne.
> He behestys[2]
> At Bedlem[3] go se
> Ther lygys[4] that fre
> In a cryb full poorely
> Betwyx two bestys.

The shepherds awake. "What a strange dream I've been having!" says one. "Nay," says another. "'Tis a real voice. 'Tis God's son he means.

> He spake of a barne
> In Bedlem, I you warne.
> That betokyns yond starne[5]
> Let us seke him there."

---

[1] Glory (to God) in the highest. [2] commands. [3] Bethlehem.
[4] Where lies. [5] star.

SCENES FROM THE LIFE OF CHRIST

From the Psalter of Robert de Lisle, English (East Anglian) illumination, early 14th century.

"Yes," says another, "though we be wet and weary let us hasten

> To that child and that lady!
> We have it not to lose.

They beguile the way with talk of remembered prophecies and when they reach the stable of Bethlehem they fall on their knees before the Child. Humble and simple folk, their hearts are divided between reverence and an awkward fatherly concern for the little helpless thing.

> Hayll, derling dere, full of godhede!
> I pray the be nere when that I have nede.
> Hayll! swete is thy chere![1] My hart wold blede
> To se the sytt here in so poore wede [2]
>> With no pennys.
> Hayll! put forth thy dall;[3]
> I bryng the bot a ball;
> Have and play the with-all,
>> And go to the tenys.[4]

Humble and simple folk! As the play ends and the crowd on the street corner begins to break up, it is just that thought that gives us the key to what we have seen. Here is a play of the "Nativity," a play woven around the familiar words: "And there were in the same country shepherds abiding in the field, keeping watch over their flock by night. And, lo, the angel of the Lord came unto them —." If the gilds of Wakefield are to have scenes from the life of Christ for their pageant on Corpus Christi Day, here, clearly, is a scene to make a play of. Luckily, the man who sets to work at it has a dramatic imagination. Mere puppets and mere recitations will not satisfy him. He wants to make the beautiful old story *real*. How else, if there are to

---

[1] face.   [2] garment.   [3] hand.   [4] tennis.

be shepherds, than by turning to the shepherds that he knows? Their rough humor does not disturb him. It is part of them. The more real, the more natural they are, the more real will be that great moment when the angels come. One truth will help the other. It is not Palestine that he is concerned about. Let the shepherds talk about the miseries of the English poor and the beastly English climate. Let the shepherds, having nothing better, give the Child a tennis-ball to play with. At least the crowd on the street corner will know that they are real shepherds — and that is, after all, the only thing that matters.

The truth is that in this old miracle play, made by the common people for the common people, we have watched the beginnings of the greatest of all forms of English literature — the drama. It is the most fascinating of all forms to study, because it is closer to our actual lives than any other form. When some one is telling us a story, the teller sometimes gets in the way. He always wants to talk *about* the characters. But a drama, a play, is a story unfolded solely through what the characters themselves say and do. We hear them talking: we guess at the kind of people they are: something happens among them: from what we have seen of them, we have an inkling what they will do: one happening leads to another: and as the events move on step by step to an outcome which somehow settles things for good or ill, the people themselves become clearer and clearer to us, until we realize that with people like that, things just had to happen in just that way. That, at least, is the way we feel about the plays of the greatest of all dramatists, Shakespeare. We are going now to follow the growth of the drama from these early miracle plays to Shakespeare; and when we get to Shakespeare, we shall find that he, just like the unknown dramatist of this old Wakefield play, was chiefly concerned to make his characters real human beings; and that, just as the old Wakefield dramatist peopled the hills of Palestine with English shepherds, so Shakespeare, though the scene of his play be laid in Italy or Bohemia, will people his plays with the English folk whom he knows and understands.

Such plays as we have just seen had their beginnings long before Chaucer's day in the form of simple little scenes or episodes from the life of Christ, acted by the priests as a part of the religious service of the Catholic church. As these little acted bits increased in popularity and in elaborateness, they became gradually detached from the religious services proper, and were taken over by outsiders. The more elaborate these dramatizations of the Bible became, the more need there was for expenditure, for careful planning, and for coöperation in the production of them. Mere casual individuals could not manage them; but the gilds, or unions of men engaged in a common craft, had both the organization and the means. For a while these scenes were given only at the appropriate festivals — Nativity plays at Christmas, for example, and Resurrection plays at Easter; but on special occasions such as Corpus Christi Day the custom grew of bringing together various plays without regard to their timeliness. Meanwhile, too, the playmakers began to draw upon the rich material of the Old Testament as well. Gradually, as one episode after another was utilized, the plays fell into an orderly sequence from the Creation to the closing scenes in the life of Christ. These sequences, or "Cycles" as they are usually called, were carefully copied out in manuscripts, some of which have been preserved. It is from one of these, the "Towneley Cycle," that our illustrations have been drawn.

Not all the cycles are alike in quality and treatment. From this same county of Yorkshire, for example, comes another cycle, that of York, in which the same themes are treated with far more dignity and decorum. But with all the grave beauty of many of the scenes, there is nothing that quite measures up to the boldness, the instinctive dramatic rightness of the Towneley Shepherds play. Somewhat like the Towneley in its humor and realism is the Chester cycle, while the plays written for the gilds of the town of Coventry are again dignified and restrained.

The actors, the gilds, and even the corporations of the towns took these plays very seriously. In some cities every person practicing a craft was required to contribute to their support. A committee of "connyng, discrete, and able players" was authorized to select those best qualified to act, and to "discharge, ammove, and avoid" all "insufficiant personnes." Actors were fined for not knowing their parts. In one of the old manuscripts directions are given for the behavior and gestures of the actor. If he names Paradise, he must always "point toward it"; he must take his cue promptly and speak his part smoothly, clearly, and with proper restraint, and he must not spoil the meter by missing out a syllable or putting in one that does not belong. The cities issued explicit instructions for the conduct of the pageant; the actors had to be at their stations "at the mydhowre" between four and five o'clock in the morning, and they must be "well arayed"; the pageants must move promptly from point to point "without tarieng." In the records of the gilds may be found items of payments to the actors — three shillings, four pence to the performer of God; one shilling to Noah (Noah's wife got less!); a "savyd sowle" received twenty pence, and, with notable fairness, a "dampnyd sowle" received the same amount. It is on record that one Fawston received four pence "for hangyng Judas" and an additional four pence "for coc croyng." The same records contain items for properties and repairs — for a pair of gloves for God, two pence; for a pair of new hose and mending of the old for the white souls, eighteen pence; for a pound of hemp to mend the angels' heads, four pence; for mending hell-mouth, six pence — and so on.

With such items, quaintly absurd to us, but just a natural part of the day's work to the fourteenth-century gildsmen, we can reconstruct alike the preparation and the performance of these old miracle plays. They must have been a very central and important thing in the lives, not only of the players themselves, but also of those who looked forward all the year to the coming of the great pageant, and thronged the street corners when the day arrived. Few could read, and even fewer could get access to the rare and precious manuscripts which were the only "books" that that age knew. The Bible itself was for most people locked in the Vulgate. But here was the living Bible, visible to any "witless" man in a succession of dramatic chapters. It was all in the odor of sanctity, and at the same time vastly entertaining — a happy, and perhaps an unusual, combination.

These gild-pageants[1] were just coming into their own in

---

[1] The pageants on Corpus Christi Day and other festivals were not confined to scenes from the Bible, though these were by far the most important, and are of most interest to us as being in the direct line of succession. With the spread of interest in acting, the lives of the saints were also drawn upon —

And, valiant George, with speare thou killed the dreadful dragon here......
Great Christopher doth wade and passe with Christ amid the brooke:
Sebastian full of feathred shaftes, the dint of dart doth feele.
There walketh Kathren, with hir sworde in hande, and cruel wheele:
The Challis and the singing Cake with Barbara is led,
And sundrie other pageants playde, in worship of this bred.

There were other themes too — such as the Robin Hood plays on Mayday — in no wise connected with religion. But it is in the dramatization of the Bible story that the real promise is to be found.

Chaucer's time (the latter half of the fourteenth century); they were to flourish for more than a century thereafter; and their slow decline will carry us to the dawn of the great dramatic period of Shakespeare. In their day, they were the "literature" of the common folk; and during most of the fifteenth century there was little enough of other literature — of literature in the stricter sense of the word. The upper classes who could read, read Chaucer, or the imitators of Chaucer who wrote in the early years of the fifteenth century. There were still poets here and there who wrote of Arthur and his knights. But the small leisure class who could read, and for whom literature was written, had other and less pleasant things to think about. Before the long war with France had drawn to a close, England had become involved in a struggle between the two great "Houses" of Lancaster and York. It was a time of civil war, of sudden depositions of kings, of sudden shifts of power from one great "House" to the other. But that was a war of the nobles and was fought chiefly by their retainers. The ordinary folk, the craftsmen and tradespeople of the towns, were not much affected by it. While the "leisure" class had actually little leisure to produce literature or to read it, the towns throve and the town gilds went on producing a "literature" which could be enjoyed alike by the literate and the illiterate.

The composers of miracle plays were content to use actual personages from the Bible story; to transform the Biblical narrative into dialogue; and (particularly in the Towneley cycle) to enlarge upon the Biblical material in such ways as would make the characters seem more real. But if the miracle plays made the Biblical characters seem more real, why not other plays in which the virtues and vices common to human nature should be represented on the stage? If the miracle plays helped to strengthen the faith of the people, why not plays which would help the people to know themselves, to practice the virtues and to abhor the vices which they saw acted before them? Out of this natural thought grew the "Morality" plays which, in the fifteenth century, began to vie with the Miracle plays in popularity. Instead of Adam or Noah or Abraham or Pilate or Judas Iscariot, the writers of the Moralities gave such names to their characters as Mercy, Mischief, Conscience, Folly, Perseverance, Imagination, Free Will, Pity. The characters so named had of course to be provided with appropriate parts. Mercy had to say and do merciful things, Folly foolish things. But these virtues and vices could not move in a vacuum. They must contend for the possession of — oneself. The spectator must say: "There am I on the stage being fought over." And so we find in one of these plays a personage called "Mankind" as the central figure, with "Myscheff" and two very up-to-date rascals named "New Gyse" and "Now-a-days" and a lively devil named "Tityvıllus" all trying to lead him into badness, and one good character, "Mercy," who is trying to save "Mankind's" soul. Another of these moralities sufficiently explains itself in its subtitle: "Here begynneth a propre newe Interlude of the Worlde and the Chylde, otherwyse called Mundus & Infans & it sheweth of the estate of Chyldehode and Manhode." It is, as the name suggests, the story of the typical child, growing up and coming into contact with the world.

"He that cometh not whan I do call,"

says the World,

"I shall hym smyte with poverte."

As *Infans* grows up, he takes new names —"Wanton,"

"Lykynge," "Manhode," "Shame" — and, at last, "Age";
and all the while "Conscyence" and "Perseverannce"
contend with "Folye" for his soul.

In yet another — and by far the finest in dignity of conception and beauty of phrase, "Everyman" is summoned
by "Death" to make his journey to the grave. He appeals
in vain to his worldly friends "Kyndred" and "Beauty"
and "Fyve Wytts" and "Strength" and "Knowledge"
to support him on his way and finds at last that only "Good
Deeds" will accompany him.

Now it is clear that such plays as this put more responsibility on the inventive powers of the composer than do
the miracle plays. But the results are disappointing. There
is indeed little actual story in the moralities — but an
endless amount of self-explanatory speech-making on the
part of each character, and an endless amount of sermoniz-
ing. It would seem at first glance as if the morality were
no more than a step backward in the evolution of the
drama; for the miracle plays were at best an attempt to
reveal character through speech and action and that is of
the very essence of the drama; while these moralities do
hardly more than put personified virtues and vices through
their paces. But if the moralities seem disappointing in
themselves, they had at least possibilities of adaptation
and growth. From personifications to real persons is but a
step; and, with the shackles of the Biblical narrative once
thrown off, the playwright, as he works gradually out of
the notion that he must *teach*, will find his way to both
plot and characterization.

This, in so far as we can guess from the few specimens
preserved, is what was taking place in them as the fifteenth
century drew to its close and the sixteenth got under way.
Of itself this might ultimately have developed into re-

spectable drama; but meanwhile great things began to happen in England — events and influences which were to change the whole spirit of English life and incidentally to stimulate this natural growth of the drama into remarkable activity.

In the first place the troubled land found peace. The accession of King Henry VII in 1485 and his marriage with Elizabeth of York put an end to the prolonged struggles of the York and Lancastrian factions and began a period of rapid growth in wealth and power.

Of greater and far more lasting importance was the introduction of printing into England. It is hard for us to realize that printing had to be introduced. To us, the "twenty bokes clad in blak or reed" of the Clerk of Oxenford suggest nothing else but a row of compact little volumes on a shelf; and an author's "writings" merely so many printed pages in covers. It is not easy for us to imagine what it would be like to live in a time when an author's "writings" would be just literally that — the very pages on which he had laboriously written out his thoughts, or a copy tediously made by some scribe, with much ink-dipping and wearing out of quill pens. But those were the only "books" to our ancestors — until, one day in November of the year 1477, a certain William Caxton, after spending a while on the continent, came back to England and set up a printing press in Westminster. He had learned the art in Bruges, where they were just beginning to experiment with it. Caxton himself didn't quite know what to make of it all. Printing, nameless yet, was "the art of writing artificially." The type must be as much like handwriting as possible. The press was clumsy, the setting up by hand a slow and bungling business. But even when he had first tried it in Bruges, the thing had thrilled him.

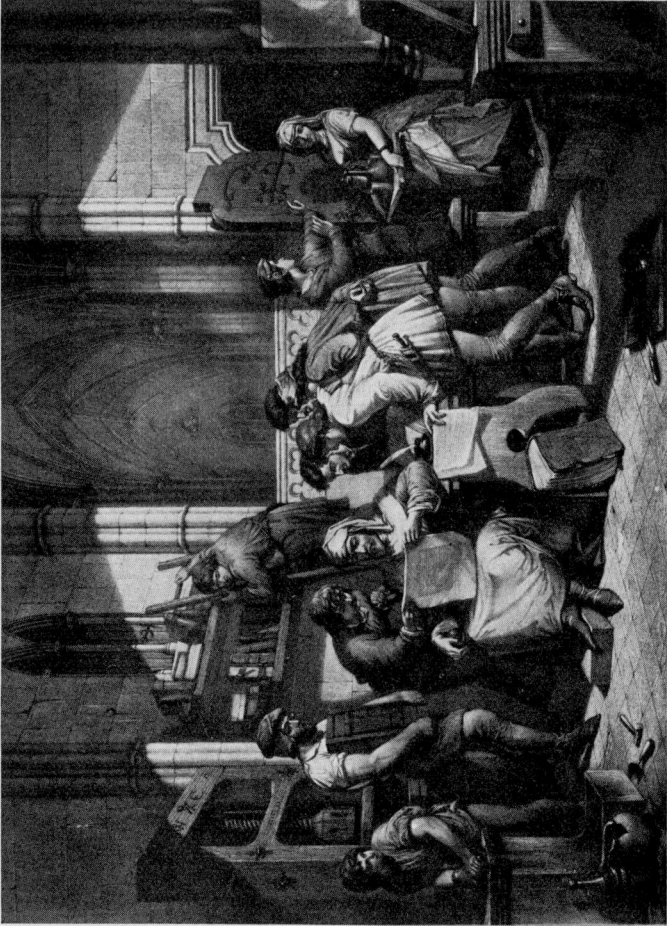

CAXTON READING FIRST PROOF AT WESTMINSTER
From an engraving by F. Bacon of a painting by E. H. Wehnert

dis /trewe /secrete /stedfast /euer kepy.z neuer ydle /Attempe
rat in spekimg /and vertuous in alle their Werkis. or atte
leste sholde be soo /For Whiche causes so euydent my sayd lord
as I suppose thoughte it Was not of necessite to sette in his
book the saiengis of his Auctor socrates touchyng Women
But for as moche as I had comademet of my saydr lordr
to correcte andr amende Where as I sholde fynde faulte /and
other fynde I none sauf that he hath left out thse dictes z
saynges of the Women of Grece /Therfore in accomplisshtg
his comandement for as moche as I am not in certayn Whe
der it Was in my lordis coppe or not +or ellis perauenture
that the Wynde had blowe ouer the leef /at the tyme of trãs
lacion of his booke /I purpose to Wryte the same saynges
of that Greke Socrates /Whiche Wrote of the Women of
grece andr nothyng of them of this Royame /Whom I sup
pose he neuer knewe /For if he had I dar plainly saye that
he Woldr haue reserued them inespeciall in his saydr dictes
Alway not presumyng to put z sette them in my saydr lor
des book /but inthende aparte in the vexer saytt of the Werkis
humbly requiryng al them that shal rede this lytyl vexer
saytt that yf they fynde ony faulte tarette it to Socrates
andr not to me Whiche Wryteth as here after foloweth

Socrates sayde That Women ben thapparaylles to
cacche men /but they take none but them that Wil
be poure /or els them that knowe hem not. And
he sayde that ther is none so grete empeshment vnto a man

A PAGE FROM "DICTES AND SAYEINGS OF THE PHILOSOPHERS,"
PRINTED BY CAXTON IN 1477

He had made a translation of a book of "strange and marvellous histories" out of French into English. His friends had besought him for copies and he had spent many months laboriously copying and recopying it in long hand. Then he had found out about this new "Art" and had learned it. "And now, behold," wrote Caxton with a little catch in his breath, "all the books [that is, copies] of this story,[1] thus imprinted as ye here see, were begun in one day and also finished in one day." To make more than one copy, even many copies, not after months of tedious transcribing, but "in one day" — it was as if the heavens had opened.

And they had. He set up his press in Westminster. Others followed him. Books multiplied. Suddenly, almost — as it seems to us through the perspective of the centuries — the Clerk's "twenty bokes" became a library.

But a library of what? By one of those curious and happy coincidences that occasionally lighten the world, a new current of thought and learning began, almost at the moment when Caxton's press started, to flow into England. Long before English literature had begun — away back into the time when, as we remember, a people called the Romans had invaded primitive Britain — there had been a great civilization and a great literature in southern and southwestern Europe. First the Greeks, and after them the Romans, had written books of searching inquiry into the moral and physical problems of life, and long narrative poems of the adventures of their national heroes, and plays in which the dramatists had shown life as in a glass — the deep and tragic things in some, the light and comic and absurd in others. For many centuries, while southern Europe had been ravaged by wars, these great writings had been practically forgotten. But just in this period

[1] "The Recuyell of the Histories of Troye."

when the English gildsmen were playing their miracle plays, and Caxton was making ready to set up his printing press in Westminster, came a widespread reawakening of interest in the "classics"— as the writings of the great period of Greek and Roman civilization were called. Stimulated by this rediscovered literature, the world seemed literally born again. Men began to think less about the church and the formulas of religion, — less about the next world and more about this. The Middle Ages wanted to possess the kingdom of Heaven. The Renaissance wanted to know, to understand, and in that sense to possess, the kingdoms of earth.

> All things that move between the quiet poles
> Shall be at my command: Emperors and Kings
> Are but obeyed in their several provinces,
> Nor can they raise the wind, or rend the clouds;
> But his dominion that exceeds in this,
> Stretcheth as far as doth the mind of man.[1]

During the first half of the sixteenth century this new spirit made its way slowly in England. In literature, certainly, there had to be a seedtime before there could be a harvest. The miracle plays, themselves so characteristic of the medieval mind, continued for a while to be popular. But the miracle plays were associated with the Roman faith. Conformity to the historic Church, already weakened by the new and independent spirit of the Renaissance, came now to an end in England. The authority of the pope was no longer admitted. The Church of England was separated from Rome. The monasteries were abolished. As the first half of the century came to an end England became a Protestant nation; and the miracle plays, looked upon as a relic of Catholicism, lost their hold.

[1] From Marlowe's *Dr. Faustus*, about 1590.

But the morality plays were more pliable. For mere abstract virtues and vices which might not at best come very close home to the onlooker, it was possible to substitute more tangible figures. In *The Play of Wyt and Science*, such characters as "Dylygence," "Instruccion" and "Honest Recreacion" teach the schoolboy devotion to study, while "Tediousnes" and "Idellness" make an effort (fortunately unavailing) to tempt him from the proper path. In *Nice Wanton*, the adage that he who spares the rod spoils the child is exemplified by the career of three quite human young persons, Barnabas and Ismael and their sister Dalila. Here the virtues and vices have at least lost their abstract names. Another morality of this period, *Kyng Johan*, turns to actual history for some of its characters. Intended as a counterblast against the Catholic Church, it is still no more than a morality in intention and in substance: but the very fact that such personages as King John and Stephen Langton rub shoulders in the play with mere personified abstractions like "Sedycyon" and "Treason" and "Veryte" prepares the way for the plays which, a few generations later, were to make English history live again on the stage.

Side by side with these late moralities, another type of play became popular. The moralities were pretty serious affairs and even in that teachable age may well have seemed rather dull. But even in the moralities the vices had a way of being more naughty than wicked — more amusing than abhorrent. If they could be amusing amid the sobriety of the morality, how much more so outside! In the "interludes," the characters are social types rather than virtues or vices, but retain a sort of cousinship to the abstractions of the moralities. Typical of these is John Heywood's playlet called *The Foure P P* (about 1530), in which a Palmer, a Pardoner, a Pedler and a 'Potecary (Apothecary) meet beside the way and, from telling of their varied experiences of human life, fall to arguing which can tell the biggest lie. The Pedler acts as judge. The Pardoner and the 'Potecary rise to the occasion. But it is the Palmer who wins — for he solemnly avers that in all his varied experience with the sex, he has never seen a woman out of patience![1]

Here, then, were various crude forms out of which a real drama was to grow — the miracle play in which actual people were dramatically presented, but in which there was little scope for the invention or the development of plots; the morality play which threw more responsibility on the dramatist, and in which the allegory was beginning to give place to reality; and the little interludes, which, already laughing at life, needed only to have their social types turned into individuals and their episodic subject matter developed into plots, to become full-fledged comedy.

And meanwhile the leaven of the Renaissance was working. As the study of Greek and Latin progressed in the schools, classical plays — especially Latin — were read and often acted as school exercises. The orderliness of these plays, their systematically developed plots, their formal arrangement into parts or acts each of which made a sort of framework for a successive stage of the plot — all

[1] The word "interlude" was loosely used in the Middle Ages. Even miracle-plays were sometimes so called. But the name was specifically applied to such playlets as that described above, which could be readily given in a banquet hall by a few hired entertainers for the amusement of the guests. Interludes of this sort were not uncommon before Heywood's day (See for example the "godely enterlude" of *Fulgens and Lucres*, written by Henry Medwall, chaplain to Cardinal Morton, as early as 1497, and recently edited by F. S. Boas and A. W. Reed); but Heywood's lively little farces popularized the type and helped to pave the way to comedy. Other interludes of Heywood's are *The Play of the Wether; A Mery Play betwene the Pardoner and the Frere, the Curate and Neybour Pratte;* and *A Mery Play betwene Iohan Iohan the Husbande, Tyb his Wyfe and Syr Ihan the Preest.*

this helped to give shape to the native drama. Plays with real home-people and home-incidents in them, but with plots developed and systematized after the Latin model, began to be written for performance by the scholars of school or university or for the entertainment of such organizations as the society of lawyers.

As the *form* thus developed, the *subject matter* became more and more diversified. The Renaissance brought into England, not only the literature of antiquity but a bewildering variety of stories, plays, poems, from Italy and Spain and France. The great Queen Elizabeth who came to the throne in 1559 had, as her tutor said, a "perfect readiness in Latin, Italian, French and Spanish." Under this well-taught and ready-witted queen it became the fashion to imitate foreign manners, to know and to read foreign languages, and to translate foreign books into English. By 1565 it could be said that "bookes of late translated out of Italian into English [are] sold in every shop in London," and that more of them have been "set out in Printe within these fewe monethes, than have bene sene in England many score yeares before." Here were stories galore — foreign, and therefore full of the enchantment which distance lends; stimulating to the imagination; offering themselves "in every shop in London" to the dramatist on the lookout for a plot.

With the stimulus from books came stimulus no less from life itself. England was become a great power, reaching out over all the world. Her explorers found their way to uncharted lands and brought back strange tales

> Of the Cannibals that each other eat,
> The Anthropophagi, and men whose heads
> Do grow beneath their shoulders.[1]

---

[1] From Shakespeare's *Othello* (about 1604).

QUEEN ELIZABETH

(Painter unknown)

The stay-at-homes marveled —

> When we were boys
> Who would believe that there were mountaineers
> Dew-lapped like bulls, whose throats had hanging at them
> Wallets of flesh? or that there were such men
> Whose heads stood in their breasts? which now we find
> Each putter-out of five for one[1] will bring us
> Good warrant of.[2]

While the stay-at-homes marveled at the strange tales of the explorers, they marveled no less at the sudden reaching out, in these great days of Queen Elizabeth, of England's commerce to all the ends of the earth: "For, which of the Kings of this land before her Majesty," exclaims Hakluyt, "had their banners ever been seen in the Caspian Sea? which of them hath ever dealt with the Emperor of Persia, as her Majesty hath done, and obtained for her merchants large and loving privileges? who ever saw before this regimen, an English lieger in the stately porch of the Grand Signor at Constantinople? Who ever found English consuls and agents at Tripolis in Syria, at Aleppo, at Babylon, at Balsara, and which is more, who ever heard of Englishmen at Goa before now? What English ships did heretofore ever anchor in the mighty river of Plate? pass and repass the unpassable (in former opinion) strait of Magellan, range along the coast of Chili, Peru, and all the back side of Nova Hispania, further than any Christian ever passed, traverse the mighty breadth of the South Sea, land upon the Luzones, in despite of the enemy, enter into alliance, amity and traffic with the princes of the Moluccas, and the Isle of Java, double the

---

[1] Ship-captains with whom the stay-at-homes had invested money to be returned fivefold in case the voyage was successful.

[2] From Shakespeare's *The Tempest* (about 1611).

famous cape of Bona Speranza, arrive at the isle of Santa Helena, and last of all return home, most richly laden with the commodities of China, as the subjects of this now flourishing monarchy have done?" [1]

From these lands, ships brought back wealth which the Elizabethans riotously spent, jewels which they gayly wore, bright garments which they promptly appropriated as the current fashion. "No people in the world is so curious in new fangles as they of England bee," said one critic of the manners of his time; and another: "It is impossible to know who is noble, who is worshipful, who is a gentleman, who is not, because all persons dress indiscriminately in silks, velvets, satens, damaskes, taffeties and such like."

And so they all, noble and baseborn alike, decked themselves

> With silken coats and caps and golden rings
> With ruffs and cuffs and farthingales and things;
> With scarfs and fans and double change of bravery. [2]

It did not please the old sobersides, who counted it "a great confusion and a general disorder, God be merciful unto us!" but it made a gay and glittering world and stimulated the imagination.

And it made everybody tremendously proud of England. They called her "The Lady of the Sea," "the most renowned and famous Isle of the whole world: so rich in commodities, so beautiful in situations, so resplendent in all glory, that if the most Omnipotent had fashioned the world round like a ring, as he did like a globe, it might have been most worthily the only gem therein." [3] And when in 1588, the little English ships defeated a great fleet or Armada

---

[1] From Hakluyt's *Principal Navigations* (1589). (See page 115.)
[2] From Shakespeare's *The Taming of the Shrew* (about 1595).
[3] From Camden's *Remains concerning Britain* (1605).

VERA TOTIUS EXPEDITIONIS NAUTICÆ

This map was probably printed in Amsterdam between the years 1588 and 1595.
Hondius (or Hondt) is known to have lived in London for some years.   He has re-

DESCRIPTIO D. FRANC. DRACI . . .

The engraver, Jodocus Hondius, the Elder, was the successor of Gerard Mercator. corded on the map the voyages both of Drake and of Cavendish.

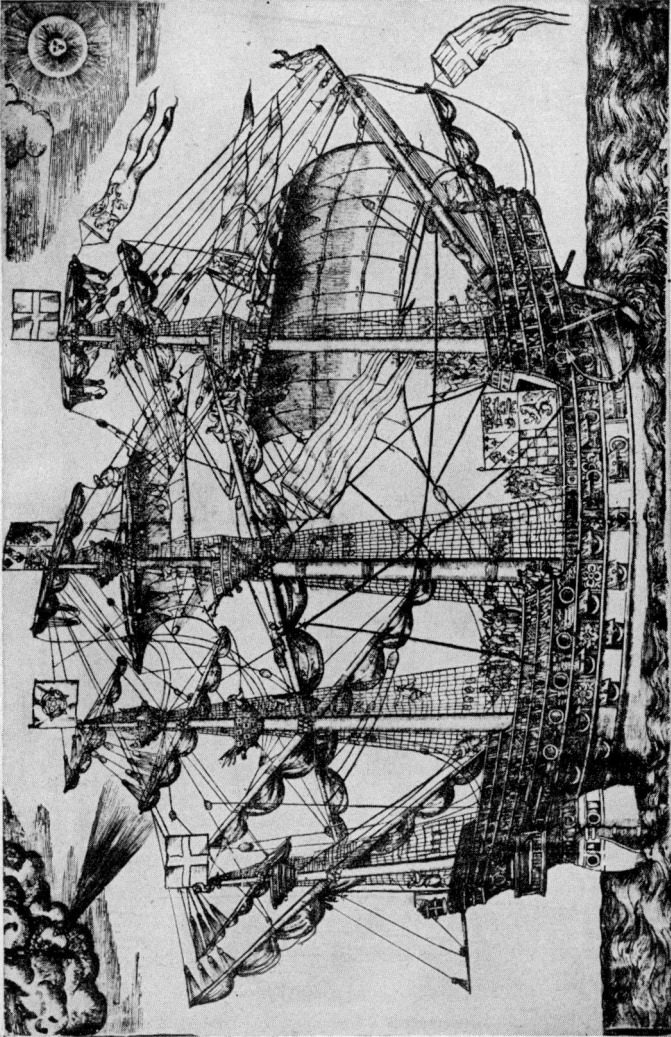

THE ARK ROYAL

The *Ark Royal*, one of the largest ships of Queen Elizabeth's navy, was built in 1587; keel, 100 feet; beam, 37 feet; 692 tons. Compare with the *Leviathan*: keel, 907 feet; beam, 100 feet; 59,957 tons.

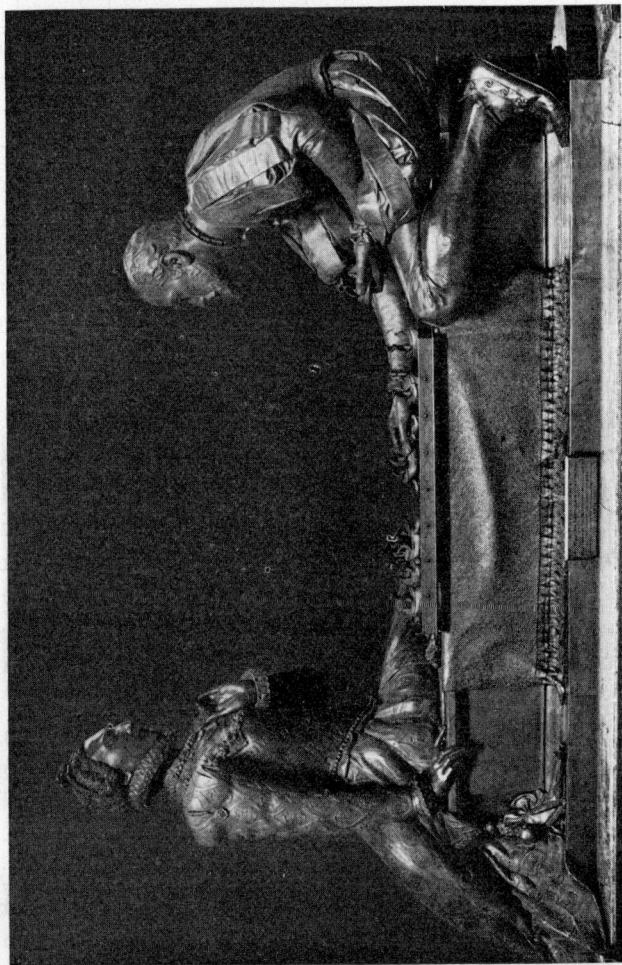

"A ROYAL GAME"

Bronze life-size statue by William Reynolds-Stephens (Tate Gallery, London), Queen Elizabeth and Philip II of Spain. The pieces with which they are playing are the little vessels of the English navy, and the great galleons of the Armada.

which the Spaniards sent against them, all this accumulated enthusiasm for England and zest for the many-sided world-life which England was bringing in to herself exploded into a tremendous activity, which made the next twenty years the golden period of English literature.

To tell here of all the wealth of prose and lyric and narrative poetry that came of this would be merely confusing. It is the drama only which concerns us — and for the drama the way had been preparing for some time before the great moment came. The plays first written and acted within the schools had gradually become the popular amusement which the miracle plays had been a few generations before. Strolling companies of actors would give performances in halls or in the yards of inns. As popular interest in the plays increased, theaters were built — usually the theater was a circular structure of several tiers of galleries, built round an unroofed space, with a stage projecting into this inclosed area. Organized companies took the place of the old haphazard groups of strolling actors, and with the increasing demand for plays a class of men developed who devoted their entire time to producing them.

There were great geniuses among these early professional playwrights — Marlowe, for example, who had a way of making human beings move like giants and speak in "high astounding terms"; Lyly, who wrote sparkling comedies, full of delightful little songs; and Kyd, who saw the grimly tragic side of life. But these, as we look back upon them, seem just to be preparing the way for the greatest of them all, William Shakespeare.

Shakespeare was born in April, 1564 (we celebrate the twenty-third as his birthday), in the little town of Stratford in Warwickshire. It was a prosperous little town with a population of, perhaps, two thousand; with the usual assortment of "crafts," each with its own society. The weavers were the most important (you will find one of them by the way, an amusing fellow named Bottom, in Shakespeare's *A Midsummer Night's Dream*); and there were various kinds of leather workers, and the usual chandlers and bakers and butchers and brewers and what not. John Shakespeare, William's father, besides owning a farm or two in the neighborhood, was a glover and "whittawer" (worker in white leather) and during William's early boyhood held in succession all the important town offices up to chief Alderman. William went to Stratford Grammar School, had a good elementary training in Latin — the bedrock of the educational system of the day; probably — though we cannot be quite sure — spent a while in a lawyer's office; and, for the rest, just "played around," watching with a quizzical eye the odd characters in which every village and small town abounds; occasionally joining his fellows in a glimpse of the life of the great folk — the Warwickshire gentry near at hand; and making one of the crowds that gathered whenever a company of strolling players obtained permission to give a play in the yard of the Swan or the Bear or the Crown. All these experiences and acquaintances were to come to life in his plays later on — the town constables in *Much Ado about Nothing;* the bumpkins giving a little play "on their own," in *Love's Labor's Lost* and in *A Midsummer Night's Dream;* the blustering English squire (albeit transferred to Italy) in *Romeo and Juliet;* one of the Warwickshire gentry, Sir Thomas Lucy, in the "Justice Shallow" of *II Henry IV* and *The Merry Wives of Windsor;* the drunken tinker in the *Induction* to *The Taming of the Shrew*, with all sorts of Stratford references worked into the tinker's talk; the "mask," as you may see it in *Romeo and Juliet*, when a group would don masks and present themselves at a neighbor's house with

> Cupid hoodwink'd with a scarf,
> Bearing a Tartar's painted bow of lath,
> Scaring the ladies like a crow-keeper;

the rustic superstitions about fairies in *Romeo and Juliet* and *A Midsummer Night's Dream*, and about ghosts, in *Hamlet*. These and a host of other things he was storing up, quite unconsciously, not guessing, one fancies, where fate was to lead him. It looked indeed as if fate were leading him to settle down in respectable commonplaceness at Stratford, for he married a woman living near-by, Anne Hathaway, and begot three children. But at some time shortly before 1590, perhaps when Lord Leicester's players visited Stratford in 1587, London and the playhouse captured his imagination. He made his way to London, and his real life began.

The next twenty years were spent as an actor in the most successful of the companies of players, and as a reviser and a writer of plays. As an actor he does not seem to have distinguished himself; but his genius as a playwright won quick recognition. He prospered, became part owner of one of the largest of the London theaters, made occasional visits to Stratford, bought a considerable house there, and, about 1613, gave up his work in London and retired to spend his declining years in his native place. He died in 1616, and was buried in Stratford Church, whither many thousands go yearly to look upon the bust which commemorates him.

Shakespeare's plays are not all masterpieces. He began, just as everyone has to begin, with 'prentice-work. A good deal of this 'prentice work consisted merely of revising, or helping others to revise, old plays so that they might be "tried out" on the stage again. Not a few of the plays which are included among his works, and some indeed which we are usually taught to treat quite reverently as his — such as *Henry V* and *Julius Cæsar* and *Richard III* and *The Taming of the Shrew* — are of this sort. In his early years, too, he was, just as we should expect, an imitator and an experimenter. He imitated and echoed Marlowe over and over again. He imitated and borrowed from John Lyly. Whatever was popular at the moment, he tried his hand at. He bungled his plots, he bungled his characterization; he had to learn through failures and half-successes before he could make a plot develop swiftly and naturally. He seldom invented or "made up" a plot. From the outset he took his stories where he found them. The people in them were what chiefly interested him. What kind of people are they, who would do the things which the old story represents them as doing? When he had studied that out, he set himself so to reshape and elaborate the borrowed framework of plot as to make it a progressive disclosure of character. While he was doing this for himself, he was helping to change the whole spirit of Elizabethan drama, to transform it into an art, in which the story itself and every possible resource of poetry and wit should be put to the use of creating real men and women.

One of the most thorough of these transformations he effected in the historical play. In a sense, the historical play is the oldest form of English drama. The fourteenth and fifteenth centuries turned Biblical history into plays. The sixteenth century, finding the miracle plays too closely associated with the Church from which they had emancipated themselves, substituted the annals of their own country. England had become a great country and the subject appealed to their pride. Up to about the middle of the sixteenth century the few serious historians who had dealt with English history had elected to write in Latin and to make their records brief and dry. With the accession of Queen Elizabeth there was a change. Histories of England, written in English, multiplied. Popular interest stimulated the historian to enliven his narrative with good stories. And all was grist that came to their mill. Brutus, great grandson of Æneas and mythical founder of Britain, or King Lear, who divided his kingdom among his three daughters, was as real as Henry VIII. The playwrights found these anecdotal histories just the thing to dramatize. But the playwrights went at it awkwardly. Like the makers of the miracle plays, their chief concern was to get everything in.   The result was what we call the "Chronicle play"— not, strictly speaking, drama at all, but a succession of dramatized scenes from the reign of this king or that.   If the playwrights found something in Hall's *Union of the Noble and Illustre Famelies of Lancastre and York* or in Holinshed's *Chronicles of England, Scotland and Ireland*, that would look rather well on the stage, they used it without worrying much as to where it would carry them.

With the one exception of a play by Marlowe — *Edward II* — the plays dealing with English history were of this rambling and inconclusive sort when Shakespeare began to experiment with them. The early history plays associated with his name are but little better. But gradually Shakespeare's interest in bringing out character wrought a change.   He began to prune away superfluous scenes and to transpose or even to alter the events narrated in Holinshed so that there would be a real growth, a development of the story. Moreover, because the pageant of history is likely to seem rather far-off and unreal, he introduced all sorts of everyday people, with their familiar foibles and absurdities, weaving their doings into the great events of court and battlefield. So, in Shakespeare's hands, the old chronicle play became the historical drama, laying bare, through its concentrated and swiftly developing plot, the hearts of men.

There is no better example of this than the first part of *Henry IV*. The long struggle between the Houses of York and Lancaster has already been referred to in the beginning of this chapter. Interesting in itself because it led up to the establishment of the royal line to which Queen Elizabeth belonged, and treated with particular fullness and color in the pages of Hall and Holinshed, it afforded good pickings for the Elizabethan dramatist. In a series of plays beginning with the deposition of Richard II by Henry of Lancaster, continuing in two plays devoted to the reign of this king, Henry IV, and in a fourth play dealing with the brief but glorious reign of Henry V, Shakespeare follows the events which led up to the final struggle between the two Houses: and in the three parts of *Henry VI* and in *Richard III* the dramatic events of that long-continued duel are set forth. The first part of *Henry IV* is, then, but one chapter in a serial story. The king, troubled with doubts about his right to the throne and his share of responsibility for the death of Richard, would leave the kingdom if he could and expiate his sins by a pilgrimage to Palestine. But his rebellious subjects give him no rest. The great barons of the north rise in revolt. Northumberland, his son Harry Hotspur and the Welshman, Glendower, league against the king. It is Henry's young son Prince Hal, the future Henry V, who inspires the army and leads them to victory over the rebels. Now, for this,

Shakespeare had not only Holinshed's history, but also an old play, to go upon; but Holinshed is a discursive narrative and the old play is puppet-chronicle. In Shakespeare these personages come to life. And what reality and what variety of human nature the struggle brings to the surface! A king, weary, conscience-stricken, timid, suspicious; rebellious Hotspur, very type of the rash and heady fighter; wild Glendower ready enough to fight, but involving himself in a mist of extravagant and erring fancies; and Prince Hal — but Hal cannot be summed up in a phrase. The character of this young man who was, as Henry V, to lead England to great victories, fascinated Shakespeare. There was a tradition, reflected alike in Holinshed and the old play, that Hal had been a wild youth. It was just enough to rouse Shakespeare's imagination. While war clouds the horizon, Hal revels in an alehouse. Among his boon companions is a fat old knight, Sir John Falstaff. To Sir John, life, the respectabilities, the prince, the king, Sir John himself, are one huge jest. Nothing escapes his dancing wit and nothing daunts him. The cronies concoct a plan to rob passers-by on the king's highway, only to turn the joke on Falstaff, by robbing him of the spoils; but Falstaff comes up smiling with a tale of being set upon by an incredible number of men in buckram. When the king summons Hal to reprove him for his wildness, Hal and Falstaff "take off" the impending scene with the fat knight playing the part of the king. When war is declared, and the prince has mended his ways and taken his proper place at the head of the forces, Falstaff leads a ragged company, with "but a shirt and a half" among them, to take part in the battle. When one of the rebel leaders attacks him he falls down and "plays dead," and when Hotspur is slain by Prince Hal, Falstaff jumps up and pretends to have slain

Hotspur himself. And all the while he is so genial in his rascality, so carefree and witty, that we can't help liking him.

So runs the story of *Henry IV*, Part I. It is an example of what Shakespeare could do with historical material. The remote figures of history have become real; and woven into the pageantry of courts and battles is the life that Shakespeare saw around him in the London taverns. It is history — but it is history interpreted and made warm and human.

Such plays as this are remarkable enough; but it is in the freer field of tragedy and comedy that his genius found full scope. A tragedy is not merely a play with a sad ending. Many of the historical plays have that. Nor need it be any the less based on history. But whereas in the historical play, the dramatist must remain a historian, adapting and interpreting but not fundamentally altering history, in tragedy he has only one problem to deal with — the problem of human nature involved in wrongdoing or disastrous mischance and the consequences that arise therefrom. In history — as in our daily experience — a thousand things may intervene between the deed and its consequences, or indeed there may seem to be no consequences whatsoever. But in a tragedy, the dramatist, by ignoring the thousand things and selecting the few significant and related things, attempts to find and to demonstrate the logic or the necessity that underlies our apparently haphazard world.

Sometimes it is necessity rather than logic, disastrous mischance rather than wrongdoing. In one of the most appealing of all Shakespeare's tragedies, two young lovers, Romeo and Juliet, belong to rival houses which are at mortal feud. The two have done no wrong. Their love for each other is natural and right. But the very fact of their love challenges and defies the bitter hatred between the two houses. The lovers, desiring only happiness and peace, find themselves involved in a linked chain of broils and disasters, ending inevitably in the death of both of them. Shakespeare calls them "star-crossed lovers," meaning that they were fated to a tragic end from the moment when they first saw each other. But their innocence, their beauty, their devotion, are not wholly frustrate. Over their dead bodies the leaders of the rival houses clasp hands, moved by the pity of it to reconciliation.

But most of Shakespeare's tragedies are of sterner stuff. One of the greatest is *Macbeth*. Here is no mischance, but the swift logic of the wages of sin. King Duncan of Scotland has sent his generals, Macbeth and Banquo, to quell a revolt. They are successful and the news of their success runs before them. Learning that the Thane of Cawdor is among the rebels, Duncan announces that he will confer the title upon Macbeth. Meanwhile, as Macbeth and Banquo are returning, they meet three witches beside the way. The witches greet Macbeth not only by his proper title of Thane of Glamis, but also as Thane of Cawdor and as future king of Scotland. Banquo they hail as one whose children shall be kings. Macbeth "seems rapt withal" by the strange greetings, and, as the two march on together, revolves them wonderingly in his mind. "King —

> And Thane of Cawdor too: went it not so?"

he says to Banquo; and again

> Your children shall be kings.

When he meets Duncan and learns that the title of Thane of Cawdor is already conferred upon him, "horrible imagin-

ings" prey upon him, but for the moment he shakes them
off —

> If chance will crown me King, why, chance may crown me
> Without my stir.

But Lady Macbeth, informed of what has happened in a
letter from her husband, has also been turning over in her
mind the witches' prophecy. To her, Macbeth is one who
is

> too full o' the milk of human kindness
> To catch the nearest way:

one who

> would not play false
> And yet would wrongly win;

and now that he has come to join her in their castle, with
Duncan on the point of arriving as their guest for the night,
she sees the dark thoughts written in his face, and whispers

> He that's coming
> Must be provided for; and you shall put
> This night's great business into my dispatch,
> Which shall to all our nights and days to come
> Give solely sovereign sway and masterdom.

Darkness gathers; and as Macbeth meditates the deed
which will bring the witches' final prophecy to pass, the
baseness and the danger of it alike give him pause. But
Lady Macbeth urges him on —

> Art thou afeard
> To be the same in thine own act and valour
> As thou art in desire?

She drugs the drink of those who will watch over the king,
and, after, goes herself to Duncan's chamber, laying bare
the daggers of the sleeping sentinels, so that when Mac-

beth has used their weapons for the deed, suspicion may rest upon them. All but the fatal stroke is hers. Nay,

Had he not resembled
My father as he slept, I had done't.

It is Macbeth at last who stabs the old king; but in his excitement and panic he brings the incriminating daggers away with him, and it remains for Lady Macbeth to take them back to Duncan's chamber and to smear the faces of the drugged sentinels with blood.

And now that the deed is done, with remorseless logic fate exacts the wages of sin. For a brief time suspicion is averted. Macbeth wins the crown. Having won, he must hold it for his heirs. But the witches' prophecy that Banquo's sons shall inherit stands in the way. He hires murderers to kill Banquo and his son, Fleance. Banquo is killed but Fleance escapes. Meanwhile the murder of the king has murdered sleep for Macbeth. His fevered mind is full of strange imaginings. At a supper given by the newly crowned king, Macbeth thinks that he sees the murdered Banquo seated, bloody as in death, at the banquet table. By Macbeth's wild words suspicion is aroused. The sons of Duncan, who have fled to England, are joined there by an influential nobleman Macduff, who aids them to gather forces to overthrow Macbeth. Macbeth, ever more anxious, goes again to consult the witches. They tell him that he is unassailable till Birnam wood shall march against him; but to beware of Macduff. Enraged, Macbeth puts Lady Macduff and her children to the sword. Lady Macbeth, her iron nerve broken at last, becomes a prey to thoughts as terrible as those that haunt her husband: "Here's the smell of the blood still; all the perfumes of Arabia will not sweeten this little hand." As word of her death is brought to Macbeth, comes also the news that the forces led by Macduff are approaching. Macbeth retreats to the castle of Dunsinane. The besiegers cut boughs from Birnam wood to protect themselves from the arrows. As Macbeth sees the waving boughs approach he remembers the prophecy of the witches. But he fights doggedly on till he meets his death at the hands of Macduff.

No mere summary can do justice to the inevitableness with which event follows event, to the effect alike of relentless pressure and of breathless speed from the moment when the first sin is committed to the tragic close. Nor can a summary convey any idea of the moving power of the great moments in the play — the words between Macbeth and Lady Macbeth just before and just after the murder of Duncan; the succession of soliloquies in which Macbeth stands face to face with his sin; Lady Macbeth walking in her sleep talking to herself of what she has done. But even in a summary it is possible to catch at least a glimpse of Shakespeare's profound and sympathetic understanding of human nature. A lesser man, undertaking as Shakespeare did to turn Holinshed's account of Macbeth into a play, would have made this murderer and murderess merely bad — unscrupulous, inhuman — and the play, while it might have been exciting, would have been in no wise moving. But the desperate struggle in Macbeth's mind between honor and ambition before he yields to the temptation, and the way in which events sweep him on after the deed is done, make us sympathize even while we condemn. And even Lady Macbeth, arch-temptress, moves our sympathy and understanding. Whatever her faults, she is at least not self-seeking. Her one thought is to accomplish Macbeth's half-realized desires, to gain his ends. Her attitude toward him, curiously blended of detached understanding and protectiveness and goading and devotion, is one of the most profound and subtle character-studies in the whole range of English literature.

The broad sympathy which enriches Shakespeare's tragedies permeates his comedies as well. Comedy is a lighter thing.

> Persons, such as Comedy would choose,
> When she would show an image of the times,
> And sport with human follies, not with crimes

allow the dramatist scant opportunity to probe to the depths of human nature. But, even here, Shakespeare made his opportunities. The story which provides the framework of *The Merchant of Venice*, for example, is light, graceful, romantic. As Shakespeare tells it, it is a thing of poetry and wit. But the story develops one character as deeply probed, as profoundly analyzed, as any in the tragedies.

The Merchant of Venice takes us into Shakespeare's workshop, gives us an opportunity to see him in the very process of molding his material. One of the familiar stories of Shakespeare's time, told and retold in various forms, was of a Jew who lent a Christian merchant a sum of money on condition that if the amount were not repaid by a certain date the Jew should cut a pound of flesh from the merchant's body. It was, in most versions, a crude and repulsive affair; but Shakespeare happened upon an Italian book in which this old tale of the pound of flesh is woven into a fantastic love-story. The Italian book tells of a certain lady of Belmonte, near Venice in Italy, who required of any suitor for her hand that he should remain awake throughout the night of his visit. If he failed to do so, the ship which had brought him to the harbor of Belmonte would be confiscated. This was a trick, for each suitor was presented with a drink of drugged wine when he arrived, and next morning when he woke up, he would be dismissed and the Lady of Belmonte would help herself to the rich cargo of his vessel. A young Venetian, whose godfather had provided him with a vessel filled with rich merchandise, moored in the harbor of Belmonte. The trick was played, the ship confiscated. The youth returned to Venice with a pitiful tale of shipwreck. His godfather gave him a second vessel richly equipped. Once more the youth tried and lost. His godfather, unable to raise the money for a third venture, borrowed from a Jew, with the fatal condition. The youth, once more arrived at Belmonte, was again about to drink the drugged wine, when a waiting-woman whispered to him to refrain. The youth fulfilled the test, was wedded to the lady, and, in his happiness, remembered all but too late the danger in which his godfather stood. Hastening back to Venice, he sought in vain to persuade the Jew to accept the money for his bond. But the date had expired, the Jew demanded his pound of flesh. At the critical moment a doctor of the law arrived in Venice. The case was tried before him, the Jew was justified of his bond. But the learned doctor warned the Jew, upon forfeit of his life, that he must fulfill the very letter of his bond, taking no more and no less, and spilling no drop of blood. Seeing himself thwarted by impossible conditions, the enraged Jew tore up his bond and left the court. The learned doctor would take no other fee than the ring which the youth wore. He protested that it had been given him by the Lady of Belmonte, but perforce yielded to the doctor's demand. The youth, taking his godfather with him, returned to Belmonte. The lady inquired for her ring, and after teasing the youth for a while, showed him the very ring, and revealed that it was she herself, disguised in the flowing robes of a doctor of the law, who had given the judgment against the Jew and received the fee. The youth was forgiven. The godfather was married to the waiting-woman who had warned the youth, and as the Italian story has it, they all "spent the rest of their lives in joy and felicity."

Now it happened that a Jew in London, no less a personage than the court physician, had just been tried, convicted and executed for complicity in a plot against Queen Elizabeth. It was an opportune moment to present a play in which a Jew should play a villain part. And there was something about the Jew in the Italian story, baited by the jeering Christians and still fiercely and bitterly demanding his rights, that appealed to Shakespeare's imagination. The general plot, too, had possibilities — except for the stupid device of the drugged wine and the confiscated ships. This Shakespeare promptly discarded, substituting a device which he had picked up from another quarter, a test in which the suitors of the lady should be confronted with three caskets, one of gold, one of silver, one of lead. He who made the right choice should find within a picture of the lady and should win her hand. He who made the wrong choice must take an oath

> Never to speak to lady afterward
> In way of marriage.

With this substitution of the caskets for the keeping-awake test, Shakespeare had his plot complete. And a good enough plot it was, with opportunity to create a charming Lady of Belmonte, a perfectly adequate young lover, an entirely respectable and benevolent merchant, and several pompous and blundering suitors to make wrong choice of the caskets before the hero arrived to pick — of course — the right one.

But the Jew! Here was a more arresting figure. Could it be that he was merely what all the old stories made him, a mere insensate figure of greed and malice? It is as if Shakespeare first said to himself words which he afterward put into the mouth of Shylock: "Hath not a Jew eyes? Hath not a Jew hands, organs, dimensions, senses, affections, passions; fed with the same food, hurt with the same weapons, subject to the same diseases, healed by the same means, warmed and cooled by the same winter and summer as a Christian is? If you prick him, does he not bleed? If you tickle him, does he not laugh? If you poison him, does he not die? And if you wrong him, will he not revenge? If he is like us in the rest, he will resemble us in that." And so Shakespeare set himself to make Shylock human. The merchant Antonio's money is invested in ships now at sea. To fit out the young Bassanio for his wooing, he must borrow of the Jew. Shylock knows — who better?— the extent of Antonio's commitments, the possibilities of shipwreck. And Shylock knows what it is to be despised, to be spat upon even, by these contemptuous Christians. Gradually, as Antonio unfolds the extent of his needs, an idea is born in Shylock's mind. This shall be no common loan. Let the bond, the surety, be a pound of Antonio's flesh. If Antonio's ships come home, the loan will be paid and the bond regarded as a merry jest. But if not. . . .

It does sound too preposterous to Antonio to be anything more than a jest. He is glad to escape the usual usurious interest and signs the bond. And then comes news of shipwrecks, one after another, till not one vessel has

scaped the dreadful touch
Of merchant-marring rocks.

Meanwhile misfortune has been hardening Shylock's determination. His daughter has fled to marry a Christian, taking her father's wealth with her. Human affection is killed in him. "The curse never fell upon our nation till now. I never felt it till now. Two thousand ducats in that; and other precious, precious jewels. I would my daughter were dead at my foot, and the jewels in her ear!" He thinks of nothing but revenge.

Then comes the trial scene, in outline much as in the old story. Shylock will give no reason for his demand that the bond be executed,

> More than a lodg'd hate and a certain loathing
> I bear Antonio.

As the doctor of the law passes from plea to argument and concedes him his legal right, Shylock's spirit soars.

> 'Tis very true!   O wise and upright judge!

he cries. But when the conditions are pronounced that frustrate the bond, he is stunned. To the judge's sentence that if he will deed his wealth to his daughter and her Christian husband, and himself become a Christian, he may go unpunished, he answers only "I am content"—and then:

> I pray you give me leave to go from hence.
> I am not well.

So Shylock disappears from the scene. The last act is all gaiety and beauty. Into it Shakespeare pours his loveliest poetry:—

> How sweet the moonlight sleeps upon this bank!
> Here will we sit and let the sounds of music
> Creep in our ears: soft stillness and the night
> Become the touches of sweet harmony.

Sit, Jessica.   Look how the floor of heaven
Is thick inlaid with patines of bright gold:
There's not the smallest orb which thou beholdest
But in his motion like an angel sings,
Still quiring to the young-eyed cherubims —

but when the curtain has fallen or the last page is turned, it is the profoundly interpreted personality of Shylock that abides with us.

Henry IV, Macbeth, The Merchant of Venice are but three of a total of thirty-seven plays that came from Shakespeare's pen.   That is a good many — more than most of us need to read; but among them are plays of such sheer delight or of such power to stir our deepest emotions, that to miss them would be a great loss out of our lives.   The best way is to go on a voyage of discovery for oneself — opening one's Shakespeare, let us say, to *A Midsummer Night's Dream,* or *As You Like It* or *Twelfth Night* or *The Tempest,* among the comedies; to *Romeo and Juliet,* or *Hamlet* or *King Lear,* among the tragedies; or to *Richard II* or *Henry V* among the plays dealing with English history; or to any one of those brilliant studies of Roman life, *Julius Cæsar, Coriolanus, Antony and Cleopatra,* which Shakespeare dug out of North's *Plutarch.*[1]   Thus we shall chance upon people who will become more real and vivid to us, and infinitely more fascinating to our imagination, than any of the folk among whom we move from day to day. Them we call real, because we can see them — though what we see is seldom more than the conventional outside — clothes, faces, lives, all of a pattern.   But of Shakespeare's people we shall know the very souls.   Whimsical Rosalind, teasing her lover; light-hearted lovely Viola, clad as a boy, unwilling messenger from the man whom she loves

[1] See page 120.

to the woman whom he thinks he loves, but braving out her disguise with all the swagger of an Elizabethan page; young Romeo and Juliet, son and daughter of families that hate each other —"star-crossed" lovers, snatching a few moments of happiness before the blood-feud between their families hurries them to separation and death; Prince Hamlet, haunted by the memory of his murdered father, ghost-driven to take vengeance on his father's murderer, troubled by the mystery of life and death, embittered, distracted, doubting, and yet ironically wise; Lear, driven out by the daughters to whom he had resigned his kingdom, wandering on the stormy heath, crazed by grief — and then, when he is in the hands of his enemies and being led to imprisonment and death, recovering his sanity for one happy moment in the presence of the daughter whom he has scorned, but who has been faithful to him: —

> Come, let's away to prison;
> We two alone will sing like birds i' the cage.
> When thou dost ask me blessing, I'll kneel down,
> And ask of thee forgiveness.   So we'll live
> And pray, and sing, and tell old tales, and laugh
> At gilded butterflies, and hear poor rogues
> Talk of court news; and we'll talk with them too,
> Who loses and who wins; who's in who's out;
> And take upon us the mystery of things,
> As if we were God's spies; and we'll wear out,
> In a walled prison, packs and sects of great ones,
> That ebb and flow by the moon.

Or, in relief of sadness, there is in *A Midsummer Night's Dream* such a fairy world as only Shakespeare's genius can create — King Oberon, Queen Titania with her lively elves Peaseblossom, Cobweb, Moth and Mustardseed; that shrewd and knavish sprite Robin Goodfellow, known also

as Hobgoblin and Sweet Puck, whose duty is to jest to
Oberon and make him smile; four lovers in an Athenian
wood, whom Puck will set at cross-purposes; and, in that
same wood, Bottom the Weaver and his fellow-artisans,
whose rehearsal of the play which they are to give before
Duke Theseus is interrupted by the pranks of the fairies.
He is very well satisfied with himself, is Bottom, and does
not know that an ass's head has been set upon his shoulders. Even when he finds Queen Titania making love to
him, it does not surprise him overmuch.

TITANIA: I pray thee, gentle mortal, sing again;
                Mine ear is much enamoured of thy note;
                So is mine eye enthralled to thy shape;
                And thy fair virtues, force perforce, doth move
                  me
                On the first view to say, to swear, I love thee.

BOTTOM: Methinks, mistress, you should have little reason
                for that: and yet, to say the truth, reason and
                love keep little company together now-a-days;
                the more the pity, that some honest neighbours
                will not make them friends. Nay, I can gleek
                upon occasion.

TITANIA: Thou are as wise as thou art beautiful.

BOTTOM: Not so, neither: but if I had wit enough to get
                out of this wood, I have enough to serve mine
                own turn.

TITANIA: Out of this wood do not desire to go:
                Thou shalt remain here, whether thou wilt or no.
                I am a spirit of no common rate:
                The summer still doth tend upon my state;
                And I do love thee: therefore, go with me;
                I'll give thee fairies to attend on thee;
                And they shall fetch thee jewels from the deep,
                And sing, while thou on pressed flowers dost sleep:

And I will purge thy mortal grossness so,
That thou shalt like an airy spirit go.
Peaseblossom! Cobweb! Moth! and Mustard-
    seed!

(*Enter* PEASEBLOSSOM, COBWEB, MOTH *and* MUSTARDSEED.)

FIRST FAIRY: Ready.

SECOND FAIRY: And I.

THIRD FAIRY: And I.

FOURTH FAIRY: And I.

ALL.   Where shall we go?

TITANIA: Be kind and courteous to this gentleman;
    Hop in his walks, and gambol in his eyes;
    Feed him with apricocks and dewberries,
    With purple grapes, green figs, and mulberries;
    The honey-bags steal from the humble-bees,
    And for night-tapers crop their waxen thighs,
    And light them at the fiery glow-worm's eyes,
    To have my love to bed and to arise;
    And pluck the wings from painted butterflies,
    To fan the moonbeams from his sleeping eyes:
    Nod to him, elves, and do him courtesies.

FIRST FAIRY: Hail, mortal!

SECOND FAIRY: Hail!

THIRD FAIRY: Hail!

FOURTH FAIRY: Hail!

BOTTOM: I cry your worships mercy, heartily: I beseech
    your worship's name.

COBWEB: Cobweb.

BOTTOM: I shall desire you of more acquaintance, good
    Master Cobweb: if I cut my finger, I shall make
    bold with you. Your name, honest gentleman?

PEASEBLOSSOM: Peaseblossom.

BOTTOM: I pray you, commend me to Mistress Squash, your
    mother, and to Master Peascod, your father. Good
    Master Peaseblossom, I shall desire you of more
    acquaintance too. Your name, I beseech you sir?

MUSTARDSEED: Mustardseed.

BOTTOM: Good Master Mustardseed, I know your patience well: that same cowardly, giant-like ox-
beef hath devoured many a gentleman of your
house: I promise you your kindred hath made
my eyes water ere now. I desire your more
acquaintance, good Master Mustardseed.

TITANIA: Come, wait upon him; lead him to my bower. . . .
Tie up my love's tongue, lead him silently.

From grave to gay, from tragedy to fairy fancies and
rollicking humor, a voyage of discovery through Shakespeare's plays follows a varied way. There is another sort
of discovery, too, which the voyager makes. New words
were pouring into the language from Latin, Italian, French
and Spanish. This "new world of words"[1] was as stimulating to the imagination of the Elizabethans as the new
world across the Atlantic. They "sported" new-fangled
words as they "sported" new-fangled costumes. The
description of Don Armado in Shakespeare's *Love's Labor's
Lost:*—

A man of fire-new words, fashion's own knight. . . .
A man in all the world's new fashion planted,
That hath a mint of phrases in his brain;
One whom the music of his own vain tongue
Doth ravish like enchanting harmony —

is applicable to the Elizabethans generally. Poets and
prose-writers alike found words enchanting, loved to play
with them, to jingle them, to make puns with them. Most
of all, they loved to try them out in new combinations, to
coin new phrases, to see what possibilities of new significance lay in the gorgeous vocabulary with which they

---

[1] John Florio (the Elizabethan translator of Montaigne's *Essays*) entitled
his English-Italian Dictionary (enlarged edition, 1611) *A New Worlde of Wordes.*

played.   The arch-experimenter was Shakespeare.   The voyager among Shakespeare's plays will discover, not only a richness of vocabulary such as no writer since has had in equal measure, but also a richness of phrase, a power of expressing a thought with such vividness that nobody since has been able to put it so well.   The result, of course, has been that thousands of Shakespeare's phrases have become imbedded in the language, have become a part of the very tissue of our thought.   Some are shopworn now.   But what a joy it is to come upon them, fire-new, so vivid and so right, in Shakespeare's pages!   Sunrise, as "jocund day, standing tiptoe on the misty mountain tops"; "the dark backward and abysm of time"; life's "insubstantial pageant"; "crossed with adversity"; "balmy" slumbers; "cudgelling one's brain"; to "stare on vacancy"; "homely" faces; men who "wear their hearts upon their sleeves"; a man's toes "looking through his shoes"; man "drest in a little brief authority"; "to patch grief with proverbs"; "devoured by the jaws of darkness"; "the strumpet wind"; "this muddy vesture of decay"; old age, as "the lean and slippered pantaloon"; "to gild refined gold, to paint the lily"; the "quiet breast" of truth; "the winter of our discontent"; "that old common arbitrator, Time"; "saint-seducing gold"; "the white wonder of dear Juliet's hand"; "life's fitful fever"; "to shuffle off this mortal coil"— these are but random samples. Every voyager will wish to do his own discovering and will enjoy making his own list.   To do so is to realize the more with every added phrase that it is the poet's vision, as well as the dramatist's power of interpreting character, that makes Shakespeare supreme — the poet's vision, shared, made visible to us, by the right describing word.

Shakespeare began his work about the year 1590.   *The Tempest*, which is thought to be his last play, is supposed

to have been written not later than 1611. These twenty
years, and the ten years following, are the great period of
the "Elizabethan" drama.[1] Of the many dramatists
whose plays have survived, we may take five as typical —
Ben Jonson, Francis Beaumont and John Fletcher, Thomas
Dekker and John Webster.

It is said that Shakespeare was instrumental in having
Ben Jonson's first comedy performed, and that he acted
parts in at least two of Jonson's plays. Tradition (recorded not long after Jonson's death) has it that Shakespeare and Jonson had many a friendly "wit-combat" at
the Mermaid Tavern, assailing each other "like a Spanish
great galleon and an English man-of-war; Master Jonson
(like the former) was built far higher in learning, solid but
slow in his performances. Shakespeare, with the English
man-of-war, lesser in bulk, but lighter in sailing, could
turn with all tides, tack about, and take advantage of all
winds by the quickness of his wit and invention." Probably many of their wit-combats turned on the drama, for
the methods of these two greatest of Elizabethan dramatists
are sharply contrasted. Shakespeare saw human nature
in the large; character, motive, personality, interested him
most. Environment, the surroundings of life, buildings,
streets, clothes, customs, the habits of the multitude, did
not matter very much — or mattered only as they might
help a little to explain why people did things. The scene
might be Venice or Verona or an Eastcheap tavern or the

---

[1] Queen Elizabeth died in 1603. Many of the most brilliant plays of the
period were actually written in the reign (1603–1625) of her successor, King
James I. It is because the creative spirit of the drama reached full tide in
"the spacious times of great Elizabeth" and did not begin to ebb till well on
in the reign of her successor that we think of the whole period as "Elizabethan."
Elizabeth's vivid personality stamped itself upon the age. James made no
such impress. To call *King Lear*, for example, "Jacobean" because it was
written after 1603, would be mere pedantry.

Merry England of the *Merry Wives;* what really mattered
was the tortured soul of Shylock, or the sudden blossoming
of love in Juliet's heart, or the gay effrontery and inexhaustible jests of Falstaff. Jonson, on the other hand, concerned himself most with the world round about him —
especially with its oddities and follies. Aside from the
"masques"[1] which he wrote for performance at court, and
his two stately Roman tragedies, Jonson's plays create
for us, in one satiric picture after another, a veritable image
of the times. That wise widow and sanctified sister, Dame
Purecraft, and her daughter, sweet Win-the-fight Little-
wit, and the Puritan preacher, Zeal-of-the-Land Busy,
rubbing shoulders with Ursula, the Pigwoman, and Lan-
thorn Leatherhead, the Hobby-horse seller, and Ezekiel
Edgeworth, the Cutpurse, and Nightingale, the Ballad-
singer, and Mooncalf, the Tapster, round the booths of
Bartholomew Fair; Captain Bobadill, the boastful soldier,
strutting through the aisles of St. Paul's; Master Stephen,
the Country Gull, getting into trouble in the City; the poor
servant, Brainworm, who is supposed to be "dreaming
on nought but idle poetry," turning out to be the most
"successful merry knave" in London; Fastidious Brisk,
the "neat spruce affecting courtier" who "wears clothes
well, practices by his glass how to salute, and speaks good
remnants"; Mistress Saviolina, the court-lady, who "does
observe as pure a phrase, and use as choice figures in her
ordinary conversation as any that be in the Arcadia";[2]
the old Londoner, Morose, who is so sick of the clack and
chatter of the town that he allows his friends to persuade
him into marrying a dumb wife — and then finds that they
have palmed off on him a noisy boy disguised as a girl;—
take Jonson by and large, there are few extravagancies or

---

[1] See page 206.   [2] See page 132.

follies or peccadillos of Elizabethan London that he misses. But by all odds the best of his plays is that exposure of the gullibility of the average Londoner which he calls *The Alchemist*. The master of a London house has gone off for a vacation. In his absence his servants pretend that they are "alchemists," who can turn base metals into gold and perform as well all other sorts of magic. A motley throng gather at the house — Dapper, the Lawyer's clerk, who wishes a "familiar" to give him skill in gambling; Drugger, a Tobacco-man, who believes that necromancy will help him to make his shop profitable; Sir Epicure Mammon, who wants limitless luxury:

> My meat shall all come in, in Indian shells,
> Dishes of agat set in gold, and studded
> With emeralds, sapphires, hyacinths, and rubies;

and, most entertaining of all, the reverend Tribulation Wholesome, Puritan preacher of Amsterdam, whom Subtle, the Alchemist, leads on to vision after vision of what the philosopher's stone may accomplish: —

> To be of power
> To pay an army in the field, to buy
> The King of France out of his realms, or Spain
> Out of his Indies. What can you not do
> Against lords spiritual or temporal
> That shall oppose you. . . .
> To win widows
> To give you legacies; or make zealous wives
> To rob their husbands for the common cause. . . .
> Nor shall you need to libel 'gainst the prelates. . . .
> Nor of necessity
> Rail against plays.[1]

---

[1] Compare generally with the foregoing quotations the account of the Puritans in Chapter VII.

The Alchemist is a great comedy. The Puritans, naturally, did not like it. But today, as in Jonson's day, no hearty reader can fail to enjoy the skill with which Jonson works out his plot, and the gleeful zest with which he displays his knaves and fools.

Dekker is a slighter, a much less important, figure. But of the enormous number and great variety of his plays, one, certainly, is worth a word here. After a course of Jonson's knaves and gulls, Dekker's *Shoemaker's Holiday* is a good play to turn to, to restore our faith in human nature. It is the sunny side of London life which Dekker gives us — the simple artisans, happy in their day's work. Simon Eyre, master shoemaker, makes shoes for the Lord Mayor of London. Rowland Lacy, nephew of the Earl of Lincoln, is in love with Rose, the Lord Mayor's daughter. To prevent the unequal match, the Earl obtains a commission for Rowland in the French war; but Rowland secretly sends a substitute, and, disguising himself as a Dutch 'prentice, enters the service of Simon Eyre, so that he may remain near Rose. How he wins her with Simon's help, and how Simon himself in due time becomes Lord Mayor, makes the main story of the play. Through it is woven another pretty romance — of how Ralph, one of Eyre's journeymen, is called to the colors, and how Ralph's young new-married wife, Jane, remains faithful to him through all temptations and discouragements. But these threads of story are mere devices to display Simon Eyre[1] and his circle — the bustling, loud-voiced, jesting, boasting, kindly, managing Simon, and his even more managing wife, Dame Margery, with her sharp tongue, her spicy bouts with the 'prentices, and her everlasting "but let that

[1] For the delightful little book from which Dekker derived Simon Eyre, see the chapter on Elizabethan prose.

pass!" and Hodge and Firk and Skipper and Hans with their merry songs:—

> Cold's the wind, and wet's the rain,
>   Saint Hugh be our good speed:
> Ill is the weather that bringeth no gain,
>   Nor helps good hearts in need.

> Trowl the bowl, the jolly nut-brown bowl,
>   And here, kind mate, to thee:
> Let's sing a dirge for Saint Hugh's soul,
>   And down it merrily.

Of all the plays by Shakespeare's contemporaries, *The Shoemaker's Holiday* is the pleasantest reading.

While Jonson in his comedies and Dekker in his *Shoemaker's Holiday* were busying themselves with the everyday world, two other dramatists were rivaling Shakespeare in his chosen field of poetic drama. Beaumont and Fletcher are named together because they worked together — jointly producing plays of such even texture that no one since their time has been able to say with certainty, "This part Beaumont wrote, that part Fletcher." The most famous fruits of this literary partnership are *The Maid's Tragedy* and a tragi-comedy *Philaster* (1609). *The Maid's Tragedy* is intensely emotional and contains passages of beautiful poetry, but it is rather painful reading. *Philaster* — though it too is not altogether free from disagreeable situations — is a pleasanter story, interesting for itself, and even more interesting because it affords a parallel to Shakespeare's *Twelfth Night*. Just as in that most delightful of romantic comedies, the young heroine, Viola, disguises herself as a page, enters the service of Duke Orsino, falls in love with him, and is compelled to act as his love-ambassador to the Lady Olivia, so in *Philaster* Euphrasia, who

is in love with Prince Philaster, enters his service as a page
and is a witness to his courtship of the Princess Arethusa.
But here the parallel ends; for whereas Viola wins Orsino,
it is Arethusa who marries Philaster; and poor Euphrasia,
with surprising amiability, asks nothing better than

> to serve the princess,
> To see the virtues of her lord and her.

But it is by more than such chance resemblances that
Beaumont and Fletcher deserve to be thought of in connection with Shakespeare. Indeed, for us, who are concerned with these fellow-dramatists of his, chiefly as they
help us to see him in the setting of his time, the resemblances of Beaumont and Fletcher to Shakespeare, and
the even more striking contrasts, are what matter most.
Beaumont and Fletcher began as Shakespeare's imitators.
They developed into his most successful rivals. Like him,
they colored life with the poet's imagination. Like him,
they were more interested in their heroes and heroines and
what was happening to them than in the material world
in which the characters lived. Like him, they had the
gift of making the story of the play intensely interesting,
of making it move with breathless speed toward its appointed climax. But what had interested Shakespeare
most was character. The person whose innermost nature
he had conceived from the outset must be true to that innermost nature throughout the play. Beaumont and
Fletcher, on the other hand, thought most (as we say today)
of "playing to the gallery." They contrived violent and
emotional scenes, they arranged unnatural and startling
situations, they strove to surprise their audiences with unexpected and unforeseeable dénouements.
This straining after effects means that the art of the

Elizabethan drama, which had reached its height in Shakespeare, was already, in the plays of his most successful rivals, beginning to decline. From this time on, more and more, this violence, this effort to surprise and startle, takes the place of Shakespeare's reasonableness and sincerity. It is not so much that genius was lacking during this period as that it was misspent. There are extraordinary flare-ups of power. One of the most remarkable is a play of John Webster's, called *The Duchess of Malfi* (first printed 1623; composed about 1617). The widowed Duchess has secretly married a man beneath her in station, the steward of her household. In the course of time her brothers discover the marriage and subject her to unimaginable tortures. She is imprisoned; she is given a dead man's hand and told that it is her husband's; through the grating of her cell she is shown waxen figures made in the semblance of her husband and their children and is led to believe that all are dead; she is placed in a madhouse among raving maniacs; and at length when her tormentors find that nothing that they can do will daunt her courage, they bring a coffin and an executioner with cords into her presence, and strangle her. One would think from this outline that the play is nothing but melodrama, a mad piling up of horror on horror, with no possible room in it for sincere delineation of character. And yet the Duchess, with her love for her husband, her tender practical solicitude for her children:—

> I pray thee, look thou givest my little boy
> Some syrup for his cold, and let the girl
> Say her prayers ere she sleep —

her indomitable courage, and that white light of her purity and beauty which shines through all the horrors of the play, is one of the noblest and truest creations of English literature.

But despite those flashes of brilliance, the art of Shakespeare was dying. The violence which had taken its place reflected the spirit of the time. The Civil War was near at hand.[1] There was a kind of madness in the air. The court of Charles I, by its frivolity, its extravagances, its excesses, was blindly fanning the flame of Puritan hate. The court patronized and encouraged the theater. The theater took its color from the court. When at length the war broke, and the court had fled to Oxford, one of the first acts of the Puritans was to close the theaters.

The edict of 1642 that "public stage-plays shall cease and be forborne" puts a final date to a period which has no counterpart in English literary history. The reopening of the theaters in 1660 spurred the drama to renewed activity for a while; but from that day to this the drama has never absorbed the best minds, the greatest creative geniuses, as it did in the height of the Elizabethan period. There has been no other Age of Dramatic Literature. Here and there, as the generations have passed, a dramatist of exceptional ability has emerged. But they can be counted almost on the fingers of one hand — Dryden, Otway and Congreve in the late years of the seventeenth century, Goldsmith and Sheridan in the eighteenth, George Bernard Shaw, perhaps, in our own day. These are few and far between. But with Shakespeare, in those thirty years between 1590 and 1620, were Marlowe and Jonson and Dekker and Beaumont and Fletcher and Webster and a score of others hardly less memorable.

[1] For the rise of Puritanism and the Civil War, see Chapter VII.

IV

ELIZABETHAN PROSE

We think of the Elizabethan period chiefly as an Age of Poetry — dramatic or lyric. English poetry had a great tradition, going back to Chaucer's day. To the Elizabethan it stood by itself, the supreme art, to be cultivated by every man of letters. That way, too, lay honor and reward. Even the mere expert craftsman, who rhymed because it was the thing to do, could hope to catch the attention of the Queen with a courtly compliment, or fatten his purse by a flattering dedication to such patrons of literature as Leicester or Essex or Southampton.

English prose had no such tradition, enjoyed no such standing, offered no such incentive. As an *art*, as a way of getting something not only intelligibly said, but also beautifully said, it was just beginning to find itself. But Elizabethan prose literature, too, has its great moments; and both in its subject matter and in its reachings after style, it is full of interest.

There is, for example, a deal of wonderfully good reading to be found in the accounts of Elizabethan voyages. Richard Hakluyt's collection of *Principal Navigations, Voyages and Discoveries*, made in 1589 and reissued, much enlarged, between 1598 and 1600, has been called "the great prose epic of the English nation." With a few exceptions, the wording of these narratives is clumsy, but there is no better way of entering into the spirit of the Elizabethan age, of realizing how present to the imagination of poet and dramatist all this matter was, than by reading *Hakluyt*. Some of the men who describe their experiences in his pages the

Elizabethans rubbed shoulders with on the London streets and listened to around tavern tables. Their stories were real as no secondhand records could have been. And even now, so much like actual rambling talk rather than planned composition are these stories, it is as if we too were listening to words new-fallen from the teller's lips.

It is much better to turn Hakluyt's pages than to get him only in brief excerpts; but a paragraph or two here and there will serve at least to show how the voyagers told their stories. Here is a bit from the narrative by John Sparke (one of Hawkins's men) of Hawkins's trading voyage to Guiana and thence past Florida along the coast to Newfoundland.

"In this river we saw many crocodiles of sundry bignesses, but some as big as a boat, with four feet, a long broad mouth, and a long tail; whose skin is so hard that a sword will not pierce it. His nature is to live out of the water as a frog doth; but he is a great devourer, and spareth neither fish, which is his common food, not beasts, nor men, if he take them, as the proof thereof was known by a negro, who, as he was filling water in the river, was by one of them carried clean away and never seen after. His nature is ever, when he would have his prey, to cry and sob like a Christian body, to provoke them to come to him, and then he snatcheth at them; and thereupon came this proverb, that is applied unto women when they weep, *lachrymæ crocodili*, the meaning whereof is, that as the crocodile when he crieth goeth then about most to deceive, so doth a woman most commonly when she weepeth."

Shakespeare and his fellow-dramatists liked the *lachrymæ crocodili:*

> and Gloucester's show
> Beguiles him as the mournful crocodile
> With sorrow snares relenting passengers.
> — *The Second Part of Henry VI*

If that the earth could teem with woman's tears,
Each drop she falls would prove a crocodile.
— *Othello*

"I will neither yield to the song of siren nor the voice of the hyena, the tears of the crocodile nor the howling of a wolf."
— *Eastward Ho*

Sometimes plain soldier Sparke pauses in his narrative to create a picture for us:

"There be also of sea-fishes, which we saw coming along the coast, flying, which are of the bigness of a smelt, the biggest sort whereof have four wings, but the others have but two. Of these we saw coming out of Guinea a hundred in a company, which being chased by the gilt-heads, otherwise called the bonitos, do to avoid them the better, take their flight out of the water; but yet are they not able to fly far, because of the drying of their wings, which serve them not to fly but when they are moist, and therefore when they can fly no further, they fall into the water, and having wet their wings, take a new flight again. . . . There is a sea-fowl also, that chaseth this flying fish as well as the bonito; for as the flying fish taketh her flight, so doth this fowl pursue to take her, which to behold is a greater pleasure than hawking; for both the flights are as pleasant, and also more often than a hundred times; for the fowl can fly no way, but one or other lighteth in her paws, the number of them are so abundant."

And here is a bit from "The Second Voyage Attempted by Master John Davis for the Discovery of the Northwest Passage, 1586":

"The people [he is speaking of the Eskimos] are of good stature, well in body proportioned, with small slender hands and feet, with broad visages, and small eyes, wide mouths, the most part unbearded, great lips, and close toothed. . . . They are idolaters and have images great store, which they wear about them, and in their boats, which we suppose they worship. They are witches, and have many kinds of enchantments, which they often used, but to small purpose, thanks be to God. . . . These people are very simple in all their conversation, but marvellous thievish, especially for iron, which they have in great account. . . . They brought us seal skins, and salmon peal, but seeing iron, they could in no wise forbear stealing: which when I perceived, it did but minister unto me an occasion of laughter, to see their simplicity, and I willed that in no case they should be any more hardly used, but that our own company should be the more vigilant to keep their things, supposing it to be very hard in so short time to make them know their evils."

And, finally, here is an altogether too brief passage from Sir Walter Raleigh's account of the fight which occurred off the Azores in the year 1591, between the little English ship, the *Revenge*, commanded by Sir Richard Grenville, and the great fleet of Spain —

The Spanish ships which attempted to board the *Revenge*, as they were wounded and beaten off, so always others came in their places, she having never less than two mighty galleons by her sides and aboard her. So that ere the morning from three of the clock the day before, there had fifteen several armadas assailed her, and all so ill approved their entertainment, as they were by the break of day, far more willing to hearken to a composition, than hastily to make any more assaults or entries. But as the day increased so our men decreased; and as the light grew more and more, by so much more grew our discomforts. For none appeared in sight but enemies, saving one small ship called the *Pilgrim*, commanded by Jacob Whiddon, who hovered all night to see the success: but in the morning bearing with the *Revenge*, was hunted like a hare amongst many ravenous hounds, but escaped.

All the powder of the *Revenge* to the last barrel was now spent, all her pikes broken, forty of her best men slain, and the most part of the rest hurt. In the beginning of the fight she had but one hundred free from sickness, and fourscore and ten sick, laid in hold upon the ballast. A small troop to man such a ship, and a weak garrison to resist so mighty an army. By those hundred all was sustained, the volleys, boardings, and enterings of fifteen ships of war, besides those which beat her at large. On the contrary, the Spanish were always supplied with soldiers brought from every squadron: all manner of arms and powder at will. Unto ours there remained no comfort at all, no hope, no supply either of ships, men, or weapons; the masts all beaten overboard, all her tackle cut asunder, her upper work altogether razed, and in effect evened she was with the water, but the very foundation or bottom of a ship, nothing being left overhead either for flight or defence. Sir Richard finding himself in this distress, and unable any longer to make resistance, having endured in this fifteen hours' fight, the assault of fifteen several armadas, all by turns aboard him, and by estimation eight hundred shot of great artillery, besides many assaults and entries, and that himself and the ship must needs be possessed by the enemy, who were now all cast in a ring round about him; the *Revenge* not able to move one way or other, but as she was moved with the waves and billow of the sea: commanded the master Gunner, whom he knew to be a most resolute man, to split and sink the ship; that thereby nothing might remain of glory or victory to the Spaniards: seeing in so many hours' fight, and with so great a Navy they were not able to take her, having had fifteen hours' time, fifteen thousand men, and fifty and three sail of men-of-war to perform it withal.

More than 250 years later the poet Tennyson retold that story —

And the sun went down, and the stars came out far over the
    summer sea,
But never a moment ceased the fight of the one and the fifty-
    three.
Ship after ship, the whole night long, their high built galleons
    came,

Ship after ship, the whole night long, with her battle thunder and
　　flame;
Ship after ship, the whole night long, drew back with her dead
　　and her shame.
For some were sunk and many were shattered, and so could fight
　　us no more —
God of battles, was ever a battle like this in the world before!—

but I doubt if you will find Tennyson's ballad, with its
carefully arranged effects, more genuinely stirring than
Raleigh's nervous and vivid prose.

Hakluyt is a part of the background of Elizabethan life
and literature.   Beside it, let us put another group of
prose-narratives, stories of men who lived in the remote
past and belonged to another race and nation, but who
were as present to the imagination of the Elizabethan
poets as their own seafarers.

Toward the end of the first century A.D., a Greek
writer named Plutarch wrote a series of biographies of the
great figures of the Greek and Roman world, devoting
each book of the series to the life of one Greek and one
Roman, and following these by a comparison of the characters of the two.   When the revival of learning came and
with it an eager interest in everything that had happened
in the classical period, the men of the Renaissance turned
to Plutarch.   The wide range of his biographies, the vividness of his characterizations, his wealth of anecdote revived for them the life of Greece and Rome.   Dryden, in
his life of Plutarch, tells a story which illustrates this
feeling.   When the question was put to Theodorus Gaza[1]
what author he would choose, if there were a general shipwreck of learning and he could preserve but one, Gaza

---

[1] One of the leaders of the revival of learning in the fifteenth century.

replied, "Plutarch"— because "in saving him, he should secure the best collection of them all."

The Elizabethans read Plutarch in the translation made by Sir Thomas North in 1575. If Plutarch recreated Greek and Roman life, North, in another sense, recreated Plutarch. North's vocabulary is rich in words newly imported — often coined, offhand — from Latin, French and Italian. It is equally rich in Elizabethan slang. When he chose, he could write with perfect dignity and restraint. But he never missed an opportunity to let himself go. Though Nash[1] comes not far short of him, his is the raciest, breeziest prose that Elizabethan literature affords.

And it is extraordinarily good reading. The combination of Plutarch's skill in weaving his story and North's dash in telling it makes North's *Plutarch* a book to live with. Certainly the Elizabethans thought . so. Shakespeare, for example, steeped himself in North, drawing from him plot, characterization, and many a casual phrase, for *Julius Cæsar, Timon of Athens, Antony and Cleopatra* and *Coriolanus*. Sometimes, the reproduction is almost literal, as when Sicinius orders that Coriolanus be put to death. North says: "He commanded the Ædiles to apprehend him and carry him straight to the rock Tarpeian, and to cast him headlong down the same." Shakespeare has Sicinius say:

> Therefore lay hold of him;
> Bear him to the rock Tarpeian, and from thence
> Into destruction cast him.

Sometimes Shakespeare takes his cue from North's racy wording, but adds an effective touch of his own. This, for example, is North's version of a saying of Cæsar's: "As

---

[1] See page 125.

for those fat men and smooth-combed heads, quoth he, I
never reckon of them; but these pale-visaged and carrion-
lean people, I fear them most; meaning Brutus and Cas-
sius."

This is Shakespeare's:

> Let me have men about me that are fat:
> Sleek-headed men, and such as sleep o' nights:
> Yond Cassius has a lean and hungry look.

Sometimes it is the picture drawn by North's swift pen
that sets fire to Shakespeare's imagination.   There is no
better example of North's power (with whatever obligation to his original) than that amazingly condensed and
breath-taking story of Cleopatra's last moments.   Antony,
whom she loves, is dead.   Now, she is captive to Cæsar —

Then having ended these doleful plaints, and crowned the tomb
with garlands and sundry nosegays, and marvellous lovingly
embraced the same, she commanded they should prepare her
bath; and when she had bathed and washed herself, she fell to
her meat, and was sumptuously served.   Now whilst she was
at dinner, there came a countryman and brought her a basket.[1]
The soldiers that warded at the gates, asked him straight what
he had in his basket.   He opened his basket, and took out the
leaves that covered the figs, and showed them that they were
figs he brought.   They all of them marvelled to see so goodly
figs.   The countryman laughed to hear them, and bade them to
take some if they would.   They believed he told them truly, and
so bade him carry them in.   After Cleopatra had dined, she sent
a certain table written and sealed unto Cæsar, and commanded
them all to go out of the tombs where she was, but the two women;
then she shut the doors to her.   Cæsar, when he had received this

---

[1] As North notes later in his narrative, Cleopatra had secretly arranged to
have brought in to her a basket in which was concealed an "asp" (a venomous
snake of the viper family).

table, and began to read her lamentation and petition, requesting him that he would let her be buried with Antonius, found straight what she meant, and thought to have gone thither himself: howbeit, he sent one before in all haste that might be, to see what it was. Her death was very sudden: for those whom Cæsar sent unto her ran thither with all haste possible, and found the soldiers standing at the gate, mistrusting nothing, nor understanding of her death. But when they had opened the doors, they found Cleopatra stark-dead, laid upon a bed of gold, attired and arrayed in her royal robes, and one of her two women, which was called Iras, dead at her feet: her other woman (called Charmion) half dead, and trembling, trimming the diadem which Cleopatra wore upon her head. One of the soldiers seeing her, angrily said unto her: "Is this well done, Charmion?" "Very well," said she again, "and meet for a princess descended from the race of so many kings;" she said no more, but fell down dead hard by the bed.

It is difficult to resist the temptation to put beside this the whole magnificent scene (*Antony and Cleopatra*, Act V, scene II) in which Shakespeare elaborates and dramatizes North's words — that scene ending with the entrance of Cæsar's soldiers —

1. GUARD Where is the queen?
CHARMIAN   Speak softly, wake her not.
1. GUARD Cæsar hath sent —
CHARMIAN   Too slow a messenger.
                          (*Applies an asp*)
              O, come apace, despatch! I partly feel thee.
1. GUARD Approach, ho! All's not well; Cæsar's beguil'd.
2. GUARD There's Dolabella sent from Cæsar; call him.
1. GUARD What work is here! Charmian, is this well done?
CHARMIAN It is well done, and fitting for a princess
              Descended of so many royal kings.
              Ah, soldier! (*Dies*)

But though all Elizabethan roads seem to lead to Shake-speare, it is North with whom we are concerned. It is not fair to treat him as if his sole or even his chief importance to us consists in what Shakespeare did with him. If it had never been North's fate to minister to a greater genius, his value would be but little lessened. With the lapse of three centuries, the mood of the Renaissance has passed. We are less anxious than the Elizabethans were to imitate the classics, less inclined to fill our writings with allusions to them, less given to spending our thoughts on the age and on the men of whom Plutarch wrote. But such changes have made little difference with North's *Plutarch*. It is because it is such a human document, because the people in his pages are so real, and because their doings are told with such dash and vividness, that it can still be read with undiminished interest and enjoyment.

So much can hardly be said of Elizabethan prose-fiction. There is no field of literature in which taste changes so greatly from generation to generation. The kind of fiction to which our novelists have accustomed us is so different from the Elizabethan that most of the invented stories which delighted that age would probably seem either hopelessly crude or intolerably artificial to us. But the beginnings of any art are interesting as beginnings; and once in a while the Elizabethans produced a tale which, like the poetry of which Sidney speaks, "holdeth children from play and old men from the chimney corner."

Elizabethan fiction falls roughly into two classes, tales of the unvarnished realities of life, and romances of love-making and adventure in an idealized world of the imagination. Of the former, two are especially interesting. A Spanish novel, *Lazarillo de Tormes,* translated into English in 1576, had started the fashion of telling stories of adventurers and tricksters. Of this sort is Thomas Nash's *The Unfortunate Traveller or the Life of Jack Wilton* (1594), the story of a page in the employ of the Earl of Surrey, who follows his master from city to city of Europe and "sees life." The variety of incident, the rapid changes of scene, the riotous vigor of the narrative make *Jack Wilton* the most genuine "thriller" in the whole range of Elizabethan fiction. It is interesting, too, as a pioneer book. Later on, we shall see such novelists as Defoe and Fielding in the eighteenth century, and Thackeray in the nineteenth century writing novels of just this sort — carrying an adventurer-hero through a succession of experiences, all of which are as *real*, as true to the rough facts of life, as the novelist can make them; involving him with all sorts of people, whom the novelist makes as real, as true to actual life, as possible; and thus making a broad, truthful picture — a veritable panoramic photograph — of the life of the times. That (although he pretended to "time" his story half a century earlier, in the reign of Henry VIII) is what Nash was trying to do in *Jack Wilton*.

The other plain-tale-of-life-as-it-is that I should like to tell you about is a little book by Thomas Deloney called *The Gentle Craft* (1597). Such stories as *Jack Wilton* have the spice of unfamiliar adventure. Deloney is content with the homely doings of working men. *The Gentle Craft* consists of three short stories, the first of St. Hugh, the patron saint of the shoemakers; the second of how the two princes, Crispin and Crispianus, found refuge with a shoemaker of Feversham; and the third of "how Sir Simon Eyre, being at first a shoemaker, became in the end Mayor of London, through the counsel of his wife; and how he broke his fast every day on a table that he said he would not sell for a thousand pounds; and how he builded Leaden-hall." The best of the three is the tale of Simon Eyre. This little tale deserves to be far better known than it is.[1] Nothing could be more delightfully natural, for example, than the bedtime talk of Simon and his wife, after the Lord Mayor's banquet. Simon the humble shoemaker has just taken his first step upward. Acting on his wife's advice, he has made a fortunate investment which has attracted public attention, and now the two have had the undreamed-of honor of sitting at the Lord Mayor's table.

"And never give me credit, husband, if I did not hear the officers whisper as they stood behind me and all demanded one of another what you were and what I was. 'O,' quoth one, 'do you see this man? Mark him well, and mark his wife well, that simple woman that sits next my lady — what are they?' 'What are they?' quoth another. 'Marry, this is the rich shoemaker that bought all the goods in the great argosy. I tell you there was never such a shoemaker seen in London since the city was builded'. . . . Credit me, husband, of mine honesty this was their communication. Nay, and do you not remember when the rich citizen drank to you — which craved pardon because he knew not your name — what my Lord mayor said? 'Sir,' quoth he, 'his name is *Master* Eyre.' Did you mark that? And presently thereupon he added these words: 'This is the gentleman that bought' — and so forth. The *gentleman* — understood you? Did you hear him speak that word?"

"In troth, wife," quoth he, "my lord uttered many good words of me, I thank his Honour, but I heard not that."

"No?" quoth she. "I heard it well enough, for by and by he proceeded further, saying: 'I suppose, though he sit here in simple sort, he is more sufficient to bear this charge than myself.' Yea, thought I, he may thank his wife for that if it came so to pass."

"Nay," said Simon, "I thank God for it."

[1] The Oxford Press has recently issued a cheap edition of *The Gentle Craft*.

"Yea, and next Him, you may thank me," quoth she. And it did her so much good to talk of it, that I suppose, if she had lived to this day, she would yet be prating thereof, and if sleep did not drive her from it.

Deloney was a humble fellow, who eked out a living by writing ballads to be crudely printed and hawked about the streets. But in *The Gentle Craft* he builded better than he knew. For that simple, artless little story is the first of a long line of novels (among them some of the best in English literature, such as Jane Austen's and George Eliot's) which depend for their interest upon the truthfulness of their studies of ordinary people and of their pictures of everyday life.

Side by side with these realistic stories, the Elizabethan age produced many romances. One of the most curious of these, both for its style (which will be discussed later) and for its subject matter, is *Euphues, the Anatomy of Wit* (1579), by John Lyly. Euphues is an Athenian youth who goes to live in Naples, falls in love and is jilted, becomes a disillusioned philosopher, and returns to Athens to write "a cooling card for all fond lovers." In the sequel, *Euphues and his England* (1580), Euphues finds his way to England, the account of his voyage and adventures being "mixed," as the sub-title explains, "with sundry pretty discourses of honest love, the description of the country, the court and the manners of that Isle." These sundry pretty discourses are indeed what the book was chiefly written for. It is in the line of succession from Hoby's *Courtier*,[1] a commentary on society, and an exemplification of the high-flown talk "polite" lovers might be supposed to engage in, if they were more interested in taking love to pieces and seeing how the wheels go round, than

[1] See page 147.

in making it. Like Nash's *Jack Wilton* and Deloney's *Gentle Craft*, *Euphues* is interesting as a pioneer-book — the first of a long line of novels written about the "polite world" and intended especially for the "gentle reader." Lyly offers *Euphues* not only as "very pleasant for all gentlemen to read and most necessary to remember," but also for the delectation of the ladies. "It resteth, Ladies, that you take the pains to read it, but at such times as you spend in playing with your little dogs, and yet will I not pinch you of that pastime, for I am content that your dogs lie in your laps, so *Euphues* may be in your hands, that when you shall be weary of the one you may be ready to sport with the other."

In subject matter, *Euphues* is a little apart from the main current of Elizabethan romance. The kind of story which the Elizabethan liked best for the story's sake transported him to a far country of brave adventure, peopled by kings and queens, and by noble gentlemen who made love to beautiful princesses. If it should happen that the princess, when an infant, had been taken away from her royal home, and been found and reared by shepherds, and had never dreamed that she *was* a princess until the prince fell in love with her (as in Robert Green's *Pandosto*, from which Shakespeare drew the plot for *The Winter's Tale*); or if a duke and his whole ducal court could be banished to the greenwood, there to live in idyllic meditation, while the hero pins sonnets to the trees in praise of his lady of high degree (as in Thomas Lodge's *Rosalind*, from which Shakespeare drew the plot of *As You Like It*) — if, in short, the romance of lordlings could be given a pastoral[1] setting, then the contrast with the busy streets of London would be all the greater and the story the more

[1] The Latin word *pastor* means a shepherd.

delightful. The most notable of these pastoral romances is Sir Philip Sidney's *Arcadia*, written in 1580 and first printed in 1590, four years after his death. Two princes, Musidorus and Pyrocles, finding their way to Arcadia, encounter in the forest the two daughters of the king of that country, Pamela and Philoclea. They fall in love with them — and of course ultimately marry them. But what with Pyrocles' disguising himself as a shepherdess and being wooed by the king, and then having his disguise discovered by the queen who thereupon falls in love with him herself; and what with the disguises and false names which the rest of them assume and the completeness and frequency with which they lose track of one another in their meanderings; and what with the knightly battles that have to be fought and the stately discourses that have to be pronounced, they are all a very long time about it.

If our interest in *Euphues* and the *Arcadia* depended upon the story, it is possible that we might not get very far. But it happens that both Lyly and Sidney were not only story-tellers but artists in words — experimenters, shaping their prose to a design, attempting to put it on a par with poetry as an instrument of beauty. In a time when poetry was looked upon as the one art that really mattered, and when prose was generally cumbrous and formless, that is the really interesting thing.

In so far as prose had developed a sense of form, it had borrowed that form from the Latin. The two principles of Latin sentence structure which were beginning to work their way into English were, first the "balancing" of phrases and clauses most closely related in sense — that is, making them somewhat similar in word order and in sound, for the sake of emphasizing the resemblance or the contrast in meaning; and second, the accumulating of these several parts of the sentence (without telling what is going to be done with them) until at length, with a fine mass effect, they are all at once propelled into action with the verb. Consider, for example, a sentence from the Latin orator, Cicero. With the English words arranged as nearly as possible in the Latin order, this is, in substance, what Cicero is saying: "Therefore, I ask you, who could blame me, who could rightly be incensed with me, if, with all the time conceded to the rest of mankind to look after their business, with all the time conceded to the rest of mankind to attend the games on public holidays, just as much time to cultivate these literary pursuits I take for myself?" But it is in Cicero's own words, rather than in this clumsy rendering of them, that the structure best appears. *Qua re quis tandem me reprehendat, aut quis mihi iure suscenseat, si, quantum ceteris ad suas res obeundas, quantum ad festos dies ludorum celebrandos . . . conceditur temporum . . . tantum mihi egomet ad haec studia recolenda sumpsero?* See how neatly balanced the two *quis* clauses are, and how the chiming of *reprehendat* and *suscenseat* adds to the effect; how neatly balanced the two *quantum* clauses are, and how the chiming of *obeundas* and *celebrandos* adds to the effect; and, finally, how Cicero leaves the two *quantum* clauses suspended till he is ready to drive the whole thing home with his *tantum . . . sumpsero.*

On this foundation of balanced clauses and periodic sentence structure, Lyly built the style of *Euphues.* There he might prudently have stopped; but he was bent on giving his carefully molded prose every possible decoration, in order to lift it out of the commonplace and put it on a par with poetry. He sought not only to make the word-order in his balanced clauses correspond and to give the paired clauses the same chime and rhythm, but also to select words beginning with the same letter. This device of alliteration he carried to such a point that words in corresponding positions in the two clauses often alliterate with each other: "Although, hitherto, Euphues, I have shrined *thee* in my *h*eart for a *tr*usty *f*riend, I will *sh*un *thee h*ereafter as a *tr*othless *f*oe." And, as if this were not enough, he chose to deck his thoughts with the strangest comparisons, the most far-fetched similes, ever collected between the covers of a single book. The nature-lore of the time furnished him with his material, and there are few observations on life, on manners, on the complicated emotions of lovers, that he neglected to spice with an allusion to some incredible beast or fish or fowl:[1]

"For as by basil the scorpion is engendered and by the same herb destroyed; so love which by time and fancy is bred in an idle head, is by time and fancy banished from the heart: or as the salamander which, being a long space nourished in the fire, at the last quencheth it, so affection having taken hold of the fancy, and living as it were in the mind of the lover, in tract of time altereth and changeth the heat and turneth it to chillness."

Euphuism seems to us rather a wit's plaything than a means of conveying thought; but it had an astonishing effect upon the literature of the time. Other story writers adopted the style, and the minor poets practiced it in their verses. From books it made its way into polite conversation, and every gallant courtier and modish fine lady of Queen Elizabeth's court tried to talk like the characters in *Euphues* — talking, as Drayton said,

[1] Most of these tricks, even the allusions to natural history, had been tried before Lyly's day — notably by Sir Thomas North in his *Diall of Princes* (1557) (itself a translation of a fantastic piece of Spanish prose) and by George Pettie, in his *Petite Palace of Pettie his Pleasure* (1576); but Lyly so far surpassed his predecessors in ingenuity that this peculiar mode of writing came to be known as Euphuism — the style of *Euphues*.

of stones, stars, plants, of fishes, flies,
Playing with words and idle similies . . .
So imitating his ridiculous tricks,
They speak and write, all like mere lunatics.

"Our nation," wrote one of Lyly's admirers some fifty
years later, "are in his debt for a new English which he
taught them. *Euphues and his England* began first that
language; all our ladies were then his scholars: and that
Beauty in Court which could not parley Euphuism was as
little regarded as she which now there speaks not French."

As a plaything for the wits, euphuism did not last long.
But it served its purpose in showing that English prose, a
humble Cinderella in the Elizabethan palace of poetry,
could be fitted with silver slippers. To construct sentences
with careful art, to proportion the parts of the sentence
one to the other, and to marshal these several parts toward
an effective finish instead of letting them hobble on any-
how — that was something worth doing. Even if, in the
first flush of his enthusiasm, Lyly carried his manipula-
tions to extravagant lengths, he deserves credit for making
the venture.

He deserves credit, too, for encouraging others to have
a try. One whom Lyly's experiment thus stimulated was
Sir Philip Sidney. In 1580, just a year after the publication of *Euphues*, Sidney retired from Elizabeth's court to
the estate of his sister, the Countess of Pembroke, and
there set to work upon the romantic tale which came to
be known as *The Countess of Pembroke's Arcadia*.

Sidney had no intention of being numbered among the
"dainty wits" who

with strange similes enrich each line
Of herbs or beasts which Ind or Affrike hold.

It is true that he enjoyed balancing sentences and playing upon words. Novel similes appealed to him too, and, in spite of his disclaimer, he was not above spicing his fancy occasionally with a tarantula or a salamander or a catoblepas. But he had a spirit above Lyly's gymnastics. What he sought to do was to make his Arcadia a "prose-poem," to tell his story of chivalric deeds and graceful love-making in words chosen for their poetic beauty and fitted musically together. And though the graces of his style become at long last a little cloying, he does often succeed in transforming the hit-and-miss stuff of daily speech into a thing of beauty — even sometimes of a rare loveliness. To describe a maiden's cheeks blushing "and withal, when she was spoken unto, a little smiling, like roses, when their leaves are with a little breath stirred," is to step so far past the faint line which divides prose and poetry that we are content to let Sidney give his style any name he chooses. And here is a longer example, which not only illustrates the delicate grace and the characteristic rhythms of Sidney's prose, but will serve also to show (especially in the last sentence) that he sometimes did imitate the tricks of Lyly's *Euphues*. It is a description of the first glimpse which the hero, Musidorus, gets of the fertile land of Arcadia, after passing through the battle-scarred waste of Laconia:

There were hills which garnished their proud heights with stately trees; humble valleys whose base estate seemed comforted with refreshing of silver rivers; meadows enamelled with all sorts of eye-pleasing flowers; thickets which, being lined with most pleasant shade, were witnessed so to by the cheerful disposition of many well-tuned birds; each pasture stored with sheep, feeding with sober security, while the pretty lambs, with bleating oratory, craved the dams' comfort: here a shepherd's boy piping, as though he should never be old; there a young shepherdess knitting, and withal singing, and it seemed that her voice comforted her hands to work, and her hands kept time to her voice's music. As for the houses of the country (for many houses came under their eye) they were all scattered, no two being one by the other, and yet not so far off as that it barred mutual succour: a show, as it were, of an accompanable solitariness, and of a civil wildness. "I pray you," said Musidorus, then first unsealing his long-silent lips, "what countries be these we pass through, which are so diverse in show, the one wanting no store, the other having no store but of want?"

The *Arcadia* found as many imitators as *Euphues*, and, on the whole, in choicer circles. "The noble Sidney," they affirmed, had for the first time so

> paced our language as to show
> The plenteous English hand in hand might go
> With Greek and Latin.

If Lyly taught the nation "a new English," Sidney taught them to modify that new English into less fantastic and more genuinely poetic forms.

But *Arcadia* is not the best of Sidney's prose-writings. The style of that book is a deliberate experiment, intended to befit the romantic theme. His choicest prose — wholly natural and easy and yet exquisitely skillful — is to be found in a little essay called *The Defence of Poesie*. Written not later than 1583, the *Defence* is among the earliest of the many treatises on the art of poetry produced during the Elizabethan period. They were all occupied with much the same topics: defence of poetry against the attacks of the Puritans, who condemned it as immoral; the establishment of the claim of poetry to outrank all other arts; the discussion of the nature of the various forms, epic, dramatic, lyric, satiric, elegiac, pastoral, and of the rules concerning them handed down from classical antiquity;

and the possibility of substituting classical meters with their orderly "feet" of "long" vowels and "short" vowels, for the natural English rhythm of "beats"or "stresses."

As his title indicates, it is the justification of poetry with which Sidney is chiefly concerned. He glances at other topics, disapproving, for example, of contemporary poetic drama (then just at the threshold of its greatness) because it seems to him a disorderly thing, mixing tragedy and comedy in the same play, and disregarding the principles of construction which the great classical dramas exemplify — "an unmannerly daughter," he calls it, "showing a bad education," causing "her mother Poesy's honesty to be called in question." He condemns the "far-fet" words which many poets affect, and their "coursing of a letter" (use of alliteration) "as if they were bound to follow the method of a dictionary;" and he turns aside to say a few wise words about the follies of euphuism; "Now for similitudes in certain printed discourses, I think all herbarists, all stories of beasts, fowls and fishes are rifled up, that they may come in multitudes to wait upon any of our conceits, which certainly is as absurd a surfeit to the ears as is possible. For the force of a similitude not being to prove anything to a contrary disputer, but only to explain to a willing hearer; when that is done, the rest is a most tedious prattling, rather overswaying the memory from the purpose whereto they were applied, than any whit informing the judgment, already either satisfied or by similitudes not to be satisfied." He is happy in such casual comments; but his golden-tongued best is devoted to the praise of poetry. Even the old ballads, the folk-songs of a bygone time, stir his pulses:

I never heard the old song of Percy and Douglas that I found not my heart moved more than with a trumpet; and yet it is sung but by some blind crowder [fiddler] with no rougher voice than rude style. [As for the poetry of great deeds greatly told, what is worthy to be compared with it? Not history, for the historian is bound to tell things as things were. He cannot select, he cannot shape life as it ought to be. Not philosophy; for though philosophy teach wisdom and virtue, it but showeth the way. It doth not move one to do that which it doth teach. The poet] doth not only show the way, but giveth so sweet a prospect into the way as will entice any man to enter it. Nay, he doth, as if your journey should lie through a fair vineyard, at the very first give you a cluster of grapes, that full of that taste you may long to pass further. He beginneth not with obscure definitions, which must blur the margent with interpretations, and load the memory with doubtfulness. But he cometh to you with words set in delightful proportion, either accompanied with, or prepared for, the well-enchanting skill of music; and with a tale, forsooth, he cometh unto you, with a tale which holdeth children from play, and old men from the chimney-corner, and, pretending no more, doth intend the winning of the mind from wickedness to virtue; even as the child is often brought to take most wholesome things, by hiding them in such other as have a pleasant taste,— which, if one should begin to tell them the nature of the aloes or rhubarb they should receive, would sooner take their physic at their ears than at their mouth. So is it in men, most of which are childish in the best things, till they be cradled in their graves,— glad they will be to hear the tales of Hercules, Achilles, Cyrus, Æneas; and, hearing them, must needs hear the right description of wisdom, valor and justice; which if they had been barely, that is to say philosophically, set out, they would swear they be brought to school again. . . .

By these, therefore, examples and reasons, I think it may be manifest that the poet, with that same hand of delight, doth draw the mind more effectually than any other art doth. And so a conclusion not unfitly ensueth: that as virtue is the most excellent resting-place for all worldly learning to make his end of, so poetry, being the most familiar to teach it, and most princely to move towards it, in the most excellent work is the most excellent workman.

The *Defence* is good prose — that excellent kind of prose which gives us the impression of good talk. It is as fresh today as when he wrote it — the companionable Sidney, chatting with us about the things he loves. But the ease and gaiety and informality never degenerate into cheapness and the shrewd judgments of his fellow-authors are never tainted with malice. It is the talk of a hearty man, a wise critic and a very great gentleman. And that, perhaps, is what gives the *Defence* its most enduring value. Many of the matters which Sidney discusses have now only an historical interest; but as a mirror of the man whom his contemporaries admired and loved beyond any other, and who left such an abiding impress upon his time, its worth is beyond estimation. "The miracle of our age," they called him. "Whatever we loved in you, . . . whatever we admired in you still continues, and will continue in the memory of man," wrote the great scholar Camden. "Gentle Sir Philip Sidney!" a fellow-craftsman said, when the news of Sidney's death was brought to him, "thou knewest what belonged to a scholar; thou knewest what pains, what toil, what travail, conduct to perfection; well couldst thou give every virtue his encouragement, every art his due, every writer his desert, because none was more virtuous, witty or learned than thyself."

In the little volume of *Discoveries Made upon Men and Matter*, left by the dramatist Ben Jonson, is a note linking two figures of the Elizabethan age whose only likeness is their mastery of English prose: "Sir Philip Sidney and Mr. Hooker (in different matter) grew great masters of wit and language, and in whom all vigor of invention and strength of judgment met." As a personality, Hooker lives for us in the biography written by Izaac Walton, some sixty years after Hooker's death. The gentle and kindly Walton, whose own personality is enshrined in the pages of *The Compleat Angler*, took a special delight in describing one whose qualities were so like his own. Hooker's sweetness of spirit, his humility and charity, his "dove-like temper," are amply set forth in those pages. What concerns us here is the quality of his English in the book by which he is chiefly remembered, *The Laws of Ecclesiastical Polity*. During his service as preacher in the Temple Church in London, he had become involved in controversies concerning the usages and mode of government and discipline of the Established Church. *The Laws of Ecclesiastical Polity* is his interpretation of the spirit and his justification of the laws of the Church of England. There is no such gaiety, companionable geniality, friendly informality, as in Sidney's *Defence*. Hooker thought only of his argument. But there are such beautiful lucidity, such grave and stately music, as English prose of later days has rarely equaled:

Albeit, therefore, much of that we are to speak in this present cause may seem to a number perhaps tedious, perhaps obscure, dark and intricate; (for many talk of the truth, which never sounded the depth from whence it springeth, and therefore when they are led thereunto they are soon weary, as men drawn from those beaten paths wherewith they have been inured); yet this may not so far prevail as to cut off that which the matter itself requireth, howsoever the nice humour of some be therewith pleased or no. . . . And if any complain of obscurity, they must consider that in these matters it cometh no otherwise to pass than in sundry the works both of art and also of nature, where that which hath greatest force in the very things we see is notwithstanding itself oftentimes not seen. The stateliness of houses, the goodliness of trees, when we behold them delighteth the eye; but that foundation which beareth up the one, that root which ministereth unto the other nourishment and life, is in the bosom of the earth concealed; and if there be at any time occasion to search into it, such labour is then more necessary than pleasant, both to them which undertake it and for the lookers-on. In like manner the use and benefit of good laws all that live under them may enjoy with delight and comfort, albeit the grounds and first original causes from whence they have sprung be unknown, as to the greatest part of men they are. But when they who withdraw their obedience pretend that the laws which they should obey are corrupt and vicious; for better examination of their quality, it behoveth the very foundation and root, the highest wellspring and fountain of them to be discovered. . . .

Of Law there can be no less acknowledged, than that her seat is the bosom of God, her voice the harmony of the world; all things in heaven and earth do her homage, the very least as feeling her care, and the greatest as not exempted from her power; both Angels and men and creatures of what condition soever, though each in different sort and manner, yet all with uniform consent, admiring her as the mother of their peace and joy.

It was said at the beginning of this chapter that the *art* of prose was just beginning to find itself in Elizabethan times. But as one considers the ease and grace of Sidney, the faultless marshaling of phrase and clause in Hooker, one realizes that, in two instances at least, Elizabethan prose had very completely found itself.

V

POETRY IN THE LATE SIXTEENTH AND EARLY SEVENTEENTH CENTURIES

It would be possible, even if our reading of Elizabethan literature were confined to the drama, to realize something of the lyric genius of the age; for the dramatists had a pleasant habit of writing songs (usually to some familiar air) to be sung by this or that character in the play. It was an age of song,— an age of notable musicians and composers of music, such as William Byrd, Edward Johnson, John Bull, Thomas Morley, John Dowland, and Thomas Campion; an age in which love of music and singing was more general, more widely diffused, than it has been in England at any other time before or since. The rich man's mansion and the poor man's tavern, both had their music. "London is so full of unprofitable pipers and fiddlers," wrote an indignant Puritan in the year 1587, "that a man can no sooner enter a tavern, than two or three cast of them hang at his heels to give him a dance before he depart." "Bands of musick" were a regular part of the household of the rich nobleman of the time — "the music of the house," as Nerissa calls Portia's musicians in *The Merchant of Venice*. Says Lorenzo, in the same play,

> The man that hath no music in himself,
> Nor is not moved with concord of sweet sounds,
> Is fit for treasons, stratagems, and spoils;
> The motions of his spirit are dull as night,
> And his affections dark as Erebus:
> Let no such man be trusted.

A person who could not sing was as much the uncomfortable exception as today a person who cannot dance. The organist and composer Thomas Morley, in his *Plain and Easy Introduction to Practical Music* (1597), tells the story of a certain "Philomathes" who was one of the guests at a supper. "Supper being ended, and music books, according to the custom, being brought to the table, the mistress of the house presented me with a part, earnestly requesting me to sing. But when, after many excuses, I protested unfainedly that I could not, every one began to wonder. Yea, some whispered to others, demanding how I was brought up."[1] When one of the actors in a play at the Globe paused in his performance to sing a song, though he might be acting the part of an Italian or a Frenchman or a Spaniard or a resident of Illyria, his audience met him on familiar ground, for his songs were English to the core. When Viola, the heroine of Shakespeare's *Twelfth Night*, finds herself shipwrecked on the coast of Illyria and decides to disguise herself as a page and enter the service of the Duke of that country, it is with the thought that

I can sing
And speak to him in many sorts of music
That will allow me very worth his service.

She doesn't, as a matter of fact, sing or play to him at all (she is too busy carrying love messages for him to the Lady Olivia), but almost all the rest of these "Illyrians" do. The attendants of the sentimental Duke make music for him. Sir Andrew and Sir Toby and the Fool sing "catches" (short compositions for three or more voices, in which, as Grove's *Musical Dictionary* explains, "the catch was for each succeeding singer to take up or catch his part in

[1] Quoted from W. B. Squire's article on "Elizabethan Music," in *Shakespeare's England* (Oxford Press).

time"). And when the Fool sings "O Mistress Mine," we may be sure that every listener at the Globe was ready to echo Sir Andrew's opinion: "I had rather than forty shillings I had so sweet a breath to sing as the Fool has."

> O mistress mine, where are you roaming?
> O, stay and hear; your true love's coming,
> That can sing both high and low:
> Trip no further, pretty sweeting;
> Journeys end in lovers meeting,
> Every wise man's son doth know.

> What is love? 'tis not hereafter;
> Present mirth hath present laughter
> What's to come is still unsure:
> In delay there lies no plenty;
> Then come kiss me, sweet and twenty,
> Youth's a stuff will not endure.

In a world so full of music and song, it is no wonder that the Elizabethan dramatists liberally scattered songs through their plays. There were other dramatists besides Shakespeare who were good song writers. Ben Jonson, though his touch was ordinarily rather heavy, has at least one good one — the hymn to Diana in *Cynthia's Revels:*

> Queen and huntress, chaste and fair,
> Now the sun is laid to sleep,
> Seated in thy silver chair,
> State in wonted manner keep;
> Hesperus entreats thy light,
> Goddess excellently bright.

> Earth, let not thy envious shade
> Dare itself to interpose;
> Cynthia's shining orb was made
> Heaven to clear when day did close:
> Bless us then with wishéd sight,
> Goddess excellently bright.

Lay thy bow of pearl apart,
And thy crystal shining quiver;
Give unto thy flying hart
Space to breathe, how short soever:
Thou that mak'st a day of night,
Goddess excellently bright.

Dekker has some lovely little songs tucked away in plays long since forgotten — as this, from *Patient Grissell:*

Art thou poor, yet hast thou golden slumbers?
    Oh, sweet content!
Art thou rich, yet is thy mind perplexéd?
    Oh, punishment!
Dost thou laugh to see how fools are vexéd
To add to golden numbers, golden numbers?
O, sweet content!   O, sweet content!

Work apace, apace, apace, apace;
Honest labor bears a lovely face;
Then hey noney, hcy noney, noney.

Beaumont and Fletcher, who were Shakespeare's rivals in the romantic drama, rivaled him no less in song. There is, for example, the exquisite little thing from *The Maid's Tragedy:*

Lay a garland on my hearse
    Of the dismal yew.
Maidens, willow branches bear.
    Say, I diéd true.

My love was false, but I was firm
    From my hour of birth.
Upon my buried body lie
    Lightly, gentle earth.

There are, too, the most rollicking drinking songs in Beaumont and Fletcher — as this, from *The Knight of the Burning Pestle:*

> For Jillian of Berry, she dwells on a hill,
> And she hath good ale and beer to sell,
> And of good fellows she thinks no ill,
> And thither will we go now, now, now,[1]
>   And thither will we go now.
> And when you have made a little stay,
> You need not ask what is to pay,
> But kiss your hostess, and go your way;
> And thither will we go now, now, now,
>   And thither will we go now.

There is that grimly humorous song (in *Rollo, Duke of Normandy*) which the yeoman of the cellar, the butler and the cook sing as they are on their way to be hanged:—

> Three merry boys, and three merry boys
>   And three merry boys are we,
> As ever did sing in a hempen string
>   Under the gallows tree.

There is no lack of good songs in the plays of Shakespeare's fellow-dramatists; but in songmaking as in playmaking, he was easily master of them all. His songs are best not only because they have such perfect grace and naturalness and melody (seeming, even without the aid of music, absolutely to *sing themselves*), but also because they fit perfectly into the context of the play. One never feels that they are inserted merely to please the audience. They are a part of the story. They "belong." The songs from Shakespeare's plays are often sung today, sometimes to the old airs to which he wrote them, sometimes to music written by modern composers. Beautiful as they are when

---

[1] At each "now" they thump their flagons on the table.

sung in this way, they lose much by being lifted out of their context. Thus when you hear sung the lovely "Who is Silvia?" (from *Two Gentlemen of Verona*), you must, to get the true quality of it, try to listen to it as Julia listened — Julia, the ingenuous and simple-hearted, who knows that the man whom she loves and to whom she is betrothed has lost his heart to this paragon:

> Who is Silvia?   What is she,
>   That all our swains commend her?
> Holy, fair and wise is she;
>   The heaven such grace did lend her,
> That she might admiréd be.
>
> Is she kind as she is fair?
>   For beauty lives with kindness,
> Love doth to her eyes repair
>   To help him of his blindness,
> And, being help'd, inhabits there.
>
> Then to Silvia let us sing
>   That Silvia is excelling;
> She excels each mortal thing
>   Upon the dull earth dwelling.
> To her let us garlands bring.

Or if you are listening to:

> Tell me where is fancy bred,
> Or in the heart or in the head
> How begot, how nourishéd?
>   Reply, reply.
>
> It is engend'red in the eyes
> With gazing fed; and fancy dies
> In the cradle where it lies.
>   Let us all sing fancy's knell;
>   I'll begin it, — Ding, dong, bell.

hear it with Bassanio's ears, as (in *The Merchant of Venice*) he ponders the caskets of gold and silver and lead. Or if it be one of the most lilting of Shakespeare's songs:

> Where the bee sucks, there suck I,
> In a cowslip's bell I lie;
> There I couch when owls do cry,
> On the bat's back I do fly
> After Summer merrily.
> > Merrily, merrily, shall I live now
> > Under the blossom that hangs on the bough.

remember that it is Ariel in *The Tempest* singing it — Ariel, the very spirit of dancing light, free at last after his long servitude.

An anthology of these little songs which Shakespeare and his fellow-dramatists scattered through their plays would make good reading; but it is not possible here to quote them further. Let us turn from these incidental expressions of the lyric genius of the age to the work of the non-dramatic poets.

It is with Edmund Spenser that the great period of Elizabethan non-dramatic poetry begins. There are several reasons why Spenser is worth reading and worth thinking about. He loved stories of adventure and was a master hand at telling them. He has the art of taking you with him into a sort of dreamworld where anything may happen, and the most extraordinary things do happen. His verse carries the tale as with a soft and haunting music. He is steeped in the spirit of the Renaissance, and, at the same time, curiously enough, reflects a new and different mood which the long religious struggles of the Reformation had brought about. There is a good deal of the Puritan[1] and

[1] For an account of the Puritan movement, see the chapter on John Milton, p. 196.

the moralist in Spenser, especially in the greatest of his poems, *The Faerie Queene.*

It was the fashion among the men of the Renaissance to write books about the education, the manners and the conduct of a gentleman. To them, with their aristocratic tradition, a "gentleman" did not mean merely (as the word means with us) anyone who conducts himself honorably and courteously. They thought of the "gentleman" much as Plato had thought of the "Guardians" whose education he discussed so fully in his *Republic,* as the men of noble birth, upon whom the responsibility for the governance of the state would fall, and who would set an example to the common folk. Early in the English Renaissance, Sir Thomas Elyot had written the *Boke of the Governour* intended to "fourm the gentill wittes of noble mennes children who . . . shall be made propise or apte to the governaunce of a publike weale." One of the most popular books at Queen Elizabeth's court was an Italian work by Castiglione which Sir Thomas Hoby translated as *"The Courtyer of Count Baldessar Castilio: very necessary and profitable for younge Gentilmen and Gentilwomen abiding in Court, Palaice or Place."* By the "courtier" was really meant the proper gentleman — for it was taken for granted that the proper gentleman would spend a while at court.[1] "Why," says jesting Touchstone to the shepherd in Shakespeare's *As You Like It,* "if thou never wast at court, thou never saw'st good manners; if thou never saw'st good manners, then thy manners must be wicked; and wickedness is sin and sin is damnation."

Inasmuch, then, as the thought of Spenser's time was so

---

[1] Courtesy, courteous, etc., derive from the Latin *cortis,* meaning court. *Courteous,* therefore, means literally having manners such as are practiced at court.

much directed toward the training, the conduct, the character and the manners of the "noble person," it was natural for Spenser to choose this theme for a poem. It was natural, also, because there was a strain of the Puritan and moralist in him, for him to think rather less of polished manners and courtly ways than the earlier Renaissance writers had thought, and rather more of the fundamental Christian virtues. "The generall end therefore of all the booke," Spenser says in his explanatory letter to Sir Walter Raleigh, "is to fashion a gentleman or noble person in virtuous and gentle discipline." He dedicates his poem to the one around whom all the courtly and noble life of the time centered: "To the most high, mightie, and magnificent Empresse, renowned for Pietie, Vertue, and all gratious Government, Elizabeth, by the Grace of God Queene of England, France and Ireland, and of Virginia." He entitles the book *The Faerie Queene* because "in that Faery Queene I meane glory in my generall intention, but in my particular I conceive the most excellent and glorious person of our soveraine the Queene, and her kingdome in Faery land." And having so explained himself, he sets out to develop his theme in a curious and fascinating way. He gives no rules or precepts. He does not say that the gentleman or noble person ought to do this or ought not to do that. Instead, he weaves the most adventurous and romantic stories about a series of knights, each one of whom embodies and illustrates in his adventures a virtue, a principle of right living. The first story is of the adventures of the Red Cross Knight, who represents Holiness; the second, of Sir Guyon, Temperance; the third, of Britomart, Chastity; the fourth, of Cambel and Triamond, Friendship; the fifth of Artegall, Justice; the sixth of Calidore, Courtesy. Such a way of teaching is called "allegory"— letting the characters of a story and their doings convey a meaning which does not lie on the surface and is not put explicitly into words, but which the reader cannot fail to grasp. Or, as Spenser thought of it, philosophy teaching by example.

It does not take Spenser long to get us well started into his own special dreamland:

> A gentle Knight was pricking on the plaine,
> Ycladd in mightie armes and silver shielde,
> Wherein old dints of deepe wounds did remaine,
> The cruel marks of many a bloudy fielde;
> Yet armes till that time did he never wield:
> His angry steede did chide his foming bitt,
> As much disdayning to the curbe to yield:
> Full jolly knight he seemed, and faire did sitt,
> As one for knightly giusts and fierce encounters fitt.
>
> And on his brest a bloudie crosse he bore,
> The deare remembrance of his dying Lord,
> For whose sweete sake that glorious badge he wore,
> And dead as living ever him adored:
> Upon his shield the like was also scored,
> For soveraine hope, which in his helpe he had:
> Right faithfull true he was in deede and word,
> But of his cheere did seeme too solemne sad;
> Yet nothing did he dread, but ever was ydrad.
>
> Upon a great adventure he was bond,
> That greatest Glorianna to him gave,
> That greatest glorious Queene of Faerie lond,
> To winne him worship, and her grace to have,
> Which of all earthly things he most did crave;
> And ever as he rode, his hart did earne
> To prove his puissance in battell brave
> Upon his foe, and his new force to learne;
> Upon his foe, a dragon horrible and stearne.

> A lovely ladie rode him faire beside,
> Upon a lowly asse more white than snow,
> Yet she much whiter, but the same did hide
> Under a vele, that wimpled was full low,
> And over all a blacke stole she did throw,
> As one that inly mournd: so was she sad,
> And heavie sat upon her palfrey snow:
> Seemed in heart some hidden care she had,
> And by her in a line a milke white lambe she lad.

Allegorically, Redcrosse, like Christian in Bunyan's story, is setting out on life's pilgrimage. He is only a fallible mortal, striving for Holiness. His companion, Una, whiter than the snow, innocent and always pure of heart, is a personification of that Holiness which Redcrosse hopes to win. A good many of the difficulties and dangers and traps that Redcrosse gets into are laid for him by the Roman Catholic Church — for Spenser remembered the old religious struggle well enough to think that most of the dangers to which the Christian pilgrim was exposed lay in that direction. But when you get into the story you can concern yourself just as much — or just as little — as you like about that. There is always the story, with tales of knightly adventure which were just as fresh to Spenser as they had been to poets all through the Middle Ages, interwoven with bright threads from classical mythology and from Italian epics of the Renaissance. There is always the story, with encounters of knights in glittering armor, and scaly monsters, and magicians, and Morpheus waiting to give Redcrosse lying dreams, and a "proud Sarazin" ready to attack him, and a giant Orgoglio who thrusts him into a dungeon, and a Cave of Despair to engulf him. After many such misadventures, Redcrosse finally finds the dragon and kills him after three days' battle. And of course Redcrosse liberates Una's parents, and Una's father treats Redcrosse and Una with the loveliest hospitality:—

> And after to his pallace he them brings
> With shaumes, and trompets, and with clarions sweet,
> And all the way the joyous people singes
> And with their garments strowes the pavéd street.

And of course Redcrosse, while he is winning Holiness, wins Una.

As for the stories of the other knights of the series, you will have to find out about them for yourself. And as for the moral, the particular "Virtue," that is veiled in the allegory, whether or not you find the story the better for that is a matter of taste. But it is worth while to remember that one of the great poets of a later time who loved Spenser's poetry for its own sake believed also that Spenser was a great teacher. Two of the philosophers whom the Middle Ages especially venerated were Duns Scotus and Thomas Aquinas. It was John Milton who called Spenser "our sage and serious poet, whom I dare be known to think a better teacher than Scotus or Aquinas."

The Faerie Queene is Spenser's lasting monument. But it is more than that. Few poems have had such vitality. A whole school of poets in the early seventeenth century imitated his style, followed him in the use of allegory, and wrote in the stanzaic form which he had devised.[1] Milton acknowledged Spenser his "original," caught Spenser's tone in such poems as *L'Allegro* and *Il Penseroso* and found suggestions for *Paradise Lost* in *The Faerie Queene*. Even the Age of Pope was not lacking in Spenserians, and in the middle years of the eighteenth century appreciation and

---

[1] You will find it interesting to study the interlaced rhyme-scheme, and the lingering cadence of the prolonged last line, in the Spenserian stanzas quoted on page 149.

imitation of *The Faerie Queene* became a touchstone of the romantic spirit in literature. And if you will turn to page 463 of this book you will see how *The Faerie Queene* stimulated and molded the genius of John Keats, the greatest of early nineteenth-century poets.

Of Spenser's minor poems, the two marriage songs, *Epithalamion* and *Prothalamion,* are the most graceful and musical, and *The Shepherds' Calendar* the most curious and interesting. *The Shepherds' Calendar* is divided into twelve books, one for each month of the year. The "shepherds" whose stories and meditations make up these books are really Spenser and his friends disguised under pastoral names. They speak a rustic — an artificially rustic — language, and the pretense of shepherd life and manners is maintained throughout; but it is Spenser's own world that passes under review in the poem — religion, politics, poetry, the glories of the Queen, life at court with its glitter and its disappointments.

It is the pastoral form of *The Shepherds' Calendar* that gives it its special interest. Among the riches of classical poetry which the Renaissance brought to light were the *Idyls* of the Sicilian poet, Theocritus, in which shepherds are represented as singing their songs and relating their experiences to one another. Virgil in his *Eclogues* imitated Theocritus. The pastoral became a favorite exercise of the poets of the Renaissance. In English poetry, *The Shepherds' Calendar* is one of the earliest of a long line of pastoral poems, of which Milton's *Lycidas* (see page 210) is the most notable example.

Spenser is also numbered among the sonnet-makers. This exacting form of verse, with its distillation of a moment's mood into fourteen lines intricately rhymed, was perfected by the Italian poet, Petrarch, and was introduced into English poetry by Sir Thomas Wyatt in 1557.[1] By Spenser's day the sonnet had become one of the most popular forms of verse. It was the custom for poets to compose "sequences" of sonnets — each little fourteen-line poem complete within itself, but the whole series of sonnets more or less related in theme. A few of Spenser's *Amoretti* (as he calls his sequence of love-sonnets) are of high quality; but as a whole they lack the intensity, the concentration of feeling, which distinguish two other son-net-sequences of the period. These are the sonnet-sequences of Sir Philip Sidney and of Shakespeare.

Sidney is an extraordinarily interesting figure. Aristo-crat, soldier, statesman, courtier; a lover of music; an athlete —

> In wrestling nimble, and in running swift,
> In shooting steady, and in swimming strong —

as his friend Edmund Spenser wrote of him; novelist, scholar, literary critic, poet, he sums up in his short in-tense life the vivid, varied spirit of the Elizabethan age. He was a visitor to European courts and the friend and correspondent of European scholars while he was yet in his 'teens; he was one of the most brilliant, and fearless, of Elizabeth's courtiers; he was the Queen's trusted am-bassador on secret missions to foreign rulers; he was killed leading his men in the battle of Zutphen (1586) when he was only thirty-two years old. No other man of his day was so admired and so beloved. To him, Spenser dedi-cated *The Shepherds' Calendar*, Hakluyt, the *Voyages* (see page 115). We have encountered Sidney already as the

---

[1] The collection of "songs and sonnets" known as *Tottel's Miscellany* (1557) contained the first fruits of the Renaissance in English poetry. It is notable as including not only the earliest sonnets, but also (from the hand of the Earl of Surrey) the first experiments in blank verse to be printed in an English book.

author of a notable romance, the *Arcadia* (see page 132), and of a notable piece of literary criticism, the *Defence of Poesy* (see page 134).

Sidney calls his sonnet-sequence *Astrophel and Stella* — Stella, the Star; Astrophel, the Star-lover. His Stella was Penelope Devereux, sister of the Earl of Essex, and Sidney's friend since childhood. All of Sidney's sonnets are worth reading — worth reading for their skill and grace, and even more for their sensitiveness and their depth and intensity of feeling. Here are two of the loveliest of them:—

With how sad steps, O Moon, thou climb'st the skies!
How silently and with how wan a face!
What! May it be that even in heav'nly place
That busy archer his sharp arrows tries?
Sure, if that long-with-love-acquainted eyes
Can judge of love, thou feel'st a lover's case:
I read it in thy looks; thy languished grace,
To me, that feel the like, thy state descries.
Then ev'n of fellowship, O Moon, tell me,
Is constant love deemed there but want of wit?
Are beauties there as proud as here they be?
Do they above love to be loved, and yet
Those lovers scorn whom that love doth possess?
Do they call virtue there ungratefulness?

Come, Sleep, O Sleep, the certain knot of peace,
The baiting-place of wit, the balm of woe,
The poor man's wealth, the prisoner's release,
The indifferent judge between the high and low!
With shield of proof shield me from out the prease
Of those fierce darts Despair at me doth throw:
O make in me those civil wars to cease!
I will good tribute pay, if thou do so:

Take thou of me smooth pillows, sweetest bed,
A chamber deaf of noise, and blind of light,
A rosy garland and a weary head;
And if these things, as being thine in right,
Move not thy heavy grace, thou shalt in me,
Livelier than elsewhere, Stella's image see.

All of the Elizabethan sonnet-sequences — and most of the poets of the day tried their hand at them — are of a conventionalized pattern. Professions of devotion to a beloved, complaints of her unresponsiveness or unfairness, are their main theme. In this respect, Shakespeare's are like the rest; but even when he is merely saying over again what his fellow-poets are saying, he expresses it with the unerring rightness of word, the perfect felicity of phrase, which the author of *Romeo and Juliet* had at his command; and when, as in many of his sonnets, he forgets these conventions and speaks out of his own heart, there is nothing in the whole range of Elizabethan poetry that can match them. Whether, as the sonnets indicate, he loved some woman higher in social station than himself, and found her unfaithful; whether he gave his heart and faith to some young nobleman of Elizabeth's court and found him a false friend; or whether all this, as some critics believe, is a mere poetic invention, there is, none the less, more of Shakespeare himself, more of his own personal feeling, in the sonnets, than we can ever expect to discover in his plays. Shakespeare would not have been the greatest of our dramatists if he had not, in the plays, lived completely in his characters — if he had not literally *become* the people whom he there presents to us. But in the sonnets this dramatizing faculty is laid aside. And certainly in some of them the veritable Shakespeare speaks — the Shakespeare who knows himself to be the genius of his age, who feels the superiority of his mind, and yet, as a mere despised actor-playwright, is condemned to make himself a motley to the view, to sell cheap upon the public stage the thoughts and feelings which are most dear to him, until his very

> nature is subdued
> To what it works in, like the dyer's hand.

It is when love and aspiration and the sense of his own intellectual greatness are fighting with this consciousness of his lowness in the social life of his day, that the sonnets become the veritable Shakespeare.

> When in disgrace with fortune and men's eyes,
> I all alone beweep my outcast state,
> And trouble deaf heaven with my bootless cries,
> And look upon myself and curse my fate,
> Wishing me like to one more rich in hope,
> Featured like him, like him with friends possessed,
> Desiring this man's art and that man's scope,
> With what I most enjoy contented least;
> Yet in these thoughts myself almost despising
> Haply I think on thee, and then my state,
> Like to the lark at break of day arising
> From sullen earth, sings hymns at heaven's gate:
> For thy sweet love remembered such wealth brings
> That then I scorn to change my state with kings.

> Like as the waves make towards the pebbled shore
> So do our minutes hasten to their end;
> Each changing place with that which goes before,
> In sequent toil all forwards do contend.
> Nativity, once in the main of light,
> Crawls to maturity, wherewith being crown'd,
> Crooked eclipses 'gainst his glory fight,
> And Time that gave, doth now his gift confound.

Time doth transfix the flourish set on youth,
And delves the parallels in beauty's brow;
Feeds on the rarities of nature's truth,
And nothing stands but for his scythe to mow:—
And yet, to times in hope, my verse shall stand
Praising Thy worth, despite his cruel hand.

Let me not to the marriage of true minds
Admit impediments.   Love is not love
Which alters when it alteration finds,
Or bends with the remover to remove:
O, no! it is an ever-fixéd mark,
That looks on tempests and is never shaken;
It is the star to every wand'ring bark,
Whose worth's unknown, although his height be taken.
Love's not Time's fool, though rosy lips and cheeks
Within his bending sickle's compass come;
Love alters not with his brief hours and weeks,
But bears it out even to the edge of doom.
If this be error and upon me proved,
I never writ, nor no man ever loved.

Or I shall live your epitaph to make,
Or you survive when I in earth am rotten;
From hence your memory death cannot take,
Although in me each part will be forgotten.
Your name from hence immortal life shall have,
Though I, once gone, to all the world must die:
The earth can yield me but a common grave,
When you entombéd in men's eyes shall lie.
Your monument shall be my gentle verse,
Which eyes not yet created shall o'er-read;
And tongues to be your being shall rehearse,
When all the breathers of this world are dead;
You still shall live — such virtue hath my pen —
Where breath most breathes, even in the mouths of men.

There is an inexhaustible mine of beautiful things in the lyric poetry of the late sixteenth and early seventeenth century. It will be possible in these pages only to tap that mine here and there. One good way of reading Elizabethan poetry is to turn the pages of any considerable collection,[1] thinking of the poems not as the work of this or that poet, but as a reflection of the moods of the time, a revelation of what the poets liked to let their fancy dwell upon. There were, of course, many moods; but two are particularly characteristic of the age. One is a sense of the shortness of life and the yearning to catch the fleeting moment of happiness — the mood of Herrick's

> Gather ye rose-buds while ye may:
>   Old Time is still a-flying;
> And this same flower that smiles today
>   Tomorrow will be dying.

The consciousness that the days of man are as grass, as a flower of the field — the wind passeth over it and it is gone and the place thereof shall know it no more — has found expression in the literature of every age. Christianity offered comfort for the brevity and vanity of this life in the contemplation of the life to come. In the centuries, so deeply imbued with the religious spirit, that lie back of the Elizabethan period, the poets thought, or strove to think, of this life rather as a preparation, than as an opportunity for snatching fleeting joys. Even Chaucer, with all his merriment and zest, felt it necessary to add to the *Canterbury Tales* a "leave-taking," in which he prayed to be

[1] For example, *The Oxford Book of English Verse* (Oxford Press); *English Poems: The Elizabethan Age and the Puritan Period,* Bronson (University of Chicago Press); *English Poetry,* Manly (Ginn and Company); *The English Poets,* Ward (The Macmillan Company); *Anthology of the Poetry of the Age of Shakespeare,* Young (The Macmillan Company); *Golden Treasury of Songs and Lyrics,* Palgrave (various editions).

forgiven for such of the tales as "sounen into sinne," and for his other "endytinges of worldly vanitees." But with the revival of interest in the pre-Christian literature of Greece and Rome, something of the pagan spirit found its way into literature once more — the spirit of this epitaph from the Greek Anthology:

> Oft have I sung — now from the tomb I cry —
> Drink, ere enveloped in this dust you lie,
> (Trans. by H. Wellesley)

and of Horace's *carpe diem* —

> Our span is brief. The niggard hour
>   in chatting, ebbs away;
> Trust nothing for tomorrow's sun:
>   make harvest of today.
> (Trans. by Gladstone)

This mood recurs again and again in Elizabethan poetry and inspires some of the loveliest of Elizabethan lyrics. Spenser had sounded the note in *The Faerie Queene:*

> So passeth, in the passing of a day
> Of mortall life, the leafe, the bud, the flowre . . .
> Gather therefore the rose whilest yet is prime
> For soone comes age that will her pride deflowre.

We have heard it in Shakespeare's "O Mistress Mine":

> Youth's a stuff will not endure;

It is sounded again in the Spring Song — "It was a lover and his lass," in *As You Like It:*—

> This carol they began that hour,
>   With a hey, and a ho, and a hey nonino,
> How that a life was but a flower;
>   In spring time, the only pretty ring time.

> When birds do sing, hey ding a ding ding;
>   Sweet lovers love the spring.
> And therefore take the present time,
>   With a hey, and a ho, and a hey nonino,
> For love is crownéd with the prime,
>   In spring time, etc. . . .

It recurs again and again in the songs and poems of the time; and it finds most beautiful expression in the last stanza of Herrick's "Corinna's Going A-Maying":

> Come, let us go while we are in our prime,
> And take the harmless folly of the time.
>   We shall grow old apace, and die
>   Before we know our liberty.
>   Our life is short, and our days run
>   As fast away as does the sun;
> And, as a vapour or a drop of rain,
> Once lost, can ne'er be found again,
>   So when or you or I are made
>   A fable, song, or fleeting shade,
>   All love, all liking, all delight
>   Lies drowned with us in endless night.
> Then while time serves, and we are but decaying,
> Come, my Corinna, come, let's go a-maying.

Carpe diem. Live today, for tomorrow we die! In the frequency with which this mood finds expression in Elizabethan poetry, there is perhaps more than a mere desire to say over again what the classical poets had said, or to fashion pretty phrases about love-making. We may not unreasonably see in it a reflection of the spirit of time,— of the intensity and recklessness which marked alike the lives of the adventurers who were carrying the flag through uncharted seas, and the lives of the poets who were living and feeling each moment for all it was worth, and caring naught for the morrow. We can catch something of that spirit in the lines in which Francis Beaumont describes the meetings of the poets at the Mermaid tavern:

> What things have we seen
> Done at the Mermaid! heard words that have been
> So nimble and so full of subtle flame
> As if that everyone from whence they came
> Had meant to put his whole wit in a jest,
> And resolved to live a fool the rest
> Of his dull life.

The other mood which seems particularly characteristic of Elizabethan poetry is the converse of the one of which we have just been thinking, and the natural reaction from it. We may call it the mood of escape — the dream of a happiness that knows no turmoil, a contentment unshadowed by the shortness of life. We have caught the note already in Dekker's song:

> Art thou poor, yet hast thou golden slumbers?
> O sweet content!

The thought strikes Shakespeare whenever he contemplates the responsibilities and anxieties of kingship.

> Methinks it were a happy life
> To be no better than a homely swain,

cries the beleaguered Henry VI; and when, dethroned, he has become an exiled wanderer,

> My crown is in my heart, not on my head;
> Not decked with diamonds and Indian stones,
> Nor to be seen. My crown is called content;
> A crown it is that seldom kings enjoy.

Or it may be Henry IV, restless with care:

> O gentle Sleep
> Nature's soft nurse, how have I frighted thee
> That thou no more wilt weigh my eyelids down
> And steep my senses in forgetfulness?
> Why rather, Sleep, liest thou in smoky cribs
> Upon uneasy pallets stretching thee . . .
> Than in the perfumed chambers of the great? . . .
> Then happy low, lie down!
> Uneasy lies the head that wears a crown;

or Henry V, watching through the night before the battle
of Agincourt:

> What infinite heart's-ease
> Must kings neglect, that private men enjoy?

In the non-dramatic poetry of the time this feeling finds
one expression in the thought that the only happy kingship
is the kingship of the mind — as in the lines by Sidney's
friend, Sir Edward Dyer:

> My mind to me a kingdom is,
>   Such present joys therein I find,
> That it excells all other bliss
>   That earth affords or grows by kind:
> Though much I want which most would have,
> Yet still my mind forbids to crave. . . .

> Content to live, this is my stay;
>   I seek no more than may suffice;
> I press to bear no haughty sway;
>   Look, what I lack my mind supplies.
> Lo, thus I triumph like a king,
> Content with what my mind doth bring;

and (as in Campion's "The man of life upright") that only
the virtuous man knows true content:—

> Good thoughts his only friends
> His wealth a well-spent age,
> The earth his sober inn,—
> And quiet pilgrimage.

But it is in the dream of simple country life that this mood
of escape most often expresses itself. Marlowe's "Come
live with me and be my love" strikes the keynote. There
is probably no other poem of the day which was so universally familiar and which the Elizabethans so loved to
quote.[1]

> Come live with me and be my Love,
> And we will all the pleasures prove
> That hills and valleys, dale and field,
> And all the craggy mountains yield.
>
> There will we sit upon the rocks
> And see the shepherds feed their flocks,
> By shallow rivers, to whose falls
> Melodious birds sing madrigals.
>
> There will I make thee beds of roses
> And a thousand fragrant posies,
> A cap of flowers, and a kirtle
> Embroidered all with leaves of myrtle.
>
> A gown made of the finest wool,
> Which from our pretty lambs we pull,
> Fair linèd slippers for the cold,
> With buckles of the purest gold.

---

[1] See, for example, even the comical Welshman, Sir Hugh Evans, struggling with it, in Shakespeare's *Merry Wives of Windsor*, III, i.

A belt of straw and ivy buds
With coral clasps and amber studs:
And if these pleasures may thee move,
Come live with me and be my Love.

Thy silver dishes for thy meat
As precious as the gods do eat,
Shall on an ivory table be
Prepared each day for thee and me.

The shepherd swains shall dance and sing
For thy delight each May-morning:
If these delights thy mind may move,
Then live with me and be my Love.

Elizabethan poetry is full of these idyllic pictures — many of them (as in this little poem of Campion's) explicitly drawing the contrast between the world of society and the happiness of the simple life:

Jack and Joan, they think no ill,
But loving live, and merry still;
Do their week-day's work, and pray
Devoutly on the holy-day:
Skip and trip it on the green,
And help to choose the Summer Queen;
Lash out at a country feast
Their silver penny with the best. . . .

— Now, you courtly dames and knights,
That study only strange delights,
Though you scorn the homespun gray,
And revel in your rich array;
Though your tongues dissemble deep
And can your heads from danger keep;
Yet, for all your pomp and train,
Securer lives the silly swain!

The popularity in Shakespeare's day of the various forms of pastoral literature is also a reflection of this mood — the shepherd poems of Spenser and his imitators; the prose romances, full of shepherd disguisings; and that pleasant habit of Shakespeare and his fellow-dramatists, of transporting all the characters to the greenwood on the slightest excuse.

Now, my co-mates and brothers in exile,

says Duke Senior in the forest of Arden,

> Hath not old custom made this life more sweet
> Than that of painted pomp?   Are not these woods
> More free from peril than the envious court?
> Here feel we not the penalty of Adam,
> The seasons' difference, as the icy fang
> And churlish chiding of the winter's wind,
> Which when it bites and blows upon my body,
> Even till I shrink with cold, I smile and say,
> "This is no flattery: these are counsellors
> That feelingly persuade me what I am" . . .
> And this our life, exempt from public haunt,
> Finds tongues in trees, books in the running brooks,
> Sermons in stones, and good in everything.

It is true that this city-born practice of depicting the quiet joys of country life is, like the theme of "Gather ye rose-buds while ye may," an inheritance from the classics. Theocritus had peopled his *Idyls* with the most poetical of shepherds; Horace had written of his Sabine farm; in Virgil's *Eclogues*, Lycidas and Mœris and Corydon and Thyrsis and Melibœus and Amaryllis talk of love and shepherding and the beauties of nature, while Tityrus on his slender pipe rehearses woodland music. With the Renaissance this theme became again a favorite literary exercise. But among the poems of this sort in Elizabethan literature there are many which are too specific and too deeply felt to be mere

Mechanic echoes of the Mantuan[1] song.

But from these random moods of Elizabethan poetry, let us turn once more to the poets themselves. It is not possible even to name here the many minor lyrists who now and again produced a memorable poem. It will suffice for us to consider a few of the more important figures. Aside from a poet here and there who refuses to be classified, we may think of the poets of the late sixteenth and early seventeenth century as falling into three groups — those who imitated Spenser or wrote somewhat in his mood; Ben Jonson and the "Sons of Ben"; and John Donne and his imitators.

The Spenserians were numerous. Let us confine ourselves to four — Samuel Daniel and Michael Drayton, who were among the most important of Spenser's immediate disciples; and Giles Fletcher and Phineas Fletcher, who belong to a later date, and who will have a special interest for us in that they handed the Spenserian tradition on to Milton. Daniel and Drayton had something of their master's pure and lofty spirit, practiced his rhythms, were fond of allegory and pastoral, and dealt with large themes in that leisured spacious way which Spenser had taught the Elizabethans to enjoy. Like him, too, they were sonnet-makers. Daniel's sonnet-sequence, *Delia*, appeared in 1592, and Drayton's *Idea's Mirror* in 1594. The best known of Daniel's sonnets is that beginning

> Care-charmer sleep, son of the sable night;
> Brother to Death, in silent darkness born.

[1] Virgil was born near Mantua.

Of the many Elizabethan sonnets and other poems dealing with sleep, Daniel's is perhaps the best; but the images, fancies, or "conceits," are much the same in them all. Shakespeare gives us, in *Macbeth*, what might almost be described as a categorical list of these images —

> the innocent sleep,
> Sleep that knits up the ravelled sleave of care,
> The death of each day's life, sore labour's bath,
> Balm of hurt minds, great nature's second course,
> Chief nourisher in life's feast.

Most of Drayton's sonnets are not remarkable; but there is one of his which for vigor and beauty is unsurpassed by any then or since.

> Since there's no help, come let us kiss and part,— *a*
> Nay I have done, you get no more of me; *b*
> And I am glad, yea, glad with all my heart, *a*
> That thus so cleanly I myself can free; *b*
> Shake hands for ever, cancel all our vows, *c*
> And when we meet at any time again, *d*
> Be it not seen in either of our brows *d*
> That we one jot of former love retain. *e*
> Now at the last gasp of love's latest breath, *e*
> When his pulse failing, passion speechless lies, *f*
> When faith is kneeling by his bed of death, *c*
> And innocence is closing up his eyes, *f*
>
> Now if thou would'st, when all have given him over, *g*
> From death to life thou might'st him yet recover! *g*

The vogue of sonnet-sequences was already near its end when Drayton's appeared. By the end of the sixteenth century the vogue had passed.

But it is not only as sonnet-makers that these two poets are interesting. The Elizabethans liked their history done

into verse.[1] Daniel supplied them with a narrative of the
Wars of the Roses, *The History of the Civil Wars*, in no less
than 7200 stanzas; and Drayton with a description of the
struggles in the reign of Edward II (*The Barons' Wars*); a
series of imaginary letters in verse from famous figures of
English history (*England's Heroical Epistles*); and a rhymed
description of England (*The Poly-Olbion*); besides a number
of lively accounts of historical episodes.

Drayton was one of the most versatile of Elizabethan
poets. Though few people today would have the patience
to read his interminable histories, there are a number of his
slighter pieces which are extraordinarily spirited and make
delightful reading. His *Ballad of Agincourt*[2] is one of the
best battle pieces ever written. It is not possible to quote
here more than the briefest sample of it, but any reader of
Shakespeare's *Henry V* who neglects to read all of Drayton's
Ballad has missed a great experience.

> They now to fight are gone:
> Armour on armour shone;
> Drum now to drum did groan,
>   To hear was wonder;
> That with the cries they make
> The very earth did shake;
> Trumpet to trumpet spake
>   Thunder to thunder. . . .
>
> With Spanish yew so strong,
> Arrows a cloth-yard long,
> That like to serpents stong,
>   Piercing the weather;

[1] With the recent success of Stephen Vincent Benet's long poem of the
Civil War, *John Brown's Body*, it is possible that the present age may see a
revival of poetical interpretations of history. The noblest poem of this sort
in modern times is Thomas Hardy's *The Dynasts*.

[2] He wrote also a long rhymed narrative, *The Battle of Agincourt*.

None from his fellows starts,
But playing manly parts,
And like true English hearts,
    Stuck close together.

When down their bows they threw,
And forth their bilbows drew,
And on the French they flew;
    Not one was tardy:
Arms were from shoulders sent,
Scalps to the teeth were rent,
Down the French peasants went;
    Our men were hardy.

And there is the gaily rippling *Nymphidia*, which every reader of Shakespeare's *A Midsummer Night's Dream* ought to read:

But listen, and I shall you tell
A chance in Faery that befell,
Which certainly may please some well
    In love and arms delighting;
Of Oberon that jealous grew
Of one of his own fairy crew,
Too well, he feared, his queen that knew
    His love but ill requiting. . . .

Her chariot ready straight is made,
Each thing therein is fitting laid,
That she by nothing may be stayed,
    For naught must be her letting.
Four nimble gnats the horses were,
Their harnesses of gossamere,
Fly Cranion, her charioteer,
    Upon the coach-box getting.

Her chariot of a snail's fine shell
Which for the colours did excell,
The fair Queen Mab becoming well,
    So lively was the limning;
The seat, the soft wool of the bee;
The cover, gallantly to see,
The wing of a pied butterfly;
    I trow 'twas simple trimming.

Drayton is at his best in these short lilting measures. He uses them to tell such stories as Spenser had loved to tell; but Drayton's way is far livelier, far less stately, than his master's. Spenser is the greater artist; but Drayton's high spirits are so infectious, he is manifestly having such huge fun out of it himself, that the reader does not stop to criticize. Who, for example, could possibly resist this, the beginning of one of the tales in the *Pastorals?*

She wore a frock of frolic green,
Might well become a maiden queen,
    Which seemly was to see;
A hood to that so neat and fine,
In colour like the columbine,
    Ywrought full featously.
Her features all as fresh above,
As is the grass that grows by Dove,
    And lythe as lass of Kent.
Her skin as soft as Lemster wool,
As white as snow on Peakish Hull,
    Or swan that swims in Trent.

This maiden in a morn betime,
Went forth when May was in the prime
    To get sweet setywall,
The honey-suckle, the barlock,
The lily, and the lady-smock,
    To deck her summer hall.

Thus as she wandered here and there,
And pickéd off the bloomy briar,
   She chancéd to espy
A shepherd sitting on a bank,
Like Chanty-clear he crowéd crank,
   And piped full merrily.

Or this, from the *Second Nymphal* of the *Muses' Elysium:*

These sprightly gallants loved a lass
Called Lirope the bright.
In the whole world there scarcely was
So delicate a wight . . .
She raised a war, appeased a strife
With turning of her eye.
Some said a god did her beget,
But much deceived were they,
Her father was a Rivulet,
Her mother was a Fay.
Her lineaments so fine that were
She from the fairy took;
Her beauties and complexion clear
By nature from the brook.

Daniel and Drayton reached their maturity while Spenser was yet alive; the work of the brothers, Giles and Phineas Fletcher (cousins of John Fletcher, the dramatist; see page 111) belongs to the second and third decades of the seventeenth century. The Fletchers wrote in Spenser's manner and with much of his spirit; and, like him, devoted themselves largely to pastoral poetry and to allegory. One of their poems, Phineas Fletcher's beautiful little story of Anchises and Venus, entitled *Brittain's Ida*, was, indeed, mistakenly attributed by its first printer to Spenser himself. How naturally, may be seen by comparing the smooth and graceful flow of this description of the "garden of delight" with the stanzas of *The Faerie Queene* quoted on page 149.

> The woode with Paphian mirtles peopled,
> (Whose springing youth felt never Winter's spiting)
> To laurels sweete were sweetely married,
> Doubling their pleasing smells in their uniting,
> When single much, much more when mixt delighting:
>   No foote of beast durst touch this hallowed place,
>   And many a boy that long'd the woods to trace,
> Entred with feare, but soone turn'd back his frighted face.

But it is for the fresh uses to which they put Spenserian allegory that the work of the Fletchers is most interesting. *The Purple Island or the Isle of Man* (1633), if not a great poem, is certainly one of the curiosities of literature. Possibly the interest aroused by Harvey's discovery of the circulation of the blood[1] suggested to Phineas the idea of describing the human body as a purple island, irrigated by the veins:

> The first in single channels, sky-like blue,
> With luke-warm waters dyed in porphyr hue,
> Sprinkle this crimson Isle with purple-coloured dew.

and the arteries:

> The next, though from the same springs first it rise,
> Yet passing through another greater fountain,
> Doth lose his former name and qualities:
> Through many a dale it flows, and many a mountain;
> More firie light and needful more than all.

---

[1] Harvey announced his theory in 1616. The book in which he describes his great discovery was printed in 1628. In one of John Donne's poems occur the lines:—

> Know'st thou how blood, which to the heart doth flow,
> Doth from one ventricle to the other go?

From this auspicious beginning the poet spurs his "lagging muse" through five of the twelve cantos of the poem, neglecting not a single detail, from the brain where

> all the senses dwell, and all the arts,

to the liver where "Plato hath disposed the seat of love," even unto "the lank and hungry gut." Having exhausted this phase of the subject, the poet proceeds to deal with the Intellect —"the Island's Prince"— and with the Will — the Prince's "beauteous Queen";

> Not that great sovereign of the Fairie land,
> Whom late our Colin[1] hath eternized,
> (Though Graces decking her with plenteous hand,
> Themselves of grace have all unfurnished;
> Though in her breast she Virtue's temple bear,
> The fairest temple of a guest so fair)
> Not that great Glorian's self with this might e'er
>   compare.

Follows a description of the vices and virtues, and finally a semblance of a story, in which the Prince and the Lady Voletta (the Will) have adventures not unlike those of Redcrosse and Una in *The Faerie Queene*.

This prodigious poem runs to 724 stanzas of seven lines each — 5068 lines! The first part of the poem — the physiological part — is of course only a curiosity — a conceit worked out with dogged patience worthy of a better cause. The second part, in which the poet contemplates the spiritual life, rises occasionally to genuine beauty.

It is in the personified figures of the vices and virtues in this second part of the *Purple Island* that Phineas Fletcher

[1] Spenser.

prepares the way for the far more magnificent personifications — the vast figures, demonic and angelic — which
move through the pages of Milton's *Paradise Lost*. No
less notable for their influence on Milton are other poems
by these two brothers. In an allegory by Phineas, *The
Apollyonists*, describing the fall of Lucifer, there are antici-
pations of Milton's description of the rebellion and downfall of Satan; and of the council of the fallen angels, in the
first book of *Paradise Lost*. And in Milton's description of
one of the grim figures guarding the portal of Hell (*Paradise Lost*, Book II) —

> The other shape —
> If shape it might be called that shape had none,
> Distinguishable in member, joint or limb;
> Or substance might be called that shadow seemed,
> For each seemed either,

You may catch an echo of Fletcher's

> The porter to th' infernal gate is Sin.
> A shapeless shape, a foul deforméd thing,
> Not nothing, nor a substance.

And in Giles Fletcher's *Christ's Victory and Triumph*,
which is a highly imaginative retelling of the Biblical story
of Satan's temptation of Christ after his forty days of
fasting, the way is prepared for Milton's *Paradise Regained*.

It will be well to remember the work of the Fletchers
when we turn to Milton. No attempt will be made in that
chapter to deal with the complicated question of Milton's
sources, or of the poetical influences that were at work
upon him. To do that would be to blur the sharp image of
the poems themselves. But we need not therefore forget
that while Milton's great themes were taking shape in his
mind, such poets as Giles and Phineas Fletcher were apply-

ing Spenserian allegory to religious and theological matters;
and that in undertaking an allegorical epic designed to

> assert Eternal Providence
> And justify the ways of God to man,

Milton was wholly in the fashion of his time.

While such poets as Daniel and Drayton and the two
Fletchers were thus continuing to write in Spenser's way,
Ben Jonson and his imitators were bringing a new spirit
into English poetry. We remember that Jonson was
"built far higher in learning" than Shakespeare (page 107).
Jonson's training at Westminster school under the great
scholar, William Camden,[1] had given him a breadth of
learning, a devotion to the Classics, a desire to imitate the
art of the classical poetry in his own compositions. As
teachers of the art of poetry, he believed that "Horace
and he that taught him, Aristotle, deserve to be the first
in estimation."[2] His comedies (page 108) he modeled
upon those of the Latin dramatists, Plautus and Terence.
And because he was himself a rather hard-headed, sharp-
eyed, clear-thinking sort of man, impatient of sentimentality
and romantic extravagance, and given to laughing at other
people's follies, he turned for his models in lyric and satiric
poetry to such Latin poets as Horace and Martial.

Thus minded, he did not fall in with the imitators of the
dreamy, smooth-flowing, honey-sweet Spenser. "Spenser's
stanza pleased him not, nor his matter," his friend, William
Drummond[2] reported him as saying. "Others there are,"
Jonson notes in his *Discoveries*, thinking perhaps of Spenser's
disciple, Daniel, "that have no composition at all; but a

---

[1] Camden! most reverent head, to whom I owe
  All that I am in arts, all that I know —
      — (From Jonson's Epigram "To William Camden.")
[2] From Jonson's *Discoveries*.

kind of tuning and riming fall in what they write. It runs
and slides, and only makes a sound. Women's poets they
are called, as you have women's tailors.

> They write a verse as smooth, as soft as cream,
> In which there is no torrent, nor scarce stream.

You may sound these wits and find the depth of them with
your middle finger. They are cream-bowl-, or but pud-
dle-deep." This matter of "composition"— the careful
planning of the whole poem, the fitting together of every
link, the definite coming to a stop when the poem had said
what it had to say — Jonson saw as vital; and beyond
that, he strove for sharper, more clear-cut images, less
flow and more precision.

He took his material where he found it; it was the form
that he could give to it that mattered. He found, for
example, several detached passages in the Greek *Epistles*
of Philostratus, which he wove together into this song —
marrying to a beautiful economy and precision of words
a lovely music of rhythm and rhyme:

> Drink to me only with thine eyes,
>   And I will pledge with mine:
> Or leave a kiss but in the cup
>   And I'll not look for wine.
> The thirst that from the soul doth rise
>   Doth ask a drink divine;
> But might I of Jove's nectar sup,
>   I would not change for thine.
>
> I sent thee late a rosy wreath,
>   Not so much honouring thee
> As giving it a hope that there
>   It could not withered be;

> But thou thereon didst only breathe
> And sent'st it back to me;
> Since when it grows, and smells, I swear,
> Not of itself but thee!

In his treatment of more exalted themes, you will find this economy of phrase becoming almost austere in its spareness, as if every excrescence and superfluity had been filed and doubly filed away, until only the shining core of the thought is left. It is so in the "Hymn to Diana," already quoted (page 142). It is so in the "Epitaph on Elizabeth, L. H."

> Wouldst thou hear what man can say
> In a little? reader, stay.
> Underneath this stone doth lie
> As much beauty as could die.
> Which in life did harbour give
> To more virtue than doth live.
> If at all she had a fault,
> Leave it buried in this vault.
> One name was Elizabeth;
> The other, let it sleep with death:
> Fitter, where it died, to tell,
> Than that it lived at all.   Farewell!

It is so in what has always seemed to me the most moving memorial verse in all English poetry — his lines "On My First Son":

> Farewell, thou child of my right hand and joy;
> My sin was too much hope of thee, loved boy.
> Seven years thou wert lent to me, and I thee pay,
> Exacted by thy fate, on the just day.
> Oh, could I lose all father now! for why
> Will man lament the state he should envy?

> To have so soon 'scaped world's and flesh's rage,
> And, if no other misery, yet age!
> Rest in soft peace; and, asked, say, "Here doth lie
> Ben Jonson his best piece of poetry;
> For whose sake henceforth all his vows be such
> As what he loves may never like too much."

And in that great Ode of his, "To the Immortal Memory . . . of Sir Lucius Cary and Sir H. Morison" (which is too long to quote in full, and which cannot fairly be represented by an excerpt), you will find no less of spareness than in the shorter pieces, and an equal energy and grave beauty.

Around Ben Jonson in his ripe years gathered the poets who liked to call themselves the "Sons of Ben." To them he was

> The Muses' fairest light in no dark time;
> The wonder of a learnéd age; the line
> Which none can pass; the most proportioned wit
> To nature, the best judge of what was fit;
> The deepest, plainest, highest, clearest pen;
> The voice most echoed by consenting men.

Of these disciples the most loyal "son" and the poet of highest quality was Robert Herrick. Herrick's religious poems, *Noble Numbers*, appeared in 1647, ten years after Jonson's death; his secular poems, *Hesperides*, in the next year.

> When I a verse shall make,

wrote Herrick,

> Know I have prayed thee
> For old religion's sake,
> Saint Ben, to aid me.

He wrote in Jonson's spirit and with all of Jonson's beautiful precision and sense of form — and with a liveliness and grace which had been denied to his master. We have already caught two glimpses of him in the opening stanza of "Gather ye rose-buds while ye may" (page 158) and in that exquisite last stanza of "Corinna" (page 160). It is hard to decide whether he is more enjoyable when he is playing or when he is serious. At play, he has a quality of sheer impishness which is absolutely irresistible —

A TERNARY OF LITTLES

Upon a pipkin of jelly sent to a lady

A little saint best fits a little shrine,
A little prop best fits a little vine,
As my small cruse best fits my little wine.

A little seed best fits a little soil,
A little trade best fits a little toil,
As my small jar best fits my little oil.

A little bin best fits a little bread,
A little garland fits a little head,
As my small stuff best fits my little shed.

A little hearth best fits a little fire,
A little chapel fits a little choir,
As my small bell best fits my little spire.

A little stream best fits a little boat,
A little lead best fits a little float,
As my small pipe best fits my little note.

A little meat best fits a little belly;
As sweetly, Lady, give me leave to tell ye,
This little pipkin fits this little jelly.

He can take some trivial thing — were it only the swish of a silken skirt — and by finding the one word in the

language that realizes the quality of the sound, make
absolute poetry of it.

> Whenas in silks my Julia goes,
> Then, then, methinks, how sweetly flows
> That liquefaction of her clothes.
> Next, when I cast mine eyes, and see
> That brave vibration, each way free,
> O, how that glittering taketh me!

He can compress into a dozen starkly simple words the
disillusionment of life:

> I have lost, and lately, these
> Many dainty mistresses:
> Stately Julia, prime of all;
> Sappho next, a principal;
> Smooth Anthea, for a skin
> White and heaven-like crystalline;
> Sweet Electra and the choice
> Myrha, for the lute and voice;
> Next Corinna, for her wit
> And the graceful use of it;
> With Perilla.   All are gone,
> Only Herrick's left alone,
> For to number sorrow by
> Their departures hence, and die.

And he can find for the mood of piety and faith words more
beautiful in their simplicity and sincerity than any other
English poet has found.

> In the hour of my distress,
> When temptations me oppress,
> And when I my sins confess,
>   Sweet Spirit, comfort me!

When I lie within my bed,
Sick in heart and sick in head,
And with doubts discomforted,
   Sweet Spirit, comfort me! . . . .

When the passing-bell doth toll,
And the furies in a shoal
Come to fright a parting soul,
   Sweet Spirit, comfort me! . . . .

When the Judgment is revealed,
And that opened which was sealed,
When to Thee I have appealed,
   Sweet Spirit, comfort me!

The Spenserians with their verse "as smooth, as soft as cream"; Ben Jonson and his "Sons" following the Latin tradition of precision and careful composition — these, with whatever difference, seem to us natural and intelligible products of the Elizabethan mood. John Donne (1573–1631) is not a very intelligible product, but he too, when we come to think about it, seems to "belong." Certainly a liking for far-fetched comparisons and startling images ("conceits"), which Donne carried to an extreme, was common enough in the literature of the time. We have seen John Lyly letting his fancy riot in *Euphues*.[1] Even Shakespeare sometimes mars the great moments of his plays by fantastic conceits.[2] Most of these Elizabethans played with conceits as a child plays with toys, allowing a whimsical or startling fancy to run its length for the pure fun of it. But John Donne lived in a strange world of his own — a world of abstractions which he was always strug-

---

[1] See page 127.
[2] See for example *Romeo and Juliet*, III, iii, 33–42.

gling to find words for, a world in which even simple things assumed as if inevitably fantastic semblances.

Donne was a queer fellow. In his early poetry, composed while he was a worldling, he writes with a brutal cynicism, trampling, rough-shod, on the Elizabethan conventions of courtly compliment and flattery to women. Donne took a rough delight in berating women and proclaiming their inconstancy —

> I can love both fair and brown;
> Her whom abundance melts and her whom want betrays;
> Her who loves loneness best, and her who masks and plays;
> Her whom the country formed, and whom the town;
> Her who believes, and her who tries;
> Her who still weeps with spongy eyes,
> And her who is dry cork and never cries.
> I can love her, and her, and you, and you;
> I can love any, so she be not true.

Though thou shouldst

> Ride ten thousand days and nights
> Till Age snow white hairs on thee,
> Thou, when thou return'st, wilt tell me
> All strange wonders that befell thee
> And swear
> No where
> Lives a woman true and fair.

But, in "Break of Day," he can phrase in six lines the loveliest of love-poems —

> Stay, O sweet, and do not rise;
> The light that shines comes from thine eyes;
> The day breaks not, it is my heart,
> Because that you and I must part.
> Stay, or else my joys will die
> And perish in their infancy.

He can involve himself in the most grotesque metaphor, —
as thus, when he imagines two lovers looking in each other's
eyes:

> Our eye-beams twisted, and did thread
> Our eyes upon one double string;

or, from a context that is hobbling and dull, he can flash
out an image as supremely beautiful as this,—

> Her pure and eloquent blood
> Spoke in her cheeks, and so distinctly wrought
> That one might almost say her body thought.

He can begin a poem with lines of arresting beauty,—

> I long to talk with some old lover's ghost
> Who died before the God of Love was born;

and then dissipate this beginning in meaningless paradoxes.
Or, again, he can begin his Elegy, "The Autumnal," with
such exquisite lines as these:

> No spring, nor summer beauty hath such grace
> As I have seen in one autumnal face;

and then, within the compass of the same short poem, drift
into such grotesque and cacophonous stuff as this:

> But name not winter faces, whose skin's slack,
> Lank as an unthrift's purse, but a soul's sack;
> Whose eyes seek light within, for all here's shade;
> Whose mouths are holes, rather worn out, than made;
> Whose every tooth to a several place is gone,
> To vex their souls at resurrection.

But it would not be fair to Donne to leave you with this
as a final impression. He could, when he chose, write

poems of consistent beauty.   There is, for example, this
noble and almost flawless sonnet:

> Death, be not proud, though some have calléd thee
> Mighty and dreadful, for thou art not so:
> For those whom thou think'st thou dost overthrow
> Die not, poor Death; nor yet canst thou kill me.
> From Rest and Sleep, which but thy picture be,
> Much pleasure, then from thee much more must flow;
> And soonest our best men with thee do go —
> Rest of their bones and souls' delivery!
> Thou'rt slave to fate, chance, kings and desperate men,
> And dost with poison, war, and sickness dwell;
> And poppy or charms can make us sleep as well
> And better than thy stroke.   Why swell'st thou then?
> One short sleep past, we wake eternally,
> And Death shall be no more: Death, thou shalt die!

That is one phase.   There is another, a mystical phase,
which was always there, but became dominant in his later
years.   And this phase, too, reflects the mood of his time.
The old theology, the literal faith of the Middle Ages, was
breaking down under the influx of the pagan classics and the
revelations of the new astronomy.[1] We have already
noticed one result of this in the mood of *carpe diem*.[2] But
Donne's tortured mind, steeped in mediæval theology with
its curious mixture of subtleties and love of paradoxes and
literal faith, could neither understand and accept the "new
philosophy," nor content itself with *carpe diem:*

> The new philosophy calls all in doubt;
> The element of fire is quite put out;
> The sun is lost, and th' earth, and no man's wit
> Can well direct him where to look for it.

[1] See the comments on Francis Bacon in the next chapter.
[2] See page 160.

And freely men confess that the world's spent,
When in the planets and the firmament
They seek so many new; they see that this
Is crumbled out again to his atomies.
'Tis all in pieces, all coherence gone.
All just supply and all relation.

This confusion drove Donne into a continual effort to disentangle the real meanings, the true significances of life, from the sense-perceptions, the "fallacies" in which they are involved, and to find words in which to express them:

In this low form, poor soul, what wilt thou do?
When wilt thou shake off this pedantry
Of being taught by sense and fantasy?
Thou look'st through spectacles; small things seem great
Below; but up into thy watch-tower get,
And see all things despoiled of fallacies.

Sometimes Donne was driven into strange and horrible imaginings:

Think that thy body rots, and — if so low,
Thy soul exalted so, thy thoughts can go —
Think thee a prince who of themselves create
Worms, which insensibly devour their state.

At other times, his imagery, so often merely strained and fantastic, rises to a height of pure and noble beauty:

Think then, my soul, that death is but a groom,
Which brings a taper to the outward room,
Whence thou spiest first a little glimmering light,
And after brings it nearer to thy sight;
For such approaches doth heaven make in death.

If you will read, from the long poem, "The Anatomy of the World," that part called "Of the Progress of the Soul," you will find many such passages, of a sustained eloquence and beauty beyond the reach of any poet since Donne's day.

Ben Jonson (who was not given to indiscriminate praise) "esteemed John Donne the first poet in the world in some things;" and there were many poets of Donne's time and the generation following, who shared Ben's opinion. Donne had many imitators. Of these, George Herbert (1593–1632), Richard Crashaw (1612?–1649?) and Henry Vaughan (1621–1695) are the most important. Perhaps of these you will enjoy most the poems of George Herbert. Herbert was almost as much of a slave to fantastic conceits as Donne was. Like Donne, Herbert turned from the world to the Church and found his purest inspiration there. But in Herbert's work you will find no trace of the brutal cynicism of Donne's early poems or the morbidness of Donne's later poems. Sometime, when you are in England, you will walk the few miles from Salisbury out to the little hamlet and church of Bemerton (it will be a sort of pilgrimage) where Herbert spent the last two years of his life. It was at Bemerton that Herbert wrote the series of poems called *The Temple* which every lover of poetry knows and treasures. This series of devotional poems begins with a group of maxims called *The Church Porch* in which Herbert (Polonius-wise) deals with the practical relationships of life. Here are two of these maxims:

Scorn no man's love, though of a mean degree
(Love is a present for a mighty king);
Much less make any one thine enemy.
As guns destroy, so may a little sling.
  The cunning workman never doth refuse
  The meanest tool, that he may chance to use.

When once thy foot enters the Church, be bare.
God is more there than thou: for thou art there
Only by his permission.   Then be ware,

And make thyself all reverence and fear.
Kneeling ne'er spoilt silk stocking: quit thy state.
All equal are within the Church's gate.

The Church Porch is a transition from the life of the world to the life of the spirit. *The Temple* is the supreme expression of the spiritual life. In *The Temple*, Herbert utilizes every conceivable metaphor (sometimes, as it will seem to you, spontaneously and sincerely appropriate, sometimes strangely far-fetched) in his effort to express the various moods of religious devotion. Thus, in "Even-Song":

Yet still thou goest on,
And now with darkness closest weary eyes,
Saying to man, *It doth suffice:*
Henceforth repose; your work is done.

Thus in thy Ebony box
Thou dost inclose us, till the day
Put our amendment in our way,
And give new wheels to our disordered clocks.

Or thus, in "Christmas":

The shepherds sing; and shall I silent be?
My God, no hymn for thee?
My soul's a shepherd too: a flock it feeds
Of thoughts, and words, and deeds.
The pasture is thy word; the streams, thy grace
Enriching all the place.

Of all the short poems which comprise the series called *The Temple*, perhaps the most beautiful is the one called "The Pulley." (It is a curious title. You will see what Herbert means by it when you reach the last stanza of the poem.)

When God at first made man,
Having a glass of blessings standing by;
Let us (said he) pour on him all we can:
Let the world's riches, which dispersèd lie,
  Contract into a span.

So strength first made a way;
Then beauty flowed, then wisdom, honour, pleasure:
When almost all was out, God made a stay,
Perceiving that alone, of all his treasure,
  Rest in the bottom lay.

For if I should (said he)
Bestow this jewel also on my creature,
He would adore my gifts instead of me,
And rest in Nature, not the God of Nature:
  So both should losers be.

Yet let him keep the rest,
But keep them with repining restlessness:
Let him be rich and weary, that at least,
If goodness lead him not, yet weariness
  May toss him to my breast.

VI

FRANCIS BACON

At the threshold of the seventeenth century stands a great figure. He belongs to English literature because he had the gift of putting his thoughts into a prose that is clear and forcible and direct and nobly phrased; and because in his hands the "essay" first established itself as a literary form in English. But he belongs also, and more, to a larger world, the world of philosophic thought. We shall have to reckon with him as a man and a thinker first, discovering as we do so how completely the style and subject matter of his Essays reflect the man.

Bacon's father, Sir Nicholas Bacon, had held the offices of Lord Keeper of the Great Seal and Lord Chancellor in the early years of Queen Elizabeth's reign. Francis Bacon (1561–1626) studied law and followed in his father's footsteps, rising to the same high offices in the reign of James I. It was as a public speaker, in the practice of his profession, that Bacon first impressed his contemporaries. "He was full of gravity in his speaking," says Ben Jonson. "His language, when he could spare or pass by a jest, was nobly censorious. No man ever spoke more neatly, more prestly, more weightily, or suffered less emptiness, less idleness in what he uttered. No member of his speech but consisted in his own graces. His hearers could not cough or look aside from him without loss. . . . The fear of every man that heard him was lest he should make an end."

Bacon wrote as he spoke. The neatness, the prestness (compactness, brevity), the gravity, the weightiness, which so impressed Ben Jonson in his speaking, are likewise the salient qualities of his writing.

Bacon's chief object in his writing was to reorganize the various fields of knowledge and to work out better methods of study and investigation in these fields. In every branch of learning, said Bacon, people were inclined to take too much for granted. They assumed that every notion or idea or principle or theory that had been handed down from the ancients must be true, and that it would be irreverent to question it. When they did set out to investigate anything in the world around them, they started with a theory and tried to make the facts fit the theory. If, Bacon contended, they would keep their eyes open, and accept nothing that was not proved, and develop their theories to fit the facts, then and only then would they begin to get at the truth.

For the greater part of his life Bacon was pondering this problem of the systematization and advancement of learning. "I confess," he wrote to his uncle, Elizabeth's chief minister, Lord Burghley, in 1592, "that I have as vast contemplative ends, as I have moderate civil ends; for I have taken all knowledge to be my province." It was his hope, he continued in this letter, to purge Learning of its faults of method and "bring in industrious observations, grounded conclusions, and profitable inventions and discoveries." Thirteen years later he published *The Advancement of Learning*, in which, after a defense of the high dignity of knowledge, he reviews the different branches of human learning, history, poetry, philosophy, and science, notes what the mind of man has accomplished in each department, points out what tasks yet remain unperformed, and analyzes the faults of method which stand in the way. *The Advancement of Learning* was intended merely as an introduction to a greater work, *Instauratio Magna*, which should present a complete systematization and reorganization of the fields of knowledge.

Another step toward this great scheme was taken in 1620, when he published his *Novum Organum*, an exposition of that "inductive" method which was to arrive at theory by observation of fact. In 1623 he translated into Latin, and expanded, his *Advancement of Learning*, under the title *De Augmentis Scientiarum*. He was still at work upon these "vast contemplative ends" when death took him in 1626.

These philosophic writings of Bacon's, some of them in English, some of them in Latin, belong to the history of scientific thought. It is in another field that he made his chief contribution to English literature. But it is impossible, even in the briefest sketch, to ignore this side of him. Bacon stands at the threshold of our modern world, with its innumerable applications of scientific method to the study of the laws of nature, and with the fruits of that study all around us, in railways and telegraphs and radio and submarines and airplanes and a thousand other things. It is because Bacon marks the dividing line between an era of superstition and unscientific thinking and an era of amazing scientific development that his major writings become so profoundly significant. While Bacon was meditating his *Instauratio Magna*, Galileo, by just such experimental methods of scientific investigation as Bacon advocated, was laying the foundations of modern astronomy, and Harvey was transforming the science of medicine by his demonstration of the circulation of the blood. Bacon himself invented nothing and discovered nothing. But because he interpreted the new age to itself and gave it not only awareness but breadth of view and a sense of co-ordination he may well be called the father of modern science.

The work of Bacon which English literature has especially appropriated to itself is only incidental to the main subject of his thought. In 1597 he printed a little volume of ten short essays, five of which were no more than expanded notes for his projected *Advancement of Learning*. In 1612 these were republished with additions, and in 1625 a third and considerably enlarged collection of his Essays appeared.

Bacon described the essay as a "dispersed meditation." In the intended dedication of the 1612 edition of his Essays to Prince Henry, he explains: "To write just treatises requireth leisure in the writer and leisure in the reader . . . which is the cause that hath made me choose to write certain brief notes, set down rather significantly than curiously, which I have called *Essays*. The word is late, but the thing is ancient."

The word *essay* is akin to assay, the process of ascertaining what metals are in an ore or other conglomerate substance. An *essay* in the literary sense is an attempt to "try out" or experiment with the possibilities of a subject by putting together the thoughts about it which are in the author's mind. It is to be distinguished, as Bacon points out, from a *treatise*, or exhaustive investigation.

Before Bacon's day the most famous essay-writer of modern times was the Frenchman, Montaigne (1533–1592). "I desire therein," wrote Montaigne in the preface to his *Essais*, "to be delineated in mine own genuine simple and ordinary fashion, without contention, art or study; for it is myself I portray." This informal, personal way of treating a subject has been characteristic of the essay from Montaigne's day to our own.

Montaigne's *Essais*, as translated by John Florio in 1603, were favorite reading in Bacon's day. Shakespeare derived hints from them for his plays. They were among the books in Ben Jonson's library. Bacon refers to them.

Bacon's *Essays* have the gravity, the wisdom, and the common sense that were characteristic of the man, and at the same time the "neatness" and "prestness" which had so struck Ben Jonson in Bacon's public speaking. They are, as we read them in their final form, the fruit of a lifetime particularly rich in experience of men and affairs. In method, even in this final form, they still reflect the way in which they originated. Most of them begin with a brief, vivid, arresting sentence — just such a sentence as we can imagine Bacon jotting down in his notebook as a nucleus around which other thoughts on the same theme should gather. Take the essay which stands first in the collection, the one entitled "Of Truth." Bacon had been reading the eighteenth chapter of the Gospel of John. "Art thou the King of the Jews?" asks Pilate, when Christ is brought before him. "My Kingdom is not of this world," Christ replies. "Thou sayest that I am a King. To this end was I born . . . that I should bear witness unto the truth. Everyone that is of the truth heareth my voice." "What *is* truth?" Pilate asks. "And when he had said this," the Biblical narrative continues, "he went out again unto the Jews." The story sets Bacon to thinking how difficult and often laborious it is to know and to practice the truth and how readily human nature slips into a lie. The essence of the Biblical story comes from Bacon's pen in a single arresting sentence: "'What is Truth?' said jesting Pilate; and would not stay for an answer." From this vivid opening, the essay grows, rather by successive jottings of examples from his wide reading and of observations derived from his experience of human nature than by any planned and organic development of the theme. Indeed it may be questioned whether this opening sentence is really an altogether apt introduction to the thoughts about truth that ultimately shape themselves into the completed essay. But the opening sentence is a fillip to the imagination. It catches the attention. And the thoughts that follow are wise thoughts and nobly expressed.

Most of Bacon's essays are made in this same fashion. The opening sentence gets hold of you, makes you want to read on. *Of Death:* "Men fear Death, as children fear to go in the dark"; *Of Revenge:* "Revenge is a kind of wild justice"; *Of Marriage and Single Life:* "He that hath wife and children hath given hostages to fortune"; *Of Great Place:* "Men in great place are thrice servants: servants of the sovereign or state; servants of fame; and servants of business"; *Of Atheism:* "I had rather believe all the fables in the *Legend* and the *Talmud* and the *Alcoran* than that this universal frame is without a Mind"; *Of Suspicion:* "Suspicions amongst thoughts are like bats amongst birds, they ever fly by twilight"; *Of Riches:* "I cannot call riches better than the baggage of virtue"; *Of Gardens:* "God Almighty first planted a garden"; *Of Studies:* "Studies serve for delight, for ornament, and for ability." Here and there in the essays the language rises to a figurative beauty; as in this passage from the essay *Of Great Place:* "Power to do good is the true and lawful end of aspiring. For good thoughts (though God accept them), yet towards men are little better than good dreams; except they be put in act; and that cannot be without power and place, as the vantage and commanding ground. Merit and good works is the end of man's motion; and conscience of the same is the accomplishment of man's rest. For if a man can be partaker of God's theater, he shall likewise be partaker of God's rest." But in general it is in a grave and unadorned dignity of expression or in a pithiness of phrase that Bacon's merit lies. Of the latter, let these oft-quoted phrases from the essay *Of Studies* serve as an example: "Some books are to be tasted, others to be swallowed, and some few to be chewed and digested: that is, some books are to be read only in parts; others to be read but not curiously; and some few to be read wholly, and with diligence and attention. . . . Reading maketh a full man; conference a ready man; and writing an exact man." As an example of the former, consider the closing words of the essay *Of Death:* "It is as natural to die as to be born; and to a little infant, perhaps, the one is as painful as the other. He that dies in an earnest pursuit is like one that is wounded in hot blood, who, for the time scarce feels the hurt. And therefore a mind fixed and bent upon somewhat that is good doth avert the dolors of death. But above all, believe it, the sweetest canticle is *nunc dimittis* when a man has attained worthy ends and expectations. Death hath this also; that it openeth the gate to good fame, and extinguisheth envy."

This plain and direct way of writing was not common in Bacon's time. He wrote so because that was the way in which he thought. His style was, literally, the man. But with most of his contemporaries English prose, to be literary, must either be tricked out with decorations, as Lyly and Sidney had tricked it out in the previous generation, or must conform to the sonorous, balanced, periodic[1] structure of the Latin prose which they were taught in school to translate and imitate. It was often rhythmical but it was all too often difficult to follow, not easy to "get" at first reading. It was not until Dryden's day, and largely by force of his example, that English prose rediscovered the fact that it could be clear and direct without being any the less rhythmical and graceful.

[1] "That form of sentence in which the sense is incomplete or suspended until the end is reached."—*Century Dictionary*. See pp. 129-130.

VII

JOHN MILTON AND THE PURITANS

When Shakespeare was yet a small boy at Stratford a sect of persons called "Puritans" were beginning to attract public attention. These Puritans thought that the "Established Church" retained too many of the ceremonies and usages of Roman Catholicism. Instead of such "idolatry" (for they were good haters and used strong words) the Puritans wanted a "purer" religion, freed from the authority of the bishops and of the elaborate machinery of the Church, simple and democratic in its methods of government. In contrast to the richness of costume and extravagance of speech characteristic of the period, they clothed themselves in sober garments and filled not only their public exhortations but their daily conversation with Biblical phrases.[1] They were not unwilling to accept the name of "Puritans," which was first applied to them in derision; but it was as "the Godly" that they always referred to themselves.

At first they were largely of the lower classes — the "psalm-singing weavers,"[2] the laborers, the petty tradesmen; but it was not long before they found support in

[1] It is commonly said that the Puritans were people of one book and that book the so-called "Authorized Version" of the Bible made in 1611. But they had coined the phraseology of Tyndale's version (1536) and of the Geneva translation (1560) into their daily speech long before the "Authorized Version" was made.

[2] So Falstaff in *I Henry IV*: "I would I were a weaver; I could sing psalms or anything."
Puritan psalm-singing was a favorite jest among the playwrights. Says the Clown in *The Winter's Tale*: "Three-man song-men all, and very good ones; but they are most of them means and bases; but one Puritan amongst them, and he sings psalms to hornpipes."

higher quarters. The authorities became alarmed. Stringent regulations were passed forbidding assemblage of Puritans. Some of the more defiant formally separated themselves from the Church, took the name of "Separatists" or "Brownists" (from the name of their leader), fled to Amsterdam to escape persecution, and in due time embarked upon the Mayflower to found a colony in America.

Meanwhile the growing power of the Puritans was making itself felt. Political changes were contributing to make Puritanism a national issue. During Queen Elizabeth's reign England had been wisely governed and had remained prosperous and at peace. Shakespeare, writing several years after the great Queen's death, but putting his words as a prophecy into the mouth of one of the characters in *Henry VIII*, had said of her:

> She shall be loved and feared; her own shall bless her. . . .
> In her days every man shall eat in safety,
> Under his own vine, what he plants, and sing
> The merry songs of peace to all his neighbours.

But Queen Elizabeth died in 1603, and her successor, King James I, was neither wise in himself nor happy in the choice of his advisers. He was a believer in the divine right of kings and was convinced that God intended a king to be "a little God to sitte on his throne and rule over other men."[1] As King of Scotland, before his accession to the English throne, he had already become bitterly prejudiced against the Puritans. "Very pestes in the Church and commonweale," he had called them,[2] "whom no deserts can oblige; neither oathes or promises binde; breathing nothing but sedition and calumnies, aspyring without measure, rayling

---

[1] The words are used in a book of advice, the *Basilikon Doron*, which James wrote for his son Prince Charles, who was to succeed him.

[2] In the *Basilikon Doron*.

without reason, and making their owne imaginations (without any warrant of the worde) the square of their conscience." When he came to the English throne, he was advised to make concessions to them. "I shall make them conform themselves," he replied, "or I shall harry them out of the land." He drove ministers with Puritan sympathies out of their livings. He enlarged the powers of the ecclesiastical courts and encouraged them to "harry" the Puritans.

Meanwhile his extravagance was piling up a mass of debts. For means of raising money he was forced to appeal to the Parliament; and when Parliament took the opportunity to make a formal protest against his unwise courses and ask for specific reforms, James sent for the journal of the House, tore up the pages in which their "Protestation" was recorded, forbade them to debate matters touching the king's government, and told them that so far from recognizing their privilege of free speech, he would punish "any insolent behavior" on their part, "as well during their sitting as after." Among a nation in which the love of freedom was so deeply ingrained, these autocratic ways served only to consolidate the opposition to king and court; and many men who on purely religious grounds would have been content to remain loyal to the established Church were driven into sympathy and coöperation with the Puritans.

When James died in 1625 and his son, Charles I, succeeded him, things had come to such a pass between the royalists on the one side and the great mass of freedom-loving Englishmen on the other, that even a wise king might not have been able to save England from civil war. But Charles was even less wise, if that were possible, than his father. With the expenses of two foreign wars on his

THE PORTRAIT OF CHARLES I BY VANDYKE

hands as well as the extravagance of the court, he tried
to force his subjects to pay all sorts of special taxes. When
Parliament refused to sanction these, he dissolved it and
for eleven years ruled by "personal government" without
summoning it again.

Meanwhile he continued to persecute the Puritans. His
most active helper was William Laud, bishop of London.
In 1633 Laud was made Archbishop of Canterbury. The
bishops who would not coöperate with Laud in the persecutions were ousted, and willing helpers put into their places.
Among Puritans and Nonconformists the feeling grew that
Laud and his bishops were gradually forcing England back
into the Church of Rome. "Prelaty" (the rule of prelates
or bishops) became a by-word for oppression, for the selfish
luxury of those in authority, for "the hateful thirst of
Lording in the Church."[1] The storm-clouds were gathering. The quarrel had become too bitter to be settled by
peaceful means. War between the opposing factions was
already seen to be inevitable.

This was what was happening in England as Milton was
growing to manhood. Milton's father was a Puritan, but
not of the severer sort. A scrivener by profession, a
musician and composer of madrigals by avocation, the
elder Milton encouraged his son to love beautiful things.
"My father," Milton wrote, "destined me from a child to
the pursuits of literature; and my appetite for knowledge
was so voracious that, from twelve years of age, I hardly
ever left my studies, or went to bed before midnight." It
was the languages which would open knowledge to him that
his father most encouraged him to study. "When at your
cost, dear father, I had mastered the tongue of Romulus

[1] The words are Milton's, used in his tract, "The Reason of Church Government Urged against Prelaty," published in 1641.

and seen all the graces of it, and had learned the noble idiom of the magniloquent Greeks . . . you persuaded me to add to these the flowers which France boasts: and the speech which the modern Italian pours from his degenerate lips . . . and the language in which the singers of Palestine speak their mysteries."

From private tuition at home and a few years at St. Paul's School, Milton proceeded to Cambridge. He spent seven years there (1625–1632), not altogether happy in the assigned tasks, but profiting by the opportunity to extend his reading. Meanwhile, he wrote. Already he felt in himself, and his friends felt in him, a promise of great things. "Both at home and in the schools it was found that whether aught was imposed upon me by them that had the overlooking, or betaken to of my own choice, in English, or other tongue, prosing or versing, but chiefly by this latter, the style, by certain vital signs it had, was likely to live." Of the poems composed while he was a student at Cambridge, one especially shows these "vital signs." In December of 1629 the twenty-one-year-old youth wrote to a friend at Oxford: "But if you will know what I am doing, I will tell you . . . I am singing the King of Heaven . . . and the stabling under a poor roof of Him who rules with his Father in the realms above; the star that led the wizards, the hymning of angels in the air, and the gods flying to their endangered fanes. This poem I made as a birthday gift for Christ; the first light of Christmas dawn brought me the theme." This is the *Ode on the Morning of Christ's Nativity*.

On the night of Christ's birth, as the poet imagines it, Nature and man were hushed to reverent silence —

> No war, or battail's sound
> Was heard the world around.

The stars waited and watched with deep amaze, the rest-less ocean forgot to rave. On the Galilean hillside the shep-herds

> Or ere the point of dawn,
> Sat simply chatting in a rustic row

until

> such music sweet
> Their hearts and ears did greet
> As never was by mortal fingers strook.

So far Milton retells the story in verse such as any good poet of his day, with an ear for the music of words, might have written. But in this youth of twenty-one was stirring a curious power such as no one in his day or since has had in equal measure. To most of us, bound down unimagina-tively to a spot of earth, the universe is at best what it was to Hamlet, "a majestical roof fretted with golden fire." But Milton, even in his early verse, had the power of putting into words, as if from some outside vantage-point, a feeling of the immensity of space:

> Such music (as 'tis said)
> Before was never made,
> But when of old the Sons of Morning sung.
> While the Creator great
> His constellation set,
> And the well-balanced World on hinges hung,
> And cast the dark foundations deep,
> And bid the weltering waves their oozy channel keep. .

It was to be many years before Milton should begin the composition of *Paradise Lost*. Heaven, the majesty of God, the battle between the rebellious and the loyal angels, the vastness and the horror of hell, the shaping of the earth out of chaos, the struggle between God and Satan for the soul of man — such things,

> Unattempted yet in prose or rhyme

he was to describe in *Paradise Lost*. But already, in this poem of his youth, are the beginnings of the art which in *Paradise Lost* was to create the picture of

> the empyreal Heaven, extended wide. . . .
> With opal towers and battlements adorned
> Of living sapphire. . . .
> And fast by, hanging in a golden chain,
> This pendent World, in bigness as a star
> Of smallest magnitude close by the moon.

Despite the Nativity Ode, the seven years at Cambridge seemed to Milton disappointingly unfruitful. "My hasting days," he wrote, in the sonnet *On His Having Arrived at the Age of Twenty-three*,

> fly on with full career,
> But my late Spring no bud or blossom shew'th.

In this year (1631) Milton finished his course at Cambridge. His father had recently retired to the village of Horton, about twenty miles from London. Through the meadows of Horton winds the Colne, emptying not far below into the Thames. Three miles away lift the gray towers of Windsor Castle.

> Meadows trim with daisies pied,
> Shallow brooks and rivers wide.
> Towers and battlements it sees
> Bosomed high in tufted trees.

In this quiet place, not yet disturbed by the "hoarse disputes" of king and Parliament, churchman and Puritan,

Milton, as he records, "enjoyed an interval of uninterrupted leisure, which I entirely devoted to the perusal of the Greek and Latin classics; though I occasionally visited the metropolis, either for the sake of purchasing books, or of learning something new in mathematics or in music, in which I at that time found a source of pleasure and amusement." During this quiet interval, too, his mind dwelt, as ever, upon the great work to come — poem it must be when he should find fit theme. His father wished him to turn his university training to the usual account by entering the ministry, but Milton, "perceiving," as he says, "what tyranny had invaded the Church, that he who would take Orders must subscribe slave and take an oath withal, which, unless he took with a conscience that would retch, he must either straight perjure, or split his faith . . . thought it better to prefer a blameless silence before the sacred office bought and begun with servitude and forswearing."   Instead, he appealed to his father, because it had been his "good chance to be born a poet," to let him devote his life to poetry.

L'Allegro, Il Penseroso, Comus, and Lycidas are the chief fruits of the five years which Milton spent at Horton. L'Allegro and Il Penseroso are companion-pieces, delicate and graceful studies of two contrasted moods. They are just such moods as Milton found himself alternating between in the quiet countryside of Horton — out of doors one day, with the healthy blood racing through his veins, and enjoying every pleasure of eye and ear; the next day, thoughtful, meditative, but enjoying himself no less. It is a mistake to think of these two poems as contrasting pictures of happiness and sadness. It is equally a mistake, as some critics have done, to describe them as "two ideal days of twelve hours each."   There is indeed a sort of framework of the passing hours of contrasted days, but Milton ignores this orderly arrangement whenever he chooses. In fact, the two little poems are too spontaneous, too natural a thinking aloud, to submit to any fixed scheme. In *L'Allegro* it is as if the young poet, waking at dawn, said to himself: It's a fine morning. Up and away! How good the world is with this morning sunshine and a frolic wind, birds singing, the mowers in the fields or coming forth to play on a sunshine holyday. And, to vary it if I will, there is London waiting for me with its thronged streets and all its glitter and revelry. There is equal delight in being here listening in the dusk to the shepherds' stories of fairy Mab and Puck the lubber fiend; or fancying myself in London where Shakespeare's *As You Like It* holds the boards. And as these thoughts play through the poet's mind, they ripple into a merry lilt of rhyme.

An equally spontaneous thinking aloud is *Il Penseroso*, the mood of pensive musing. Away with yesterday's sportive pleasures! Not the lark's bright morning song, but the voice of the nightingale,

> Most musical, most melancholy,

shall blend with my thoughts. Yesterday I watched. Tonight I would dream. I would wonder with Plato what becomes of that immortal part of us when it leaves the body; or I would let my thoughts dwell upon the great themes of tragedy; or listen in fancy to the music of Musæus or Orpheus; or hark to the tale of magic which Chaucer's Squire began on the road to Canterbury, and left half-told. For it is mystery and enchantment that move me now. And when the magic night is over and morning dawns, I would have no garish day, no gaiety of young men and maidens upon the green, but shadowy groves and the

cathedral's dim religious light — and at length a mossy
cell where I may keep my solitary watch

> Till old Experience do attain
> To something like prophetic strain.

Comus is of a different pattern. During the first decade
of the seventeenth century "Masques"[1] became fashionable. Like the dramas in the professional theaters, the
masque was intended to be played before an audience, the
participants speaking and acting their parts; and in most
of the masques there is at least a thread of story; but the
seventeenth-century audience was chiefly interested in the
beauty of the spectacle and of the poetry. A masque was
usually performed at court or in a nobleman's house. Elaborate and costly settings and costumes were provided, and
the major parts — the kings and queens and gods and
goddesses — were often acted by the titled folk for whose
pleasure the masque was written. For a number of years
Ben Jonson, next to Shakespeare the most distinguished
of Elizabethan dramatists, had supplied the masques an-
nually performed at court; and the King's architect, Inigo
Jones, had prepared the scenery for them.

That Milton, with his Puritan background, should have
composed an entertainment of this sort may seem surprising. The Puritans hated the stage and everything
associated with it, and were always rushing into print to
denounce it. Only two years before *Comus* was written,
the Puritan Prynne had startled England with the violence
of his attack upon "plays and common actors and all those
several mischievous and pestiferous fruits of hellish wickedness that issue from them" and had boasted that "one

---

[1] So called because traditionally the actors of mythical or allegorical characters wore masques.

grand badge of a Puritan is . . . to condemn stage-plays, players, and play-haunters, and wholly to renounce these pomps of the devil." To the average Puritan certainly, masques were to be numbered among the mischievous and pestiferous fruits. Milton himself, though he was far from being an average Puritan, had, only a few years before, denounced his fellow-students of Christ's College for acting in a play which was performed in honor of one of King Charles's state visits to Cambridge. It was beneath the dignity of these students for the ministry, he averred, "to writhe their clergy-limbs upon the stage. . . . They thought themselves gallant men and I thought them fools."

But it was wholly characteristic of Milton to go his own way. His friend and his father's friend, the musician and composer Henry Lawes, was tutor in music to the family of the Earl of Bridgewater. Lawes invited Milton to write the words, for which Lawes himself would write the music, for a masque to be given at the Earl's castle of Ludlow, on Michaelmas night (September 29th), 1634. Milton would write the masque — but to his intensely serious mind no other theme was possible than one of spiritual beauty and ennoblement. That was, he felt, what the poetic drama was for. Young students, he wrote a few years later in his tractate *Of Education*, ought to be taught the laws that govern the structure of a dramatic poem, because the knowledge of these laws "would make them soon perceive what despicable creatures our common rhymers and play-writers be, and show them what religious, what glorious and magnificent use might be made of poetry both in divine and human things." Had not Milton's master, Spenser, used poetry thus — Spenser, whom Milton thought "a better teacher than Scotus or Aquinas"?

The masque in Milton's hands becomes an allegory

of the strength, the invulnerability, of moral purity. *Comus* is the story of a "Lady" (not otherwise named), who strays from her two brothers and becomes lost in a wood. The evil-minded sorcerer, Comus,[1] finds her there, disguises himself as a gentle shepherd, and, persuading her that he is guiding her back to her brothers, leads the way to his own stronghold. There he creates by his magic a stately castle, seats her in an enchanted chair, and tempts her with all sensuous delights. Powerless to rise, she yet daunts the tempter by her eloquence. An "Attendant Spirit" appears to the two brothers and warns them of their sister's plight. The younger brother is anxious, the elder confident:

> Virtue, may be assailed, but never hurt;
> Surprised by unjust force, but not enthralled.

Under the guidance of the attendant spirit they make their way to the sorcerer's stronghold. Comus flees, but his spell still holds the Lady in durance. The attendant spirit summons to their aid a gentle nymph

> That with moist curb sways the smooth Severn stream,
> Sabrina is her name, a virgin pure.

This "goddess of the silver lake," whose pathetic story Milton had read in Spenser (the "Meliboeus old" of *Comus*) annuls the sorcerer's spell, and the Lady is united to her brothers.

---

[1] Comus is represented as the son of Circe. In Classic myth, Circe lures travelers to her island and gives them a magic potion which turns them into swine. In Milton's play, likewise, Comus offers travelers a potion by which

> their human countenance,
> The express resemblance of the gods, is changed
> Into some brutish form.

Milton's conception of Comus was probably influenced, if not suggested, by Spenser's story of the Bower of Bliss, presided over by the enchantress Acrasia. (*The Faerie Queene*, Book II, Canto XII.)

At this point the scene suddenly changes from the enchanter's castle to Ludlow Town. Country dancers come thronging round Ludlow Castle; and the three noble actors who have played the chief parts (for the Lady Alice Egerton, fifteen-year-old daughter of the Earl, played the Lady, and her two brothers, thirteen and twelve respectively, were the Elder Brother and the Younger Brother) are restored to their parents by the Attendant Spirit.

This little play, with its lofty moral tone, with the music and the romantic beauty of the Sabrina scene —

> Sabrina fair,
>   Listen where thou are sitting
> Under the glassy, cool, translucent wave,
>   In twisted braids of lilies knitting
> The loose train of thy amber-dropping hair;
>   Listen for dear honour's sake,
>   Goddess of the silver lake,
>   Listen and save! . . .

and with the whimsical charm of the close, is altogether typical of the blended impulses of this first phase of Milton's poetic genius. The lyrist of *L'Allegro*, responsive to

> Such sights as youthful poets dream
> On summer eves by haunted stream;

the disciple of Spenser; the Puritan moralist, for whom

> Evil on itself shall back recoil
> And mix no more with goodness, when at last,
> Gathered like scum and settled to itself,
> It shall be in eternal restless change
> Self-fed and self-consumed. . . .

are happily at one in *Comus*.

Between *Comus* and *Lycidas*, three years elapsed. During this time the people of England were growing more and more restless under the heavy fines and special taxes which the King was imposing.   The court called "the Star Chamber" was meting out fines and imprisonments at the will of the King and the King's party, without regard to the common law.   The measures of Laud, now Archbishop of Canterbury, to force the Puritans into conformity, were growing daily more severe.   The bishops who were enforcing his measures and who thus came into direct contact with the people were the special objects of hatred. To the oppressed Puritans the bishops seemed no longer conscientious overseers[1] and true shepherds of their flocks, but selfish and designing men, destroyers of liberty and enemies of the truth.

To understand *Lycidas*, it is necessary to see it against this background of popular feeling.   For *Lycidas* is not merely an elegy woven in a conventional pattern[2] and phrased with exquisite art.   The oppressions of the last few years had stirred Milton's emotions too deeply for him to content himself with mere artistry.   The poet-dreamer of *L'Allegro* and *Il Penseroso* is developing into the fighting Puritan.   In his hands the conventional elegy becomes a symbol, a challenge, and a warning.

The "sad occasion dear" of *Lycidas* was the death of Edward King, who had been a fellow-student with Milton

---

[1] "Bishop" is made up of two Greek words meaning *to oversee.*

[2] An elegy is a funeral song or song of bereavement.   A favorite form in Greek and Latin poetry was the "pastoral elegy," in which the person mourned for is represented as a shepherd.   In the imitations of the classical pastoral elegy common in Renaissance literature, there was a conventional pattern or established way of treating the subject.   The poet represented himself and his dead friend as having been shepherds together, feeding their flocks; it was regularly assumed that all nature mourned for the dead shepherd; spirits which were personified forces of nature were summoned in procession to lament the dead; and, finally, the poet turned for comfort to the thought of the dead shepherd's immortality.   The intense personal feeling that vibrates through *Lycidas* becomes the more remarkable when we realize how strictly Milton was following the conventional pattern of the pastoral elegy.

at Cambridge. A volume of *Obsequies to the Memory of Mr. Edward King* was planned by King's Cambridge friends. *Lycidas* was Milton's contribution. There is no evidence that Milton knew King intimately at Cambridge. But the death of a fellow-student, himself a poet, was enough to set Milton's imagination going — an imagination at once creative in itself and teeming with literary reminiscence. It has been pointed out that phrase after phrase of Lycidas is translation or paraphrase or echo — "Where were ye, Nymphs, etc.?" from the *Idyls* of Theocritus; "Who would not weep for Lycidas" and "Phœbus replied and touched my trembling ears" and "Visit'st the bottom of the monstrous world" from Virgil's *Eclogues;* the opening lines of *Lycidas,* suggested by an anonymous elegy lamenting the death of Sir Philip Sidney's sister, the Countess of Pembroke; Spenser's *Eclogue* for April and Shakespeare's *The Winter's Tale* for hints for the flowers strewn on Lycidas' "laureate hearse"; the last line of the poem from Phineas Fletcher's "Tomorrow shall ye feast in pastures new," in *The Purple Island.* Around these remembered phrases and motives, Milton wove his own flawless imagery. English poetry has nothing more beautiful than the picture of the two shepherds, together tending their flock; than the enumeration of the flowers that "strew the laureate hearse where Lycid lies;" than the ebb and flow of Milton's music; than the tranquil loveliness of the closing lines:

> Thus sang the uncouth swain to th' oaks and rills,
> While the still moon went out with sandals gray;
> He touched the tender stops of various quills,
> With eager thought warbling his Doric lay:
> And now the sun had stretched out all the hills,
> And now was dropped into the western bay;

> At last he rose and twitched his mantle blue:
> Tomorrow to fresh woods, and pastures new.

This was Milton, the creative artist — and by 1637, Milton the creative artist had reached the full maturity of his powers. But by 1637 the world of actualities, the struggle of Puritanism against the oppressions of the church, was closing in upon him. Interesting as a work of art, *Lycidas* is even more interesting as a reflection of Milton's state of mind, as a transition to the nearing time when he was reluctantly to give over his beloved poetry and devote himself entirely to helping the Puritan cause.

At Cambridge, King had been preparing himself for the ministry. It was impossible for Milton to think of him as a shepherd in the traditional poetical sense without thinking of him at the same time as a minister of God, a pastor shepherding his spiritual flock. In Milton's mind, King becomes a symbol. What *is* a *good* shepherd? One, surely, who is willing to sacrifice himself; to "scorn delights, and live laborious days;" to be, at every moment, the conscientious watcher, the overseer of his flock; to look for his reward, not in earthly, mortal fame, but in that fame which

> lives and spreads aloft by those pure eyes
> And perfect witness of all-judging Jove;
> As he pronounces lastly on each deed. . . .

Not, surely, the shepherd who is a kind of blind mouth; who does not take the trouble to oversee; who thinks only of feeding himself instead of feeding his flock; who, indeed, poisons the flock by the rank mist of his false teachings. Let such beware — for their punishment is already at the door. It is from the lips of Peter, founder of the church, that the denunciation comes — Peter, so strangely and daringly numbered among the pagan-classical personifications that lament for Lycidas . . . .

> Last came and last did go,
> The Pilot of the Galilean Lake.
> Two massy keys he bore of metals twain
> (The golden opes, the iron shuts amain).
> He shook his mitered locks and stern bespake:
> How well could I have spared for thee, young swain,
> Enow of such as, for their bellies sake,
> Creep, and intrude, and climb into the fold!
> Of other care, they little reckoning make
> Than how to scramble at the shearers' feast,
> And shove away the worthy bidden guest.
> Blind mouths! that scarce themselves know how to hold
> A sheep-hook, or have learned aught else the least
> That to the faithful herdsman's art belongs!
> What recks it them? What need they? They are sped;
> And, when they list, their lean and flashy songs
> Grate on their scrannel pipes of wretched straw;
> The hungry sheep look up and are not fed,
> But swoln with wind and the rank mist they draw
> Rot inwardly and foul contagion spread;
> Besides what the grim wolf with privy paw
> Daily devours apace, and nothing said.
> But that two-handed engine at the door
> Stands ready to smite once, and smite no more.

And, lest any misunderstand, when Milton reprinted *Lycidas* seven years later in a collection of his own poems, he set under the title these words: "In this Monody the Author bewails a learned friend, unfortunately drowned in his passage from Chester on the Irish seas, 1637. And by occasion foretells the ruin of our corrupted clergy then in their height."

The years between the first appearance of *Lycidas* in

1638, and its reappearance with this inscription in Milton's *Poems Both Latin and English*, 1645, saw that ruin which the poem had foretold. It will be remembered that at the time when the poem was written, King Charles was refusing from year to year to call Parliament together. If, as is thought by some critics, Milton meant by the "two-handed engine at the door" that

> Stands ready to smite once, and smite no more,

the two houses of Parliament, his grim warning was justified by the event. Indignation against the king and the oppression of the corrupt clergy was increasing yearly. Without a parliament, this indignation was without a voice. But when at length new needs for money forced Charles to call Parliament together again, that body made it clear that there would be no grants without redress of grievances. Once more (it was his last royal gesture) the king dismissed them in a rage. But, like it or not, he had to have them back. When they reassembled, their patience was exhausted. They took matters into their own hands, ignored the authority of the king, abolished the Star Chamber and the ecclesiastical Court, and impeached and executed Laud and a few others of the King's most active agents. Charles gathered his supporters about him — for there were still many who were loyal both to the king in person and to the age-old tradition of the monarchy. The Puritans gathered round the Parliament. Everywhere men seized arms; and every town and hamlet and countryside suddenly found itself peopled, not with old friends and neighbors, but with bitter enemies — cavaliers against roundheads,[1] royalists against parliament-men, church-

---

[1] It was the fashion of the day for gentlemen to wear long curling locks. The Puritan tradesmen and apprentices with their close-cropped hair were called "roundheads."

OLIVER CROMWELL

Painting by R. Walker

men against Puritans. With the battle of Edgehill (1642) began the civil war which was to result in the defeat of the King's forces, the beheading of Charles (1649), and the rule of Oliver Cromwell as "Protector."

Milton's part in this struggle was with the pen rather than with the sword. He began with pamphlets urging the abolition of the episcopal system, the machinery of government of the "Established Church." When Charles was executed, and England was a-gasp at the beheading of a king who ruled "by divine right," Milton published his *Tenure of Kings and Magistrates* (written while the King's trial was going on, and printed only two weeks after the King's death) arguing that government is by the consent of the governed, and that subjects are not bound to endure an unjust rule. Soon after this pamphlet appeared Milton was appointed Secretary for Foreign Tongues to the Council of State. His duties were to translate official communications from foreign countries, to put into Latin official communications from the Council of State to foreign countries and to answer the attacks made upon the new form of government by its enemies abroad. This last involved Milton in many violent and protracted controversies on political and theological subjects. With these controversies, as Milton said, "all Europe rang from side to side"; but their interest for us today is chiefly in the occasional references which Milton makes in them to himself — his past doings, his judgment of his own character, his aims and ideals — references occasioned by the personal accusations and affronts which his opponents were constantly leveling against him.

Meantime, also, his pen was busy with various other matters of public welfare. From the vast mass of these prose writings of Milton's, official and unofficial, one work stands out, as vital today as when he wrote it. In 1643, Parliament had passed an act that no book or pamphlet should be printed until it had been read and licensed by an official censor. In 1644 Milton published the *Areopagitica*,[1] his plea for freedom of thought and freedom of the press. The royalists had used the Star Chamber to suppress freedom of thought. In the three years which had elapsed since the Star Chamber was abolished in 1640, every man had been free to think and print what he pleased. And now the Presbyterians in their turn were trying to destroy this freedom. What censor or body of censors, said Milton, could decide what was truth and what was error? Time would tell. The good books would live, the bad books would die. No board of censors, Milton insisted, could keep out bad books, false ideas. And no board of censors ought even to try, for life is not lived that way. "He that can apprehend and consider vice with all her baits and seeming pleasures, and yet abstain, and yet distinguish, and yet prefer that which is truly better, he is the true warfaring Christian. I cannot praise a fugitive and cloistered virtue, unexercised and unbreathed, that never sallies out and sees her adversary, but slinks out of the race, where that immortal garland is to be run for, not without dust and heat. . . . And though all the winds of doctrine were let loose to play upon the earth, so Truth be in the field, we do injuriously by licensing and prohibiting to misdoubt her strength. Let her and Falsehood grapple; who ever knew Truth put to the worse in a free and open encounter?"

Freedom of thought, freedom of choice, strength through struggle, self-discipline, a proved integrity of character —

---

[1] Milton addresses his discourse to the "Lords and Commons," the court of final authority in England, just as the Assembly of the Areopagus was the court of final authority in Athens. Hence, the title.

these were Milton's watchwords, the key to his thinking in both prose and verse.

For verse, indeed, there was little time in these years. A few personal sonnets and a few political sonnets are his only return to the kind of writing which was always nearest his heart. One of the noblest and most characteristic of the political sonnets is that *On the Late Massacre in Piedmont.* The Duke of Savoy had tried to force the Vaudois, his Protestant subjects in Piedmont, to attend mass. The troops whom he sent to enforce the edict massacred the Vaudois. As Latin Secretary to Cromwell, Milton had written on behalf of the English government to the Duke of Savoy and to Louis XIV, eloquently denouncing the massacre. On this theme Milton the official spokesman of his country and Milton the poet could speak with the same voice.

> Avenge, O Lord, thy slaughtered saints whose bones
> Lie scattered on the Alpine mountains cold;
> Even them who kept Thy truth so pure of old
> When all our fathers worshipped stocks and stones,
> Forget not: In Thy book record their groans
> Who were Thy sheep, and in their ancient fold
> Slain by the bloody Piedmontese that rolled
> Mother with infant down the rocks. Their moans
> The vales redoubled to the hills, and they
> To Heaven. Their martyred blood and ashes sow
> O'er all the Italian fields, where still doth sway
> The triple tyrant; that from these may grow
> A hundredfold, who, having learnt Thy way,
> Early may fly the Babylonian woe.

A great poet of the nineteenth century, William Wordsworth, said of the use to which Milton put the sonnet-form

in his hand
The Thing became a trumpet, whence he blew
Soul-animating strains — alas, too few!

During this busy period of his Secretaryship, the blindness which had been growing upon him for a number of
years became total.   In another of his sonnets Milton tells
us how he felt about it.

When I consider how my light is spent
Ere half my days, in this dark world and wide,
And that one talent which is death to hide
Lodged with me useless, though my soul more bent
To serve therewith my Maker, and present
My true account, lest He returning chide, —
Doth God exact day-labour, light denied?
I fondly ask: — But Patience, to prevent
That murmur, soon replies; God doth not need
Either man's work, or His own gifts: who best
Bear His mild yoke, they serve Him best: His state
Is kingly; thousands at His bidding speed
And post o'er land and ocean without rest: —
They also serve who only stand and wait.

But blindness itself was powerless to hide the one talent.
Dictating where before he had written, Milton went on.
The years passed.   Cromwell died.   The Puritan commonwealth which Cromwell's authority as "Protector" had
held together, began to go to pieces.   In the general break-
up, the old controversies died away.   Milton's fighting pen
was no longer needed.   With greater leisure and with the
greater concentration of mind induced by his blindness
(My blindness, he came to feel, "keeps from my view only
the coloured surfaces of things, while it leaves me at liberty to contemplate the beauty and stability of virtue and
of truth") Milton could turn at length to the writing of

the great poem which he had so long thought about. When Charles II, son of that king whose execution Milton had justified, came to the throne, the blind poet was already well on in the writing of *Paradise Lost*.

Each morning, Milton would rise at four. Soon after, his secretary would come in and read to him — chiefly from the Hebrew Bible — till breakfast time. After breakfast, till noon, Milton would dictate. Thus, for the space of about five years, the poem grew.

The central theme is the story told in the book of *Genesis* of the temptation and fall of man. Drawing upon other passages in the Bible, passages in the Apocrypha,[1] and the writings of various interpreters and elaborators of the Biblical story, Milton leads up to and surrounds this central theme with a magnificent drama — the rebellion in Heaven of Satan and the great array of angels who followed him; their defeat and expulsion,

> Hurled headlong flaming from the ethereal sky;

the creation of the earth in its setting of tributary stars; the creation of life upon the earth and of Adam and Eve; the plot of Satan and the other fallen angels to revenge themselves upon God by injuring his new creation; the escape of Satan from hell, his flight to earth and his appearance to Eve in the guise of a serpent. Nearly 8000 lines of the poem are occupied with these things. But amid all this magnificent pageantry, one never loses sight, if one reads the poem understandingly, of the great moment toward which all of it is moving. To Milton, believing with utter literalness that the earth, instead of being merely one of a million such bodies moving in infinite space, is the

---

[1] Biblical writings which, because of their doubtful origin, are not included in the "authorized" version of the Bible.

veritable footstool of God[1] and that God fashioned it in
order that man, "created in the image of God," should
occupy it — to Milton, there was no anti-climax, no insignificance of outcome in the fact that a drama set amid
the sublimities of heaven and hell should culminate in that
human act of disobedience which

> Brought death into the world and all our woe.

Upon that sin, punishment follows swiftly.   Man, whom
God "made

> Sufficient to have stood but free to fall,"

has not met the test.   Justice must be satisfied.   As in the
story of *Genesis*, the sinner must depart from Paradise into
a world which shall be labor and sorrow.   And yet it is
upon a note, not of sorrow, but of serenity, that the poem
closes.   Adam learns of One who shall redeem the sins of
the world.   From the lips of the angel who has shown him
this vision fall the words of Milton's own creed:

> Only add
> Deeds to thy knowledge answerable; add faith;
> Add virtue, patience, temperance; add love,
> By name to come called Charity, the soul
> Of all the rest: then wilt thou not be loth
> To leave this Paradise, but shalt possess
> A Paradise within thee, happier far.

Thus Adam and Eve depart from Paradise — and it is as
if their departure were not so much an end as a beginning:

> All in bright array
> The Cherubim descended, on the ground
> Gliding metéorous, as evening mist

---

[1] "Thus saith the Lord, the heaven is my throne, and the earth is my
footstool."   *Isaiah* lxvi, 1.

Risen from a river o'er the marish glides,
And gathers ground fast at the labourer's heel
Homeward returning.   High in front advanced,
The brandished sword of God before them blazed,
Fierce as a comet; which with torrid heat,
And vapour as the Libyan air adust,
Began to parch that temperate clime; whereat
In either hand the hastening Angel caught
Our lingering Parents, and to the eastern gate
Led them direct, and down the cliff as fast
To the subjected plain — then disappeared.
They, looking back, all the eastern side beheld
Of Paradise, so late their happy seat,
Waved over by that flaming brand; the gate
With dreadful faces thronged and fiery arms.
Some natural tears they dropped, but wiped them soon;
The world was all before them, where to choose
Their place of rest, and Providence their guide.
They, hand in hand, with wandering steps and slow,
Through Eden[1] took their solitary way.

So Milton would have wished us to read and remember his great poem. But poetry is queer stuff. It does not live by reason of its logic or by the success of its author in proving or demonstrating or "justifying" something, but by the imaginative power which finds its way into it.   And this imaginative power does literally seem to find its own way in, even sometimes by a side door instead of the main entrance. To Milton the struggle in heaven and the evil design of Satan were merely a setting, a way of leading

[1] Eden is the general area in the midst of which is the walled garden called *Paradise*.

> Eden where delicious Paradise...
> ...crowns with her enclosure green
> As with a rural mound, the champain head
> Of a steep wilderness.
>
> *Paradise Lost* iv, 132

up to the central moral theme; and yet it is this panorama beyond the bounds of earth, this way Milton has of giving us a sense of space wholly beyond our own vision and experience, and of beings unimaginably vast and remote and yet in some strange way visible and real — it is this which does most to keep the poem alive for generation after generation of readers. This, and, of course, the magnificent organ-music of Milton's verse. To illustrate this adequately would require far more quotation than there is space for; but it is possible to get some notion of it from Milton's description of the flight of Satan earthward, when Sin has opened for him the gates of Hell.

> . . . On a sudden open fly,
> With impetuous recoil and jarring sound,
> The infernal doors, and on their hinges grate
> Harsh thunder, that the lowest bottom shook
> Of Erebus.   She opened; but to shut
> Excelled her power: the gates wide open stood,
> That with extended wings a bannered host,
> Under spread ensigns marching, might pass through
> With horse and chariots ranked in loose array;
> So wide they stood, and like a furnace-mouth
> Cast forth redounding smoke and ruddy flame.
> Before their eyes in sudden view appear
> The secrets of the hoary Deep — a dark
> Illimitable ocean, without bound,
> Without dimension; where length, breadth, and highth,
> And time, and place, are lost; where eldest Night
> And Chaos, ancestors of Nature, hold
> Eternal anarchy, amidst the noise
> Of endless wars, and by confusion stand . . .
> . . . At last his sail-broad vans
> He spread for flight, and, in the surging smoke
> Uplifted, spurns the ground; thence many a league,

As in a cloudy chair, ascending rides
Audacious; but, that seat soon failing, meets
A vast vacuity.   All unawares,
Fluttering his pennons vain, plumb-down he drops
Ten thousand fathom deep, and to this hour
Down had been falling, had not, by ill chance,
The strong rebuff of some tumultuous cloud,
Instinct with fire and nitre, hurried him
As many miles aloft.   That fury stayed —
Quenched in a boggy Syrtis, neither sea,
Nor good dry land — nigh foundered, on he fares,
Treading the crude consistence, half on foot,
Half flying; behoves him now both oar and sail . . .
. . . But now at last the sacred influence
Of light appears, and from the walls of Heaven
Shoots far into the bosom of dim Night
A glimmering dawn.   Here Nature first begins
Her farthest verge, and Chaos to retire,
As from her outmost works, a broken foe,
With tumult less and with less hostile din;
That Satan with less toil, and now with ease,
Wafts on the calmer wave by dubious light,
And, like a weather-beaten vessel, holds
Gladly the port, though shrouds and tackle torn;
Or in the emptier waste, resembling air,
Weighs his spread wings, at leisure to behold
Far off the empyreal Heaven, extended wide
In circuit, undetermined square or round,
With opal towers and battlements adorned
Of living sapphire, once his native seat,
And, fast by, hanging in a golden chain,
This pendent World, in bigness as a star
Of smallest magnitude close by the moon.
Thither, full fraught with mischievous revenge,
Accurst, and in a cursèd hour, he hies.

But perhaps the most curious and interesting example of the way in which the imaginative power found its way in by a side door instead of the main entrance is Milton's characterization of Satan. There can be no doubt about what Milton *meant* to do with Satan. Satan is the spirit of evil. He is a rebel, a liar, and a trickster. The brightness, as of archangel ruined, that clings to him for a while, diminishes until, as one of the angelic guardians of Paradise tells him:

> Thou resemblest now
> Thy sin and place of doom obscure and foul.

When at length he has lured Adam and Eve into sin, and returns to Hell, erect in majesty and pride, to announce the success of his mission — suddenly

> His visage drawn he felt to sharp and spare;
> His arms clung to his ribs, his legs entwining
> Each other, till, supplanted, down he fell,
> A monstrous serpent on his belly prone.
> Reluctant, but in vain; a greater power
> Now ruled him, punished in the shape he sinned
> According to his doom.

Yet, for the life of him, Milton couldn't keep his heart from going out to Satan. Milton was a rebel too, challenging alike the authority of King or Church, "resolved not to repose upon the faith or judgment of others" and "determined to lay up as the best treasure of a good old age . . . the honest liberty of a free speech." I do not think that any reader of *Paradise Lost* ever remembers Satan as the ignominious figure, in aspect progressively obscure and foul, of Milton's conscientious portrayal. It is, rather, the Satan of the earlier part of the story who remains in our minds — the Satan who

> Above the rest
> In shape and gesture proudly eminent,
> Stood like a tower.   His form had yet not lost
> All her original brightness, nor appeared
> Less than Archangel ruined, and the excess
> Of glory obscured. . . . Darkened so, yet shon
> Above them all the Archangel: but his face
> Deep scars of thunder had intrenched, and care
> Sat on his faded cheek, but under brows
> Of dauntless courage, and considerate pride
> Waiting revenge; —

the Satan who, cast down by the Almighty power, exclaims

> What though the field be lost?
> All is not lost — the unconquerable will,
> And study of revenge, immortal hate,
> And courage never to submit or yield:
> And what is else not to be overcome.
> That glory never shall his wrath or might
> Extort from me.   To bow and sue for grace
> With suppliant knee . . .
> That were an ignominy and shame beneath
> This downfall! —

the Satan who, when he reaches the Garden of Eden, can see nor sense nor reason in God's forbidding Adam and Eve to taste of the tree of the knowledge of good and evil:

> Knowledge forbidden?
> Suspicious, reasonless!   Why should their Lord
> Envy them that?   Can it be sin to know?
> Can it be death?   And do they only stand
> By ignorance?   Is that their happy state,
> The proof of their obedience and their faith?
> O fair foundation laid whereon to build
> Their ruin! —

It is as if in telling this part of Satan's story, Milton forgot
for the moment his moral theme, and those ways of God
to man which he was "justifying," and remembered only
his own spiritual independence and isolation, his own love
of freedom and desire above all things to *know*, his own
staunch adherence to the Puritan cause, though that cause
were wholly lost and he himself

> fallen on evil days,
> On evil days though fallen, and evil tongues.

When Milton finished *Paradise Lost*, there were left to
him but nine years of life.[1] He filled them full. His *History of Britain*, probably composed some years before, was
given to the press. He wrote a textbook of Latin Grammar and a treatise on Logic. He published an appeal to
the churches for greater tolerance in their relations to one
another. He composed two notable poems. One of these,
Paradise Regained, is a portrayal[2] of the efforts made by
Satan to tempt Christ, after the forty days' fast in the
wilderness. Milton intended it as a sort of companion-
piece or sequel to *Paradise Lost;* but the theme did not lend
itself to the dramatic effects of the earlier poem, and the
narrative is much encumbered with theological argument.

The other poem of these late years, *Samson Agonistes*, is
arranged as a drama, with dialogue and chorus, after the
manner of the Greek tragedies. There was a special appeal
to Milton in the story of Samson,[3] the strong man of the
Israelites, who had sinned and lost his strength and then
repented and regained it; and who having been captured
and blinded by the Philistines and led into their temple "to
make them sport," had brought down the temple upon

[1] *Paradise Lost*, completed in 1665, was printed in 1667.
[2] Based on the account in the fourth chapter of *Matthew*.
[3] See the *Book of Judges*, Chapters XIII to XV.

their heads and involved them with himself in a common ruin. When the Messenger has brought the news of Samson's death, the last words of Samson's father, Manoa, and the closing words of the Chorus, have much of the dignity, the fortitude, the steadfastness, of Milton himself, unshaken in defeat.

> *Manoa:* Come, come; no time for lamentation now,
> Nor much more cause. Samson hath quit himself
> Like Samson, and heroicly hath finished
> A life heroic. . . .

> *Chorus:* All is best, though we oft doubt
> What the unsearchable dispose
> Of Highest Wisdom brings about . . .
> His servants he, with new acquist
> Of true experience from this great event,
> With peace and consolation hath dismissed,
> And calm of mind, all passion spent.

Samson Agonistes was printed in 1671. Milton died three years later. He died, says a contemporary biographer, "with so little pain or emotion, that the time of his expiring was not perceived by those in the room. And though he had been long troubled with . . . disease, yet was he not ever observed to be very impatient." If we were to seek an epitaph for him, it would be in his own words — that his one great object in life was "the promotion of real and substantial liberty; which is rather to be sought from within than from without; and whose existence depends, not so much on the terror of the sword, as on sobriety of conduct and integrity of life."

VIII

JOHN BUNYAN'S WORLD — AND JOHN DRYDEN'S

In November, 1637, when Milton was foretelling the ruin of the "corrupted clergy," and when the clouds of civil war were gathering fast, two little boys were living in villages not far apart in central England. One was the son of a poor and ignorant tinker — a mender of pots and kettles — in the village of Elstow in Bedfordshire. The other, son of a family of comfortable means and good connections, lived in the vicarage of the parish of Aldwinkle All Saints, some twenty miles northwest of Elstow, in the adjoining county of Northampton. There was only three years difference in the ages of the two boys. They were to grow to manhood during the civil war and the Protectorate, and the really important part of their lives was to begin with the Restoration — the accession of Charles II to the throne. One of these boys, the tinker's son, was to spend the most important part of his life in jail. The other boy was to spend the most important part of his life as a favorite of the court. The tinker's son was to write one of the great books of the world's literature. The boy at the vicarage was to become the most famous poet and satirist of his day and one of the wisest and wittiest critics that English literature possesses. The tinker's son was John Bunyan. The boy at the vicarage was John Dryden.

Bunyan never became an educated man, in the usual sense of that word. Dryden grew up to be one of the most finished masters of both English prose and English verse. Bunyan wrote for people like himself. The chief character of his famous story, "after a little laying of letters together," could "pick out the meaning" of the signs on the highway. Many of Bunyan's readers were not much better educated than that. Dryden's writings were the delight of scholars and wits. Bunyan and Dryden lived in different worlds. If, from this point on, we attempt to see Bunyan's world through his eyes, and then attempt to see Dryden's world through his eyes, we must not forget that the two worlds moved on side by side, and that it took ˙oth worlds to make up the England of the late seventeenth century.

Bunyan's world, not only during his boyhood and early manhood but also after the Restoration had put an end to the Puritan régime, was a deeply serious and religious one. In the year of Bunyan's birth, 1628, King Charles I was forced to make his first important concession to the growing power of the Puritans. In the years during which Bunyan was growing into manhood the civil war was fought and finished, King Charles was beheaded, and Cromwell began his rule. In this clash of creeds, with a whole nation fighting among themselves for their religious convictions, the problems of religion were in every man's heart, the phrases of religion on every man's lips. Every Puritan was very much concerned to find out whether he was among the "elect"— that is, whether he had been divinely chosen to be saved at the last day. It was necessary for him to have a "conviction of sin" and to reach a state of mind in which he was acutely conscious of "conversion" and of being "saved by grace." He must then lead a "Godly life," which meant that he should refrain not only from what we think of as real sins, but also from things which we think of as mere play and diversion — such things, for example,

Courtesy of National Portrait Gallery, London

JOHN BUNYAN

Portrait by T. Sadler

as sports and games and light reading and dancing. This way of thinking was most prevalent among the lower classes. They were poor. They had not, at best, many amusements. Their whole lives became centered in their chapels and assemblies, in the exhortations of the preacher, in their professions of religion. They ransacked the Bible for texts which would guide them or relieve their troubled minds. They read little else, and they had the Bible at their finger tips.

Bunyan was born into this atmosphere. He says of himself that he came "of a low and inconsiderable generation, my father's house being of that rank which is meanest and most despised of all the families in the land." He went to school only long enough to learn "to read and write according to the rate of other poor men's children" and "did soon lose that little I learnt." The ignominy of his position as the son of a tinker threw him with the roughest of the village boys; he learned to lie and to curse and became, as he records, "the very ringleader of all the youths that kept me company, in all manner of vice and ungodliness." But from his childhood he was tormented with visions and warnings. While he was playing with other boys on the village-green he heard a voice from heaven saying, "Wilt thou leave thy sins and go to heaven, or have thy sins and go to hell?" He gave up playing games. He was one of the bell-ringers in Bedford Church. He gave that up. He loved to dance. After a year of struggle he gave that up. For years he was puzzling over Scripture texts which seemed at one moment to promise him salvation and at the next moment to place him beyond the pale. He spent all of his boyhood and a good part of his younger manhood in such confusions of mind and torments of conscience.

Meanwhile he learned the tinker's trade, sometimes working at his father's forge and sometimes carrying his tools about the country as a wandering tinker. These journeys took him chiefly along the great highway which ran through Bedford, south to London and north through Nottingham and Sheffield. In after time, that main road through Bedford was to become transformed in his mind into "the King's highway" leading to the Celestial City, and many of those whom he met or beside whom he trudged were to come to life again in the pages of his book.

The eager and curious eyes of young John Bunyan gazed upon a varied scene. The problem of unemployment was never more acute than in the days of Bunyan's boyhood. The roads were full of vagrants, "masterless men," as the laws described them. Like Autolycus in Shakespeare's *A Winter's Tale*, there were many men "out of service," who had turned peddler and whose musical

> Come buy of me, come; come buy, come buy;
> Buy, lads, or else your lassies cry.
> Come buy,

sounded along the highway. Like Autolycus, too, they did not limit themselves to fair sales, but would pick your pockets with one hand, while they handed you something out of their "sow-skin budget" with the other. But the casual pickpockets did no great harm. It was the highwaymen who were the real menace. Many of them were what Bunyan calls "journeyman highwaymen," working not for themselves but for a manager, such as the famous "Roaring Girl," Moll Cutpurse, who lived in London and had a host of highwaymen all through the country under her command. Every traveler was in mortal fear of these highwaymen. If he carried a large sum of money with him, he waited till a body of travelers could be collected large enough to protect one another. If he could not get such an escort, he would ride by night rather than by day, on the chance of not being seen. Especially he would avoid riding on Sunday, for the highwaymen were more numerous then, because there were fewer constables about. On Sunday, too, the local posses would refuse to turn out to chase the highwaymen, and the magistrates would not punish them. Sunday, they said, was a day of rest. If a traveler did not stay at home on Sunday, then he could take his medicine. Every "hundred,"[1] or subdivision of a county, was supposed to provide its own guards against highwaymen; but the "hundreds" were often lax, and the constables were all too often disposed to follow the advice of Dogberry in Shakespeare's *Much Ado about Nothing:* "The most peaceable way for you, if you do take a thief, is to let him show himself what he is and steal out of your company."

Often the rogues and vagabonds themselves would band together for protection. "Some whereof," as one of the regulations observes, "pretend to be petty chapmen, others pedlars, others glassmen, tinkers, others palmsters, fortune-readers, Egyptians, and the like," who "sometime . . . meet by thirty in a company both upon the highway and in the night-times in ale-houses and other cottages and obscure places and houses of evil report, so as his majesty's better subjects are not only much prejudiced but terrified."

Punishments for vagabondage and for highway robbery were very severe. Confinement in the stocks, where the vagabond would sit beside the highway with his ankles locked

---

[1] So called, originally, as the area occupied by "ten times ten families." (Blackstone.)

between heavy boards and be hissed and pelted by the passers-by, was the least of his troubles. It was worse to be branded with a big R on cheek or forehead; worse still to be "stripped naked from the middle upwards, and openly whipp'd, until his or her body be bloody, and then pass'd to his or her birthplace or last place of residence"; worse still to be deported for life to the colonies; and worst of all to be executed (if he were a highwayman or indeed if he had committed any one of a score of flagrant offenses) and his body left dangling in chains from a gallows. The stocks or the pillory for the minor offender, the gallows for the rotting body of the major offender — such gruesome reminders were common sights beside the highway.

There is a grim little story which Bunyan tells in one of his minor works — an incident typical of the mood of the time. It was a time of such spiritual excitement that conversion swept the sinner off his feet and lashed him into public confession of his sins. It was a time when human life was lightly valued and when punishment was swift and terrible. The story concerns "one old Tod that was hanged . . . at Hartford, for being a thief. . . . At a summer assizes holden at Hartford, while the judge was sitting upon the bench, comes this old Tod into the court, clothed in a green suit, with his leathern girdle in his hand, his bosom open, and all on a dung sweat, as if he had run for his life; and being come in, he spake aloud as follows: 'My Lord,' said he, 'here is the veryest rogue that breathes upon the face of the earth. I have been a thief from a child: when I was but a little one, I gave myself to rob orchards, and to do other such like wicked things, and I have continued a thief ever since. My Lord, there has not been a robbery committed these many years, within so many miles of this place, but I have either been at it, or privy to it.' The judge thought the fellow was mad, but after some conference with some of the justices, they agreed to indict him; and so they did of several felonious actions; to all which he heartily confessed Guilty, and so was hanged with his wife at the same time."

But the things seen beside the highway were not all gruesome, neither were the most of the travelers dishonest. There were honest folk trudging from village to village to sell their goods, glass-men with baskets of drinking-glasses, crate-men with earthen jars of butter at their backs, knife-grinders pushing little carts on which were an emery wheel and an array of shiny new knives from Sheffield, portly clothiers a-horseback with a roll of holland at the saddle-bow. Here would be a stout-booted farmer riding along, with his wife on a pillion behind him; there a fine lady, likewise on a pillion but with her face masked by a "visard" against the vulgar gaze or the heat and dust of the highway. Here a drover driving his herd of cattle to Bedford market, there a gentleman's coach lumbering along, with the coachman cracking his whip over the four horses, and two outriders pushing ahead and shouting, "Make way, good people, make way."

And at evening, as John Bunyan trudged along with his pack upon his back, he would find himself near a roadside inn. If his day had been a particularly profitable one, he might, for once, indulge himself in the best that the inn afforded. They must have been pleasant places, those wayside inns. Here is a picture, drawn by an English traveler just a few years before Bunyan's time, of the way in which the guests were treated: After the ostler has taken his horse (poor John Bunyan would not have needed this attention) and shown him in, "another servant gives the passenger his private chamber, and kindles his fire, the

third pulls off his boots, and makes them clean. Then the
host or hostess visits him, and if he will eat with the host,
or at a common table with others, his meal will cost him
sixpence . . . but if he will eat in his chamber, he commands what meat he will according to his appetite, and as
much as thinks fit for him and his company, yea, the kitchen
is open to him, to command the meat to be dressed as he
best likes; and when he sits at table, the host or hostess will
accompany him, or if they have many guests, will at least
visit him, taking it courtesy to be bid to sit down: while
he eats, if he have company, he shall be offered music,
which he may freely take or refuse, and if he be solitary,
the musicians will give him the goodday with music in the
morning."

Or, more probably, John Bunyan will stop at one of the
smaller inns, "less honourable, and not used by Gentlemen," where "his meal will cost him . . . four pence"
and where he will get less attention.

If you would see how Bunyan's memories of these havens
of rest and refreshment became transformed in his allegory, you must read his description of "the house built
by the Lord of the Hill for the relief and security of pilgrims."

There was another memory, also, of these early days of
wandering, which remained with him very vividly when
he wrote his great book. Usually there would be about as
many people going north as south on the Bedford road.
But as mid-August approached the tide would flow chiefly
southward, with tricksters and honest travelers alike bound
for London and Bartholomew Fair. They were great
events, these fairs. Intended for the exhibition and sale
of goods and livestock, they had become occasions when
country-folk from far and near foregathered with the

town folk to have a good time. Here were whole streets or rows of booths for the sale of this commodity and other streets or rows for the sale of that. Here were little roast pigs for the buying — pigs so appetizing, with their sweet sauce and cracklings, that they were like to run off the spit into your mouth. Here were tobacco at three pence the pipeful, and ale well frothed in the can, and "comfortable" (*i.e.* spiced) gingerbread, and a fine hobby-horse, to make your son a tilter, and a drum to make him a soldier and a fiddle to make him a reveler. Here were rattles, and little dogs, and fine whistling birds for the ladies, and purses and pouches and pipes for the gentlemen; and ballads to paste up over the nursery chimney at home — and, best of all, puppet-shows, where you might see Jerusalem or Nineveh or the destruction of Sodom and Gomorrah or the Gunpowder Plot — or even the ancient modern history of Hero and Leander played not according to the printed book, but with the Thames for the Hellespont, and Leander a dyer's son of Puddle-wharf and Hero a wench o' the Bankside. There would be a mort of rascals too at the fair, and when they made trouble, they would be hauled before the Pie-powder Court[1] and put in the stocks.[2]

When the fair was over, honest folk would be coming home again and rascals would be seeking fresh fields, and the flow along the Bedford road would set northward once more. I like to imagine young John Bunyan watching that flow of travel, and wondering where they were all going! To London, to the fair? Or, northward, to Nottingham perhaps to buy laces, or to Sheffield to buy knives? I like

[1] From the French words *pieds poudreux, dusty feet*. This informal court, held on the fair grounds, was intended primarily to settle disputes between the peddlers and traveling merchants and their customers.

[2] These glimpses of the fair are culled chiefly from Ben Jonson's comedy *Bartholomew Fair*, which was written in 1614.

to fancy him as stopping, some wet day, when the highway was ankle-deep in mud, and unslinging his pack and sitting down to rest on a square milestone beside the road. A traveler pauses beside him. "Where are you going?" says the stranger. "To Elstow, by Bedford," says John Bunyan. "Where, then?" says the stranger. "Nowhere," says John Bunyan. "I live there." "Nay," says the stranger, "I think you do but sojourn there. The city that hath foundations, whose builder and maker is God — that is journey's end. Is it not time for you to start on that pilgrimage?" Puzzled and in two minds whether to laugh or run, the boy simply sits and stares. The man seems suddenly to have forgotten him and, in a kind of dream, is half singing, half murmuring to himself. In a lull of the noise from the highway John Bunyan can catch some of the words:

There lust and lucre cannot dwell;
    There envy bears no sway;
There is no hunger, heat, nor cold,
    But pleasure every way. . . .

Thy gardens and thy gallant walks
    Continually are green;
There grows such sweet and pleasant flowers
    As nowhere else are seen.

Quite through the streets, with silver sound,
    The flood of life doth flow;
Upon whose banks on every side
    The wood of life doth grow.

There trees forevermore bear fruit,
    And evermore do spring;
There evermore the angels sit,
    And evermore do sing. . . .

The noise increases again, a crowd of wayfarers goes pushing by, the man seems to melt into them, and John Bunyan gets up and kicks the kinks out of his legs. "Well-a-
day," he says, as he shoulders his pack, "Bedford will do
me for a while — but I rather like that part about the
gardens and the gallant walks, and the flood of life."

The next few years of John Bunyan's life were full of
excitement. The civil war began. Just turned sixteen,
he was mustered into a Bedfordshire regiment. He seems
to have been present at at least one siege and to have
narrowly missed getting killed there; but where this was,
or what other experiences he had, we do not know. He
must have been mustered out and gone back to Elstow
while he was still in his 'teens. He resumed his trade.
The old tormenting struggle between his better and his
worser self was renewed. At length he found peace and
the assurance of salvation. He discovered that he had a
gift for preaching. When he preached, the country people
round about "came in to hear the Word by hundreds."

He had been preaching for five years when the Puritan
government collapsed and Charles II came to the throne.
Laws were passed requiring every one to conform to the
faith and practice of the Established Church and forbidding Nonconformists to assemble together. Bunyan continued to preach and was arrested. Refusing to promise to
give up his preaching he was kept in prison for twelve years.
A friend who visited him there found him possessed of a
"library, the least and yet the best that ever I saw, consisting only of two books — a Bible and the *Book of Martyrs*."[1]

----

[1] John Foxe's *Book of Martyrs*, written in Latin and first published on the
Continent, was translated into English and printed in England in 1563,
under the title: *Acts and Monuments of these latter and perilous Days*, etc.
It gives a vivid account of the sufferings and the heroism of the Protestant
martyrs in the persecutions under the Roman Catholic Queen Mary.

In these long quiet years, Bunyan read and reread these two books until not merely their subject matter, but also their style, their way of saying things, had soaked into his very marrow.

It is worth while to stop and think about this for a minute. In his brief schooling Bunyan had learned little, and had soon forgotten that little. Toward the end of this imprisonment Bunyan himself was to write a great book. Meanwhile, these two books were his real school. If you will turn the pages of Foxe's *Books of Martyrs*, you will find there a kind of homely simplicity and straightforwardness, which never changes into "fine writing" and "heroics," even when Foxe is describing tragic and heroic moments. Here, for example, is a bit from his description of the martyrdom of Latimer and Ridley: "Then Master Ridley, looking back, espied Master Latimer coming after, unto whom he said, 'Oh, be ye there?' 'Yea,' said Master Latimer, 'have after as fast as I can follow.' So he following a pretty way off, at length they came both to the stake."

That plain, downright, unexcited style was a part of Bunyan's school. As for the other book, where else could Bunyan learn so well how to tell a story? You have only to turn, for example, to the story of the Prodigal Son, to realize that.

And he arose and came to his father. But when he was yet a great way off, his father saw him, and had compassion and ran, and fell on his neck, and kissed him.

And the son said unto him, Father, I have sinned against heaven and in thy sight, and am no more worthy to be called thy son.

But the father said to his servants, Bring forth the best robe, and put it on him; and put a ring on his hand, and shoes on his feet:

And bring hither the fatted calf, and kill it; and let us eat, and be merry:

For this my son was dead, and is alive again; he was lost, and is found.

This also is very plain writing, very straightforward and direct and sure; but there is a kind of sweep to it, too, as if something sang within the man who wrote it. This is the school in which Bunyan learned to write; and after he had read such passages as this many times over, he began to write like this himself.

The first books which he wrote in prison are not of much importance. His imagination was not yet awake. But, one day, while he was writing a little sermon called "The Strait Gate, or the Great Difficulty of going to Heaven," he fell to thinking of the journey which all must make along the highway of life toward that gate which opens into the eternal city. Then it was as if he were no longer in his cell, but back once more in the highway out of Bedford. The Christian pilgrimage became, in his imagination, such a journey as he had taken himself, the travelers those with whom he had shared the way, the "great difficulties" such as he and they had encountered together. Here, then, was not a sermon but a story. Bunyan conscientiously finished his sermon about the Strait Gate, and then turned to the story — and the story wrote itself. He named the story *The Pilgrim's Progress from this World to that which is to come*.[1] Bunyan tells the story as a dream which came to him in that "den" which was his prison cell. "As I walked through the wilderness of this world, I lighted on a certain place, where was a den, and I laid me

---

[1] *The Pilgrim's Progress* was printed in 1678. In 1684 Bunyan published a "Second Part," describing the journey of Christian's wife, Christiana, and their children, to the Celestial City.

down in that place to sleep: and as I slept, I dreamed a dream." He saw a man named Christian reading in a Book. The Book told Christian that the city in which he dwelt would be destroyed. Christian became very unhappy and knew not how he might be saved. At length, Evangelist pointed the way to a wicket gate, through which Christian could escape. On his way to the gate Christian fell into the Slough of Despond. Christian was nearly drowned in the Slough, but at last Help dragged him out and set his feet on solid ground. So he got through the wicket and started on his long journey on the King's highway.

This was the highway of the heavenly King, straight and narrow, but needful to be followed, however tempting the paths on either side. It was the highway to the Celestial City; but as Bunyan sat in his cell, with memories crowding thick and fast upon him, the Bedford road gave substance and reality to the allegorical highway. Where the road ran in low places, there was "a ditch on one hand and a quag on the other" and the road itself was "so full of pits, pitfalls, deep holes, and shelvings" that no one would dare risk it in the dark. There were pickpockets on the road and the unwary traveler might find himself in the hands of highwaymen. "At the entering in of this passage, there came down from Broad-way-gate a lane called Deadman's-lane; so called because of the murders that are commonly done there. And this Little-Faith . . . chanced to sit down there and slept. Now there happened, at that time, to come down that lane from Broad-way-gate three sturdy rogues and their names were Faint-heart, Mistrust, and Guilt, (three brothers) and they espying Little-Faith where he was, came galloping up with speed. Now the good man was just awaked from his sleep, and was getting up to go on his journey. So they came all up to him, and with threatening language bid him stand. At this Little-Faith looked as white as a clout, and had neither power to fight nor fly. Then said Faint-heart, 'deliver thy purse'; but he, making no haste to do it, (for he was loth to lose his money,) Mistrust ran up to him, and thrusting his hand into his pocket, pull'd out thence a bag of silver. Then he cried out, 'Thieves, thieves!' With that, Guilt with a great club that was in his hand, strook Little-Faith on the head, and with that blow fell'd him flat to the ground, where he lay bleeding as one that would bleed to death. All this while the thieves stood by: but at last, hearing that some were upon the road . . . they betook themselves to their heels, and left this good man to shift for himself. Now after a while, Little-Faith came to himself, and getting up, made shift to scrabble on his way."

Beside the road, too, were gallows from which, in creaking chains, swung the bodies of wrongdoers. "It is well that they hang so near the highway that others may see and take warning. . . . I think it a high favour that they were hanged afore we came hither, who knows else what they might a done?"

Here and there along the highway were the walled parks of the gentry, and now and then a garden-wall — "and some of the fruit-trees that grew in that garden shot their branches over the wall, and being mellow, they that found them did gather them up and oft eat of them to their hurt." All too often there was "a most cruel dog thereabout." The traveler might well wonder why the owner kept "such a filthy cur in his yard," and would "persuade him to hang him" if he dared.

Sometimes there were groves beside the way where birds were singing. "They sing these notes but seldom except it be at the spring, when the flowers appear, and the Sun shines warm, and then you may hear them all day long. . . . They are very fine company for us when we are melancholy, also they make the woods, and groves, and solitary places desirous to be in."

But the road was beset with dangers. Before he had traveled very far, Christian and his friend, Faithful, who had joined him on the way, found themselves entering the town of Vanity. In the town of Vanity was a fair which ran all the year round. "As in other fairs of less moment, there are the several rows and streets, under their proper names, where such and such wares are vended. . . . Here is the Britain row, the French row, the Italian row, the Spanish row, the German row, where several sorts of Vanities are to be sold." Bunyan means the state-churches, the authorized formal religions of these several countries, to which his own plain and simple faith was so much opposed. These, and worldly pleasures and indulgences, were the commodities for sale in Vanity Fair. The traders in Vanity Fair raised a great hubbub when they saw Christian and Faithful coming in. These visitors, said they, were outlandish men and must be fools or Bedlam Toms. They wore strange clothes and spoke the speech of Canaan, not the speech of men of the world. And worst of all they would not buy their wares, saying only "We buy the Truth." So poor Christian and Faithful were beaten and besmeared with dirt and put in a cage, and then taken out and led in chains up and down the fair and at length hailed before Pie-powder court, where they were indicted for disturbing trade and causing commotions in the town. Judge Hate-good called three witnesses, Envy, Superstition and Pickthank[1] who testified against them. Faithful, it ap-

[1] a tale-bearer, a busybody.

peared, had been more outspoken against the customs of Vanity Fair, so his case was first given to the jury. Bunyan's picture of that jury is worth remembering. "Then went the jury out, whose names were, Mr. Blind-man, Mr. No-good, Mr. Malice, Mr. Love-lust, Mr. Live-loose, Mr. Heady, Mr. High-mind, Mr. Enmity, Mr. Lyar, Mr. Cruelty, Mr. Hate-light, and Mr. Implacable, who every one gave in his private verdict against him among themselves, and afterwards unanimously concluded to bring him in guilty before the judge. And first Mr. Blind-man, the foreman, said 'I see clearly that this man is an heretick. Then said Mr. No-good, 'Away with such a fellow from the earth.' 'Ay,' said Mr. Malice, 'for I hate the very looks of him.' Then said Mr. Love-lust, 'I could never endure him.' 'Nor I,' said Mr. Live-loose, 'for he would always be condemning my way.' 'Hang him, hang him,' said Mr. High-mind. 'My heart riseth against him,' said Mr. Enmity. 'He is a rogue,' said Mr. Lyar. 'Hanging is too good for him,' said Mr. Cruelty; 'Let's dispatch him out of the way,' said Mr. Hate-light. Then said Mr. Implacable, 'Might I have all the world given me, I could not be reconciled to him, therefore let us forthwith bring him in guilty of death.' And so they did, therefore he was presently condemned, To be had from the place where he was, to the place from whence he came, and there to be put to the most cruel death that could be invented."

This was the end of Faithful. But Christian, after being imprisoned for a while, was allowed to continue his journey. With him came a new friend, Hopeful, who had decided to give up the vanities of the Fair and take the narrow way.

Vanity Fair had been a sore experience for Christian. He had had to endure the hatred and abuse of those who

could not understand him. But the worldly vanities had
not tempted him. He had played the man there and had
nothing to be ashamed of. There were other temptations,
however, which it was not so easy to withstand. The way
was hard and the journey very tiring. Christian and Hopeful
got frightfully discouraged sometimes and longed for easier
ways. Once beside the road they saw a low-lying meadow.
There was a convenient stile over the roadside fence and
beyond the stile a pleasant-looking path. Christian and
Hopeful took it and got into trouble. Night fell, there was
a heavy rain, water rose in the meadow, they lost their way.
Worn out, they lay down on the wet ground and fell asleep.
Next morning Giant Despair seized them for trespassing
on his grounds and cast them into a dungeon of Doubting
Castle. It was "a very dark dungeon, nasty and stinking
to the spirit of these two men. Here then they lay, from
Wednesday morning till Saturday night, without one bit
of bread, or drop of drink, or any light, or any to ask
how they did." Giant Despair beat them with "a grievous
Crab-tree Cudgel" and left them with the suggestion that
as he would never release them, "their only way would be,
forthwith to make an end of themselves, either with Knife,
Halter, or Poison." Christian was so downcast and sore
with stripes that he was minded to do as Giant Despair
said. But Hopeful counseled him to patience. At last
Christian bethought himself of "a key called Promise"
which had been in his possession all the while. With it
they tried the dungeon door and opened it easily. The
heavy iron gate of the castle yard still stood between them
and liberty. "That lock went damnable hard, yet the key
did open it; then they thrust open the gate to make their
escape with speed, but that gate, as it opened, made such
a creaking, that it waked Giant Despair, who hastily rising

to rescue his prisoners, felt his limbs to fail, for his fits took him again, so that he could by no means go after them. Then they went on, and came to the King's highway again, and so were safe."

That experience of Christian's gives us a glimpse of the art which makes *Pilgrim's Progress* such a great book. Bunyan knew what it meant for the Christian to go astray and lose faith and heart and feel as if life were not worth living. He knew, too, perhaps at first hand, what trouble common folk got into if they strayed off the public road and were caught trespassing in some rich man's park. It did not require much exaggeration to transform an irate country squire into Giant Despair. In such episodes, the commonplaces of daily life and the spiritual experiences common to all mankind and the specific Christian allegory are perfectly blended. Even that "damnable," which probably slipped off Bunyan's pen unawares, he was too much of an artist to cut out. After all, isn't that just what Christian would have said, with the key grating in the rusty lock, and the Giant about to get after him?

Not all of Christian's experiences have this homely flavor. As a boy, Bunyan had liked storybooks better than the Bible. "The Scriptures, thought I, what are they? A dead letter, a little ink and paper, of three or four shillings worth. Give me a ballad, a news-book, George on horseback, or Bevis of Southampton." Bunyan was probably thinking of the *Seven Champions of Christendom* in which is the story of St. George and the Dragon; and of the old narrative poem, *Bevis of Hampton*, retold as a prose romance in the sixteenth century, in which Bevis does battle with the giant, Ascapart. Giants and Dragons abound in *Pilgrim's Progress*. In the Valley of Humiliation Christian was confronted by a monster named Apollyon.[1] "He was clothed with scales like a fish . . . he had wings like a dragon, feet like a bear, and out of his belly came fire and smoke, and his mouth was as the mouth of a lion." This Apollyon "straddled quite over the whole breadth of the way" and threw "darts as thick as hail." They fought for "above half a day" till Christian grew weak and his sword flew out of his hand. But Christian grasped Apollyon's sword and gave him such a thrust with it that Apollyon "spread forth his dragon's wings and sped him away." There were even lions in the way; and, when Christiana and the children are on their journey, their escort, Great-heart, defends them against two giants in quick succession, Giant Grim and Giant Maul. Great-heart disposes of Giant Grim in short order by slashing off his arm; but Giant Maul is a terrible fighter. He springs out of his cave and downs Great-heart with a single blow of his club. They fight for an hour, stop for a rest and go at it again. Great-heart stretches the giant on the ground. "Nay, hold, and let me recover," says the giant. Great-heart politely waits till he is on his feet again and then cuts off his head with a single blow of his sword.

But even these storybook monsters are powerless to rob the story of its reality. If Christian and his friends escape now and then into the dreamworld of romance or into a strained figure of allegory, they are back, the next minute, on solid ground. They never cease to be themselves — or ourselves. I suppose this is because Bunyan was such a human sort of fellow himself, with a healthy hatred of meanness and wrong, and with an amused and sympathetic

---

[1] "And they had a king over them, which is the angel of the bottomless pit, whose name in the Hebrew tongue is Abaddon, but in the Greek tongue hath his name Apollyon." *Revelation* ix, 11.

Apollyon means *destroyer*.

understanding of human nature. However seriously he took his religion, he never ceased to love life. And he managed to write about it with such unaffected simplicity and such heartiness! It is often the most trivial things that do most to make a story seem real to us. Chaucer and Shakespeare knew that, long before Bunyan's day. But, in the field of prose fiction, Bunyan was one of the first to realize it, and he passed the lesson on. It was an illiterate age in which Bunyan lived. Beside the highway in which Christian and Hopeful are journeying, there were signs. Hopeful could not read. Christian ("for he was learned") could. So Christian, "after a little laying of Letters together," managed to "pick out the meaning." Little Matthew, the son of Christian and Christiana, having eaten green plums from Beelzebub's orchard, had a pain so severe "that he was with it, at times, pulled as 'twere both ends together." Mr. Skill prescribed for him, but Matthew did not like the medicine. "'Come, come,' said the Physician, 'you must take it.' . . . 'Pray, Sir,' said Christiana, 'how does it taste?' 'It has no ill taste,' said the Doctor, and with that she touched one of the pills with the tip of her Tongue. 'Oh, Matthew,' said she, 'this potion is sweeter than Honey. If thou lovest thy Mother . . . take it!' So with much ado . . . he took it, and it wrought kindly with him." When Christiana's guide, Mr. Greatheart, had killed Giant Despair, the little company were so rejoiced that they stopped and had a dance. "Now when Feeble-mind and Ready-to-halt saw that it was the head of Giant Despair indeed, they were very jocund and merry. Now Christiana, if need was, could play upon the viol, and her daughter Mercy upon the lute: so, since they were so merry disposed, she plaid them a lesson, and Ready-to-halt would dance. So he took Despondency's Daughter, named Much-afraid, by the hand, and to dancing they went in the road. True, he could not dance without one crutch in his hand, but I promise you, he footed it well; also the girl was to be commended, for she answered the music handsomely. As for Mr. Despondency, the music was not much to him; he was for feeding rather than dancing, for that he was almost starved. So Christiana gave him some of her bottle of spirits for present relief, and then prepared him something to eat: and in little time the old gentleman came to himself, and began to be finely revived."

It is such quaintly simple and homely touches as this that keep the story alive and make it seem true to every generation of readers. And because Bunyan's religious faith was as unaffectedly sincere and hearty as his love of life, the allegory graces the story, and the story gives body to the allegory.

In an old edition of *Pilgrim's Progress* there is an illustration depicting Vanity Fair. In the middle distance are Christian and Faithful in the cage surrounded by scoffers. In the foreground is a playhouse into which fashionably dressed folk are thronging. Over the entrance is a signboard naming the play which they are about to see. It is *All for Love, or the World Well Lost*, with which, in the same year in which *Pilgrim's Progress* was published, John Dryden scored one of his greatest dramatic successes. But on the signboard the play is represented as "by Beelzebub." To the people of Bunyan's world London, with its gay court, its glittering shops, its crowded theaters, summed up all that they knew or imagined of worldliness and sin —"all that is there sold or that cometh thither, is Vanity." Vanity Fair, and John Dryden its Beelzebub!

To us, however, as we look back, Dryden does not seem

Places Reformancie
Political and
Ecclesiastical
to be sold by Auction
Simony Salleiry

ALL for LOVE
or the World
well lost
by Beelzebub
&c.

REGATTA

RELIGION
A FARCE
the Chorus
by S Foote

SACRED
ORATORIOS
by the
DEVILS
Servants

VANITY FAIR

From an early edition of *The Pilgrim's Progress*

252

a very wicked Beelzebub. He was the creature of his time, just as Bunyan was. While Bunyan, plying the tinker's trade, was forgetting the little he had learnt, Dryden was at the famous old Westminster school, studying the classics and getting well birched by Dr. Busby. A great teacher and a great believer in the rod was Dr. Busby. Many of the famous men of that generation passed through his hands — and over his knee. The monuments to Busby the teacher and to Dryden the poet are not far apart in the South Transept of Westminster Abbey. "A great man," said Sir Roger de Coverley, as he stood before Dr. Busby's tomb; "he whipped my grandfather; a very great man! I should have gone to him myself, if I had not been a blockhead; a very great man!" Dryden honored him, in spite of the birchings. It was at Westminster, by constant practice in translating the classical satirists into English verse, that Dryden developed the edged precision which was to make him the master of poetic satire. — One of these translations, made as a "Thursday night's exercise" while he was a boy at Westminster, he included long afterwards among his published works, prefacing it with the comment: "I believe that it, and many other of my exercises of this nature in English verse, are still in the hands of my learned master, Dr. Busby."

From Westminster Dryden went to Cambridge. All that is known of his university life is that he got into a few scrapes, remained at Cambridge for seven years, and left with no liking for his Alma Mater. In later years he took a number of occasions when his plays were performed at Oxford to pay the most flattering tributes to that institution. One of these prologues says of the author of the play:

> Oxford to him a dearer name shall be
> Than his own mother-university.

Nowhere does he speak a good word for Cambridge. Possibly, like Milton, Dryden found the prescriptions of the university irksome and preferred to go his own way as student and poet.

In 1657, when Dryden left Cambridge to seek a career, Cromwell had but one more year to live, the Restoration was only three years away. It was Dryden's lot to be in at the disastrous finish. His cousin, Sir Gilbert Pickering, was Cromwell's Lord Chamberlain. Dryden became Sir Gilbert's secretary. As such, he found himself a part of the machinery of Puritan government, but he was neither the Milton kind of Puritan nor the Bunyan kind of Puritan. To them, in their very diverse ways, Puritanism was a cause to fight for and if necessary to die for. It may be doubted whether to Dryden, coming at the tired end of the whole affair, Puritanism was anything more than an existing form of government, providing a convenient opening for a young man looking for something to do. And whatever he might be doing, poetry was the one thing he cared to do. The sudden death of Cromwell furnished a theme.

Dryden's "Poem upon the Death of His Late Highness, Oliver, Lord Protector of England, Scotland and Ireland" is a just tribute to a great man. It praises his disinterestedness —

> No borrow'd bays his temples did adorn,
>> But to our crown he did fresh jewels bring;
> Nor was his virtue poisoned, soon as born,
>> With the too early thoughts of being king;

it recounts his victories, and rightly emphasizes his success in forcing the European monarchies to treat republican England with respect. It closes nobly —

His ashes in a peaceful urn shall rest,
His name a great example stands to show
How strangely high endeavours may be blessed
Where piety and valour jointly go.

It moves to a brave music, and is at the same time dignified and restrained. Panegyric poetry — poetry in praise
of some great or supposedly great man or great deed —
was all the rage in Dryden's day. The presses poured it
out by the ream. Most of it was extraordinarily fulsome
stuff. If Dryden's tribute to Cromwell was not great
poetry, it was at least so immeasurably better than anything of the sort being done by anybody else, that it made
Dryden a marked man.

But within a year after the poem was published the ashes
of the Protector were resting no longer in a peaceful urn,
and open admiration of him became an unsafe thing to be
marked for. King Charles the Second entered London.
Here is the way in which his coming impressed that devoted Royalist, Mr. John Evelyn:

"29 May, 1660. This day his Majestie Charles II came to
London after a sad and long exile and calamitous suffering both
of the King and Church, being 17 years. This was also his birthday, and with a triumph of above 20,000 horse and foote, bran-
dishing their swords and shouting with inexpressible joy; the
wayes strew'd with flowers, the bells ringing, the streetes hung
with tapistry, fountaines running with wine; the Mayor, Aldermen, and all the Companies in their liveries, chaines of gold and
banners; Lords and Nobles clad in cloth of silver, gold, and velvet; the windowes and balconies well set with ladies; trumpets,
music, and myriads of people flocking, even so far as from Rochester, so as they were seven houres in passing the Citty, even
from 2 in the afternoone till 9 at night.

"I stood in the Strand and beheld it, and bless'd God. And
all this was don without one drop of bloud shed, and by that

very army which rebell'd against him; but it was the Lord's doing, for such a Restauration was never mention'd in any history antient or modern, since the returne of the Jews from the Babylonish captivity; nor so joyfull a day and so bright ever seene in this Nation, this hapning when to expect or effect it was past all human policy."

Seeing what Evelyn saw, and finding himself in a changed world, Dryden became a Royalist. He let no grass grow under his feet. By the twenty-first day after the king's entrance, he had finished and published "Astræa Redux,[1] A Poem on the Happy Restoration and Return of his Sacred Majesty Charles the Second." Dryden's enemies, quick to recall the tribute to Cromwell, labeled him turncoat. But many another, who had at least acquiesced in Cromwell's rule, was likewise swept off his feet by the wave of rejoicing and hope that had so moved Evelyn, and Dryden's heart was in the traditional authority and stability of a royal succession as it had never been in the Protectorate.

"Astræa Redux" is not so good a poem as the tribute to Cromwell. Cromwell was a Man. Charles was not very much of a man. He was only a king, and to write a long poem in praise of him was more a matter of ingenuity than of inspiration. But Dryden had limitless ingenuity. "Astræa Redux" is at least a very fervent tribute. If it did not win immediate recognition from Charles, it served to give Dryden prominence both as a poet and as a supporter of the crown.

But he still had his way to make. The theater gave him his opportunity. Since the great day of Shakespeare, the English stage had had a chequered history. Shakespeare

---

[1] Astræa was the Goddess of Justice who was supposed to have lived on the earth during the Golden Age. With the advent of Charles, she resumes her sway.

had been interested in human character — its temptations, its struggles, its victories and defeats. After his death, the drama had slowly but surely deteriorated. More and more, witty dialogue, or startling effects, or situations intended to arouse the baser emotions of the audience, had taken the place of that mirror which Shakespeare held up to nature. When the Puritans became strong enough, they had closed the theaters. With the Restoration, the pendulum swung to the other extreme, the restraints and prohibitions of Puritanism were thrown off, the theaters started full blast, the pleasure-loving king and court led the way in attending them. Two kinds of plays became the fashion — comedies in which some of the worst elements of the dying drama of the earlier period were revived, and in which witty dialogue, and the schemes of men and women of fashion to outwit one another in dubious ways, afforded the chief entertainment; and the "heroic play," which provided a sort of set-off to the comedies, by representing the hero as a man of prodigious valor and prodigious virtue, making declamatory love to a virtuous heroine, in a court full of enemies and villains. The scenes of these heroic plays were always laid in some romantically remote part of the world, it mattered not where, as long as the names rolled strangely on the tongue and the events were such as no ordinary person could check by his knowledge or experience.

Dryden tried his hand at both kinds, the improper comedies and the heroic plays. His first dramatic successes were with the heroic plays written in rhymed couplets. His heroes are super-men, unconquerable fighters, irresistible wooers. Duels, battles, ghosts, palaces raised by enchantment, kept the spectators on the *qui vive*. Even the fact that the heroes and heroines talk philosophy and politics, and argue at length the subtlest distinctions of love and honor, did not detract from the popularity of these plays. The fashionable world thronged to see them; some of them were acted at court, where the Duke and Duchess of Monmouth (the Duke was King Charles's son) acted the principal rôles; and when these plays were printed, romantic young ladies pored over them in their boudoirs and dreamed of them at night. Here are a few of the entries in Clarinda's journal, as Addison reports them in the *Spectator:* "Thursday. From eight to ten in the morning. Chocolate. Read two acts of *Aurengzebe*[1] a-bed. . . . One in the afternoon. Called for my flowered handkerchief. Worked half a violet leaf in it. Eyes ached and head out of order. Threw by my work, and read over the remaining part of *Aurengzebe.* . . . Between twelve and one. Dreamed that Mr. Froth lay at my feet and called me Indamora. . . . Monday. Eight o'clock in the morning. Waked by Miss Kitty. *Aurengzebe* lay upon the chair by me. Kitty repeated without book the eight best lines in the play."

Dryden rapidly became famous as a playwright. But he was not content merely to let his plays take their course upon the stage. He wanted to think of them as dramatic experiments, to defend his methods, to analyze his art. With each play as it appeared in print, he published a preliminary essay, and the controversies which these essays aroused led him into further excursions in the field of literary criticism. Probably Dryden thought of these essays as merely incidental; but it is his vivid racy prose, rather than his plays, that has stood the test of time.

[1] *Aureng-Zebe* (1675) was the last of Dryden's heroic plays. It was still being acted in Addison's day. Indamora is the captive queen in *Aureng-Zebe.*

Let us stop for a minute and think about this. Why is Dryden's prose a landmark? Why is Dryden called "the Father of Modern Prose"?

Here and there before Dryden's day, men wrote plain, simple, vigorous prose. But it was generally because they were writing for plain people, as Bunyan did, or because their hearts were so full of the subject that they cared more for getting the thing said than for the way in which they were saying it. But to write *well* in prose, to produce prose that could be considered literature, meant, before Dryden's day, to make your sentences march like an army with banners. A regiment of words; coördinate clauses marshaled in companies; relative clauses, phrases, parentheses in sections; adjectives and adverbs waving in the breeze, drums rolling, a crescendo of sound — a very regiment of words between capital and period. Magnificent, sometimes; but not infrequently of the sort to be read twice over — once, to fill the ear with a noble music, and again, to be sure just what it was all about. The conscious imitation of the classics, the training of the schools in translating the involved sentences of the Latin rhetoricians, had a good deal to do with the shaping of these elaborate sentence-structures. Here, for example, is the way in which a famous seventeenth-century historian wrote about Cromwell: "He must have had a wonderful understanding in the nature, and humours of men, and as great a dexterity in applying them; who, from a private and obscure birth, (though of a good family) without interest or estate, alliance or friendship, could raise himself to such a height, and compound and knead such opposite and contradictory tempers, humours, and interests into a consistence, that contributed to his designs, and to their own destruction; whilst himself grew insensibly powerful enough to cut off those by whom he had climbed, in the instant that they projected to demolish their own building." Or, if you would catch the music that often transformed the pomposity of these old sentences into magnificence, listen to Milton's vision of the London of the Commonwealth, rising triumphant from her struggles: "Methinks I see her as an eagle muing her mighty youth, and kindling her undazzled eyes at the full mid-day beam, purging and unscaling her long abused sight at the fountain itself of heavenly radiance, while the whole noise of timorous and flocking birds, with those also that love the twilight, flutter about, amazed at what she means, and in their envious gabble would prognosticate a year of sects and schisms."

Milton, and a few other stout old classicists, clung to this grand manner to the end of their days. But during the period in which the Restoration makes a convenient milestone, a change was taking place. French prose, by which the Royalists had learned to profit during their long exile, taught its lesson of clearness, directness and simplicity. The rising wave of interest in science brought with it a desire for simplification. The newly formed Royal Society, to which Dryden was promptly elected, went on record as rejecting "all the amplifications, digressions, and swellings of style"; as exacting from its members "a close, naked, natural way of speaking; positive expressions; clear senses; a native easiness: bringing all things as near the mathematical plainness as they can; and preferring the language of artisans, countrymen and merchants, before that of wits and scholars."

Here was Dryden's heaven-sent opportunity. It is easy to say that the language of artisans, countrymen, and merchants shall be preferred to that of wits and scholars, and no one would question that plain talk is better than mere fine writing. But, outside of mechanic matters, the language of artisans seldom holds our attention and almost never stirs our pulses. Something more is needed if a man is to write books that will be remembered with delight through generation after generation. Dryden could write with a crisp brevity, a plain directness, that might have made any scientist of his time green with envy. Any one can do that, who has had the right sort of training and who tries hard enough. But beyond that lies genius. Dryden's genius wrought this crisp prose of his into a style that is intimate and easy without ever being cheap, that is full of figure and fancy without ever being artificial or ornate, that is precise and symmetrical without ever being formal or mechanical, that is clear and simple and plain — but never dull. And now that that is said, let it be sorrowfully admitted that this is mere talk about Dryden's style — not a definition of it. Beyond all that is the fact that in any style, if it be truly the work of genius, the man who wrote it comes to life again — is visibly with us as we read — though his pen may have moved over the paper a thousand years ago. Slip a paragraph of Dryden's prose into any book by a modern author; print it, unidentified, between the paragraphs of some recent page, and if you have read enough of Dryden to become acquainted with the man, you will say to yourself: "Why, how did that get here? That is not Mr. So-and-So whose name is on the title page. That is John Dryden talking."

That is it. These volumes, duly labeled "The Essays of John Dryden," that lie before us on the table, and that look, with their board covers and numbered pages, as if they were just a book like any other book, are not mere cold print. They are still, after the lapse of more than two centuries, John Dryden talking. Listen to him as he sits at his ease in Will's coffee-house and chats about the rich variety of characters in Chaucer's *Canterbury Tales:* "Some of his persons are vicious, and some virtuous; some are unlearned, or (as Chaucer calls them) lewd, and some are learned. Even the ribaldry of the low characters is different; the Reeve, the Miller, and the Cook, are several men, and distinguished from each other as much as the mincing Lady Prioress, and the broad-speaking, gap-toothed Wife of Bath. But enough of this; there is such a variety of game springing up before me, that I am distracted in my choice, and know not which to follow. 'Tis sufficient to say, according to the proverb, that *here is God's plenty.* We have our forefathers and great-grandames all before us, as they were in Chaucer's days; their general characters are still remaining in mankind, and even in England, though they are called by other names than those of monks and friars, and canons and lady abbesses, and nuns; for mankind is ever the same, and nothing lost out of Nature, though everything is altered."

This passage is quoted from an essay which Dryden wrote in the last year of the century and in the last year of his life. It is pleasant to come upon it — to come upon part of it for a second time, in fact[1]— because it is about an old friend, and because happily chosen words about an old friend may be the better for being said twice over. But, for style, an earlier essay would have served as well. There is the same easy grace in them all. Listen to Dryden, in, for example, the very first of his essays, defending himself against the charge of *unnaturalness* in making the characters of his plays talk in rhymed couplets instead of in prose: rhymed couplets are unnatural, says he, only when the words have to be put out of their proper place to make

---

[1] See pages 51–52.

the rhyme; "but when 'tis so judiciously ordered, that the first word in the verse seems to beget the second, and that the next, till that becomes the last word in the line, which, in the negligence of prose, would be so; it must then be granted, rhyme has all the advantages of prose, besides its own."

"It is a naturall, simple, and unaffected speech that I love," said the old French essayist, Montaigne, as Elizabethan Florio translates him; "a pithie, sinnowie, full, strong, compendious and materiall speech, so written as it is spoken, and such upon the paper, as it is in the mouth." That is a good description of Dryden's style.

With Dryden's adroitness in catching the popular taste in his plays, with his skill in verse, and his genius in what he called "the other harmony of prose," he soon found himself on the highroad to success. His skill, too, in the celebration of passing events — a sort of inspired journalism in the days before the newspaper as we know it had come into existence — stood him in good stead.

For instance, in 1665, a great plague swept London. On the sixth of June, 1665, Mr. Samuel Pepys, an officer of the Admiralty, records in his Diary:[1] "This day, much against my will, I did in Drury Lane see two or three houses marked with a red cross upon the doors, and 'Lord, have mercy upon us' writ there; which was a sad sight to me, being the first of the kind that, to my remembrance, I ever saw. It put me into an ill conception of myself and my smell, so that I was forced to buy some roll-tobacco to smell to and chaw, which took away the apprehension." The wisdom

[1] The Diary runs from 1659 to 1669. It is a minute — and remarkably frank — record of his own daily doings and of the life of the City as he saw it. Pepys wrote his diary in cipher, for his private satisfaction. Printed for the first time in the nineteenth century, it affords a vivid and absorbing picture of Restoration London.

of Mr. Pepys was the wisdom of his generation. It was before the day of modern sanitation. The plague spread. The court scurried to safety. Theaters and shops were closed. The docks were deserted. The population of London in that day was about 350,000. When the fatal summer of 1666 had drawn to a close, nearly 100,000 were dead of the plague.

Then came the fire. Pepys saw it first at three o'clock of a Sunday morning, the second of September. It had started in the King's baker's house in Pudding Lane and was burning along the river-front. Pepys hurried to tell the King. The King sent Pepys to order the Lord Mayor to pull down houses and stop the fire. Pepys found the Lord Mayor in Canning street, "like a man spent, with a handkercher about his neck. To the King's message he cried, like a fainting woman, 'Lord! What can I do? I am spent: people will not obey me. I have been pulling down houses; but the fire overtakes us faster than we can do it!'" Then Pepys went home and "had an extraordinary good dinner, and as merry as at this time we could be." But by nightfall Pepys was carrying his furniture into his garden and burying his money in the cellar, and when he went down to the river, the fire was spreading "up the hill of the City in a most horrid malicious bloody flame. We saw the fire as only one entire arch of fire from this to the other side the bridge, and in a bow up the hill for an arch of above a mile long: it made me weep to see it." "God grant," exclaims Mr. John Evelyn, "that mine eyes may never behold the like, who now saw above 10,000 houses all in one flame; the noise and cracking and thunder of the impetuous flames, the shrieking of women and children, the hurry of people, the fall of Towers, Houses and Churches, was like an hideous storme, and the aire all about so hot and inflam'd that at the last one was not able to approach it, so that they were forc'd to stand still and let the flames burn on . . . London was, but is no more!"

But the fire, too, spent itself. Within a week, Mr. John Evelyn was presenting to the King "a survey of the ruines and a plot for a new Citty." The great architect, Sir Christopher Wren, made another. And though ultimately nobody's plan was followed, the City grew again. Even St. Paul's, "that most venerable Church, one of the most antient pieces of early piety in the Christian world," the destruction of which had nearly broken Evelyn's heart — even St. Paul's, under Wren's magic touch, rose triumphant from its ashes.

The plague and the fire; and, to balance accounts, naval victories over the Dutch, with whom the English had been at war since 1662. A year of wonders, with Dryden, poet-journalist, to celebrate them in *Annus Mirabilis*. "I have chosen," wrote Dryden in his preface, "the most heroic subject, which any poet could desire: I have taken upon me to describe the motives, the beginning, progress, and successes, of a most just and necessary war; in it, the care, management, and prudence of our King; the conduct and valour of a Royal Admiral, and of two incomparable Generals; the invincible courage of our captains and seamen, and three glorious victories, the result of all. After this, I have in the Fire, the most deplorable, but withal the greatest argument[1] that can be imagined; the destruction being so swift, so sudden, so vast and miserable, as nothing can parallel in story."

These high themes, Dryden continues, "inspired me with thoughts above my ordinary level"; but to the modern reader the poet seems, in the homely phrase, to be pulling

[1] Theme.

himself up by his own bootstraps.   Here and there in the descriptions of battle at sea there is a stirring image —

> Borne each by other in a distant line,
>   The sea-built forts in dreadful order move;
> So vast the noise, as if not fleets did join,
>   But lands unfixt, and floating nations strove.

But most of the naval part is merely grandiose and full of far-fetched images.   Even the account of the great fire, which he had seen with his own eyes and might well have coined into living words, is largely given over to flattery of the King.   Even Dryden sometimes locked up his sense of humor when he was in panegyric vein.   Behold the "Merry Monarch"—

> Meantime he sadly suffers in their grief,
>   Out-weeps an hermit, and out-prays a saint;
> All the night long he studies their relief,
>   How they may be supplied, and he may want.

As for his suffering people bereaved and destitute —

> No thought can ease them but their sovereign's care,
>   Whose praise th' afflicted as their comfort sing;
> E'en those whom want might drive to just despair,
>   Think life a blessing under such a King.

But it is just because *Annus Mirabilis* is such unabashed flattery that it is worth pausing over.   It was a time when poets, with very few exceptions, fawned at the feet of power and patronage.   Dryden was a creature of his time.   This was the way to advancement.   He took it — and was, on the whole, rather complacent about it.

Advancement came with reasonable promptness.   One mark of recognition was Dryden's appointment as poet laureate. In the early years of the seventeenth century, Shakespeare's friend and fellow-dramatist, Ben Jonson, had written a series of masques for performance at court. These were dramatic spectacles, with gorgeous costumes and stage settings. As the principal rôles were often played by the lords and ladies or even by the members of the royal family, and as Ben came to be considered — or to consider himself — the official author of court-masques, he styled himself the "Court Poet" or (in revival of an ancient tradition) the "Poet Laureate."[1] When Ben died, the title was unofficially handed on to Sir William Davenant, poet and dramatist, who, upon the accession of Charles II, was made manager of one of the theatrical companies. When Davenant died in 1668, the quasi-official laureateship became a salaried office of the crown, with the appointment of John Dryden.

To Dryden the appointment meant something more than an excuse for continuing his panegyrics. His powers as a poet could be used to mold public opinion on behalf of his royal master. Most people, today, think of poetry, if they think of it at all, as the satisfaction of a leisure hour, as an occasional titillation of the senses. Especially, we do not expect the poet to meddle with politics. That is the business of the newspapers. But in Dryden's day the man who could turn a witty rhyme on a political issue could count on its being read. Hot from the press, in pamphlet form, a verse-satire on My Lord This or an exposure of the dishonest schemes of Mr. Politician So-and-So would be hawked about the streets, or read aloud to eager listeners in the coffee-houses.

---

[1] The great Italian poet Petrarch was crowned poet-laureate in Rome in 1341. The title of *versificator regis* or King's poet occurs occasionally in the household lists of the early English Kings. A "Poet Laureate" appears in the household list of Henry VIII.

Dryden's adroitness as a panegyrist was known. The opportunity to show what he could do as a satirist soon presented itself. The heir to the throne was James, Duke of York, the King's brother. But the chief object of Charles II's affection was an illegitimate son, whom he made Duke of Monmouth. "The Duke of Monmouth," writes Pepys in 1662, "is in so great splendour at Court, and so dandled by the King, that some doubt, if the King should have no child by the Queen . . . whether he would not be acknowledged for a lawful son; and that there will be a difference follow upon it between the Duke of York and him; which God prevent!" And again the next year: "I do suspect that all is not kind between the King and the Duke (of York), and that the King's fondness to the little Duke do occasion it; and it may be that there is some fear of his being made heir to the Crown." Now, the Duke of York was an avowed Roman Catholic, and the old feeling against the Catholics was still so strong in England, that a powerful Protestant party were ready to go to any length to prevent the Duke of York from becoming King. The leader of that party, the Earl of Shaftesbury, brought a bill into the House to exclude Catholics from the royal succession; and, counting on the King's affection for his son, attempted to have the Duke of Monmouth declared heir to the throne. But this was going too far. Despite his affection for Monmouth, the King would brook no interference with the rights of the Crown. He dissolved the House, banished Monmouth, and threw Shaftesbury into the Tower.

This is where Dryden came in. A bill of indictment for treason was about to be brought against the imprisoned Shaftesbury. But the sympathy of Protestant England was with Shaftesbury and against the King. Could not the tide of feeling be turned? Could not Shaftesbury be made ridiculous, and the King's course justified, while, at the same time — a most delicate matter — the young Duke of Monmouth be made to appear, not as a plotter for the crown, but as the innocent victim of Shaftesbury's wicked schemes?

At the psychological moment, Dryden published his *Absalom and Achitophel*. On the face of it, it is a mere re-telling, in rhymed couplets, of the Biblical story (*II Samuel*, xv–xviii) of how the wicked counsellor Ahithophel[1] be-beguiled Absalom to revolt against his father, David. But the allegory was wholly transparent. Not only was Absalom unmistakably Monmouth and Achitophel unmistakably Shaftesbury, but every one of the Biblical characters conspiring against good King David was made to fit to a nicety some conspirator against King Charles. As for Shaftesbury, with his wizened body and fiery, restless spirit, no such biting characterization had ever before been spread upon the pages of English poetry.

> Of these, the false Achitophel was first;
> A name to all succeeding ages curst:
> For close designs and crooked counsels fit;
> Sagacious, bold and turbulent of wit;
> Restless, unfixt in principles and place,
> In pow'r unpleased, impatient of disgrace;
> A fiery soul, which working out its way
> Fretted the pigmy body to decay,
> And o'er-informed the tenement of clay.
> A daring pilot in extremity;
> Pleased with the danger, when the waves went high
> He sought the storms; but for a calm unfit,
> Would steer too nigh the sands to boast his wit . . .

[1] A Hebrew word meaning Brother of Ruin.

> In friendship false, implacable in hate,
> Resolved to ruin or to rule the state;
> To compass this, the triple bond he broke;
> The pillars of the public safety shook,
> And fitted Israel for a foreign yoke;
> Then seized with fear, yet still affecting fame,
> Usurped a patriot's all-atoning name.

Even more damning, because the subject afforded no gold amid the dross, is the picture of another plotter, the Duke of Buckingham —

> A man so various that he seemed to be
> Not one, but all mankind's epitome.
> Stiff in opinions, always in the wrong;
> Was everything by starts and nothing long:
> But, in the course of one revolving moon,
> Was chemist, fiddler, statesman and buffoon;
> Then all for women, painting, rhyming, drinking,
> Besides ten thousand freaks that died in thinking.
> Blest madman, who could every hour employ,
> With something new to wish or to enjoy!

Great satire never perverts the truth, though it may acidify it. It was not merely the brilliant wit, but the measured justice, the fatal accuracy, of these pictures that took the town by storm. If *Absalom and Achitophel* did not altogether succeed in serving the purpose for which the King and the King's poet laureate had designed it, it served to make Dryden the best known and the most admired — albeit in some quarters the best hated — man in London.

This was the heyday of "Glorious John," as his admirers called him. The coffee-houses had become the social centers of London life. From 1652, when a Greek had opened the first coffee-house in St. Michael's Alley, Cornhill, the coffee-

JOHN DRYDEN

Portrait by Sir Godfrey Kneller

271

houses had spread. Within a decade they had become the
centers of gossip and political intrigue. As hotbeds of
sedition King Charles had ordered them closed in 1675.
But within a year they were running again full blast.
Each coffee-house had its own group of frequenters. At
Will's, No. 1, Bow St., the poets and wits consorted.
"In Covent Garden tonight," records Pepys in 1664,
"going to fetch home my wife. I stopped at the great
Coffee-house there, where I never was before; where Dryden, the poet (I knew at Cambridge), and all the wits
of the town, and Harris the player, and Mr. Hoole of our
College. And had I had time then, or could at other times,
it will be good coming thither, for there, I perceive, is very
witty and pleasant discourse."   Will's prospered on Dryden's reputation. A chair was reserved for him, by the
fireplace in winter, on the balcony in summer. There, enthroned, he discoursed of the Ancients and Moderns, of
French plays and English, of rhyme and blank verse, of his
admiration for Ben Jonson and his love for Shakespeare.
There gathered about him the would-be wits and the aspiring poets, "conceited," says a writer of the day, "if they
had but once the honour to dip a finger and thumb in Mr.
D —'s snush-box, it was enough to inspire 'em with a
true Genius of Poetry, and make 'em write verse as fast
as a tailor takes his stitches."

It was a brave time while it lasted, and a time of tireless
activity. Heroic plays, operas, comedies, and one great
tragedy, the title of which we have already encountered
adorning a signboard in Vanity Fair, and in which Dryden
challenged his beloved Shakespeare by dramatizing once
again the story of Antony and Cleopatra — and brought
it off rather magnificently. It is worth remembering, too,
that in this same *All for Love*, Dryden threw over the

rhymed couplets which he had used regularly and defended
so eloquently, and showed that he too could be a master of
blank verse —

> Men are but children of a larger growth;
> Our appetites as apt to change as theirs;
> And full as craving too, and full as vain;
> And yet the soul, shut up in her dark room,
> Viewing so clear abroad, at home sees nothing;
> But like a mole in earth, busy and blind,
> Works all her folly up, and casts it outward
> To the world's open view.

And, meanwhile, he was pouring out satire after satire,
sometimes in furtherance of his royal master's plans, sometimes in retaliation of the attacks which his personal enemies made upon him. It would take too long to tell here
of these battles of the wits. Suffice it that those who tried
to bury Dryden under the weight of their satire are remembered today only because he has pilloried them —

> Who by my Muse, to all succeeding times
> Shall live in spite of their own doggerel rhymes.

There is space to tell only briefly of the closing years of
Dryden's life. Despite the momentary flare-up over the
Duke of Monmouth, the Duke of York, when Charles died,
succeeded to the throne as James II. Under James, Dryden, who was nothing if not adaptive, embraced Catholicism, and, as poet laureate to the new sovereign, wrote another allegorical poem, *The Hind and the Panther*, to show
that the Catholic was the older and the better faith.
Again his enemies called him a turncoat — and with perhaps more justification than before. But Dryden was by
instinct and conviction more a King's man than a churchman. In a country in which church and state were one,

Dryden felt that the faith of the King should be the faith of his loyal subjects. At any rate, right or wrong, he went his chosen way in apparent sincerity and paid no attention to his detractors.

But his heyday came abruptly to an end. The epitaph which the witty Earl of Rochester is said to have written on the bedchamber door of Charles II —

> Here lies our sovereign lord the King,
>   Whose word no man relies on;
> He never says a foolish thing,
>   Nor ever does a wise one

is equally applicable to his successor. Despite James's professions of fair intentions, nobody trusted him. England could not brook the idea of returning to Catholicism. After a brief reign of four years, James was driven out of England, and the Protestant William of Orange and his wife Mary, eldest child of James II, were brought in to reign in his stead. Dryden lost his laureateship, found no further favor at court, and retired quietly into private life. He engaged no more in controversies, but busied himself still with plays, with poetical versions of the classical poets, with poems such as the universally familiar *Alexander's Feast* —

> 'Twas at the royal feast, for Persia won
>   By Philip's warlike son —

and with those essays whose infinite variety age could not wither nor custom stale. "I think myself as vigorous as ever in the faculties of my soul," he wrote in the last year of his life, "excepting only my memory, which is not impaired to any great degree; and if I lose not more of it, I have no great reason to complain. What judgment I had, increases rather than diminishes; and thoughts, such as they are, come crowding in so fast upon me, that my only difficulty is to choose or to reject, to run them into verse, or to give them the other harmony of prose." He died on the first of May, 1700, and was nobly buried in the "Poets' Corner" of Westminster Abbey. He lives as one of the greatest English satirists, the author of a few poems and plays which the world will not willingly let die, and the creator of a prose unrivaled since his day.

IX

MEN OF THE WORLD

Three things especially will strike you in your reading of the poets and prose writers of the first half of the eighteenth century. First, that they were mainly interested in the morals and manners, the social virtues and vices of their own civilized world. Second, that though some of them tried to interpret life imaginatively as Shakespeare had interpreted it, their chief impulse was to criticise it — not happy-go-luckily, but according to the accumulated experience and common sense of mankind.[1] Third, that in both poetry and prose, but especially in poetry, they were concerned to say what they had to say with the utmost possible clearness and neatness. Good form, a clear and polished style, and that "fine taste" in expression which one of them calls "the utmost perfection of an accomplished man," were their watchwords. To explain their feeling that clearness and good form were so important, it is necessary to look back to Elizabethan times.

There had been a sort of unbridled power in the Elizabethan Age. At its best that unbridled power gave us Shakespeare. But even Shakespeare often let his imagination, his quick fancy, run away with him. Ben Jonson, a shrewd critic, said of him: "The players have often mentioned of Shakespeare that in his writing, whatsoever he penned, he never blotted a line. My answer hath been,

---

[1] It was the task of his generation, Addison said, in what they should write about life and literature, "to represent the common sense of mankind in more strong, more beautiful, or more uncommon lights."

'Would he had blotted a thousand!' . . . His wit was in his power; would the rule of it had been so too." At its worst, among many of the minor poets and playwrights of the age, this unrestrained vigor resulted in mere wildness. We remember, for example, what a strange mixture of genuine creative power and of mad extravagance there is in Webster's *Duchess of Malfi* (see page 113), and to what absurd lengths that late disciple of Spenser, Phineas Fletcher, let his fancies run in the allegory of *The Purple Island* (see page 172).

Ben Jonson himself, in his plays, and especially in his poems, had sought to set an example to his age of greater restraint, of more orderly thinking, of greater reasonableness, of a more careful filing of the phrase (see page 176). As the seventeenth century progressed, other poets, reacting, as he had reacted, against the looseness and extravagance of the Elizabethan way, strove especially for correctness and precision and a greater smoothness. A form of verse which lent itself particularly well to such an effort was the rhymed couplet — lines ten syllables in length, rhyming in pairs. This form was no new thing in English poetry. Chaucer himself had used it in many of his narrative poems — how skilfully, you may see by turning back to the quotation from the *Prologue* on page 43. It had not been uncommon in Shakespeare's day. But always, or almost always, it had flowed rather loosely and freely. What could be more tempting to these seventeenth-century seekers for order than to box a complete thought within each couplet; to balance one line of the couplet against the other; and to contrive a pause within the line (toward the middle, but varying somewhat to avoid monotony) so that each line should have first a rise and then a fall of sound?

Madam! new years may well expect to find

Welcome from you, to whom they are so kind;

Still as they pass, they court and smile on you,

And make your beauty, as themselves, seem new.

The author of these lines is Edmund Waller. He wrote them in the year 1650. He had been writing just such fluent, regular, perfectly modulated couplets for nearly thirty years before that date. He continued to write them for more than thirty years thereafter. The late seventeenth and early eighteenth century honored him as the creator of the form of verse which satisfied them best. Earlier English poets, said Dryden, had written "nothing so even, sweet and flowing as Mr. Waller." The editor of Waller's *Poems* (1690) called him "the parent of English verse and the first that showed us our tongue had beauty and numbers in it," and dismissed all earlier poets as mere "rhymers" in whose verse "there was no distinction of parts, no regular stops, nothing for the ear to rest upon."

If the wiser critics and poets of the day did not put Waller on such a pinnacle as this, they at least believed that the polished instrument which he had handed on to them was the best possible one for their purpose. And in a way they were right. Shakespeare's notion of "the poet's eye in a fine frenzy rolling" was not theirs. They did not try wild flights. The things that they wanted to write about were reasonable things, real life, average life, as they saw it around them. And above all they wanted to be clear, to "make their points." For this, no better form could be devised than these neat couplets with their even, carefully balanced parts. You cannot balance phrases in a poetical mist.

But "correctness" meant more to them than mere rightness of phrase. It meant also something which is best summed up in the word *urbanity*, which the dictionary defines as "that civility or courtesy of manners which is acquired by associating with well-bred people." This looks like an equivalent for politeness, the faculty of saying pleasant and courteous things. But the urbanity of the eighteenth century was not wholly that. The most urbane poet of the century wrote of a half-starved Grub-street[1] critic who had been finding fault with him:

I wished the man a dinner, and sat still.

That was not exactly polite, but it was said with an air. It was the retort, not of a gentleman, but of a fine gentleman — which is a very different thing. To be graciously polite and to be politely contemptuous fitted equally into the kind of urbanity which the eighteenth century cultivated.

This polished manner was a part of the literary tradition to which they prided themselves on belonging. The tradition went back to Roman literature, and especially to Horace. Horace was not a creative poet. The great creative period of classical literature lay among the Greeks, three centuries earlier. It is because of his perfect skill and easy grace, and because (the words are Professor Mackail's), in interpreting Greece to the world, he added "that peculiarly Roman urbanity — the spirit at once

---

[1] A London street, traditional haunt of needy writers.

of the grown man as distinguished from children, of the man of the world, and of the gentleman," that Horace is numbered among the great poets.

This "Roman urbanity" had come into England largely by way of France. During the harsh times of Puritanism, the court and many of the literary men who had depended upon the patronage of the court, took refuge in that country. France, then, was having its "classical age," with Corneille, Molière, Racine and Boileau among its dramatists, poets, and critics. It was a place of polished writing and of fine manners. When Charles II and his court came back to England in 1660, these refinements seemed to them more right, and far more pleasant, than the grim and sour ways of the Puritans. And England, sick of Puritanism, thought so too. The standards of the late seventeenth century, following the accession of Charles II, were largely French standards. The early eighteenth century carried on the tradition of the Restoration. What they thought that France had done for them can be best put in the words of the greatest of eighteenth-century poets, Alexander Pope:

> We conquered France,[1] but felt our captive's charms;
> Her arts victorious triumphed o'er our arms;
> Britain, to soft refinements less a foe,
> Wit grew polite, and numbers learned to flow.

Pope (1688–1744) is the best representative of this eighteenth-century spirit. When he was beginning to write, an old friend gave him a piece of advice which Pope liked afterward to recall: "Walsh used to tell me that

[1] Pope wrote these words in 1737. He refers to the Treaty of Utrecht (1713) which brought to a close, advantageous to England, the long war in which England, Holland and Austria had been fighting against France, to prevent the union of France and Spain.

THE ONLY FULL-LENGTH PORTRAIT OF POPE

Drawn without his knowledge while he was conversing with Mr. Allen at Prior Park, by William Hoare, who had painted a portrait of Pope.

there was one way left of excelling; for though we had several great poets, we never had any one great poet who was *correct*, and he desired me to make that my study and aim." It was, indeed, the way. Waller, however even and flowing, had not been precise. Dryden, at his best a perfect master of the couplet, had not known how to restrain himself. In the hurry of his energy, he had let many bad lines — careless in form and faulty in taste — slip in. Pope did make correctness his study and aim. He published nothing hastily. Every phrase, with the most patient care, he filed and smoothed and sharpened. The rhymes, to suit him, must seem as if they had grown there. Every couplet must be compact. The flow and ebb must be varied from line to line by a frequent shifting of the pause. The meaning of the line and its movement (its effect upon the ear) must be in accord. Lesser poets, blindly imitating Waller, were trying to make all of their lines equally smooth; and this uniform smoothness, this even flow, was being hailed by the critics as perfection in verse. Pope knew better.

> 'Tis not enough no harshness gives offence,
> The sound must seem an echo to the sense.
> Soft is the strain when zephyr gently blows,
> And the smooth stream in smoother numbers flows;
> But when loud surges lash the sounding shore,
> The hoarse rough verse should like the torrent roar.

But, above all, in the thought, the meaning, the sense of the line, there must be no lapses — nothing hazily or vaguely said, no mere poetical trick of fancy played up for its own sake, nothing that could detract from the perfect clearness and directness of the thought.

One result of all this care has been that Pope stands next to Shakespeare and Milton in the number of "familiar quotations"— condensations of human experience into an apt phrase or two — which he has supplied to the language. A case in point is an early poem of Pope's, the *Essay on Criticism*, written when he was only twenty-one. It is not a particularly original poem — hardly more than a re-stating of the views about poetry generally held in his day. But he manages to put a number of general truths about the difference between good poetry and bad, and about the way one should judge poetry — manages to put them so effectively that the world has gone on quoting them ever since. Turn for example to Bartlett's *Familiar Quotations* and see how many phrases from this poem written by a twenty-one-year-old youth have a familiar ring. "So that," you will find yourself saying, "is where

> To err is human, to forgive divine,

and

> The bookful blockhead, ignorantly read,
> With loads of learned lumber in his head,

come from!"

You will have the same experience with another didactic poem of Pope's, the *Essay on Man*. Again, it is not a particularly original poem. It is a philosophical inquiry into "the nature and state of man," with respect, first, "to the universe," second, "to himself as an individual," third, "to society," and, fourth, "to happiness." The philosophy is largely borrowed from Pope's friend, Lord Bolingbroke. But, once more, it is the clearness, the condensation, and the finish with which Pope expresses the thoughts that makes them memorable.

> Hope springs eternal in the human breast:
> Man never is, but always to be blest.

> All are but parts of one stupendous whole,
> Whose body Nature is, and God the soul.
>
> Slave to no sect, who takes no private road,
> But looks through Nature up to Nature's God.

The jingle of the rhyme as well as the aptness of the wording prints such passages on our memory. But there are also, in the *Essay on Man*, many chance phrases and "sayings," long since bereft of their reminder-rhymes, that spring so naturally to our lips that we never stop to think whence they come, and indeed hardly realize that they are quoted at all. "Order is heaven's first law"; "worth makes the man"; "damned to everlasting fame"; "guide, philosopher and friend"; "an honest man's the noblest work of God" are a few of many familiar ones.

The *Essay* is interesting too because it reflects so well the state of mind of Pope's world. They were not given to dreams, or un-worldly or other-worldly speculations, or rash experiments. Why theorize? Things are so because they have been made so.

> For forms of government let fools contest;
> Whate'er is best administered is best.
>
> All nature is but art, unknown to thee;
> All chance, direction which thou canst not see;
> All discord, harmony not understood;
> All partial evil, universal good;
> And spite of pride, in erring reason's spite,
> One truth is clear, whatever is, is right.

Pope was the spokesman of a rather complacent, self-satisfied world — and at the same time one of its sharpest and bitterest faultfinders. No doubt all things were as they should be, but the individuals who made up this excellent world were fair game for his biting wit. This, too, was in the literary tradition. Dryden had put the whole thing in a nutshell: "Moral doctrine, and urbanity, or well-mannered wit, are the two things which constitute the Roman satire." Horace and Juvenal (of whom, as it happens, Dryden was thinking in the foregoing quotation) were the Roman satirists upon whom these eighteenth-century wits patterned themselves. Satire was a nice art. "How easy it is to call rogue and villain and that wittily!" Dryden had said; "But how hard to make a man appear a fool, a blockhead, or a knave, without using any of these opprobrious terms!" Addison somewhere describes the Genius of Satire "with smiles in her look and a dagger under her garment." Pope made himself the master of this trick of being politely contemptuous. His *Moral Essays*, his *Satires* and, most notably, his *Dunciad*, are a sort of rogues' gallery of the 1720's and 1730's — a gallery, that is, of those who had become rogues by happening to affront or to disagree with Pope, or who had incurred his wrath by their meanness or pretentiousness or folly. He was a hard hitter, and when he did not name them by their own names, he made the reference so palpable that nobody could misunderstand. Dean Swift (see page 313) advised Pope "to reform and not to chastise" — to correct folly in the large, instead of going after the individual fools. Pope replied: "To reform and not to chastise, I am afraid, is impossible. To attack vices in the abstract, without touching persons, may be safe fighting, indeed, but it is fighting with shadows." So Pope chastised. The innumerable little men (half-starved critics, Grub-street writers, turning a penny by a pamphlet or a poem) whom he pricked or stabbed or flayed, are not worth naming here. They would have been forgotten overnight, if he had not named them. Pope himself dismisses them in four lines of characteristic irony —

> Ye little Wits, that gleamed awhile,
>   When Pope vouchsafed a ray,
> Alas! Deprived of his kind smile,
>   How soon ye fade away!

But he did not confine himself to the little fellows. How some of the beruffled and periwigged fine gentlemen must have writhed at the things he said about them! There was the notorious Lord Hervey,[1] for instance, whom, in his satires, Pope variously names as "Lord Fanny," "Sporus," "Paris," "Adonis" and "Narcissus," and whom he describes as:

> . . . this bug with gilded wings,
> This painted child of dirt, that stinks and stings;
> Whose buzz the witty and the fair annoys,
> Yet wit ne'er tastes, and beauty ne'er enjoys:
> So well-bred spaniels civilly delight
> In mumbling of the game they dare not bite.
> Eternal smiles his emptiness betray,
> As shallow streams run dimpling all the way.
> Whether in florid impotence he speaks,
> And as the prompter breathes, the puppet squeaks;
> Or, at the ear of Eve, familiar toad,
> Half froth, half venom, spits himself abroad,
> In puns, or politics, or tales, or lies,
> Or spite, or smut, or rhymes, or blasphemies.
> His wit all see-saw, between that and this,
> Now high, now low, now master up, now miss,
> And he himself one vile antithesis.

[1] Friend and adviser to Queen Caroline, wife of George II. Queen Caroline is the "Eve" of the following quotation.

I fear that it would be difficult to stretch our definition of urbanity to include that passage; but in the following lines, in which Pope paid off a score against his old friend Addison, though the manners are open to question, the manner is above reproach. Addison (whose work we shall consider a little later) was a man of wisdom, of wit, and of stainless reputation. It was hard to find a weak joint in his armor. But Pope found it. Addison was not, like Pope, outspoken in his criticisms. And he was vain. He liked to gather an admiring circle of wits and politicians and poets around him at Button's coffee-house and listen to their praises. And so Pope, having in one of his satires poured out his scorn upon a medley of worthless poet-asters, exclaims:

> Peace to all such! but were there one whose fires
> True genius kindles and fair fame inspires;
> Blest with each talent, and each art to please,
> And born to write, converse, and live with ease:
> Should such a man, too fond to rule alone,
> Bear, like the Turk, no brother near the throne,
> View him with scornful, yet with jealous eyes,
> And hate for arts that caused himself to rise;
> Damn with faint praise, assent with civil leer,
> And, without sneering, teach the rest to sneer;
> Willing to wound, and yet afraid to strike,
> Just hint a fault and hesitate dislike;
> Alike reserved to blame, or to commend,
> A timorous foe and a suspicious friend;
> Dreading e'en fools, by flatterers besieged,
> And so obliging, that he ne'er obliged;
> Like Cato, give his little senate laws,
> And sit attentive to his own applause;
> While wits and Templars every sentence raise,
> And wonder with a foolish face of praise . . .

> Who but must laugh if such a man there be?
> Who would not weep if Atticus were he?

The Dunciad is Pope's most comprehensive collection of fools and knaves and contains some of the sharpest of his thrusts.   Dryden had written a satire (*MacFlecknoe*) in which he described one of his rivals as King of the realm of Dulness and surrounded him with a court of dunces. In the first edition of *The Dunciad*, Pope makes *his* king of the dunces a certain Lewis Theobald who had ventured to point out mistakes in Pope's edition of Shakespeare. Theobald himself had subsequently edited Shakespeare. To the Goddess of Dulness, who is considering candidates for the crown, "Tibbald" pleads his cause:

> Here studious I unlucky moderns save,
> Nor sleeps one error in its father's grave,
> Old puns restore, lost blunders nicely seek,
> And crucify poor Shakespeare once a week.

The Goddess places the crown of Dulness on his head, and

> God save King Tibbald! Grub-street alleys roar.

Whereupon Pope turns from the king to his subjects, and in the course of the "high heroic games" in which they take part, ridicules the Grub-street wits.

After this first form of *The Dunciad* had been in circulation for some time, Pope dethroned Theobald and published a new version in which Colley Cibber appears as King of the Dunces.   Cibber was a second-rate poet and rather better than second-rate dramatist and actor, who had been appointed poet laureate and had written some ridiculous New Year's and Birthday odes to King George.   Pope had been gibing at Cibber for years, and Cibber had finally retaliated by publishing an unsavory story at Pope's expense. As King of the Dunces, Cibber is

> formed by nature, Stage and Town to bless,
> And act, and be, a coxcomb with success.

It is in this later form, with Cibber as King, that *The Dunciad* is familiar to readers of today.

The *Moral Essays*, the *Satires*, and *The Dunciad* are not pleasant reading. One admires the marksmanship but grows weary of the slaughter — especially as so many of the victims seem hardly worth the killing. If all of Pope's satire were like that, we might well begin to doubt whether the "urbanity" on which the poets prided themselves were anything more than abuse dexterously worded. It is in an earlier poem, which Pope wrote before he had begun to nurse so many grievances, that the urbanity of eighteenth-century literature finds its perfect example. It is satire still — urbanity with an edge; but it is satire at play, satire on a holiday.

"Women are only children of a larger growth," said Lord Chesterfield. "A man of sense only trifles with them, humours and flatters them, as he does with a sprightly forward child; but he neither consults them about, nor trusts them with serious matters, though he often makes believe that he does both." It is in this spirit (the spirit of eighteenth-century society generally) that Pope wrote *The Rape of the Lock*. It is a dramatization of the play-world of society with woman as the plaything.

A young gallant, Lord Petre, had slyly snipped a lock of hair from the head of Arabella Fermor, one of the belles of the day. The families of the two became angry. The suggestion was made to Pope (not very reasonably, one would think) that a playful poem about the episode might reconcile them.　Pope made two versions of the story. The first, which appeared in a miscellany with other poems by various hands, tells the story with an air of mock-seriousness, an ironical loftiness of manner, which makes every triviality doubly trivial and wholly absurd.　In the second version which appeared two years later, Pope added to the mock-serious effect by introducing supernatural beings into the story.　In playful imitation of the Homeric epics in which the gods direct the affairs of mortals, Pope has *his* belles and beaux attended by fantastic little spirits — airy "sylphs" who befriend human beings, and ugly little "gnomes" who delight in mischief.　It is Uriel, an attendant sylph, who tries to save Belinda from the humiliation of losing her lock.　It is Umbriel, a dusky melancholy sprite, who stirs up the ill-feeling over "the Baron's" deed.

A delightful example of this mock-serious manner is the description of Belinda's toilet, as her maid, the "inferior priestess," prepares her for the party at Hampton Court.

> And now, unveiled, the toilet stands displayed,
> Each silver vase in mystic order laid.
> First robed in white, the nymph intent adores,
> With head uncovered, the cosmetic pow'rs.
> A heav'nly image in the glass appears,
> To that she bends, to that her eyes she rears;
> Th' inferior priestess, at her altar's side,
> Trembling begins the sacred rites of pride.
> Unnumbered treasures ope at once, and here
> The various offerings of the world appear;
> From each she nicely culls with curious toil,
> And decks the goddess with the glitt'ring spoil.
> This casket India's glowing gems unlocks,
> And all Arabia breathes from yonder box.

> The tortoise here and elephant unite,
> Transformed to combs, the speckled and the white.
> Here files of pins extend their shining rows,
> Puffs, powders, patches, bibles, billets-doux.

Not less charming — not easily to be matched, indeed, for its smoothness and grace — is the description of the boat-ride of the belles and beaux on the Thames to Hampton Court.

> But now secure the painted vessel glides,
> The sun-beams trembling on the floating tides;
> While melting music steals upon the sky,
> And softened sounds along the water die;
> Smooth flow the waves, the zephyrs gently play.
> Belinda smiled, and all the world was gay.

The party itself gives Pope an opportunity for some of his deftest touches of playful satire.

> Close by those meads, for ever crowned with flow'rs
> Where Thames with pride surveys his rising towers,
> There stands a structure of majestic frame,
> Which from the neighb'ring Hampton takes its name.
> Here Britain's statesmen oft the fall foredoom
> Of foreign tyrants, and of nymphs at home;
> Here thou, great ANNA! whom three realms obey,
> Dost sometimes counsel take — and sometimes tea.
> Hither the heroes and the nymphs resort,
> To taste awhile the pleasures of a court.
> In various talk th' instructive hours they past,
> Who gave the ball, or paid the visit last;
> One speaks the glory of the British Queen,
> And one describes a charming Indian screen;
> A third interprets motions, looks, and eyes;
> At ev'ry word a reputation dies.

Ombre, the fashionable card-game of the period, occupies the party for a while — and then comes the fatal moment.

> The Peer now spreads the glitt'ring forfex wide,
> T' inclose the Lock; now joins it, to divide.
> Ev'n then, before the fatal engine closed,
> A wretched Sylph too fondly interposed;
> Fate urged the shears, and cut the Sylph in twain
> (But airy substance soon unites again):
> The meeting points the sacred hair dissever
> From the fair head, for ever, and for ever!
> Then flashed the living lightning from her eyes,
> And screams of horror rend th' affrighted skies.
> Not louder shrieks to pitying heav'n are cast,
> When husbands, or when lapdogs breathe their last;
> Or when rich China vessels fall'n from high,
> In glittering dust and painted fragments lie!

Belinda reduces the Baron to helplessness by throwing snuff into his eyes, and menaces him with a bare bodkin.

> 'Restore the Lock!' she cries; and all around,
> 'Restore the Lock!' the vaulted roofs rebound.

But the lock has vanished —

> A sudden star, it shot thro' liquid air,
> And drew behind a radiant trail of hair . . .
> The Sylphs behold it kindling as it flies,
> And pleased pursue its progress through the skies.

It is delightful fooling — and at the same time a vivid picture of the world of "heroes" and "nymphs," of puffs, powders, patches, billets-doux, of elaborate gallantries and light mockery, in which so much of the liveliest and cleverest and wittiest of eighteenth-century literature had its being. Round the card tables they sit, the ladies in dresses of Indian chintz printed in bright patterns; their skirts be-

frilled and distended by enormous hoops; their heads
crowned with a vast structure of false hair built up on
cushions, powdered and curled, and surmounted by imitation fruits and flowers; and, gently waving while they
watch their cards, the inevitable fan, an exquisite creation
of silk and ivory, adorned with allegorical paintings in
miniature —

> Loves in a riot of light,
> Roses and vaporous blue.

Opposite, the gentlemen, no less gay; heads crowned with
periwigs, "toupees," curl on curl of powdered hair, built
high above the forehead; suit, it might be of lavender;
shirt of costly Holland linen; a ruffle of lace at the neck,
a lace frill at the wrist; here and there a gallant clinging to
the waning fashion of shoulder-knots of bright ribbon;
waistcoats of white embroidered silk; knee breeches, gold
buckles, silk stockings. Talk, lightly of politics, deeply of
gossip, darkly of scandal —

> At every word a reputation dies.

But talk, too, we may guess, of Mr. Pope's *Pastorals*, and
of those charming little poems by Mr. Prior — and in a
lull of the game a beruffled and periwigged gentleman
catches the ear of the belles and beaux and quotes one of
Mr. Prior's. "Never," says he, "was anything so courtly
writ. 'Twas to a child of five years old — a child of the
Quality, who would be a belle herself some day: and Mat
Prior was forty when he wrote it —."

> Lords, knights, and 'squires, the numerous band,
>   That wear the fair Miss Mary's fetters,
> Were summoned by her high command,
>   To show their passion by their letters.

My pen among the rest I took,
  Lest those bright eyes that cannot read
Should dart their kindling fires, and look
  The power they have to be obeyed.

Nor quality, nor reputation,
  Forbid me yet my flame to tell,
Dear Five-years-old befriends my passion,
  And I may write till she can spell.

For, while she makes her silk-worms beds
  With all the tender things I swear;
Whilst all the house my passion reads,
  In papers round her baby's hair;

She may receive and own my flame,
  For, though the strictest prudes should know it,
She'll pass for a most virtuous dame,
  And I for an unhappy poet.

Then too, alas! when she shall tear
  The lines some younger rival sends;
She'll give me leave to write, I fear,
  And we shall still continue friends.

For, as our different ages move,
  'Tis so ordained, (would Fate but mend it!)
That I shall be past making love,
  When she begins to comprehend it.

Talk, too, it may be, of Dean Swift (see pages 317–318) of
the bitter tongue and kindly heart, whose latest witticism
one of the beaux had overheard, as the Dean bustled in and
out among the courtiers; or laughter over Mr. Addison's
gibe at the ladies in yesterday's *Spectator* (see page 299);
— but if all this happened that afternoon at Hampton

Court, before the Baron spoiled everything, Pope was too busy with his story to mention it.

Pope's picture of the belles and beaux at Hampton Court (with perhaps such supplementing as we have ventured) gives us one part of the background of early eighteenth-century literature. Another is the coffee-house life. The coffee-houses had had their start about the middle of the seventeenth century. Says the author of *A New View of London*, published in 1708: "I find it recorded that one James Farr, a barber, who kept the coffee-house, which now is the Rainbow, by the Inner Temple Gate (one of the first in England) was in the year 1657 presented by the Inquest of St. Dunstans in the West for making and selling a sort of liquor called Coffee as a great nuisance and prejudice of the neighborhood. And who would have thought London would ever have had 3000 such nuisances, and that coffee should have been (as now) so much drank by the best of Quality and Physicians?" Of the best-known coffee-houses in these early eighteenth-century days, there were Will's, made famous a generation earlier by Dryden's patronage, and still the resort of wits and poets; Button's, where Addison "ruled the roost," much as Dryden had done at Will's; St. James's, resort of Whig politicians, the fountain head of political gossip and of "foreign and domestic" news; the Grecian, which was near the Temple where the lawyers lived, and at which they would lounge in their dressing gowns in the early morning; and White's Chocolate house, patronized by men of fashion. At any one of these you could have, for your penny, your seat by the fire, your "dish" of coffee, and, if you were lucky, a glimpse of the *Daily Courant*, or Defoe's *Little Review;* or the *Flying Post*, conveniently printed with one side blank, so that you could scribble the latest political or social gossip upon it and send the precious sheet to your friends in the country. These coffee-houses were the centers, and in a way, the mainspring of London life. Whigs in one place, Tories in another, concocted their political schemes; the wits put their heads together over the newest volume of verse; the lawyers wrangled over their cases; the fine gentleman retailed the latest gossip.

On Tuesday, April 12, 1709, a little paper called the *Tatler* made its first appearance on the streets of London. It was printed on a single folio sheet, it sold for a penny, and it announced that it would appear every Tuesday, Thursday and Saturday. It offered a variety of entertainment. The writer, who called himself "Mr. Bickerstaff," proposed to drift about from one coffee-house to another, listening to the talk of the "men about town" who regularly gathered at White's, to the poets and other men of letters who assembled at Will's, to the lawyers from the Temple sipping their coffee at the Grecian, and to the politicians who came together at Saint James's. Writing from each of these coffee-houses in turn, and enlarging upon whatever topic the talk of that circle suggested to him, "Mr. Bickerstaff" would go the round for each issue of his paper. As a sample, the first number contained an account, written from White's, of "the deplorable condition of a very pretty gentleman"; a description, written from Will's, of a performance of Congreve's comedy, *Love for Love;* and, from Saint James's, news of the war with the Dutch, and political gossip on the authority of a "Mr. Kidney who has the ear of the greatest politicians."

The actual writer of this ingenious medley was Richard Steele, a captain in the Tower Guard and the author of several successful plays. He was an engaging fellow, a wit, and a scapegrace with a gift for preaching. He wanted not only to entertain, but to improve the morals of the town. As he had been something of a rascal himself, he thought it wise to keep his identity a secret. For a while the secret was pretty well kept from the general public; but fortunately for the success of the venture, a chance phrase in the sixth number of the *Tatler* revealed the identity of "Mr. Bickerstaff" to Steele's friend, Joseph Addison.

Addison and Steele had been schoolfellows at Charterhouse, and from there had gone up to Oxford together. Since that time, their ways had parted. Addison had made a name for himself, first by verse-translations from the classics, then — and far more widely — by a poem, *The Campaign*, celebrating Marlborough's victory over the French at Blenheim. The politicians had taken him up. He had been appointed to several political offices. He had become a much more important figure in the life of the time than Steele. But his real forte, the natural outlet of his genius, was in exactly the sort of thing which Steele had just launched. Like Steele he was by nature a humorist, an amused observer of the parade of London life. Like Steele, too, he had a helpful spirit. He was not content to be a mere detached observer. If human folly could be cured by laughing at it, if men and women could be made more sensible, more thoughtful, wiser, by a little gentle satire, he wanted to have a hand in it. What Steele was attempting to do in the opening numbers of the *Tatler* captured his imagination. He offered to contribute. With Steele's delighted acceptance, was born the happiest of literary partnerships.

Under Steele's nominal control, but with Addison becoming more and more the guiding spirit, the *Tatler* ran for two years. Then Steele discontinued it, because, as he frankly explained to the public, everybody had found out by that time that "Mr. Bickerstaff" was Dick Steele, and Dick Steele could not be taken seriously as a censor of "fashionable vices." When the *Tatler* stopped, the poet and dramatist John Gay wrote: "His disappearance seemed to be bewailed as some general calamity. Everyone wanted so agreeable an amusement, and the coffee-houses began to be sensible that the Esquire's[1] lucubrations alone had brought them more customers, than all other newspapers put together."

But the best of the partnership was yet to come. The *Spectator* began on March 1, 1711 and continued till December 6, 1712. It appeared daily and was printed on both sides of a single folio sheet. Most of this space was occupied with an essay on some topic of current interest, the rest being given over to advertisements. The good-natured satire, which had made the *Tatler* so popular, was continued in the *Spectator*. In its pages, the partnership is at its best. Steele's was the more alert and suggestive mind; but Addison, with no less natural humor, had far more steadfastness, greater patience in elaboration, and a finer sense of form.

They sought chiefly to ridicule the follies and reform the manners of the age. The follies were those of society at large. The Spectator "would not draw a faulty character which did not fit at least a thousand people." The reforms were of the sort to make their compact little world a better and a pleasanter place to live in. "I shall be ambitious," wrote Addison, "to have it said of me that I have brought Philosophy[2] out of closets and libraries, schools and colleges, to dwell in clubs and assemblies, at tea-tables and in coffee-houses."

---

[1] "Isaac Bickerstaff, Esquire."
[2] Principles of good conduct and right living.

There was little that escaped the Spectator's roving eye. The evils of party-strife in politics; the harsh religious prejudices, inherited from the old days of strife between Puritan and Royalist; the evil ways of the town; the bad influence of the stage on which were still being played comedies depicting life falsely, as if it consisted of nothing but intrigues and deceptions and smart sallies of wit — such serious faults as these he exposed and ridiculed again and again. Moreover, finding his contemporaries largely ignorant of the greatest poem which the preceding age had produced, he devoted many numbers (not now in ironic vein) to pointing out the beauties of *Paradise Lost.*

But, in their zeal for reformation, Addison and his fellow-contributors[1] did not confine themselves to serious matters. "There are none," wrote Addison, "to whom this paper will be more useful than to the female world." Certainly there was no subject more useful to the Spectator. What a deal of fun he poked at the ladies! There was a craze for beautiful and costly fans. Tea-tables, receptions, the theater, the whole town were a-flutter with them. Wherefore, on a June day in 1711, appeared a letter in the *Spectator*, purporting to be from a professional instructor in the use of the fan. In his "great hall," writes he, "a regiment of ladies" assemble twice a day for fan-drill. The master snaps his orders like any sergeant-major: *Handle your fans, Unfurl your fans, Discharge your fans, Ground your fans, Recover your fans, Flutter your fans.* "The *fluttering of the fan* is the last and indeed the masterpiece of the whole exercise; but if a lady does not mis-spend her

---

[1] Of the 635 issues of the *Spectator* (including those of 1714, when it was revived for six months, appearing thrice a week), Addison wrote 274, Steele 240, Budgell 37, and Hughes 11. There were a number of other contributors — among them Swift and Pope — of occasional papers or parts of papers. There were 53 anonymous contributions.

time, she may make herself mistress of it in three months.
. . . There is an infinite variety of motions to be made use
of in the flutter of a fan. There is the angry flutter, the
modest flutter, the timorous flutter, the confused flutter,
the merry flutter, and the amorous flutter. Not to be
tedious," concludes the drill-master, "there is scarce any
emotion in the mind which does not produce a suitable
agitation in the fan; insomuch, that if I only see the fan
of a disciplined lady, I know very well whether she laughs,
frowns, or blushes."

Fashions in head-gear, the Spectator found equally
diverting. The "commode," imported from Paris in the
late seventeenth century, was a wire framework, on which
the hair was built up, and elaborately decorated with laces
and ribbons. "There is not so variable a thing in nature
as a lady's head-dress," wrote Addison. "Within my own
memory I have known it rise and fall above thirty degrees.
About ten years ago it shot up to a very great height, insomuch that the female part of our species were much
taller than the men. The women were of such enormous
stature that *we appeared as grasshoppers before them.*"[1]
But, of late, Addison notes, "the ladies have been in a kind
of moulting season, with regard to that part of their dress,
having *cast* great quantities of ribbon, lace, and cambric,
and in some measure reduced that part of the human figure
to the beautiful globular form which is natural to it. We
have for a great while expected what kind of ornament
would be substituted in place of those antiquated com-
modes. But our female projectors were all the last summer so taken up with the improvement of their petti-

---

[1] An ingenious use of a biblical quotation: "And there we saw the giants,
the sons of Anak, which come of the giants: and we were in our sight as grasshoppers, and so we were in their sight." *Numbers* xiii, 33.

coats, that they had not time to attend to anything else."

This "improvement of their petticoats" was the fashion of hoop-skirts.

"Since your withdrawing from this place," writes an indignant townsman to the Spectator,[1]

"the fair sex are run into great extravagancies. Their petticoats, which began to heave and swell before you left us, are now blown up into an enormous concave, and rise every day more and more. In short, Sir, since our women know themselves to be out of the eye of the Spectator, they will be kept within no compass. You praised them a little too soon, for the modesty of their head-dresses. For as the humour of a sick person is often driven out of one limb into another, their superfluity of ornaments, instead of being entirely banished, seems only fallen from their heads upon their lower parts. What they have lost in height they make up in breadth, and contrary to all rules of architecture widen the foundations at the same time that they shorten the superstructure . . .

Should this fashion get among the ordinary people, our public ways would be so crowded that we should want street-room. Several congregations of the best fashion find themselves already very much straitened, and if the mode increases, I wish it may not drive many ordinary women into meetings and conventicles.[2] Should our sex at the same time take it into their heads to wear trunk-breeches (as who knows what their indignation at this female treatment may drive them to?) a man and his wife would fill a whole pew . . .

When I survey this new-fashioned rotunda in all its parts, I cannot but think of the old philosopher, who after having entered into an Egyptian temple, and looked about for the Idol of the

---

[1] The Spectator was supposed to be visiting his friend, Sir Roger, in the country. The letter is of course by Addison himself.

[2] The ironical suggestion is that many women will find themselves crowded out of the Established Church, where the fashion prevails, and will join the Dissenters.

place, at length discovered a little black monkey enshrined in the midst of it, upon which he could not forbear crying out (to the great scandal of the worshippers), What a magnificent palace is here for such a ridiculous inhabitant!

The Spectator is not usually so biting as this. Ordinarily he is content to let his humor play gently upon My Lady's follies, and leave it to his readers to point the moral. If he finds her head full of "shepherds, knights, flowery meads, groves and streams," as Biddy Tipkin's was in Steele's comedy *The Tender Husband*, he will quietly describe his visit to Leonora's library, and leave the books in it to tell their own tale. All the classic authors are ranged on Leonora's shelves — but these, he discovers, are wooden blocks, dummy books. The books which show signs of actual use are the extravagantly sentimental French romances — "the Grand Cyrus, with a pin stuck in one of the middle leaves," and "Clelia, which opened of itself in the place that describes two lovers in a bower." Madame de Scuderi's *Grand Cyrus* and *Clelia* must have been among those

> Twelve vast French romances, richly gilt,

of which the Baron in Pope's *Rape of the Lock* constructed his altar of love. They are enormous many-volume stories, full of interminable stilted conversations on the art of gallantry. In the former, the hero, Cyrus, son of Cambyses, King of Persia, is cast away as an infant, is found by shepherds and reared as a shepherd lad. In the latter, Clélie, the daughter of a noble Roman, is brought up as an exile in Carthage, where her hand is sought by three aristocratic lovers of as many countries. From the *Grand Cyrus*, Dryden had taken the plots of three of his plays, *Secret Love*, *Marriage à la Mode*, and *Aureng-Zebe*. Besides the sentimentality, Leonora no doubt enjoyed the thinly disguised portraits of the noblemen and wits and fair ladies of the French court which Madame de Scudéri introduced into both stories. Leonora's library is well supplied with books of this sort. Madame la Calprenède's *Cassandra* and *Cleopatra* and D'Urfé's *Astræa* are waiting for her, if she ever finishes *Clelia* and the *Grand Cyrus*. Addison wishes that Leonora "had been guided to such books as have a tendency to enlighten the understanding . . . as well as those which are of little more use than to divert the imagination," and lets it go at that.

Silly women, masculine women, female athletes, pretentiously learned women, female politicians,— the Spectator had his own suave little ways of disturbing their complacency. No doubt, when he reminded them that the sex should "distinguish themselves as tender mothers and faithful wives" and that "the family is the proper province for private women to shine in," they retaliated by calling him "old-fashioned." It is one of the delights of the *Spectator* papers, with their vivid and varied portrait gallery, that in the reading of them the gulf of time between the eighteenth century and the twentieth vanishes. "Mankind is ever the same, and nothing lost out of nature, though everything is altered."

Certainly in that picture which Addison touched most lovingly and elaborated most carefully, there is this enduring quality. The Spectator's country friend, the Tory squire, Sir Roger de Coverley, is, as far as the mere shell of him is concerned, a vanishing, an almost vanished type. But the inside of Sir Roger, his Tory conservatism, his foibles and his virtues, his quirks and oddities, his rough ways and tender heart, make him as real, as much alive today, as when Addison drew him more than two hundred years ago.

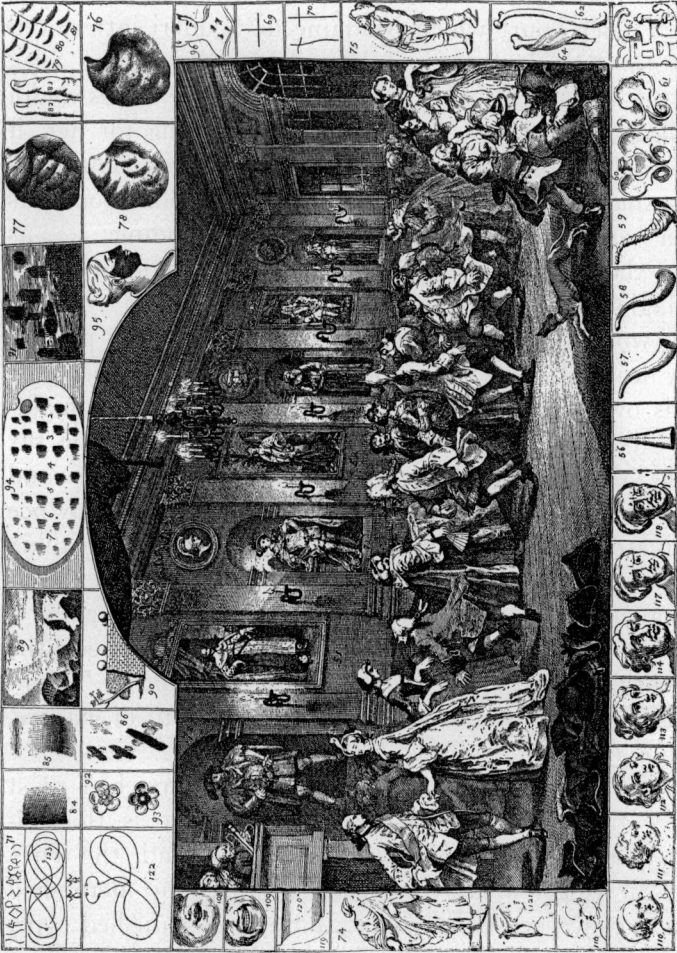

An Eighteenth Century "Rout"
(Hogarth's *Analysis of Beauty*, Plate II)

The truth is that Addison, who had meant merely to make fun of the Tory Squire, fell in love with Sir Roger. The hint for him had come from one of Steele's characters in the *Tatler* — Sir Jeoffery Notch, "a gentleman of an ancient family, that came to a great estate some years before he had discretion." Here was fair game. But to develop Sir Jeoffery Notch into a caricature would have been as impolitic as untrue. London knew her country squires. She laughed at their rusticities when they came up to town, but she loved their homely virtues. As Addison played with these possibilities, he found Sir Roger growing under his hand into a delightfully whimsical and altogether lovable person.

It was Steele who sketched the outline which Addison was to fill in:

The first of our society[1] is a gentleman of Worcestershire, of ancient descent, a baronet, his name Sir Roger de Coverley. His great-grandfather was inventor of that famous country-dance which is called after him. All who know that shire are very well acquainted with the parts and merits of Sir Roger. He is a gentleman that is very singular in his behaviour, but his singularities proceed from his good sense, and are contradictions to the manners of the world, only as he thinks the world is in the wrong. However this humour creates him no enemies, for he does nothing with sourness or obstinacy; and his being unconfined to modes and forms, makes him but the readier and more capable to please and oblige all who know him. When he is in town, he lives in Soho Square. It is said, he keeps himself a bachelor by reason he was crossed in love by a perverse beautiful widow of the next county to him. Before this disappointment, Sir Roger was what you call a Fine Gentleman, had often supped with my Lord

[1] That is, the little group of the Spectator's friends who, as he had announced in the opening number, "are concerned with me in this work" and with whom "a plan of it is concerted."

Rochester and Sir George Etherege, fought a duel upon his first coming to town, and kicked Bully Dawson [1] in a public coffee-house for calling him youngster.   But being ill-used by the above-mentioned widow, he was very serious for a year and a half; and though, his temper being naturally jovial, he at last got over it, he grew careless of himself, and never dressed afterwards.   He continues to wear a coat and doublet of the same cut that were in fashion at the time of his repulse, which, in his merry humours, he tells us, has been in and out twelve times since he first wore it. He is now in his fifty-sixth year, cheerful, gay, and hearty; keeps a good house both in town and country; a great lover of mankind; but there is such a mirthful cast in his behaviour, that he is rather beloved than esteemed.   His tenants grow rich, his servants look satisfied, all the young women profess love to him, and the young men are glad of his company.

Having thus introduced Sir Roger, the Spectator turns for a time to other matters, with only an occasional quotation of the knight's opinions to whet the curiosity of the public.   It is not until the 106th *Spectator* that Sir Roger appears in flesh and blood.[2]   He is at his country-seat in Worcestershire, where the Spectator is visiting him. Among his servants and dependents Sir Roger is at once the father and the master of the family.   His servants "have grown old with their master. You would take his valet de chambre for his brother, his butler is gray-headed, his groom is one of the gravest men that I have ever seen, and his coach-

---

[1] Lord Rochester, whom Evelyn called "a very profane wit," and Pepys described as an "idle rogue," was a prominent figure in the court of Charles II. Etherege was a Restoration dramatist. Bully Dawson was a notorious gambler of White Friars.

[2] Forty-nine of the *Spectator* papers are concerned with Sir Roger. Of these Addison wrote twenty-seven, Steele fifteen, Budgell six. One is of undetermined authorship. Of Steele's fifteen, only four add materially to the picture, the rest containing no more than a casual quotation from Sir Roger or an incidental reference to him. Of Budgell's six only two deal directly with Sir Roger. It was Addison who displayed Sir Roger's character under a variety of aspects and endeared him to his contemporaries and to posterity.

man has the look of a privy-counsellor." They are happy
when he is happy, sad when he is sad. "If he coughs, or
betrays any infirmity of old age, it is easy for a stander-by
to observe a secret concern in the looks of all his servants."
Sir Roger rules his little world according to his own notions.
In the village church on his estate, he has installed a clergyman whose qualifications are good sense, a clear voice, a
sociable temper and a knowledge of backgammon. Sir
Roger has no desire to listen to the good man's own sermons. "At his first settling with me," Sir Roger explains,
"I made him a present of all the good sermons which
have been printed in English, and only begged of him that
every Sunday he would pronounce one of them from the
pulpit. . . . As Sir Roger is landlord to the whole congregation, he keeps them in very good order, and will suffer
nobody to sleep in it besides himself; for if by chance he
has been surprised into a short nap at sermon, upon recovering out of it he stands up and looks about him, and
if he sees anybody else nodding, either wakes them himself, or sends his servant to them."

Sir Roger's tenants relish his kindly rule, come to him
in their troubles, and make him the arbiter of all their differences. So, in fact, do all the countryside; and when he
has heard their quarrels out, and "paused some time with
an air of a man who would not give his judgment rashly,"
he pronounces that "much might be said on both sides."
He is a great fellow for smoothing things out. One of his
former tenants, having set up as an inn-keeper, has Sir
Roger's face painted on the sign, and calls his inn *The
Knight's Head*. This will not do, decides Sir Roger, when
he discovers himself creaking in the wind, but he would
not hurt the old tenant's feelings for the world. "This,"
he explains to the inn-keeper, "is too great an honour for

any man under a Duke," but the face on the sign may be readily changed by a few touches and he himself will bear the expense of it. "Accordingly they got a painter by the knight's directions to add a pair of whiskers to the face, and by a little aggravation of the features to change it into the *Saracen's Head.*" Even the taciturn Spectator is moved to mirth when in this monstrous face he can still discover a distant resemblance to his old friend. Poor Sir Roger is much disturbed. "Upon the Knight's conjuring me to tell him whether it was not still more like himself than a Saracen, I composed my countenance in the best manner I could, and replied, *That much might be said on both sides.*"

The Spectator spends some time with Sir Roger; and not long after his return to London Sir Roger comes to town to visit him. It is characteristic of Addison's happy combination of the journalist and the man of letters, that he should represent Sir Roger as coming "to get a sight of Prince Eugene." Only three days before the date (Jan. 8, 1712) on which Addison records Sir Roger's arrival, Prince Eugene of Savoy, who as leader of the Austrians had shared with Marlborough the glory of defeating the French at Blenheim and Oudenarde, had come on a special mission to England, and all London had thronged to see him.

Sir Roger, then, sees Prince Eugene; and having duly applauded the great man, sets out with the Spectator to see the town. They visit Westminster Abbey, where Sir Roger stops in front of the tomb of every national hero to exclaim: "A great man, Sir! a very great man!" The good old Knight has been reading Baker's *Chronicle of the Kings of England* and observes with some surprise that Sir Richard Baker has a great many kings in him whose tombs are not to be found in the Abbey; but inasmuch as there are enough royal tombs to keep Sir Roger busy displaying to the Spectator all that he has just learned from Baker, the Knight soon forgets his disappointment. But when he comes upon the mutilated statue of Henry V and hears the guide explain that "the head, which was of beaten silver, had been stolen away several years since: 'Some Whig, I'll warrant you,' says Sir Roger; 'you ought to lock up your kings better; they will carry off the body too, if you do not take care.'"[1]

After the Abbey, the theater. Sir Roger has not been at a play these twenty years, and is a little dubious about London streets, at night. The Mohocks[2] are abroad. Sir Roger remembers that a neighbor of his was robbed on the streets of London in Charles the Second's time. But the Spectator reassures him by promising to bring Captain Sentry along. They make quite a procession, the Captain in front, and Sir Roger's servants armed with oaken clubs bringing up the rear. The play is Ambrose Philips's blank-verse tragedy *The Distrest Mother*, which Addison had already "puffed" several times in the *Spectator*. The distressed mother is Andromache, the widow of Hector. After the fall of Troy she is wooed by Pyrrhus, who is already betrothed to Hermione, the beautiful daughter of Menelaus and Helen. In the fifth act of the tragedy Pyrrhus is slain by Orestes to whom Hermione had previously been promised. "Upon the entering of Pyrrhus," says the Spectator, "the knight told me that he did not believe the King of France himself had a better strut. . . . When Sir Roger saw Andromache's obstinate refusal to her lover's

---

[1] It was probably at the dissolution of the monasteries, about a century and a half before there was a Whig party, that the mutilation had taken place; but Sir Roger is too good a Tory to let that worry him.

[2] Bands of young ruffians who roamed the streets and often insulted and sometimes dangerously wounded passers-by.

importunities, he whispered me in the ear, that he was sure she would never have him; to which he added, with a more than ordinary vehemence, you cannot imagine, Sir, what it is to have to do with a widow.[1] Upon Pyrrhus his threatening afterwards to leave her, the Knight shook his head, and muttered to himself, Ay, do if you can. This part dwelt so much upon my friend's imagination, that at the close of the third act, as I was thinking of something else, he whispered in my ear, These widows, Sir, are the most perverse creatures in the world. But pray, says he, you that are a critic, is this play according to your dramatic rules, as you call them? Should your people in Tragedy always talk to be understood? Why, there is not a single sentence in this play that I do not know the meaning of."

Sir Roger gets home safely from the play and a few days later, accompanies the Spectator to Vauxhall Gardens. Vauxhall had been a popular pleasure-place since the 1660's. In those early days, Pepys liked to go there: "A great deal of company; the weather and gardens pleasant, and cheap going thither: for a man may go to spend what he will, or nothing at all: all is one. But to hear the nightingale and other birds, and here fiddles and there a harp, and here a Jew's harp, and there laughing, and there fine people walking, is very diverting." Dr. Johnson's friend, Boswell (see page 331), writing some time later than the date of Sir Roger's visit, called it "an excellent place of public amusement . . . peculiarly adapted to the taste of the English nation, there being a mixture of curious show, gay exhibition, music, vocal and instrumental; not too refined for the general ear; — for all which only a shilling

---

[1] Sir Roger, it will be remembered, had been "crossed in love by a perverse beautiful widow of the next county to him" and continued "to wear a coat and doublet of the same cut that were in fashion at the time of his repulse."

is paid; and though last, not least, good eating for those who choose to purchase that regale." As Vauxhall is on the other bank of the Thames, Sir Roger and the Spectator take a boat at Temple stairs. Among the crowd of boatmen looking for a "fare," Sir Roger spies one with a wooden leg. "You must know," says Sir Roger, "I never make use of anybody to row me, that has not either lost a leg or an arm. I would rather bate him a few strokes of his oar, than not employ an honest man that has been wounded in the Queen's service." As they are rowed up the river, Sir Roger is, for the moment, more interested in the appearance of the City than the gaieties of Vauxhall. "The old Knight, turning about his head twice or thrice, to take a survey of this great metropolis, bid me observe how thick the city was set with churches, and that there was scarce a single steeple on this side Temple-bar.[1] A most heathenish sight! says Sir Roger. There is no religion at this end of the town. The fifty new churches[2] will very much mend the prospect; but church-work is slow, church-work is slow!" Sir Roger is so accustomed to greeting every one whom he meets on the country-roads that, to the great amusement of the young sports in the other boats on the river, he calls a genial *good night* to every one they meet; but when they reach the gardens, with throngs of people moving back and forth and the birds singing in the trees overhead, he is moved to a sentimental melancholy. "Sir Roger told me," says the Spectator, "it put him in mind of a little coppice by his house in the country which his chaplain

[1] When Sir Roger looked back, they were opposite the Houses of Parliament and Westminster Abbey. A little more than half a mile beyond this point, their boatman landed them on the southern bank, near where Vauxhall Bridge now spans the river.

[2] A statute of 1710 had provided for the erection of "fifty new Churches in and about the cities of London and Westminster," but few of them were ever erected.

used to call an aviary of nightingales. You must understand, says the Knight, there is nothing in the world that
pleases a man in love so much as your nightingale. Ah,
Mr. Spectator! the many moonlight nights that I have
walked by myself, and thought on the widow by the music
of the nightingale!" And, aside from reproving a pert
young woman who invites him to drink a glass of mead with
her, that is all the notice Sir Roger takes of the gaieties of
Vauxhall.

And so, except for one final word, Sir Roger passes out
of the picture. But that final word is perhaps the choicest
touch of all Addison's fine artistry. "Mr. Addison was so
fond of this character," wrote his friend and fellow-con-
tributor, Eustace Budgell, "that a little before he laid down
the Spectator (foreseeing that some nimble gentleman
would catch up his pen the moment he quitted it), he said
to an intimate friend . . . I'll kill Sir Roger, that nobody
else may murder him." Not long after Sir Roger's return
to Worcestershire, the Spectator receives a letter from Sir
Roger's butler, telling of the old knight's death. After
describing his bequests the letter concludes:

The chaplain tells everybody that he made a very good end,
and never speaks of him without tears. • He was buried according
to his own directions, among the family of the Coverleys, on the
left hand of his father, Sir Arthur. The coffin was carried by six
of his tenants, and the pall held by six of the Quorum:[1] The
whole parish followed the corpse with heavy hearts, and in their
mourning suits, the men in frieze, and the women in riding-hoods.
Captain Sentry, my master's nephew, has taken possession of the

---

[1] Sir Roger as a justice of the peace was one of the "Quorum" or associa-
tion of justices who constituted a bench for the trial of cases. On one occasion during his visit to Worcestershire, the Spectator had accompanied Sir
Roger to a sitting of the court and had listened to him speak "two or three
sentences with a look of much business and great intrepidity."

hall-house, and the whole estate. . . . The captain truly seems a courteous man, though he says but little. He makes much of those whom my master loved, and shows great kindnesses to the old house-dog, that you know my poor master was so fond of. It would have gone to your heart to have heard the moans the dumb creature made on the day of my master's death. He has never joyed himself since; no more has any of us. It was the melancholiest day for the poor people in Worcestershire.

To the light pleasantries and good-humored mockery of Addison, the writings of Jonathan Swift (1667–1745) afford a striking contrast. Swift lashed even more mercilessly than Pope; but, unlike the author of *The Dunciad,* Swift "spared the name." What moved his wrath were the wrongs that seem so inevitably to arise when men act together, in masses, in sects, in organizations. "When you think of the world," he wrote to Pope, "give it one lash the more at my request. I have ever hated all nations, professions, and communities, and all my love is toward individuals; for instance, I hate the tribe of lawyers, but I love Counsellor Such-a-one; so with physicians — I will not speak of my own trade — soldiers, English, Scotch, French and the rest. But principally I hate and detest that animal called man, although I heartily love John, Peter, Thomas, and so forth. This is the system upon which I have governed myself many years, but do not tell, and so I shall go on till I have done with them."

Born in Ireland of English parentage, Swift was sent to Trinity College, Dublin. Some two years after he had obtained his degree, a distant connection, Sir William Temple, who was spending an old age of wealthy leisure on his estate in Surrey, invited Swift to act as his secretary. Except for a few intervals, in one of which he returned to Ireland to take holy orders, Swift spent the ensuing ten years with Sir William Temple; and there in 1696-7, he wrote the first of his two greatest satires, *A Tale of a Tub*.

It is characteristic of Swift's outspokenness, that he should have struck his first blow at the three great religious organizations of his time — The Church of England, to which he himself had just been ordained, the Roman Catholic, and, third, the various sects which were grouped under the name of "Nonconformists" or "Dissenters." "The Grandees of Church and State," Swift explains in his mock-serious "Preface" to the *Tale*, are afraid that the Wits of the present Age will "find leisure to pick holes in the weak sides of religion and government." They have appointed him, he pretends, to divert the Wits by this *Tale*, just as seamen when a whale is about to attack the ship, throw a tub overboard to divert the whale.[1] With this Swift launches his allegory, which turns out to be itself an attack more open and unsparing than any other Wit of the day would have dared to make.

"Once upon a time," he begins, as innocently as if he were telling a nursery tale, "there was a man who had three sons by one wife, and all at a birth. . . . Their father died while they were young; and upon his death-bed, calling the lads to him, spoke thus:

Sons; because I have purchased no estate, nor was born to any, I have long considered of some good legacies to bequeath you; and at last, with much care, as well as expense, have provided each of you (here they are) a new coat." [The three coats, the father explains, will last them as long as they live, and will grow as they grow, so as always to fit.] "You will find in my will (here it is)," he continues, "full instructions in every particular concerning the wearing and management of your coats; wherein

---

[1] The phrase "A Tale of a Tub" was seventeenth-century slang for *a joke, a hoax, an idle discourse*. Ben Jonson calls one of his plays *A Tale of a Tub*.

you must be very exact to avoid the penalties I have appointed for every transgression or neglect, upon which your future fortunes will entirely depend. I have also commanded in my will, that you should live together in one house like brethren and friends, for then you will be sure to thrive and not otherwise."

It is already apparent that the "father" is meant for Christ, the coats the Christian faith and practice, the will the New Testament, the three sons the three Churches. Peter (the Roman Catholic Church), Martin (the Church of England), and Jack (the Dissenting bodies)[1] do carry out their father's commands for a time. They keep their coats clean and live together like brethren and friends. But as they grow prosperous they begin to yield to the temptations of the world. Fashions have changed, and, instead of being content to let their coats grow as they grow, they try to find warrant for adapting their coats to the current fashion. Their efforts to deceive themselves into thinking that the plain words of the will mean something that they do not mean; the shifts they are put to to find what is not there; their unavailing search, for example, for something which will permit them to adorn their coats with shoulder-knots, and their satisfaction when at length Peter suggests that if they cannot find shoulder-knots mentioned in the will, they can at least pick out a letter from this word and a letter from that, and *spell* shoulder-knots — of such things as these Swift tells his tale. And point by point, as he does so, he makes his arraignment of the churches — how century by century they have, as Swift thinks, departed from the humility and self-sacrifice and simple faith which Christ taught, and how they have built on that pure foundation a super-

[1] Martin Luther; John Calvin.

structure of worldly display and intrigue and spurious doctrine and feud and hatred of one another.

Upon the death of his patron in 1699, Swift was appointed to several small livings[1] in the vicinity of Dublin. It was the beginning of what was to be a lifetime of "banishment," as Swift called it, from his beloved London. He did not like Ireland or the Irish, and resented being called an Irishman. "I happened by a perfect accident to be born here," he wrote, "and thus I am a Teague, or an Irishman, or what people please." He called Ireland "a wretched, dirty dog-hole," a place of "slaves and knaves and fools." He spent as much time as he decently could in England. And yet, because it was his nature to fight against wrong wherever he found it, he made himself the champion of the Irish against English oppression. In pamphlet after pamphlet he attacked the English Government for discouraging Irish manufactures and debasing Irish coinage; and on their behalf, he wrote the most terrible of his satires. *A Modest Proposal for Preventing the Children of Poor People in Ireland from being a Burden to their Parents or Country, and for making them beneficial to the Public* describes "the streets, the roads, and cabindoors, crowded with beggars of the female sex, followed by three, four or six children, all in rags, and importuning every passenger for alms"; explains that no employment can be found for these children and that they "can very seldom pick up a livelihood by stealing till they arrive at six years old"; and proposes, as plainly and soberly as if the writer meant every word, that they be fattened and butchered for the English market. "A young healthy child, well nursed, is,

---

[1] In Swift's day, it was possible to hold several Church appointments (livings) at the same time, the reading of the services and other duties being left in each instance to an assistant clergyman, or curate.

at a year old, a most delicious, nourishing and wholesome food, whether stewed, roasted, baked, or boiled. . . . As to our city of Dublin, shambles may be appointed for this purpose in the most convenient parts of it, and butchers, we may be assured, will not be wanting; although I rather recommend buying the children alive, then dressing them hot from the knife, as we do roasting pigs." Moreover, adds Swift, it will be good economy to "flay the carcass, the skin of which, artificially dressed, will make admirable gloves for ladies, and summer-boots for fine gentlemen."

This, Swift means, is what your treatment of the Irish really amounts to. You have beggared them, body and soul. Is my plan much worse than what you have done already? But there was no need to point the moral. Swift was content to let the cold-blooded brutality of the *Modest Proposal* speak for itself.

Meanwhile, in the course of several prolonged sojourns in London, he had begun to take an active part in English political life. His pen came to be much in demand for political pamphlets. He was dined and praised and consulted by the leaders of the party in power. Himself without office, and with no other authority than his vigorous intellect and quick wit gave him, he became the adviser of ministers, and the friend at court of many petitioners. Here is a picture of him, at the high tide of his career, from the pen of a contemporary diarist.

"When I came to the antechamber to wait before prayers, Dr. Swift was the principal man of talk and business, and acted as minister of requests. He was soliciting the Earl of Arran to speak to his brother the Duke of Ormond to get a chaplain's place established in the garrison of Hull, for Mr. Fiddes, a clergyman in the neighbourhood, who had lately been in jail, and published sermons to pay fees. He was promising Mr. Thorold to undertake with my Lord Treasurer that according to his petition he should obtain a salary of 200£ per annum, as minister of the English Church at Rotterdam. He stopped F. Gwynne, Esq., going in with the red bag to the queen, and told him aloud he had something to say to him from my Lord Treasurer. He talked with the son of Dr. Davenant to be sent abroad, and took out his pocket-book and wrote down several things as *memoranda*, to do for him. He turned to the fire, and took out his gold watch, and telling him the time of day, complained it was very late. A gentleman said, "it was too fast." "How can I help it," says the Doctor, "if the courtiers give me a watch that won't go right?" Then he instructed a young nobleman that the best poet in England was Mr. Pope (a Papist), who had begun a translation of Homer into English verse, for which, he said, he must have them all subscribe. 'For,' says he, 'the author *shall not* begin to print till *I have* a thousand guineas for him.' Lord Treasurer, after leaving the Queen, came through the room, beckoning Dr. Swift to follow him; both went off just before prayers."

He could get advancement for others, but when he sought a high appointment in the Church for himself, his political friends failed him. Possibly they feared his bitter tongue; certainly his attack on the Churches in *A Tale of a Tub* stood in his way. At length he was made Dean of St. Patrick's (Dublin), and with that "banishment" had to be content.

And then Queen Anne died, and the political party with which Swift had allied himself collapsed. Swift's declining years were years of disappointment and bitterness. But it was during this period that he produced the book which has done most to keep his name alive.

Gulliver's Travels is perhaps the only book ever written that has two distinct existences — two reasons for being, each of which is sufficient unto itself, and independent of the other. It is, in the first place, the most fascinating of

storybooks for children. Few of us will ever forget the
moment when we first came upon an illustrated edition of
Gulliver, and opened to a picture of a man,— a giant of a
man, he seemed — lying upon a sandy sea-shore. Around
him were hundreds of little men, busily tying him down
with ropes fine as cobwebs. The giant had evidently just
waked from a sound sleep and was turning his head to look
with helpless wonder at his Lilliputian enemies. There was
no resisting that picture. We read on and on — of the
mariner, Gulliver, who swam ashore from a wrecked vessel
and slept the sleep of exhaustion and woke to find himself
in the toils of a pygmy race; of how they took him to their
capital, where he met their king who was taller by the
breadth of a finger-nail than any of his subjects; of how
these Lilliputians went to war with the neighboring island
of Blefuscu, and Gulliver waded the channel and towed
the entire Blefuscan fleet into the Lilliputian harbor; and
of countless adventures no less wonderful. And then,
when we thought the limit of marvels had been reached,
the whole thing got going again, with the fated Gulliver
wrecked on an island of giants, beside whom he looked as
tiny as the Lilliputians had looked beside him. Again there
were pictures — of a fabulously gigantic young servant-
girl, who had been deputed to look after the diminutive
Gulliver, and who held him wonderingly in the palm
of a vast and ridgy hand; and of Gulliver permitted to go
boating in a giant's bath-tub, and, like that other mariner
of whom Coleridge tells, finding himself alone on a wide,
wide sea. And again we read on and on and found countless adventures no less wonderful.

The best of it was that these things, however strange,
were manifestly true. How could they not be, when every
detail was so scrupulously recorded? Five hundred Lilli-

putian carpenters were employed in making the wagon in
which Gulliver was conveyed to the Emperor's palace.
Fifteen hundred horses, each four and a half inches high,
drew the wagon. Six hundred Lilliputian beds sewn together made a sleeping place for Gulliver. The Emperor
granted him a "daily allowance of meat and drink sufficient for the support of 1728 of our subjects." The two
main streets of the Lilliputian capital "which run cross
and divide it into four quarters, are five foot wide." In
the land of the giants (Brobdingnag), the farmer's dinner-
table is "thirty feet high from the floor." His dish of meat
is twenty-four feet in diameter. Here, clearly was no
fairy-tale, but plain matter of fact. We did not know that
Swift had carefully worked the whole thing out on a mathematical scale, computing the proportion of Gulliver to the
Lilliputians as 12 to 1, and of Gulliver to the Brobding-
nagians as 1 to 12; but we felt instinctively the reasonableness, the rightness of it all. As to the existence of pygmies
and giants, a few measurements, soberly set down, were
all that were necessary to confirm our natural faith. What
else should there be on new-found islands?

A strange man was Swift. When he was thirty-two,
he composed some "good resolutions" for his guidance as
he grew toward old age. One of these is worded: "Not to
be fond of children, or let them come near me hardly."
He was rough and arrogant and harsh and bitter. And
yet he was extraordinarily tender-hearted and had a vein
of childlike playfulness in him — a playfulness which appears especially in the "little language," a kind of prattle
of made-up words and abbreviations, in which he wrote
to a young woman whom he had known and befriended
since her girlhood. He never tired of writing playful
doggerel verses, many of which are sheer nursery rhymes.

And when he was nearing sixty, he wrote this amazing storybook.

That is one side, one existence, of *Gulliver's Travels*. Its other self is a satire so searching and so wide-ranging that much knowledge and experience are required to read it understandingly. In the descriptions of Lilliput and Brobdingnag, Swift is bent chiefly on making a good story. Only here and there are we conscious that Lilliput is England reduced to the scale of pettiness and triviality and trickery which Swift thought characteristic of her political and national and religious life. Sir Robert Walpole, English Prime Minister and Chancellor of the Exchequer, becomes Flimnap, lord high treasurer of Lilliput, expert on the tight-rope, who "can cut a caper an inch higher than any other Lord in the Empire." The controversy over whether the bread and wine used at communion are really, in that act, transformed into the flesh and blood of Christ, becomes a controversy as to whether a boiled egg should be broken at the big end or the little end — a controversy so bitter that the Lilliputians and the Blefuscans are ready to cut one another's throats to settle the question. And just as Lilliput is England diminished into pettiness, so Brobdingnag is, here and there, England grotesquely magnified, as if through a lens which makes every little thing ridiculously big. But as Swift goes on to tell of Gulliver's further adventures in Laputa and in the land of the Houyhnhnms, his early zest in the telling of the story loses itself more and more in his absorbing hatred of "that animal, man." *Laputa* is primarily a satire on the scientists of Swift's day, who, under the auspices of the Royal Society[1] were engaged in all sorts of queer investigations. On the island of Laputa, which

[1] See page 260.

floats in mid-air, bald-headed gentlemen with abstracted countenances spend uneventful lives in meditating the wonders of mathematics and astronomy; and down below, in the Grand Academy of Lagado, scientists are trying to extract sunbeams from cucumbers, and teach spiders to manufacture silk, and soften marble into pillows and pincushions, and write learned books by shaking words together on a board; while, in the School of Political Projectors, who, Gulliver thinks, must certainly be out of their senses, schemes are being proposed "for persuading monarchs to choose favorites upon the score of their wisdom, capacity and virtue, and of teaching ministers to consult the public good . . . with many other wild impossible chimaeras, that never entered before into the heart of man to conceive." In another part of this strange land Gulliver is permitted to summon before him the spirits of great men of the past. From the lips of famous generals he learns (for spirits always tell the truth) of cowardice and treachery masquerading as courage and loyalty; and from the lips of kings, that no royal throne "could be supported without corruption, because that positive, confident, restive temper, which virtue infused into a man, was a perpetual clog to public business."

But it is in the description of Gulliver's experiences among the Houyhnhnms that Swift's satire becomes most bitter. Here horses rule, and men are the stupid, brutal beasts of burden. These men — "Yahoos," the Houyhnhnms call them — are so filthy and repulsive that Gulliver is ashamed of his kinship with them. When the horses, the wise and decent Houyhnhnms, admit Gulliver to their companionship and question him about how his fellow Yahoos live in the country whence he came, Gulliver finds that he cannot gloss things over. He must tell the plain truth, for there is no lying in Houyhnhnm land. And so Gulliver gives them the unvarnished facts about the "civilization" of which he has been a part. When, for example, he has succeeded in explaining to those peaceful beings what War is, it becomes necessary to explain why "civilized" nations make war upon one another:

Sometimes the quarrel between two princes is to decide which of them shall dispossess a third of his dominions, where neither of them pretend to any right. Sometimes one prince quarrelleth with another, for fear the other should quarrel with him. Sometimes a war is entered upon, because the enemy is too strong, and sometimes because he is too weak. Sometimes our neighbours want the things which we have, or have the things which we want; and we both fight, till they take ours or give us theirs. It is a very justifiable cause of war to invade a country after the people have been wasted by famine, destroyed by pestilence, or embroiled by factions among themselves. It is justifiable to enter into war against our nearest ally, when one of his towns lies convenient to us, or a territory of land, that would render our dominions round and complete. If a prince sends forces into a nation where the people are poor and ignorant, he may lawfully put half of them to death, and make slaves of the rest, in order to civilize and reduce them from their barbarous way of living. It is a very kingly, honourable, and frequent practice, when one prince desires the assistance of another to secure him against an invasion that the assistant, when he hath driven out the invader, should seize on the dominions himself, and kill, imprison, or banish the prince he came to relieve. Alliance by blood or marriage is a frequent cause of war between princes; and the nearer the kindred is, the greater is their disposition to quarrel; poor nations are hungry, and rich nations are proud; and pride and hunger will ever be at variance. For these reasons, the trade of a soldier is held the most honourable of all others; because a soldier is a

Yahoo hired to kill in cold blood as many of his own species, who
have never offended him, as possibly he can.

As Gulliver thus finds himself compelled to face the
truth about the world whence he came, it becomes a horror
to him. "When I thought of my family, my friends, my
countrymen, or the human race in general, I considered them
as they really were, Yahoos in shape and disposition —
perhaps a little more civilized, and qualified with the gift
of speech, but making no other use of reason than to improve and multiply those vices whereof their brethren in
this country had only the share that nature allotted them.
When I happened to behold the reflection of my own form
in a lake or fountain, I turned away my face in horror and
detestation of myself, and could better endure the sight
of a common Yahoo than of my own person."
There can be no doubt that in this, and many similar
passages, Gulliver speaks with the voice of Swift. Ill-
health, ungratified ambition, a lifetime's experience of
human selfishness and meanness, had brought Swift to a
state of mind in which he could not think of the world
without hatred and disgust. He had become one-sided,
morbid, mentally as well as physically unhealthy. On
this account, the latter part of *Gulliver* is inferior to some
of Swift's earlier satire. A satirist may caricature but he
must not falsify. We know that our fellow-Yahoos are
not so gross and so unrelievedly vile as Swift represents
them. We resent the unfairness of the picture; but there
are few books more profitable to read. Swift has a way of
probing beneath the comfortable surface of life and forcing us to ask ourselves the *why* of things which we have
always taken for granted.
It is in this fearless probing, and in the energy of his

attack, the fertility of his invention, and the absolute
simplicity and clearness of his style, that Swift's greatness
consists. He had not Addison's lightness of touch, and
friendly humor. He could not cajole. His style is like
himself — plain, and hard-hitting. He hated wrong. His
unmatched gift of story-telling he forged into a deadly
weapon. Even in his decline there was great-mindedness;
for the wrongs which he fought were always real wrongs,
and he fought them for the sake of humanity.

Swift and Addison and Pope are the great figures of their
age — possibly the only ones whose work will not be forgotten as time goes on. To this day, each in his own peculiar quality remains unequaled. No satirist since has been
able to approach Swift either in deadly power or in that
"droll sobriety" by which he

> raised a smile
> At folly's cost, himself unmoved the while.

There have been greater poets than Pope but none who
could touch him in brilliance of wit and mastery of phrase.
There have been many delightful essayists since Addison's
day but none who have so perfectly combined wisdom and
sweet reasonableness with charm of humor and grace of
style.

The age to which they belonged pinned its faith to good
sense. It distrusted enthusiasm and emotionalism and
sentimentality and raptures of any sort, and very definitely
disagreed with Shakespeare's notion that "seething brains"
could sometimes

> apprehend
> More than cool reason ever comprehends.

Addison, we remember, said that the task of his generation was "to represent the common sense of mankind in more strong, more beautiful, or more uncommon lights." In their occasional criticism of literature, and in their criticism of morals and manners, that is what Addison and Swift and Pope did.

With them it will be interesting to consider another apostle of common sense, in spite of the fact that he belongs later in the century and was just beginning his career as Swift and Pope were ending theirs. Samuel Johnson was born in 1709, the year in which Steele started the *Tatler.* Johnson's boyhood was spent in his father's bookshop in Lichfield. There, as he said, he had "looked into a great many books, which were not commonly known at the Universities . . . so that when I came to Oxford, Dr. Adams, now master of Pembroke College, told me I was the best qualified for the University that he had ever known come there."

His funds gave out. He left Oxford without taking a degree. He tried to support himself by teaching school; but his nervousness and awkwardness made him a laughing-stock among his pupils. He decided to try his fortune in London, and "reached the City with two pence half penny in his pocket."

His life was a continuous struggle against poverty and disease. He translated for the booksellers. For a London magazine he wrote reports of speeches in the House of Commons, and instead of reproducing what had actually been said, chose to stay in his garret and write what he thought the speakers ought to have said. Long afterward, when a group of his friends were praising the eloquence of a speech by the great statesman and orator, William Pitt, Johnson listened in silence for a while and then said quietly:

"That speech I wrote in a garret in Exeter Street." He wrote a blank-verse tragedy, *Irene,* which failed. He wrote two poems, *London* and *The Vanity of Human Wishes,* which won him recognition. But it was through personal contact, the give and take of offhand argument, that his powers became known. He loved to talk. "I dogmatize and am contradicted, and in this conflict of opinions and sentiments I find delight." Those who encountered him in these word-battles realized, as Adam Smith[1] put it, that "Johnson knew more books than any man alive." It is true that he was dictatorial. He had a way of roaring his opponents down which was rather terrifying. But his wisdom, the vigor with which he slashed to the core of a problem, his homely telling illustrations, made him worth listening to. Those who were stunned one day came back next day for more. In spite of his crusty ways, he had a genius for making friends, and, as he said, keeping his friendships in repair.

When he announced his intention of undertaking a dictionary of the English language, it was apparent that there was no one else so well fitted for the task. It needed doing. Henry Cockeram's *Dictionary* (1623) and Edward Phillips's *New Worlde of Wordes* (1658) were insignificant compilations. Nathaniel Bailey's *Universal Etymological English Dictionary* (1721), in common use in Johnson's time, was not much better. The language was constantly changing. Johnson hoped to give it stability, to establish a standard of correctness by illustrating the use of each word from the best writers and defining it accordingly. "If the language of theology were extracted from Hooker and the translation of the Bible; the terms of natural knowledge

---

[1] Author of *The Wealth of Nations,* and one of the most learned men of the time.

from Bacon; the phrases of policy, war, and navigation from Raleigh; the dialect of poetry and fiction from Spenser and Sidney; and the diction of common life from Shakespeare, few ideas would be lost to mankind, for want of English words in which they might be expressed."

Aided by advance payments from several booksellers, Johnson employed amanuenses, and set to work on his long task of reading, selecting and defining — gleaning "as industry should find, or chance should offer it, in the boundless chaos of a living speech."

During two of the seven years in which he was thus engaged, he published, in imitation of Addison's *Spectator*, a periodical which he called the *Rambler*. He had not Addison's lightness of touch. To Johnson the *Rambler* seemed a proper place in which to express with grave sincerity the fruit of his experience and sober thinking. Much wisdom and good sense may be found in its pages, but no such delight as Addison affords.

The *Dictionary* came from the press in 1755, in two massive folio volumes. It had a wealth of quotations. For example, the various uses of the word *for* are illustrated by thirteen quotations from Shakespeare, three from Spenser, ten from Bacon, two from Milton, twenty-nine from Dryden, five from Addison, five from Swift, and three from Pope, besides a scattering from a dozen others. But, as was to be expected from a man of Johnson's vigorous and independent mind, the definitions are the thing. He went at his defining as zestfully as if no English word had ever been defined before. The "Whig," or Liberal, party was then in power. Johnson was a "Tory," a Conservative. A *Tory*, he defines as "one who adheres to the ancient constitution of the State, and the apostolical hierarchy of the Church of England"; but *Whig* is "the name of a faction,"

Courtesy of National Portrait Gallery, London

Dr. Samuel Johnson

Painting by Sir Joshua Reynolds

and *Whiggism*, "the *notions* of a Whig." A tax called "excise" was favored by the Whig government. Johnson defines *excise* as "a hateful tax levied upon commodities, and adjudged not by the common judges of property, but wretches hired by those to whom excise is paid." One of Johnson's most emphatic prejudices was against the Scotch. The word, *oats*, he explains as "a grain which in England is generally given to horses, but in Scotland supports the people." But if he allowed his dislikes to get into the *Dictionary*, he was no less downright in matters which concerned himself. A *lexicographer* he defines as "a writer of dictionaries, a harmless drudge," and *grubstreet*, where he had himself eked out a living for many years, is explained as "originally the name of a street in Moorfields in London, much inhabited by writers of small histories, dictionaries, and temporary poems; whence any mean production is called *grubstreet*."

As a book of reference, an authority on meaning and usage, Johnson's *Dictionary* has of course long since been superseded. But just because Johnson did thus speak his mind about things, it will always be one of the most delightful of books to dip into. He wrote at a happy moment. The day of dictionaries prepared by whole syndicates of scholars, and with definitions as colorless as they are scientific, was yet to come. For reference, it is probably much more precise to have a certain variety of insect defined as "the *cimex lectularius*, the bedbug or house-bug, or any member of this genus or of the family *Cimicidae*"; but it is more enlivening to turn to Johnson and see the same creature defined as "a stinking insect bred in old household stuff." It is no doubt much more accurate to define *revenge* as "retaliation for wrongs real or fancied; hence, the gratification of vindictive feeling"; but it would be hard to better the terse completeness of Johnson's "the return of an injury." It is fascinating to consider in the light of modern usage Johnson's judgment on the standing of words — to find him, for example, describing *gratefulness* as "now obsolete," characterizing the verb *to restrict* as "a word scarce English," and curtly dismissing *flirtation* as "a cant word among women." It is no less fascinating to come upon a definition here and there which reminds us of the road that science has traveled — to read, for example, his long discussion of *electricity*, closing with the words: "The philosophers are now endeavouring to intercept the strokes of lightning."

The *Dictionary* had been before the public for eight years, and Johnson was at the height of his fame, when he met his future biographer. Johnson was in his fifty-fourth year. James Boswell, twenty-two, well-to-do, and on the lookout for experiences, had just come down from Scotland, bent on beholding "Dictionary Johnson." One of Boswell's acquaintances was Tom Davies, a retired actor, who kept a bookshop. Boswell was drinking tea with Tom and his wife in the "back-parlour," when, through the glass door opening into the shop, they saw Johnson approaching. "Don't tell him I come from Scotland," said Boswell. But Tom did. "I do indeed come from Scotland," stammered poor Boswell, "but I cannot help it." "That, Sir," thundered Johnson, "is what a very great many of your countrymen cannot help." Johnson began to talk with Tom and his wife and once more Boswell tried to break in and again was snubbed. "I now felt myself much mortified," Boswell records, "and began to think that the hope which I had long indulged of obtaining his acquaintance was blasted. And, in truth, had not my ardor been uncommonly strong, and my resolution uncommonly persevering, so rough a reception might have deterred me forever from making any further attempts. Fortunately, however, I remained upon the field not wholly discomfited, and was soon rewarded by hearing some of his conversation, of which I preserved a short minute."

There are the whole inception, process, and art of Boswell's *Life of Johnson* in a nutshell. With a resolution uncommonly persevering, Boswell devoted himself to overcoming the great man's prejudices and getting on friendly terms with him. He preserved a short minute that day and he kept on preserving minutes. At dinners, he would sit behind Johnson's shoulder, suddenly spring up and rush to the end of the room, turn his back on the company and make jottings in his notebook. Pestered within an inch of his life, Johnson would fall on him like a mountain. "Sir, you have but two subjects, yourself and me. I am sick of both." And next day Boswell would come back for more. Boswell contrived situations, impartially maneuvered Johnson into meetings with enemy or friend, just to see what he would do. Pleasant or unpleasant, the results went down in the notebook. "I would not," said Boswell, "cut off Johnson's claws to please anybody." Boswell ferreted out Johnson's acquaintances, got from them whatever they knew, and that went into the notebook. Johnson made fun of him, Johnson's friends made fun of him; but Boswell knew what he was doing and never faltered in his plan. "He will be seen," determined Boswell, "as he really was; for I profess to write, not his panegyric, which must be all praise, but his Life." "When I delineate him without reserve, I do what he himself recommended, both by his precept and his example." "I will venture to say that he will be seen in this work more completely than any man who has ever yet lived."

He is. Boswell records the bad as well as the good, the rough with the smooth, Johnson's bearishness, his bad table-manners, his ferocious appetite; his unquenchable thirst for tea — sixteen cups at a meal; his boisterous laughter, resounding in the silence of the night from Temple-bar to Fleet-ditch; his twitching muscles and rolling walk; his queer habit of touching every post which he passed; his habit of whistling in the midst of conversation, of talking to himself, of "blowing out his breath like a whale" at the end of an argument; his violent prejudices — against Scotland and the Scotch; against the Whigs ("Sir, he is a cursed Whig, a bottomless Whig, as they all are now"); against Presbyterians and Roman Catholics; against stage-players, "fellows who exhibit themselves for a shilling"; but with these, his splendid courage, his benevolence toward the needy, his inexhaustible humor, and, above all, the extraordinary blend of learning and philosophic wisdom and plain, homely, common sense which made and still makes his conversation memorable. "As Dr. Johnson said" has prefaced many an apt quotation, from his day to our own — and is likely to preface many another in time to come.

The most definite and lasting impression which you will get from Boswell's pages is of Johnson's entire straightforwardness and honesty of mind. "My dear friend," he said to Boswell one day, "clear your mind of *cant*. You may *talk* as other people do: you may say to a man, 'Sir, I am your most humble servant.' You are *not* his most humble servant. You may say, 'These are bad times; it is a melancholy thing to be reserved to such times.' You don't mind the times. You tell a man, 'I am sorry you had such bad weather the last day of your journey, and were so much wet.' You don't care sixpence whether he is wet or dry. You may *talk* in this manner; it is a mode of talking in Society: but don't *think* foolishly."

When you turn from Boswell's *Life* to Johnson's own writings, you will get this same impression of straightforwardness and honesty of mind, and abhorrence of cant and sentimentality. You will see it in his moving little allegory, the story called *Rasselas,* in which the young Abyssinian Prince who has grown up in a happy valley, where everything is arranged for his comfort and pleasure, goes forth into the world, expecting to find his happy valley on a larger scale, equally well-ordered. Instead he finds that while each person whom he meets has made a choice of life which, he thinks, will bring him happiness, all have been disappointed. "Human life," it appears, "is everywhere a state in which much is to be endured and little to be enjoyed." It is the Prince's sister, who has accompanied him, who sums up the only possible conclusion: "To me, the choice of life is become less important; I hope hereafter to think only on the choice of eternity."

You will get this same impression of straightforwardness and honesty of mind in Johnson's criticisms of literature. The most important of these are his Introduction and Notes to Shakespeare and his *Lives of the Poets.* When Johnson's Introduction to Shakespeare appeared, Adam Smith characterized it as "the most manly piece of criticism that was ever published in any country." It is still, despite all the modern developments of scholarship, considered one of the great pieces of Shakespeare criticism. The same plainness and directness and honesty which characterize his talk, he applied to his criticism of Shakespeare. He found many faults in Shakespeare, and in his usual downright way enumerated them. Many of his

contemporaries were angry at this and accused him of be-
littling their idol; but, today, we are inclined to see in most
of Johnson's criticisms only the reasonable judgments of a
thoughtful and independent mind. And no one can read
the Introduction without a better understanding of the
true elements of Shakespeare's greatness.

Doctor Johnson[1] was sixty-seven when he undertook the
Lives of the Poets. A comprehensive collection of the works
of English poets was to be published in London. Johnson
was asked to write a brief notice of each poet represented.
The expectation was that each notice would be confined,
as he explained, to "a few dates and a general character,
but I have been led beyond my intention, I hope, by the
honest desire of giving useful pleasure." These critical
biographies, into which his "few dates and general character" grew, have taken their place among lasting works
of literary criticism.

They are by no means of equal merit. A man of Doctor
Johnson's strong prejudices could not but have his blind
spots. But his judgments in the *Lives* are generally extraordinarily fair and sound; and, now and again, he puts
into a few grave and stately words the very essence of a
poet's life. Here, for example, is the concluding paragraph
of his biography of Milton: "He was naturally a thinker
for himself, confident of his own abilities and disdainful
of help or hindrance; he did not refuse admission to the
thoughts or images of his predecessors, but he did not
seek them. From his contemporaries he neither courted
nor received support; there is in his writings nothing by

---

[1] Oxford conferred upon him the honorary degree of Doctor of Laws in
1775, when he was sixty-six years old. He did not use the title himself or
expect his friends to use it; but posterity has joined it to his name. "Doctor"
means a well-taught or learned man. Many other men of letters have received the title, but it never seems to have settled so appropriately or so
firmly upon the head of any other man.

which the pride of other authors might be gratified or favor gained, no exchange of praise nor solicitation of support. His great works were performed under discountenance and in blindness, but difficulties vanished at his touch; he was born for whatever is arduous; and his work is not the greatest of heroic poems, only because it is not the first."

The *Lives of the Poets* was the last notable production of Johnson's pen. He died on the 13th of December, 1784, being then seventy-five years old. Not long before his death, he wrote to one of his friends: "I hope scarcely any man has known me closely but for his benefit, or cursorily but to his innocent entertainment." That was, in truth, the experience of his own generation; and it has been the experience of every one since, who has turned the pages of his writings and of Boswell's *Life*.

X

ROMANTIC POETS

Till toward the middle of the eighteenth century, Pope set the fashion for English verse. "The public," wrote Joseph Warton in 1746, "has been so much accustomed to didactic poetry alone, and essays on moral subjects, that any work where the imagination is much indulged will perhaps not be relished or regarded." But poets here and there were beginning to find the social themes, the cool, rational tone, and the urbane manner of the fashionable poetry unsatisfying, and were turning to themes in which the imagination could be "indulged."

One such theme they found in the contemplation of nature. It is a mistake to assume, as people fond of cut and dried distinctions sometimes do, that the fashionable poets of the first half of the eighteenth century had no appreciation of the beauties of nature. No one had a better eye for what we now call the picturesque than Pope himself: —

> Here waving groves a chequered scene display,
> And part admit, and part exclude the day . . .
> There, interspersed in lawns and opening glades,
> Thin trees arise that shun each others shades,
> Here in full light the russet plains extend;
> There wrapt in clouds the blueish hills ascend:
> Even the wild heath displays her purple dyes,
> And 'midst the desert fruitful fields arise,
> That crowned with tufted trees and springing corn,
> Like verdant isles the sable waste adorn.
>
> "Windsor Forest"

But it is true that Pope and his kind cared more for human nature, and that they usually saw the natural world as a setting for human life rather than as worth writing about for its own sake. For example, in Pope's "Windsor Forest," such passages as that just quoted form no more than a background — and indeed a rather scanty background — for the historical, the human, associations of the place, and for his moralizings about them.

Probably James Thomson (1700–1748) did more than anyone else to bring back the feeling that nature was worth writing about for its own sake, and that the simple lives and daily tasks of country folk were interesting as part of the picture. Born in Scotland, educated at Edinburgh, Thomson had come to London in his twenty-fifth year to live by his pen. In a poem written in his student days he had professed his hatred of "the clamour of the smoky towns," his love of the "pleasant sounds" and "delightful prospects" of the country,

Through every season of the sliding year.

Now, "for his own amusement," as he wrote to a friend, he devoted himself to "painting nature in her most lugubrious dress, describing Winter as it presents itself." Instead of using the rhymed couplet, he chose to write in blank verse, modeled somewhat on Milton's flowing measure in *Paradise Lost*. "Winter" appeared in 1726. Its success encouraged Thomson to describe with equal fulness the other parts of the year. The completed poem, *The Seasons*, its four parts totaling something more than six thousand lines of blank verse, was published in 1730.

Thomson's description of the approach of winter is a fair example of his manner.

The keener tempests come; and, fuming dun
From all the livid east or piercing north,
Thick clouds ascend, in whose capacious womb
A vapoury deluge lies, to snow congealed.
Heavy they roll their fleecy world along,
And the sky saddens with the gathered storm.
Through the hushed air the whitening shower descends,
At first thin wavering, till at last the flakes
Fall broad and wide and fast, dimming the day
With a continual flow. The cherished fields
Put on their winter robe of purest white;
'T is brightness all, save where the new snow melts
Along the mazy current; low the woods
Bow their hoar head; and ere the languid sun
Faint from the west emits his evening ray,
Earth's universal face, deep-hid and chill,
Is one wild dazzling waste, that buries wide
The works of man. Drooping, the labourer-ox
Stands covered o'er with snow, and then demands
The fruit of all his toil. The fowls of heaven,
Tamed by the cruel season, crowd around
The winnowing store, and claim the little boon
Which Providence assigns them. One alone,
The redbreast, sacred to the household gods,
Wisely regardful of th' embroiling sky
In joyless fields and thorny thickets leaves
His shivering mates, and pays to trusted man
His annual visit: Half-afraid, he first
Against the window beats, then brisk alights
On the warm hearth; then, hopping o'er the floor,
Eyes all the smiling family askance,
And pecks, and starts, and wonders where he is,
Till, more familiar grown, the table-crumbs
Attract his slender feet. The foodless wilds
Pour forth their brown inhabitants. The hare,
Though timorous of heart and hard beset

By death in various forms — dark snares, and dogs,
And more unpitying men, — the garden seeks,
Urged on by fearless want. The bleating kine
Eye the black heaven, and next the glistening earth,
With looks of dumb despair; then, sad dispersed,
Dig for the withered herb through heaps of snow.

And thus, in "Summer," he describes the shearing of the
sheep:

At last, of snowy white, the gathered flocks
Are in the wattled pen innumerous pressed,
Head above head; and, ranged in lusty rows,
The shepherds sit and whet the sounding shears.
The housewife waits to roll her fleecy stores,
With all her gay-drest maids attending round:
One, chief, in gracious dignity enthroned,
Shines o'er the rest, the pastoral queen, and rays
Her smiles, sweet-beaming, on her shepherd-king,
While the glad circle round them yield their souls
To festive mirth and wit that knows no gall.
Meantime their joyous task goes on apace:
Some, mingling, stir the melted tar, and some
Deep on the new-shorn vagrant's heaving side
To stamp his master's cipher ready stand;
Others the unwilling wether drag along;
And, glorying in his might, the sturdy boy
Holds by the twisted horns th' indignant ram.
Behold where, bound and of its robe bereft
By needy man, that all-depending lord,
How meek, how patient the mild creature lies!
What softness in its melancholy face,
What dumb complaining innocence, appears!
Fear not, ye gentle tribes, 't is not the knife
Of horrid slaughter that is o'er you waved;
No, 't is the tender swain's well-guided shears,

Who having now, to pay his annual care,
Borrowed your fleece, to you a cumbrous load,
Will send you bounding to your hills again.

Thomson's interest in nature was genuine and deep.

For me, when I forget the darling theme,
Whether the blossom blows, the summer-ray
Russets the plain, inspiring Autumn gleams,
Or Winter rises in the blackening east,
Be my tongue mute — my fancy paint no more,
And dead to joy, forget my heart to beat.

But it is only in the freshness of the material and the minute detail with which it is described that *The Seasons* stands apart from the main current of early eighteenth-century poetry. In spite of the shift from couplet to blank verse, Thomson's way of expressing himself is not unlike Pope's. Compare, for example, this passage from one of Pope's *Pastorals:*

Soon as the flocks shook off the nightly dews,
Two swains, whom Love kept wakeful, and the muse,
Poured o'er the whitening vale their fleecy care,
Fresh as the morn and as the season fair:
The dawn now blushing on the mountain's side
Thus Daphnis spoke, and Strephon thus replied.

Daphnis

Hear how the birds, on every blooming spray
With joyous music wake the dawning day!
Why sit we mute, when early linnets sing,
When warbling Philomel salutes the spring?
Why sit we sad, when Phosphor shines so clear,
And lavish nature paints the purple year?

Strephon

Sing then, and Damon shall attend the strain,
While yon' slow oxen turn the furrowed plain,
Here the bright crocus and blue violet glow,
Here western winds on breathing roses blow.

Thomson's "tender swain" wielding the "well-guided shears," his "pastoral queen" "raying her smiles" upon her "shepherd King," the housewife's "fleecy stores," the regular pairing of adjective and noun so that every thing-word should be properly graced with an epithet, are in the accepted manner. Thomson's method, too, and his attitude of mind are not greatly unlike Pope's. Thomson was systematic, orderly. He arranged his picture, catalogued its beauties, presented it objectively. He could even moralize about it on occasion just as Pope might have done:

Ye generous Britons, venerate the plough!
And o'er your hills and long withdrawing vales
Let Autumn spread his treasures to the sun,
Luxuriant and unbounded! As the sea,
Far through his azure turbulent domain
Your empire owns, and from a thousand shores
Wafts all the pomp of life into your ports,
So with superior boon may your rich soil,
Exuberant, Nature's better blessings pour
O'er every land, the naked nations clothe,
And be the exhaustless granary of a world!

The Seasons was a guidepost pointing the way to nature as a theme for poetry; but it is not, in the strict sense of the word, a "romantic" poem. The words quoted at the beginning of this chapter from Joseph Warton's Preface to his little volume of *Odes* reflect a more definite break with the kind of poetry then in fashion. "The author of these

pieces," Warton continues, "is convinced that the fashion
of moralizing in verse has been carried too far, and as he
looks upon invention and imagination to be the chief faculties of a poet, so he will be happy if the following Odes
may be looked upon as an attempt to bring back poetry
into its right channel."

The romanticist was not content to see nature as a
spectacle, to describe it objectively, as Thomson had described it. The romanticist *felt* its beauties and wanted
to put his emotions into words. Warton entitles one of
his poems "The Enthusiast: or the Lover of Nature:"—

> O taste corrupt! that luxury and pomp
> In specious names of polished manners veiled,
> Should proudly banish Nature's simple charms!
> All-beauteous Nature! by thy boundless charms
> Oppressed, O where shall I begin thy praise,
> Where turn th' ecstatic eye, how ease my breast
> That pants with wild astonishment and love!

In his "Ode to Fancy," he invokes that "warm, enthusiastic maid" to

> Animate some chosen swain,
> Who, filled with unexhausted fire,
> May boldly smite the sounding lyre . . .
> O deign t'attend his evening walk,
> With him in groves and grottos talk,
> Teach him to scorn with frigid art
> Feebly to touch th' unraptured heart;
> Like lightning let his mighty verse
> The bosom's inmost foldings pierce,
> With native beauties win applause,
> Beyond cold critics' studied laws.

And the romanticist, in Warton's phrase, wished to *indulge* his imagination. He let his fancy play upon the

beauties and wonders of nature, found magic in it, felt it
as the abode of mysterious presences, had a sense of communion with nature as if it too were sentient. Night cast
its spell for him, moldering churchyards and ivy-clad
ruins lured him, he brooded and dreamed. Thomas Warton, Joseph's brother, sounds a characteristic note in his
Pleasures of Melancholy. (He was seventeen when he
wrote it. Romanticism, in its beginnings, was the mood
of youth):

> Beneath yon ruined abbey's moss-grown piles
> Oft let me sit, at twilight hour of eve,
> Where through some western window the pale moon
> Pours her long-levelled rule of streaming light,
> While sullen, sacred silence reigns around,
> Save the lone screech-owl's note, who builds his bow'r
> Amid the mould'ring caverns dark and damp,
> Or the calm breeze that rustles in the leaves
> Of flaunting ivy, that with mantle green
> Invests some wasted tow'r. Or let me tread
> Its neighb'ring walk of pines, where mused of old
> The cloistered brothers: through the gloomy void
> That far extends beneath their ample arch
> As on I pace, religious horror wraps
> My soul in dread repose. But when the world
> Is clad in midnight's raven-coloured robe,
> 'Mid hollow charnel let me watch the flame
> Of taper dim, shedding a livid glare
> O'er the wan heaps, while airy voices talk
> Along the glimm'ring walls, or ghostly shape,
> At distance seen, invites with beck'ning hand
> My lonesome steps through the far-winding vaults.
> Nor undelightful is the solemn noon
> Of night, when, haply wakeful, from my couch
> I start: lo, all is motionless around!

Roars not the rushing wind; the sons of men
And every beast in mute oblivion lie;
All Nature's hushed in silence and in sleep:
O then how fearful is it to reflect
That through the still globe's awful solitude
No being wakes but me! till stealing sleep
My drooping temples bathes in opiate dews.
Nor then let dreams, of wanton folly born,
My senses lead through flow'ry paths of joy:
But let the sacred genius of the night
Such mystic visions send as Spenser saw
When through bewild'ring Fancy's magic maze,
To the fell house of Busyrane, he led
Th' unshaken Britomart; or Milton knew,
When in abstracted thought he first conceived
All heav'n in tumult, and the seraphim
Come tow'ring, armed in adamant and gold.

Spenser and Milton — these, rather than Pope and his
kind, were the poets to imitate; Milton, not only when he

> First conceived
> All heaven in tumult,

but also, and even more, in the early romantic mood of
L'Allegro and *Il Penseroso*, when his fancy was caught by

> Such sights as youthful poets dream
> On summer eves by haunted stream,

or when, under the spell of "divinest Melancholy" he
walked, unseen,

> On the dry smooth-shaven green
> To behold the wandring moon
> Riding near her highest noon;

Spenser, not only luring these eighteenth-century romanticists with his "mystic visions," but tempting them as well

with the soft lingering music of his stanzas, and his antique style. One of the best of these imitations of Spenser was written by the author of *The Seasons*. Thomson's *Castle of Indolence* appeared in 1748 — just a year after Warton's *Pleasures of Melancholy*. It is full of such mystic visions as Spenser had loved. Here is Thomson's picture of the land in which the wizard Indolence built the castle to which he lured lovers of slothful ease. You will be interested in comparing it with the stanzas from *The Faerie Queene*, quoted on page 149.

> A pleasing land of drowsy-hed it was:
> Of dreams that wave before the half-shut eye;
> And of gay castles in the clouds that pass,
> Forever flushing round a summer sky,
> There eke the soft delights that witchingly
> Instil a wanton sweetness through the breast,
> And the calm pleasures, always hovered nigh;
> But whate'er smacked of noyance or unrest
> Was far, far off expelled from this delicious nest.

Thomson and the Wartons are interesting as pioneers, but they are not great poets. Among the romantically minded group represented in that popular mid-eighteenth century anthology of contemporary verse known as "Dodsley's Miscellany,"[1] only two — William Collins (1721-1759) and Thomas Gray (1716–1771) — have won lasting fame. Like Joseph Warton and the other "enthusiasts," Collins and Gray found the form of verse known as the

---

[1] *A Collection of Poems in Six Volumes by Several Hands, 1748–1758.* The poems of Pope and his kind still bulk large in Dodsley's pages; but along with them are poems by John Dyer, Thomson, William Mason, Mark Akenside, William Shenstone, Gray, Collins, and the two Wartons. If you will turn the pages of any considerable modern collection of poetry of this period (for example, the *Oxford Book of Eighteenth Century Verse*), you will be struck by the contrast between the mood and interests of these poets and the mood and interests of the school of Pope.

"Ode"[1] especially suited to their mood. In the slender sheaf of Collins's *Odes* which appeared in 1746, when the author was only twenty-five years old, are two which are among the most perfect poems in English literature. One is the "Ode to Evening," with its delicate imagery, and its harmonies so attuned that the ear does not note the absence of rhyme:

If aught of oaten stop or pastoral song
May hope, chaste Eve, to soothe thy modest ear,
    Like thy own solemn springs,
    Thy springs and dying gales,

O nymph reserved, while now the bright-haired sun
Sits in yon western tent, whose cloudy skirts,
    With brede ethereal wove,
    O'erhang his wavy bed:

Now air is hushed, save where the weak-eyed bat,
With short, shrill shriek, flits by on leathern wing;
    Or where the beetle winds
    His small but sullen horn,

As oft he rises 'midst the twilight path,
Against the pilgrim borne in heedless hum:
    Now teach me, maid composed,
    To breathe some softened strain,

Whose numbers, stealing through thy dark'ning vale,
May not unseemly with its stillness suit,
    As, musing slow, I hail
    Thy genial loved return!

[1] "A lyric poem expressive of exalted or enthusiastic emotion, especially one of complex or irregular metrical form; originally and strictly, such a composition intended to be sung." *Century Dictionary*.

For when thy folding-star, arising, shows
His paly circlet, as his warning lamp
    The fragrant Hours, and elves
    Who slept in flow'rs the day,

And many a nymph who wreathes her brows with sedge
And sheds the fresh'ning dew, and, lovelier still,
    The pensive Pleasures sweet,
    Prepare thy shadowy car.

Then lead, calm vot'ress, where some sheety lake
Cheers the lone heath, or some time-hallowed pile
    Or upland fallows grey
    Reflect its last cool gleam.

But when chill blust'ring winds or driving rain
Forbid my willing feet, be mine the hut
    That from the mountain's side
    Views wilds, and swelling floods,

And hamlets brown, and dim-discovered spires,
And hears their simple bell, and marks o'er all
    Thy dewy fingers draw
    The gradual dusky veil.

While Spring shall pour his show'rs, as oft he wont,
And bathe thy breathing tresses, meekest Eve;
    While Summer loves to sport
    Beneath thy ling'ring light;

While sallow Autumn fills thy lap with leaves;
Or Winter, yelling through the troublous air,
    Affrights thy shrinking train,
    And rudely rends thy robes;

So long, sure-found beneath the sylvan shed,
Shall Fancy, Friendship, Science, rose-lipped Health,
   Thy gentlest influence own,
   And hymn thy fav'rite name!

The other is the Ode "Written in the Beginning of the Year 1746." Few poems are so widely known. For these twelve lines of grave and tender beauty, composed in commemoration of the men who gave their lives at Fontenoy in 1745, have been freshly spread before the eyes of our own generation on many a memorial tablet to that greater host who also gave their lives on Flanders fields. No commemorative verse inspired by the late war had been found worthy to displace it. There is a rightness, an exquisite fitness in every word of it, that makes one think no poem ever will.

> How sleep the brave who sink to rest
> By all their country's wishes blest!
> When Spring, with dewy fingers cold,
> Returns to deck their hallowed mould,
> She there shall dress a sweeter sod
> Than Fancy's feet have ever trod.
>
> By fairy hands their knell is wrung,
> By forms unseen their dirge is sung;
> There Honour comes, a pilgrim grey,
> To bless the turf that wraps their clay;
> And Freedom shall awhile repair,
> To dwell a weeping hermit there!

Collins, as Dr. Johnson said, "loved fairies, genii, giants, and monsters and delighted to rove through the meanders of enchantment."

These are the themes of simple, sure effect,

he exclaims in the "Ode on the Popular Superstitions of the Highlands of Scotland."

'Tis Fancy's land to which thou[1] sett'st thy feet,
Where still, 'tis said, the fairy people meet
Beneath each birken shade on mead or hill . . .
Such airy beings awe th' untutored swain:
Nor thou, though learn'd, his homelier thoughts neglect,
Let thy sweet Muse the rural faith sustain:
These are the themes of simple, sure effect,
That add new conquests to her boundless reign,
And fill, with double force, her heart-commanding strain. . .
Unbounded is thy range; with varied style
Thy Muse may, like those feath'ry tribes which spring
From their rude rocks, extend her skirting wing
Round the moist marge of each cold Hebrid isle, . . .

Nor needst thou blush that such false themes engage
Thy gentle mind, of fairer stores possest:
For not alone they touch the village breast,
But filled in elder time th' historic page.
There Shakespeare's self, with ev'ry garland crowned,
In musing hour, his wayward sisters found,
And with their terrors drest the magic scene;
From them he sung, when, mid his bold design,
Before the Scot afflicted and aghast,
The shadowy Kings of Banquo's fated line
Through the dark cave in gleamy pageant passed.
Proceed, nor quit the tales which, simply told,
Could once so well my answering bosom pierce.
Proceed, in forceful sounds and colors bold,
The native legends of thy land rehearse:
To such adapt thy lyre and suit thy powerful verse.

[1] The Ode is addressed to the poet and dramatist, John Home, then returning to his native Scotland.

Collins's genius flashed and died. His mind broke down before he reached his thirtieth year. Gray's was a cooler spirit. He spent his life in leisured seclusion at Cambridge, writing slowly and endlessly revising. He lived to a ripe age; but all of his published verse makes only a slender volume.

Gray had not Collins's energy and daring; nor was he, like Collins, from the outset whole-heartedly romantic. Not Pope himself was more classical in style, more coolly rational, more given to moralizing, than Gray in his early poems.

> Beside some water's rushy brink
> With me the Muse shall sit and think
>   (At ease reclined in rustic state)
> How vain the ardour of the crowd,
> How low, how little are the proud,
>   How indigent the great.

That is (of all places!) from an "Ode to Spring" which Gray wrote when he too was in his twenties. His much over-rated "Ode on a Distant Prospect of Eton College," with its melancholy musings on the destiny of Eton youths who

>   chase the rolling circle's speed
> Or urge the flying ball,

and its closing words that have become a proverb —

>   where ignorance is bliss
> 'Tis folly to be wise —

was written at twenty-six. Between the pure genius of Collins's youthful poems and the carefully filed phrases of Gray's, the contrast seems obvious; but Gray's were popular in the 1750's, and the 1746 volume of Collins's *Odes* had so little sale that the author, in a fit of despair,

destroyed all the unsold copies.   While Dodsley's pages bear
witness that the romantic mood was beginning to get a
hearing, popular taste still preferred clearness and elegance
and sententious phrases to dreams and raptures.

It was the *Elegy Written in a Country Churchyard* which
established Gray's fame.   The poem enjoyed an immediate
and immense popularity.[1]   The moralizing mood, the
chiseled perfection of phrase, the stately march of the
verse —

> Th' applause of listening senates to command,
> The threats of pain and ruin to despise,
> To scatter plenty o'er a smiling land,
> And read their history in a nation's eyes,
>
> Their lot forbade —

were in the great tradition.   But with these qualities were
others which belonged to the newly developing romantic
mood.   Meditation in churchyards was a favorite exercise of
poets who wanted to get as far away as possible from Pope's
polite world.   Notable examples are Parnell's "Night-
Piece on Death" (1721) —

> a place of graves
> Whose wall the silent water laves . . .
> There pass, with melancholy state,
> By all the solemn heaps of Fate,
> And think, as softly-sad you tread
> Above the venerable dead,
> "Time was, like thee they life possessed,
> And time shall be that thou shalt rest" —

[1] Gray notes that the *Elegy* was "published in February 1751 by Dodsley
and went through four editions in two months; and afterwards a fifth, sixth,
seventh and eighth, ninth and tenth and eleventh.   Printed also with Mr.
Bentley's designs, of which there is a second edition and again by Dodsley
in his Miscellany, volume 7th, and in a Scotch collection called the Union.
Translated into Latin by Christopher Anstey, Esq., and the Reverend Mr.
Roberts and published in 1762; and again the same year by Robert
Lloyd, M.A."

and Blair's "The Grave" (composed about 1735; printed
1743) —

> the task be mine
> To paint the gloomy horrors of the tomb,
> Th' appointed place of rendezvous.

And we have not forgotten Warton's

> When the world
> Is clad in midnight's raven-coloured robe,
> 'Mid hollow charnel let me watch the flame
> Of taper dim, shedding a livid glare
> O'er the wan heaps.

The darkness, the "solemn stillness" which broods over
Gray's meditations, the ivy-mantled tower and moping owl,
the lonely youth, marked by melancholy for her own,
are typical romantic touches.

But how we classify the *Elegy* doesn't really matter. It
has outlasted its time. There are critics who deny it a
place among great poems on the ground that it is merely
a collection of commonplaces felicitously phrased; that it
does no more than express the thoughts that occur to all
of us when we are "mindful of the unhonored dead." It is
true that Gray does not startle or exalt. There is nothing
in his meditations on the mystery of life and death to stir
our pulses as does Shelley's

> Life, like a dome of many-coloured glass,
> Stains the white radiance of Eternity.

No thought of Gray's, suggested by these futile and forgotten lives, has the grim magnificence of Shakespeare's

> And all our yesterdays have lighted fools
> The way to dusty death.

And yet even Dr. Johnson, who disliked most of Gray's poems, and did not hesitate to say that their author "had a kind of strutting dignity, and was tall by walking on tiptoe"—even Dr. Johnson concurred with "the common sense of readers uncorrupted with literary prejudices" in thinking highly of the *Elegy*. "Had Gray written often thus, it had been vain to blame, and useless to praise him." Johnson's comment on part of the poem is worth wider application: "The four stanzas beginning *Yet even these bones* [lines 77 to 92], are to me original: I have never seen the notions in any other place; yet he that reads them here, persuades himself that he has always felt them." That is the reason, or one of the reasons, for the undiminished hold of the *Elegy* upon generation after generation of readers. If it has not the exaltation of Shelley or the profundity and power of Shakespeare, or even the "grey and silver" beauty of Collins, its genuineness of feeling and beautiful clearness and simplicity of style make Gray's thoughts our thoughts. We are possessed by them and possess them — and persuade ourselves that we have always felt them.

So easily and surely right seems every word, so unforced the rhymes, so natural the transition from thought to thought, that it is as if the poem had flowed from Gray's pen at a sitting; but it was probably begun in 1742 and finished in 1750; many stanzas were discarded, some of them as admirable as any which Gray retained; the lines and phrases that seem to us spontaneously right became so only through much revision. Few poems as short have given so many familiar quotations to the language. In those one hundred and twenty-eight lines, you will come upon not less than fifteen lines or parts of lines that have become stock phrases. Some indeed have grown stale from overmuch quotation. But if rather too many flowers since Gray's time have been born to blush unseen, ourselves are to blame — not Gray. It is at any rate a curious trick of fate that this scholarly recluse, with his almost morbid dread of public contacts, should have written a poem which has so woven itself into the heart and thought of the world at large.

After writing the *Elegy* Gray turned to purely romantic themes. Norse mythology furnished him with subjects for "The Fatal Sisters" and "The Descent of Odin"; Welsh legends, and Evan Evans's *Specimens of the Poetry of the Ancient Welsh Bards* provided material for "The Bard," "The Triumphs of Owen," "The Death of Hoel," "Caradoc" and "Conan." The most ambitious of these poems is "The Bard: A Pindaric Ode,"[1] based on the legend that King Edward I of England, when he conquered Wales, ordered that all of the Bards (the singers of heroic deeds) be put to death. The Bard of Gray's poem is the last survivor — a typically romantic figure, as, from his mountain height, he calls down vengeance upon the royal invader and his descendants:—

> On a rock whose haughty brow
> Frowns o'er old Conway's foaming flood,
> Robed in the sable garb of woe,
> With haggard eyes the Poet stood
> (Loose his beard and hoary hair
> Streamed, like a meteor, to the troubled air),

---

[1] That is, an imitation of the Odes in which the Greek poet, Pindar, celebrated the victories in the Olympic games. Interest in this form had been stimulated afresh by the appearance in 1749 of Gilbert West's metrical translation of the Odes of Pindar. Pindar's Odes were constructed according to a very complex, but precise and regular pattern. Gray's two Pindarics, "The Bard" and "The Progress of Poesy," are thus constructed. Many of the so-called Pindaric Odes written in the seventeenth and eighteenth centuries are merely "free" lyrical poems, varying more or less haphazardly in line-length and rhythm and rhyme-scheme.

And with a master's hand and prophet's fire,
Struck the deep sorrows of his lyre.
"Hark, how each giant oak, and desert cave
Sighs to the torrent's awful voice beneath!
O'er thee, O King! their hundred arms they wave,
Revenge on thee in hoarser murmurs breathe;
Vocal no more, since Cambria's fatal day,
To high-born Hoel's harp, or soft Llewellyn's lay.

   Cold is Cadwallo's tongue,
That hushed the stormy main:
Brave Urien sleeps upon his craggy bed;
Mountains, ye mourn in vain
Modred, whose magic song
Made huge Plinlimmon bow his cloud-topped head.
On dreary Arvon's shore they lie,
Smeared with gore and ghastly pale:
Far, far aloof th' affrighted ravens sail;
The famished eagle screams and passes by.
Dear lost companions of my tuneful art,
Dear as the light that visits these sad eyes,
Dear as the ruddy drops that warm my heart,
Ye died amidst your dying country's cries —

   No more I weep.   They do not sleep.
On yonder cliffs, a griesly band
I see them sit; they linger yet,
Avengers of their native land:
With me in dreadful harmony they join,
And weave with bloody hands the tissue of thy line.

"The Bard" and its companion Pindaric, "The Progress of Poesy," have been highly praised. They are spirited and move swiftly to an effective climax. But somehow, with all their apparent fire, they leave one a little cold. In reading them, it is possible to stop at any moment to

think how well-made and well-phrased they are. They are
striking experiments rather than great poems.

But if they lack the final perfection of the *Elegy*, these
later Odes of Gray's are interesting as examples of what
the romantic poets were thinking about. The Norse legends sprang from a people's childhood. "The Bard" describes a happening of the thirteenth century. Especially
to this remote past the thoughts of the romanticists turned.
The medieval cathedrals, which the previous generation,
contrasting them with the pure and regular lines of classical architecture, had looked upon as little better than
monstrosities, and which had moved Addison to marvel
over "the prodigious pains and expense that our forefathers have been at in these barbarous buildings," began
once more to be admired. "Gothic architecture[1] became
a fad. We remember Warton's lines —

> Beneath yon ruined abbey's moss-grown piles
> Oft let me sit, at twilight hour of eve,
> Where through some western window the pale moon
> Pours her long-levelled rule of streaming light.

Sham ruins (towers, pointed windows, disintegrating walls)
were set up at the ends of vistas in gentlemen's gardens.
The poet, William Mason, in his *English Garden*, even advocated erecting farm buildings "in castle semblance":

[1] That is, the form of buildings erected by the "Goths" or northern invaders, during the centuries between the decline of Roman architecture and
the revival of it in the Renaissance. The literature of the Middle Ages was
likewise "Gothic."   English classicists of the early eighteenth century
applied the word to anything that offended their classical taste. Says Addison: "Poets who want this strength of genius to give that majestic simplicity
to nature, which we so much admire in the works of the ancients, are forced
to hunt after foreign ornaments. . . . I look upon these writers as Goths in
poetry, who, like those in architecture, not being able to come up to the
beautiful simplicity of the old Greeks and Romans, have endeavored to supply
its place with all the extravagancies of an irregular fancy."

Some tower rotund
Shall to the pigeons and their callow young
Safe roost afford, and every buttress broad
Whose proud projection seems a mass of stone
Give space to stall the heifer and the steed.

Horace Walpole, son of the great statesman Sir Robert Walpole, built for himself a Gothic castle on Strawberry Hill, adorned the interior with suits of medieval armor, and started a whole school of "Gothic" novelists, by writing a romance *The Castle of Otranto: a Gothic Story*, full of specters, mysterious subterranean passages, and violent deaths.

And in the face of time-honored tradition, the romanticists ventured to think that "Gothic" literature was better than classical literature. "Much has been said, and with great truth," wrote Richard Hurd in his *Letters on Chivalry*, *1762*, "of the felicity of Homer's age, for poetical manners. But as Homer was a citizen of the world, when he had seen in Greece, on the one hand, the manners he has described, could he, on the other hand, have seen in the west the manners of the feudal ages, I make no doubt but he would certainly have preferred the latter. And the grounds of this preference would, I suppose, have been the improved gallantry of the feudal times; and the superior solemnity of their superstitions. . . .

"On the whole, though the spirit, passions, rapine, and violence of the two sets of manners were equal, yet there was a dignity, a magnificence, a variety in the feudal, which the other wanted.

"The current popular tales of elves and fairies were even fitter to take the credulous mind, and charm it into a willing admiration of the specious miracles which wayward fancy delights in, than those of the old traditionary rabble of pagan divinities. And then, for the more solemn fancies of witchcraft and incantation, the horrors of the Gothic were above measure striking and terrible. The mummeries of the pagan priests were childish, but the Gothic enchanters shook and alarmed all nature."[1]

This new appetite for the literature of the "Gothic" past grew by what it fed on. Some of the food was spurious —"made up" to satisfy the demand. Most curious and appealing is the story of the youthful forger, Chatterton. A poor and uneducated (or rather self-educated) Bristol boy, Chatterton spent such time as he could spare from earning his daily bread in poring over old folios and the tattered and faded manuscript records in the muniment-room of the Church of which his uncle was sexton. Surrounded by ancient monuments, among them those to the Canynges, father, son, and grandson, rich merchants and mayors of Bristol in the fourteenth and fifteenth centuries, whose money built the church, Chatterton lived wholly in the past. He imagined Master William Canynge as the center of a literary circle and as the patron of poets. Using a vocabulary partly gleaned from old books and manuscripts, partly made up according to his own notions, Chatterton (then in his fourteenth year) began a series of poems, purporting to be by a member of this circle — "Thomas Rowley, priest of St. John's in the city of Bristol." After vain efforts (by correspondence) to interest Dodsley

---

[1] Hurd cites Prospero's "rough magic" in the *Tempest* —

> The strong-based promotory
> Have I made shake, and by the spurs plucked up
> The pine and cedar; graves at my command
> Have waked their sleepers.

Although Shakespeare and Spenser were products of the Renaissance, their free play of fancy, and indifference to classical rules, and their choice of subject matter, made them the great stand-bys of the lovers of "Gothic Literature."

and Horace Walpole in his "discovery" of these "ancient manuscripts," Chatterton left Bristol and established himself in a London garret. A few of his poems were accepted by London magazines but not paid for. On the verge of starvation, and too proud to ask for help, the eighteen-year-old boy committed suicide.

The closing stanzas of "An Excelente Balade of Charitie" will give you an inkling of the vividness and vigor of Chatterton's style, and of his would-be archaic vocabulary. The pilgrim meets the Abbot of St. Godwins:

An almes, sir prieste! the droppynge pilgrim saide,
O! let me waite within your covente dore,
Till the sunne sheneth hie above our heade,
And the loude tempeste of the aire is oer;
Helpless and ould am I, alas! and poor;
No house, ne friend, ne moneie in my pouche;
All yatte I call my owne is this my silver crouche.

Varlet, replyed the Abbattee, cease your dinne,
This is no season almes and prayers to give;
Mie porter never lets a faitour in;
None touch mie rynge who not in honour live.
And now the sonne with the black clouds did stryve,
And shettynge on the grounde his glairie raie,
The abbatte spurrde his steede, and eftsoones roadde awaie.

Once moe the skie was blacke, the thounder rolde;
Faste reynenge oer the plaine a prieste was seen;
Ne dighte full proude, ne buttoned up in golde;
His cope and jape were graie, and eke were clene;
A Limitour he was of order seene;
And from the pathwaie side then turnèd hee
Where the pore almer laie binethe the holmen tree.

An almes, sir priest! the droppynge pilgrim sayde,
For sweete Seyncte Marie and your order sake.

The Limitour then loosen'd his pouche threade,
And did thereoute a groate of silver take;
The mister pilgrim dyd for halline shake.
Here take this silver, it maie eathe thie care;
We are Goddes stewards all, nete of our owne we bare.

But ah! unhailie pilgrim, lerne of me,
Scathe anie give a rentrolle to their Lorde.
Here take my semecope, thou arte bare, I see;
'Tis thyne; the Seynctes will give me mie rewarde.
He left the pilgrim, and his waie aborde.
Virgynne and hallie Seyncte, who sitte yn gloure,
Or give the mittee will, or give the gode man power!

Few were deceived by the Rowley poems, when they found their way into print seven years after Chatterton's death; but the public were quick to realize the originality of his genius, and the completeness with which he had absorbed the atmosphere of the time to which he had pretended that the poems belonged. His work is uneven and — naturally — immature. His sham-archaic words make hard reading. But here and there in the Rowley poems and in his *Miscellanies*, the reader is rewarded with passages of extraordinary intensity and lyric beauty.[1] He was a genuinely creative poet. He bade fair to become a great one. Certainly the great romantic poets of later times have counted of their company,

> that lone spirit who could proudly sing
> His youth away, and die.

Wordsworth paid tribute to

> the marvellous Boy,
> The sleepless Soul that perished in his pride.

[1] Try the *Mynstrelles Songe* from *Aella*, and *The Dethe of Syr Charles Bawdin*.

Keats dedicated his first long poem, "Endymion," "with bowed mind, to the memory of the most English of poets except Shakespeare, Thomas Chatterton." Shelley numbered him, with Keats and Sir Philip Sidney, among

> The inheritors of unfulfilled renown.

Coleridge honored

> the wondrous boy,
> An amaranth, which earth seemed scarce to own,
> Blooming 'mid poverty's drear wintry waste.

But, for the moment, our interest in Chatterton is as one of those who responded to the craving of his time for things out of the remote past. Another who fed this appetite — and with food almost as dubious — was the Scotchman, James Macpherson. In 1762, Macpherson excited Londoners with an alleged "translation" of a long narrative poem supposed to have been written about 250 A.D. by a Gaelic[1] poet, Ossian, the son of Fingal. Just how much of it Macpherson made up himself, and how much he pieced together from old Gaelic song and story, has never been settled. Dr. Johnson called Macpherson an impostor, and when asked whether he thought any man of a modern age could have written such poems, replied: "Yes, Sir, many men, many women and many children. . . . A man might write such stuff forever, if he would abandon his mind to it." But Ossian's swelling periods enthralled the romantics —

"U-thorno, hill of storms, I behold my race on thy side. Fingal is bending in night over Duth-Marino's tomb. Near him are the steps of his heroes, hunters of the boar. By Turthor's stream the host of Lochlin is deep in shades. The wrathful Kings stood on

[1] The Gaels were a Celtic race inhabiting the Highlands of Scotland.

two hills: they looked forward from their bossy shields. They
looked forward to the stars of night, red wandering in the west.
Cruthloda bends from high, like a formless meteor in clouds. He
sends abroad the winds, and marks them with his signs."

"I was so struck," wrote Gray, "so *extasié* with the infinite beauty of these translations, that I writ into Scotland to make a thousand enquiries. . . . This man is the
very Daemon of poetry, or he has lighted on a treasure
hid for ages." Not only romantic England but Italy,
Germany and France raved over the "Celtic Homer."
Misty mountain tops and mysterious melancholy became
fashionable. "Whatever men may now think of the Ossianic poems," wrote the poet Wordsworth in the early
nineteenth century, "there cannot be a doubt that these
mountain monotones took the heart of Europe with a new
emotion and prepared it for that passion for mountains
which has since possessed it." Of the romantic poets of
the early nineteenth century, Lord Byron (see pages 439 ff.)
most strongly shows the influence of Ossian. In his 'teens
Byron produced an imitation of Macpherson's lyric prose
— "The Death of Colmar and Orla"— which (in confirma-
tion of Dr. Johnson's theory) is quite as good as anything
in the original; and a fair share of responsibility for the
characteristic Byronic mood —

> Where rose the mountains, there to him were friends . . .
> But in man's dwellings he became a thing
> Restless and worn, and stern and wearisome,
> Drooped as a wild-born falcon with clipt wing
> To whom the boundless air alone were home —

may be laid at the door of James Macpherson.

Not less influential than the Ossianic poems — and far
more wholesome in their influence — were the old Eng-

lish ballads. *Ossian* took the 1760's by surprise. Nothing like it had ever been heard of or dreamed of. But interest in the ballads — the old songs, of warfare and adventure, of loves and hates and spells and grimly ghosts, handed down from father to son throughout the Middle Ages — had been gradually accumulating. Addison started it with an essay in the *Spectator* on the ballad of "Chevy Chase," in which he professed himself "an admirer of this antiquated poem." Only by pointing out its conformity to the rules of the classical epics could Addison justify his liking for a poem of "the common people." "I feared my own judgment would have looked too singular, had not I supported it by the practice and authority of Virgil." Equally apologetic was the anonymous editor of a collection of old ballads published in 1723, who feared that "many will think it ridiculous enough to enter seriously into a dissertation upon ballads," but encouraged himself by the example of "the great Mr. Addison." It required courage; for critics had made fun of Addison for discussing such "old dogrel." But here and there people were beginning to express a liking for the ballads for their own sake, rather than for chance likenesses to the classical epics. In the prologue to one of his plays the dramatist Rowe praised "those venerable ancient song-inditers"—

> Their words no shuffling double-meaning knew.
> Their speech was homely but their hearts were true.
> With rough majestic force they moved the heart,
> And strength and nature made amends for art.

In *The Tea-Table Miscellany* and *The Evergreen,* the Scottish poet, Allan Ramsay, collected ancient — as well as modern — Scottish verse and wrote in his Preface: "I have observed that readers of the best and most exquisite discernment frequently complain of our modern writings, as filled with affected delicacies and studied refinements, which they would gladly exchange for that natural strength of thought and simplicity of style our forefathers practiced."

Gray was as enthusiastic about ballads as about *Ossian*. He happened upon the old Scotch ballad of "Gil Maurice"—

> Gil Maurice was an Earle's son,
> His fame it wexed wide,
> It was nae for his grete riches,
> Nae for his mickle pride;
> But it was for a ladie gay
> That lived on Carron's side —

"It is divine, and as long as from hence to Aston," he wrote in 1757 to his friend Mason. "Have you never seen it? Aristotle's best rules are observed in it in a manner that shows the author never had heard of Aristotle."

These straws show which way the wind was blowing. A few years later, the old ballads came definitely into their own. Young Thomas Percy chanced upon a dirty old folio manuscript on the floor of the house of a friend in Shropshire. The manuscript was "sadly torn," for the maids had been using it to light the fire. On what was left of it, transcribed in an early seventeenth-century hand, were ballads — ballads ranging from fourteenth-century tales of the outlaw, Robin Hood[1], to poems of a much later date. Percy too was in doubt whether poems which were of such "great simplicity" and "seemed to have been merely written for the people," could "in the present state of improved literature be deemed worthy the attention of the public." But he rescued the manuscript and set to work. Friends in London, and correspondents "in Wales,

---

[1] Sloth, in the fourteenth-century poem, *Piers Plowman* (see page 23) says that he knows "rymes of Robyn Hood."

in the wilds of Staffordshire and Derbyshire, in the West
Indies and in Ireland," ferreted out and copied ballads to
add to the collection. Percy was a careless, even unprin-
cipled editor. He did not scruple to "improve" the style
and to supply stanzas of his own to take the place of those
which had been torn off. But most of what he printed
was genuine. The publication in 1765 of *Reliques of Ancient English Poetry* (Percy's *Reliques*, as it is familiarly
known) aroused tremendous interest. Hard-headed Dr.
Johnson, though he "took pains to serve Dr. Percy in
regard to his *Ancient Ballads*," ridiculed Percy's enthusiasm,
and "observed one evening at Miss Reynolds' tea-table
that he could rhyme as well, and as elegantly, in common
narrative and conversation." For instance, says he,

> As with my hat upon my head
> I walked along the Strand,
> I there did meet another man
> With his hat in his hand.

Or, to render such poetry subservient to my own immediate use,

> I therefore pray thee, Renny dear,
> That thou wilt give to me,
> With cream and sugar softened well,
> Another dish of tea.
>
> Nor fear that I, my gentle maid,
> Shall long detain the cup,
> When once unto the bottom I
> Have drunk the liquor up.
>
> Yet hear, alas! this mournful truth,
> Nor hear it with a frown; —
> Thou canst not make the tea so fast
> As I can gulp it down.

Of some of the old ballads this prattle is a fair parody; but many of them have a real story to tell, and tell it with a blunt directness that is extraordinarily dramatic. One has only to recall an example or two to realize what must have been their effect upon readers accustomed to "studied refinements." Take "Sir Patrick Spence" with its whole story from inception to tragic climax compressed into forty-four lines — and almost every line setting the imagination flying —

> The king sits in Dumferling toune,
>   Drinking the blude-reid wine:
> "O whar will I get guid sailor,
>   To sail this schip of mine?"
>
> Up and spak an eldern knicht,
>   Sat at the kings richt kne:
> "Sir Patrick Spence is the best sailor
>   That sails upon the se."
>
> The king has written a braid letter,
>   And signd it wi his hand,
> And sent it to Sir Patrick Spence,
>   Was walking on the sand.
>
> The first line that Sir Patrick red,
>   A loud lauch lauched he;
> The next line that Sir Patrick red,
>   The teir blinded his ee.
>
> "O wha is this has don this deid,
>   This ill deid don to me,
> To send me out this time o' the yeir,
>   To sail upon the se!
>
> "Mak hast, mak haste, my mirry men all,
>   Our guid schip sails the morne:"
> "O say na sae, my master deir,
>   For I feir a deadlie storme.

"Late late yestreen I saw the new moone,
  Wi the auld moone in hir arme,
And I feir, I feir, my deir master,
  That we will cum to harme."

O our Scots nobles were richt laith
  To weet their cork-heild schoone;
Bot lang owre a' the play wer playd,
  Their hats they swam aboone.

O lang, lang may their ladies sit,
  Wi their fans into their hand,
Or eir they se Sir Patrick Spence
  Cum sailing to the land.

O lang, lang may the ladies stand,
  Wi thair gold kems in their hair,
Waiting for thair ain deir lords,
  For they'll se thame na mair.

Haf owre, haf owre to Aberdour,
  It's fiftie fadom deip,
And thair lies guid Sir Patrick Spence,
  Wi the Scots lords at his feit.

Or, if it were a question of romantic love-stories, Percy's readers could turn to such ballads as "Lord Thomas and Fair Annet" (Lord Thomas married his nut-browne bride for her money, but loved fair Annet. Annet came to the wedding):

And whan she cam into the kirk,
  She shimmered like the sun;
The belt that was about her waist
  Was a' wi pearles bedone.

She sat her by the nut-browne bride,
  And her een they wer sae clear,
Lord Thomas he clean forgat the bride,
  Whan Fair Annet drew near.

He had a rose into his hand,
   He gae it kisses three,
And reaching by the nut-browne bride,
   Laid it on Fair Annet's knee.

Up than spak the nut-browne bride,
   She spak wi meikle spite:
"And whair gat ye that rose-water,
   That does mak yee sae white?"

"O I did get the rose-water
   Whair ye wull neir get nane,
For I did get that very rose-water
   Into my mither's wame."

The bride she drew a long bodkin
   Frae out her gay head-gear,
And strake Fair Annet unto the heart,
   That word spak nevir mair.

Lord Thomas he saw Fair Annet wex pale,
   And marvelit what mote bee;
But when he saw her dear heart's blude,
   A' wood-wroth wexéd hee.

He drew his dagger, that was sae sharp,
   That was sae sharp and meet,
And drave it into the nut-browne bride,
   That fell deid at his feit.

"Now stay for me, dear Annet," he sed,
   "Now stay, my dear," he cry'd;
Then strake the dagger untill his heart.
   And fell deid by her side.

Lord Thomas was buried without kirk-wa,
   Fair Annet within the quiere,
And o the tane thair grew a birk,
   The other a bonny briere.

> And ay they grew, and ay they threw,
>   As they wad faine be neare;
> And by this ye may ken right weil
>   They were twa luvers deare.

One influence of the old ballads was toward a greater simplicity and directness in poetical style. The fashion of studied refinements was already waning. The ballads helped to kill it. There is a passage in "An Essay on Poetry" by James Beattie published in 1779, which illustrates this change of taste. Writing on figures of speech, Beattie recalls the movingly simple words in which Desdemona, in Shakespeare's *Othello*, grieves over the loss of her husband's love:

> My mother had a maid called Barbara;
> She was in love, and he she loved proved mad
> And did forsake her. She had a song of "willow";
> An old thing 'twas, but it expressed her fortune,
> And she died singing it.

These lines, the critic amuses himself by rewriting in the earlier eighteenth-century manner. The maid called Barbara becomes

> The nymph Dione, who with pious care,
> My much loved mother, in my vernal years
> Attended.

Shakespeare's "she was in love" is transformed into

> O luckless was the day, when Cupid's dart,
> Shot from a swain's alluring eye
> First thrilled with pleasing pangs her throbbing breast,

and "she had a song of willow; an old thing 'twas," to

> From morn to dewy Eve,
> From Eve till rosy-fingered morn appeared,

In a sad song, a song of ancient days,
Warbling her wild woe to the pitying winds,
She sat; the weeping willow was her theme.

"I hope my young readers are all wiser," Beattie adds, "but I believe there was a time when I should have been tempted to prefer this flashy tinsel to Shakespeare's fine gold."

It is of this influence of the old ballads toward greater simplicity and naturalness in poetry that Wordsworth was thinking, when he wrote in 1815: "I have already stated how much Germany is indebted to the *Reliques;* and for our own country, its poetry has been absolutely redeemed by it. I do not think there is an able writer in verse of the present day who would not be proud to acknowledge his obligations to the *Reliques;* I know that it is so with my friends; and for myself, I am happy in this occasion to make a public avowal of my own."

Aside from this far-reaching influence of the ballads, it is interesting to think of them as preparing the way for the greatest of eighteenth-century lyric poets, the Scottish peasant, Robert Burns. The ballads, it is well to remind ourselves, were not "polite literature." They were folk-songs, originally recited, in singing fashion, among the common folk of the Middle Ages when there was no printed page. They do not seem quite to "belong" in a book. Goldsmith's was the better way, when his "old dairy-maid sang him into tears with 'Johnny Armstrong's Last Good-Night.'" Thus she would begin:

Sum speiks of lords, sum speiks of lairds,
    And siclyke men of hie degrie;
Of a gentleman I sing a sang,
    Sumtyme called Laird of Gilnockie.

The ballads were story-songs — songs out of the hearts of the people. The poetry of the first half of the eighteenth century had been predominantly head poetry — critical, didactic, rather stand-offish and cynical and amused when it had to do with feeling or emotion. But the themes of the old ballads which were now catching the imagination of eighteenth-century readers were "the essential passions of the heart," directly and uncritically represented, story-wise — or, as it might be, presented with no story whatsoever, in pure song —

> O gin my love were yon red rose
>   That grows upon the castle wa',
> And I mysel' a drop of dew,
>   Down on that red rose I would fa'.
> O my love's bonny, bonny, bonny;
>   My love's bonny and fair to see;
> Whene'er I look in her weel-fared face,
>   She looks and smiles again to me.

And they were, in the main, Scottish, rather than English. Allan Ramsay's *Ever Green* (1724) was, as the sub-title says, "A collection of Scots poems, wrote by the ingenious before 1600." In 1725, W. Thomson had published his "*Orpheus Caledonius*, or, a collection of the best Scotch Songs." Most of the ballads in the *Reliques* originated in Scotland or on the border. Four years after the appearance of the *Reliques*, David Herd published his "*Ancient and Modern Scots Songs, Heroic Ballads, etc.*, now first collected into one body from the various Miscellanies wherein they formerly lay dispersed."

In 1765, when Percy published his *Reliques*, Robert Burns was a six-year-old boy, living in a straw-thatched cottage not far from the Town of Ayr. On your map you will find Ayr —

Auld Ayr, wham ne'er a town surpasses
For honest men and bonie lasses —

in the southwestern corner of Scotland, about thirty miles
southwest of Glasgow, on the Firth of Clyde. Burns's father
was a gardener. Burns drew a picture of him in "The
Cotter's Saturday Night"—

The toil-worn Cotter frae his labour goes,
This night his weekly moil is at an end,
Collects his spades, his mattocks, and his hoes,
Hoping the morn in ease and rest to spend,
And weary, o'er the moor, his course does hameward bend.

At length his lonely cot appears in view,
Beneath the shelter of an aged tree;
Th' expectant wee-things, toddlin', stacher through
To meet their Dad, wi' flichterin' noise and glee.
His wee bit ingle, blinkin bonilie
His clean hearth-stane, his thrifty wifie's smile,
The lisping infant prattling on his knee,
Does a' his weary kiaugh and care beguile,
An' makes him quite forget his labour an' his toil.

As a child, Burns listened to ballads from his mother's
lips. Older, he found among the books on the cottage
shelves — for his father was a reading man — a collection
of songs. "I pored over them," said Burns, "driving my
cart, or walking to labour, song by song, verse by verse;
carefully noting the true, tender or sublime, from affectation and fustian. I am convinced I owe to this practice
much of my critic-craft, such as it is."

The family fortunes went from bad to worse, the family
moved from place to place, the father died, the family
established themselves on the little farm of Mossgiel.
Burns was twenty-five when they settled there. He re-

corded in his commonplace book his longing to immortalize the scenery and life of his "dear native country" as other poets had immortalized the scenery and life of other parts of Scotland. "But, alas! I am far unequal to the task, both in native genius and in education. Obscure I am, obscure I must be, though no young poet's nor young soldier's heart ever beat more fondly for fame than mine." The farmhouse of Mossgiel consisted of two rooms and a garret. An early biographer records that when Burns "had returned from his day's work, the poet used to retire to the garret, and seat himself at a small deal table, lighted by a narrow skylight in the roof, to transcribe the verses which he had composed in the fields. His favorite time for composition was at the plough." He got rather close to nature's heart at such times; and his tenderness for all living harmless things — a feeling which became one of the characteristics of the developing romantic mood in English poetry — finds expression in words which every reader of Burns loves.

To a Mouse

On Turning Her Up in Her Nest, with the Plough, November, 1785

Wee, sleekit, cowrin, tim'rous beastie,
O, what a panic's in thy breastie!
Thou need na start awa sae hasty,
    Wi' bickering brattle!
I wad be laith to rin an' chase thee,
    Wi' murdering pattle!

I'm truly sorry man's dominion
Has broken Nature's social union,

An' justifies that ill opinion
    Which makes thee startle
At me, thy poor, earth-born companion,
    An' fellow-mortal!

I doubt na, whyles, but thou may thieve;
What then? poor beastie, thou maun live!
A daimen icker in a thrave
    'S a sma' request;
I'll get a blessin wi' the lave,
    An' never miss't!

Thy wee bit housie, too, in ruin!
Its silly wa's the win's are strewin!
An' naething now to big a new ane,
    O' foggage green!
An' bleak December's win's ensuin,
    Baith snell an' keen!

Thou saw the fields laid bare an' waste,
An' weary winter comin fast,
An' cozie here, beneath the blast,
    Thou thought to dwell —
Till, crash! the cruel coulter passed
    Out thro' thy cell.

That wee bit heap o' leaves an' stibble
Has cost thee monie a weary nibble!
Now thou's turned out, for a' thy trouble,
    But house or hald,
To thole the winter's sleety dribble,
    An craneuch cauld!

But, mousie, thou art no thy lane
In proving foresight may be vain:
The best-laid schemes o' mice an' men
    Gang aft agley,

An' lea'e us naught but grief an' pain
For promised joy!

Still, thou art blest compared wi' me!
The present only toucheth thee:
But och! I backward cast my e'e,
    On prospects drear!
An' forward, tho' I canna see,
    I guess an' fear!

At Mossgiel, where Burns remained from his twenty-fifth to his twenty-ninth year, he did his best work. The fruit of his labors was the *Poems, chiefly in the Scottish Dialect* published at Kilmarnock in 1786. These poems made "the heaven-taught ploughman" known in literary circles in Edinburgh. Thence the fame of them spread to England. Appointment as an exciseman gave Burns a living wage and leisure to continue his writing. He died in 1796, in his thirty-seventh year.

On his songs and short lyrics, and on a number of extraordinarily spirited narrative, descriptive, and satirical poems, his fame rests. The familiar "Cotter's Saturday Night" has already been mentioned. For verve and vividness, and zest in the telling, the story of Tam O'Shanter's ride from Ayr has no match in English poetry. Burns's satires, many of which were leveled against the church-life, and hell-fire-and-damnation theology, of his day, shocked the pious when they first appeared; but in our own times it must be a pretty stolid reader who could fail to relish the rollicking fun, the impish laughter, that pervade them. The spirit of these satires can best be interpreted in Burns's own words — his choice of companions on the way to the "tent-preaching," which he impudently calls the "Holy Fair." Three women there were on the road —

The twa appeared like sisters twin,
  In feature, form and claes;
Their visage withered, lang an' thin,
  An' sour as onie slaes:
The third cam up, hap-step-an'-lowp,
  As light as onie lambie,
An' wi' a curchie low did stoop,
  As soon as e'er she saw me,
      Fu' kind that day.

Wi' bonnet aff, quoth I, "Sweet lass,
  I think ye seem to ken me;
I'm sure I've seen that bonie face,
  But yet I canna' name ye."
Quo' she, an' laughin as she spak,
  An' takes me by the han's,
"Ye, for my sake, hae gi'en the feck
  Of a' the Ten Comman's
      A screed some day.

"My name is Fun — your cronie dear,
  The nearest friend ye hae;
An' this is Superstition here,
  An' that's Hypocrisy.
I'm gaun to Mauchline Holy Fair,
  To spend an hour in daffin:
Gin ye'll go there, yon runkled pair,
  We will get famous laughin
      At them this day."

At the Holy Fair Nanse Tinnock's tavern divides the
allegiance of the congregation for a while:

But now the Lord's ain trumpet touts,
  Till a' the hills are rairin,
And echoes back return the shouts;
  Black Russell[1] is na spairin:

[1] John Russell, minister at Kilmarnock.

His piercin words, like Highlan' swords,
    Divide the joints an' marrow;
His talk o' hell, where devils dwell,
    Our verra sauls does harrow,
        Wi' fright that day.

A vast unbottomed, boundless pit,
    Filled fou o' lowin brunstane,
Whase ragin flame an' scorching heat
    Wad melt the hardest whun-stane!
The half-asleep start up wi' fear,
    And think they hear it roarin,
When presently it does appear
    'Twas but some neebor snorin,
        Asleep that day.

One of the keenest of Burns's satires is "Holy Willie's Prayer," leveled against hypocritical believers in the good old Scotch doctrine of predestination —

O Thou, wha in the Heavens does dwell,
Wha, as it pleases best thysel',
Sends ane to heaven and ten to hell,
    A' for thy glory,
And no for ony guid or ill
    They've done afore thee!

I bless and praise thy matchless might,
Whan thousands thou hast left in night,
That I am here afore thy sight
    For gifts and grace
A burnin' an' a shinin' light
    To a' this place.

Satirical poetry is likely to lose something of its point and sting, as times and manners change. But Burns's lyrics

renew their hold upon the hearts of every passing generation. They are simple unpretentious things. There is no
lack of art in them — Burns's "critic-sense" was highly
developed — but they spring so naturally and flow so
freely from the moment's mood that they seem as artless
as bird-song.

> My love is like a red red rose
>   That's newly sprung in June:
> My love is like the melodie
>   That's sweetly played in tune.
>
> As fair art thou, my bonnie lass,
>   So deep in love am I:
> And I will love thee still, my dear,
>   Till a' the seas gang dry.
>
> Till a' the seas gang dry, my dear,
>   And the rocks melt wi' the sun:
> And I will love thee still, my dear,
>   While the sands o' life shall run.
>
> And fare thee weel, my only love,
>   And fare thee weel a while!
> And I will come again, my love,
>   Tho' it were ten thousand mile.

Burns's genius was a natural flowering from the soil of
Scottish song. In the preface to the Kilmarnock edition,
he records that, in composing, he "often had in his eye"
the songs of Allan Ramsay and Robert Fergusson, "but
rather with a view to kindle at their flame than for servile
imitation." But a host of nameless singers also provided
him with models. He refurbished old songs for James
Johnson's *Scots Musical Museum* and for George Thomson's *Select Collection of Original Scottish Airs*, and by his

genius so recreated old things that they became his own.
He wove old phrases into new patterns. *My love is like a
red, red rose* is typical of this process. In an old ballad,
he found the lines:

> Her cheeks are like the Roses
> That blossom fresh in June,
> O, she's like a new-strung instrument
> That's newly put in tune.

In another, the line

> And the rocks melt with the sun.

In another,

> The seas they shall run dry
> And rocks melt into sands;
> Then I'll love you still, my dear,
> When all those things are done.

And in yet another,

> Fare you well, my own true love,
> And fare you well for a while,
> And I will be sure to return back again,
> If I go ten thousand mile.

You have only to put these, line by line, beside Burns's
song to see how, when he wrote, old phrases were lilting in
his mind; but the song is as truly Burns's own as if not a
phrase of it had existed elsewhere. It is his because these
bits have become a single, a complete, an integral thing,
transformed by his magic touch — though it were but the
alteration of a word — into pure music. In the old phrases,
something is lacking. When Burns has touched them, they
glow.

"Auld Lang Syne," "John Anderson, My Jo," "Ye
Banks and Braes O' Bonnie Doon," "Highland Mary,"

"Scots, wha hae wi' Wallace bled," "O, Wert thou in the Cauld Blast"— these, so diverse in their music and in the nature of their appeal, and all so spontaneous and instinct with life, are among the lasting things which came from Burns's pen.

> Gie me ae spark o' Nature's fire,
> That's a' the learning I desire;
> Then, tho' I drudge thro' dub an' mire
>   At pleugh or cart,
> My Muse, though hamely in attire,
>   May touch the heart.

Three years before Burns's *Poems* were printed in Kilmarnock, a little volume entitled *Poetical Sketches* came from an English press. The author, like Burns, was of humble origin and self-taught. He was destined to live obscurely, to die almost unknown, and, ultimately, to be ranked among the few great lyric poets of the eighteenth century. It would be hard to imagine a more striking contrast than between Burns's lyrics and Blake's — Burns's so hearty and red-blooded, Blake's so other-worldly and dreamlike.

William Blake was the son of a poor shopkeeper of London. The shopkeeper was a follower of the Swedish mystic, Emanuel Swedenborg, who taught that the world was just entering upon a new dispensation — the New Jerusalem which St. John, in prophetic vision, saw "coming down from God out of heaven" (*Rev.* xxi, 2). The little group of disciples who gathered round Swedenborg during his residence in London[1] shared his belief that God now dwelt visibly among them (*Rev.* xxi, 3), and that it was

---

[1] It was in London, in 1788, that the followers of Swedenborg organized the "Society of the New Church signified by the New Jerusalem."

possible to hold converse with angels and the spirits of the dead. In this atmosphere of visions and supernatural presences, William Blake grew up. Bound apprentice to an engraver, he developed a genius for drawing. He earned his living as an engraver, but lived in his visions and tried to express them, both in his verses and in his drawings. When he had finished composing his second group of poems, *Songs of Innocence*, the spirit of his dead brother showed him how to make the book by engraving the songs upon copper plates, and gave him the design for the marginal decorations. St. Joseph, husband of Mary, the mother of Jesus, appeared to him in a vision, to give him the secret of making unfading colors with which to tint the pages of his book.

Blake became as a little child to enter into the Kingdom of poetry. The purest and loveliest of his lyrics in *Songs of Innocence* (1789) and *Songs of Experience* (1794) are not so much works of art as acts of faith — the unspoiled faith of a child to whom it is given

> To see a world in a grain of sand,
> And a heaven in a wild flower;
> Hold infinity in the palm of your hand,
> And eternity in an hour.

They are visions and moods, put into words that are as simple and direct as a child's — and almost as little composed into sentences. They are naïve, and yet curiously charged with significances — significances that grow upon one with every rereading; and running through their short, and sometimes even abrupt, lines is a most delicate and subtle music. Consider, for example, these three little poems, in which the child's wonder and the poet's sense of the significance of life are exquisitely blended:

The Lamb

Little lamb, who made thee?
　Dost thou know who made thee?
Gave thee life, and bid thee feed
By the stream and o'er the mead;
Gave thee clothing of delight,
Softest clothing, woolly, bright;
Gave thee such a tender voice,
Making all the vales rejoice?
　Little lamb, who made thee?
　Dost thou know who made thee?

Little lamb, I'll tell thee;
　Little lamb, I'll tell thee:
He is calléd by thy name,
For He calls Himself a Lamb.
He is meek, and He is mild,
He became a little child,
I a child and thou a lamb,
We are calléd by His name.
　Little lamb, God bless thee!
　Little lamb, God bless thee!

A Dream

Once a dream did weave a shade
O'er my angel-guarded bed,
That an emmet lost its way
Where on grass methought I lay.

Troubled, 'wildered, and forlorn,
Dark, benighted, travel-worn,
Over many a tangled spray,
All heart-broke, I heard her say:

"Oh my children! do they cry,
Do they hear their father sigh?
Now they look abroad to see,
Now return and weep for me."

Pitying I dropped a tear;
But I saw a glow-worm near,
Who replied: "What wailing wight
Calls the watchman of the night?

"I am set to light the ground,
While the beetle goes his round:
Follow now the beetle's hum;
Little wanderer, hie thee home!"

The Tiger

Tiger! tiger! burning bright
In the forests of the night,
What immortal hand or eye
Could frame thy fearful symmetry?

In what distant deeps or skies
Burnt the fire of thine eyes?
On what wings dare he aspire?
What the hand dare seize the fire?

And what shoulder and what art
Could twist the sinews of thy heart?
And when thy heart began to beat,
What dread hand? and what dread feet?

What the hammer? what the chain?
In what furnace was thy brain?
What the anvil? what dread grasp
Dare its deadly terrors clasp?

When the stars threw down their spears,
And watered heaven with their tears,
Did He smile His work to see?
Did He Who made the lamb make thee?

Tiger! tiger! burning bright
In the forests of the night,
What immortal hand or eye
Dare frame thy fearful symmetry?

Blake lived on for nearly forty years after the publication of *Songs of Experience* — for nearly the space of a generation into the changed world of the nineteenth century. He continued to write — strange "Prophetical Books," in which he withdrew himself ever more and more from the realities of life into a world of symbols. He decorated these books with drawings — the stuff of dreams — of mighty angels with vast sweeping pinions. These books are hard, and perhaps not very profitable, reading — and yet in them you will happen upon passages of extraordinary beauty and simplicity.

Thou perceivest the Flowers put forth their precious Odours:
And none can tell how from so small a centre come such sweets; . .
First, ere the morning breaks, joy opens in the flowery bosoms,
Joy even to tears, which the Sun rising dries: first the Wild Thyme
And Meadow-sweet, downy and soft, waving among the reeds,
Light springing on the air lead the sweet Dance: they wake
The Honeysuckle sleeping on the Oak: the flaunting beauty
Revels along upon the wind: the White-thorn lovely May
Opens her many lovely eyes: listening the Rose still sleeps;
None dare to wake her: soon she bursts her crimson-curtained bed,
And comes forth in the majesty of beauty.
                        — From the poem entitled *Milton* (1804).

The illustration contains the following inscriptions:

Canst thou bind the sweet influences of Pleiades or loose the bands of Orion

14

Let there Be

Light

Let there be A

Firmament

Let the Waters be gathered together into one place

& let the Dry Land appear

And God made Two Great Lights

Sun

Moon

Let the Waters bring forth abundantly

Let the Earth bring forth

Cattle & Creeping thing & Beast

When the morning Stars sang together, & all the
Sons of God shouted for joy

W Blake inven & sc

Copyright by R. B. Fleming & Co., London

ONE OF WILLIAM BLAKE'S ILLUSTRATIONS OF THE BOOK OF JOB

The young Elihu and Job and his three friends listen as God "answers Job out of
the whirlwind"

As we look back from this vantage-point of the 1780's we realize how greatly poetry has changed since the early years of the century. The change has consisted chiefly of a letting loose of imagination and feeling. The glamour of the remote past; the fancies and superstitions of simple people living close to nature; the beauty, the grandeur and the magic of nature itself, have rewarded the poet's search for themes in which the imagination could be indulged. And after passing through a period during which poets distrusted emotion and schooled themselves to avoid it, poetry has again become the voice of the heart. It has shifted its ground from *I think* to *I feel*.

There has been a change, too, in the poet's attitude toward human nature. In the late seventeenth and early eighteenth century, poetry was an aristocratic diversion. Lords and lordlings dabbled in it. Fine gentlemen patronized and encouraged aspiring poets. When Pope was beginning to write,

> The courtly Talbot, Somers, Sheffield read;
> Even mitred Rochester would nod the head,
> And St. John's self (great Dryden's friend before)
> With open arms received one poet more.

The poets caught the tone of their patrons, looked at life through their eyes. The work-a-day world, human nature in the rough, was a curious and entertaining spectacle. If, for example, you will turn the pages of the fashionable Mr. Gay's[1] *Trivia; or the Art of Walking the Streets of London* (1716), you will enjoy, with the polite readers of Gay's own day, his picture of the chairmen lounging round the tavern-door, the draggled damsel bearing her "fishy traffic"

---

[1] John Gay's name is still known to theater-goers through his *Beggar's Opera* (1728) which reappears every now and then upon the modern stage. In this tuneful burlesque, highwaymen and pickpockets dance and sing their way through Newgate prison.

from Billingsgate, the little chimney-sweeper "marking with sooty stains the heedless throng," the bully "keeping the wall" and crowding luckless passers-by into the muddy street, the skulking thief whose "unfelt fingers make the pocket light," the "nickers" and "scowrers" and "mohocks." Or, in the "Shepherd's Week" (1714), you may share Mr. Gay's smile at the doings of the yokels —

> To show their love, the neighbours far and near,
> Followed with wistful look the damsel's bier.
> Sprigged rosemary the lads and lasses bore,
> While dismally the Parson walked before.
> Upon her grave the rosemary they threw,
> The daisie, butter-flower and endive blue.
>
> After the good man warned us from his text,
> That none could tell whose turn would be the next;
> He said, that heaven would take her soul, no doubt,
> And spoke the hour-glass in her praise — quite out.
>
> To her sweet mem'ry flow'ry garlands strung,
> O'er her now empty seat aloft were hung.
> With wicker rods we fenced her tomb around,
> To ward from man and beast the hallowed ground,
> Lest her new grave the Parson's cattle raze,
> For both his horse and cow the church-yard graze.
>
> Now we trudged homeward to her mother's farm,
> To drink new cyder mulled, with ginger warm.
> For gaffer Tread-well told us by the by,
> Excessive sorrow is exceeding dry.
>
> While bulls bear horns upon their curléd brow,
> Or lasses with soft stroakings milk the cow;
> While paddling ducks the standing lake desire,
> Or batt'ning hogs roll in the sinking mire;
> While moles the crumbled earth in hillocks raise,
> So long shall swains tell Blouzelinda's praise.
>
> Thus wailed the louts in melancholy strain,
> 'Till bonny Susan sped a-cross the plain;

> They seized the lass in apron clean arrayed,
> And to the ale-house forced the willing maid;
> In ale and kisses they forget their cares,
> And Susan Blouzelinda's loss repairs.

You do not feel that these poets entered into the joys and sorrows of common folk or felt that they were made of the same clay as themselves. Even the dramatists, when they presented a heroine of common clay, felt that such a choice needed justification —

> Long has the fate of Kings and Empires been
> The common business of the tragic scene,
> As if misfortune made the throne her seat,
> And none could be unhappy but the great.
> Stories like these with wonder we may hear
> But far remote, and in a higher sphere,
> We ne'er can pity what we ne'er can share;
> Therefore an humbler theme our author chose
> A melancholy tale of private woes.
> — Rowe, Prologue to *The Fair Penitent* (1703)

But gradually as the century drew towards the half-way point, conditions changed. The old aristocratic tradition, with its conception of poetry as a gentleman's diversion, was dying. Poets were coming to depend less upon a patron's gifts, and upon publication of their work by private subscription solicited from fashionable people;[1] more upon direct relation to the reading public. The make-up of the reading public was changing. The aristocracy was becoming less literate, the middle classes more literate. Literature was becoming less exclusive. Time

---

[1] In the preceding chapter (page 318) we caught a glimpse of Dean Swift obtaining subscribers at court for Pope's forthcoming translation of the *Iliad*. The list of subscribers published with Pope's *Iliad* is a "Who's Who" of the polite world of the second decade of the century.

was, wrote Pope in 1737, when the average middle-class Englishman contented himself with worshiping like his fathers, sending his wife to church, his son to school, practicing the frugal virtues, and lending money on good security.

> Now times are changed, and one poetic itch
> Has seized the court and city, poor and rich:
> Sons, sires and grandsires, all will wear the bays.

The poet found himself writing for a different public, and became one with them in sympathy and understanding.

Among this middle-class public, new theories of social equality and the brotherhood of man were beginning to get a foothold. Pope's generation had comfortably taken for granted a social system which played into the hands of a privileged few and did not bother about the rights of the ordinary man (see page 284). The new generation were beginning to doubt and question. In other parts of the world these doubts and questionings were destined to have great consequences. England's American colonies were to sever their connection with the mother country, and write into their Declaration of Independence their belief that "all men are created equal and are endowed by their Creator with the inalienable right to life, liberty and the pursuit of happiness." In France, these doubts and questionings were to culminate in a revolution, with "liberty, equality and fraternity" as its watchwords. In more conservative England, these doubts and questionings were to bear fruit, ultimately, in social and political reforms[1];

---

[1] In "The Task" (1785), the poet William Cowper (see page 400) thus expresses the English feeling:

> We love
> The King who loves the law, respects his bounds,
> And reigns content within them: him we serve
> Freely and with delight, who leaves us free:

and, meanwhile, in a change in the way in which men felt
and thought and wrote about their fellow-men — a change
which is reflected in Burns's words —

> The rank is but the guinea's stamp,
> The man's the gowd for a' that . . .

> A prince can mak a belted knight,
> A marquis, duke an' a' that,
> But an honest man's aboon his might;
> Guid faith, he mauna fa' that!
> The pith o' sense an' pride o' worth
> Are higher rank than a' that.

There must have been a time long ago, the poets felt,
when there were no artificial distinctions of rank — a
"Golden Age" in which men enjoyed equally the fruits of
the earth.

> When first th' Almighty sire his work began,
> And spoke the mingling atoms into man,
> To all the race with gracious hand was given
> One common forest, and one equal heaven;
> They shared alike this universal ball,
> The sons of freedom, and the lords of all.
> The poets too this sacred truth displayed,
> From cloud-topped Pindus to the Latian shade,
> They sung, that ere Pandora, fond of strife,
> Let loose each embryo-misery of life,

> But recollecting still that he is man,
> We trust him not too far. King though he be,
> And King in England too, he may be weak,
> And vain enough to be ambitious still:
> May exercise amiss his proper powers,
> Or covet more than free men choose to grant:
> Beyond that mark is treason. He is ours,
> To administer, to guard, to adorn the state,
> But not to warp or change it. We are his,
> To serve him nobly in the common cause,
> True to the death, but not to be his slaves.

> All nature brightened in one golden age,
> Each sire a monarch, and each son a sage;
> Eternal blessings flowed to all the race,
> Alike in riches, as alike in place.

And no "new distinctions since,"

> Which place a slave some leagues below a prince,

affect their common humanity or make the joys and sorrows of the one less worth entering into and writing about than the joys and sorrows of the other.

During the second half of the century, with Gray's *Elegy* as a convenient starting point, poetry was increasingly occupied with the short and simple annals of the poor. Two of these later poems are of especial interest. Oliver Goldsmith's *The Deserted Village* (1770) is a picture — a little idealized, perhaps — of another sort of Golden Age — of a time, not long past, when English rural life was simple and peaceful and happy —

> When every rood of ground maintained its man;[1]
> For him, light labor spread its wholesome store,
> Just gave what life required, but gave no more;
> His best companions, innocence and health;
> And his best riches, ignorance of wealth.

With memories, perhaps, of Lissoy, the little Irish village in which he had spent his boyhood, Goldsmith paints his picture of

> Sweet Auburn, loveliest village of the plain,

and its simple, kindly folk — the village preacher —

> to all the country dear,
> And passing rich with forty pounds a year;

---

[1] A statute of Queen Elizabeth's reign attempted to secure to every cottage four acres of land. The statute had become a dead letter when Goldsmith wrote *The Deserted Village*, and was repealed in 1774.

Remote from towns he ran his godly race,
Nor e'er had changed, nor wished to change his place; . . .
His house was known to all the vagrant train;
He chid their wanderings but relieved their pain;
The long-remembered beggar was his guest,
Whose beard descending swept his aged breast;
The ruined spendthrift, now no longer proud,
Claimed kindred there, and had his claims allowed;
The broken soldier, kindly bade to stay,
Sat by the fire, and talked the night away . . .
Thus to relieve the wretched was his pride,
And e'en his failings leaned to virtue's side;
But in his duty prompt at every call,
He watched and wept, he prayed and felt for all;
And, as a bird each fond endearment tries
To tempt its new-fledged offspring to the skies,
He tried each art, reproved each dull delay,
Allured to brighter worlds, and led the way . . .
At church, with meek and unaffected grace,
His looks adorned the venerable place;
Truth from his lips prevailed with double sway,
And fools, who came to scoff, remained to pray . . .
   Beside yon straggling fence that skirts the way,
With blossomed furze unprofitably gay
There, in his noisy mansion, skilled to rule,
The village master taught his little school.
A man severe he was, and stern to view;
I knew him well, and every truant knew;
Well had the boding tremblers learned to trace
The day's disasters in his morning face;
Full well they laughed with counterfeited glee
At all his jokes, for many a joke had he;
Full well the busy whisper circling round
Conveyed the dismal tidings when he frowned.
Yet he was kind, or, if severe in aught,
The love he bore to learning was in fault;

The village all declared how much he knew:
'Twas certain he could write, and cipher too;
Lands he could measure, terms and tides presage,
And even the story ran that he could gauge;
In arguing, too, the parson owned his skill,
For, even though vanquished, he could argue still;
While words of learned length and thundering sound
Amazed the gazing rustics ranged around;
And still they gazed, and still the wonder grew,
That one small head could carry all he knew.

Around these the village life groups itself — the games upon the green, the pleasant homely sounds at evening's close —

The swain responsive as the milkmaid sung;
The sober herd that lowed to meet their young;
The noisy geese that gabbled o'er the pool;
The playful children just let loose from school . . .

These *were* thy charms — but all these charms are fled.

The rich are grasping the land and evicting the small land-holders. The open commons upon which, time out of mind, poor folk grazed their cattle, are being fenced in. The old contented poverty is gone. Pauperism is on the increase — and sweet Auburn is deserted.

Amidst thy bowers the tyrant's hand is seen,
And desolation saddens all thy green:
One only master grasps the whole domain,
And half a tillage stints thy smiling plain.
No more thy glassy brook reflects the day,
But, choked with sedges, works its weedy way;
Along the glades, a solitary guest,
The hollow sounding bittern guards its nest;
Amidst thy desert walks the lapwing flies,
And tires their echoes with unvaried cries.

Sunk are thy bowers in shapeless ruin all,
And the long grass o'ertops the mouldering wall;
And trembling, shrinking from the spoiler's hand,
Far, far away thy children leave the land.

A picture — and a warning:

Ill fares the land, to hastening ills a prey,
Where wealth accumulates and men decay;
Princes and lords may flourish or may fade;
A breath can make them, as a breath has made:
But a bold peasantry, their country's pride,
When once destroyed can never be supplied.

Gray liked *The Deserted Village*. "That man is a poet," he exclaimed when, in the last year of his life, he heard it read aloud. The *Elegy* and *The Deserted Village* have much in common — the meditative mood, the concern with humble lives, the apparently effortless ease of the verse, the exquisite rightness of word, the beautiful finish of phrase. Gray, with infinite leisure, spent years perfecting the *Elegy*. Goldsmith, though he was in a whirl of pot-boiling projects when he wrote *The Deserted Village*,[1] was hardly less fastidious. He made his first draft with wide spaces between the lines, and filled the spaces with revisions before he gave the poem to the press. A good many of Goldsmith's phrases — though not so many as those of Gray — have become current coin. "Passing rich with forty pounds a year"; "e'en his failings leaned to virtue's side"; "allured to brighter worlds, and led the way"; "fools, who came to scoff, remained to pray";

and still the wonder grew
That one small head could carry all he knew,

[1] A *Life of Parnell*, a *Life of Bolingbroke*, a *History of the Earth and of Animated Nature* (eight volumes), a *History of England* (four volumes.)

are among those which will have a familiar ring to you. Goldsmith did not have Gray's craftsmanship. In comparison with the *Elegy*, *The Deserted Village* seems diffuse and ill-constructed. But Goldsmith had a whimsical, humorous, and yet wholly sympathetic understanding of the hearts and minds of simple folk. It is not easy to preserve a nice balance between an acute sense of humor and a warm and tender sympathy. That gift had enabled Goldsmith to make *The Vicar of Wakefield* the most delightful of eighteenth-century novels. It enabled him to make *The Deserted Village* the most delightful of eighteenth-century poems. Delightful is the word. No one would think of putting *The Deserted Village* in the first rank. But there are few poems that have so held the affection of generation after generation of readers.

It is interesting to place beside *The Deserted Village* another poem about humble lives, written only ten years later. George Crabbe, author of *The Village* (composed about 1780; printed, 1783), thought that Goldsmith had been idealizing and sentimentalizing. Crabbe made up his mind to tell the plain truth.

> I grant indeed that fields and flocks have charms
> For him that grazes or for him that farms;
> But when amid such pleasing scenes I trace
> The poor laborious natives of the place,
> And see the mid-day sun, with fervid ray,
> On their bare heads and dewy temples play;
> While some, with feebler heads, and fainter hearts
> Deplore their fortune, yet sustain their parts —
> Then shall I dare these real ills to hide,
> In tinsel trappings of poetic pride?
>   No; cast by Fortune on a frowning coast,
> Which neither groves nor happy valleys boast;

Where other cares than those the Muse relates,
And other shepherds dwell with other mates;
By such examples taught, I paint the Cot,
As Truth will paint it, and as Bards will not . . .

Ye gentle souls, who dream of rural ease,
Whom the smooth stream and smoother sonnet please;
Go! if the peaceful cot your praises share,
Go look within, and ask if peace be there;
If peace be his, that drooping weary sire;
Or theirs, that offspring round their feeble fire;
Or hers, that matron pale, whose trembling hand
Turns on the wretched hearth the expiring brand.
    Nor yet can Time itself obtain for these
Life's latest comforts, due respect and ease;
For yonder see that hoary swain, whose age
Can with no cares except its own engage . . .

Oft may you see him, when he tends the sheep,
His winter charge, beneath the hillock weep;
Oft hear him murmur to the winds that blow
O'er his white locks and bury them in snow,
When, roused by rage and muttering in the morn,
He mends the broken hedge with icy thorn: —
    "Why do I live, when I desire to be
At once from life and life's long labor free?
Like leaves in spring, the young are blown away,
Without the sorrows of a slow decay;
I, like yon withered leaf, remain behind,
Nipped by the frost, and shivering in the wind."

It will interest you to compare, first with Gay's description of Blouzelinda's Funeral,[1] and, second, with Goldsmith's description of the Parson in *The Deserted Village*,[2]

[1] See page 388.   [2] See page 393.

Crabbe's description, in *The Village,* of the burial of an inmate of the poor-house:

> But ere his death some pious doubts arise,
> Some simple fears which "bold bad" men despise;
> Fain would he ask the Parish Priest to prove
> His title certain to the Joys above;
> For this he sends the murmuring Nurse, who calls
> The holy Stranger to these dismal walls;
> And doth not he, the pious man, appear,
> He, "passing rich with forty pounds a year?"
> Ah! no, a Shepherd of a different stock,
> And far unlike him, feeds this little flock;
> A jovial youth, who thinks his Sunday's task,
> As much as God or Man can fairly ask;
> The rest he gives to loves and labours light,
> To Fields the morning and to Feasts the night;
> None better skilled the noisy pack to guide,
> To urge their chase, to cheer them or to chide;
> A Sportsman keen, he shoots through half the day,
> And skilled at Whist, devotes the night to play;
> Then, while such honours bloom around his head,
> Shall he sit sadly by the Sick Man's bed
> To raise the hope he feels not, or with zeal
> To combat fears that ev'n the pious feel?
> Now once again the gloomy scene explore,
> Less gloomy now; the bitter hour is o'er,
> The Man of many Sorrows sighs no more. —
> Up yonder hill, behold how sadly slow
> The Bier moves winding from the vale below;
> There lie the happy Dead, from trouble free,
> And the glad Parish pays the frugal fee:
> No more, O Death! thy victim starts to hear
> Churchwarden stern, or kingly Overseer;
> No more the Farmer claims his humble bow,
> Thou art his lord, the best of tyrants thou!

Now to the Church behold the Mourners come,
Sedately torpid and devoutly dumb;
The Village Children now their games suspend,
To see the Bier that bears their antient Friend;
For he was one in all their idle sport,
And like a monarch ruled their little court;
The pliant Bow he formed, the flying Ball,
The Bat, the Wicket, were his labours all;
Him now they follow to his grave, and stand
Silent and sad, and gazing, hand in hand;
While bending low, their eager eyes explore
The mingled relicks of the Parish Poor:
The bell tolls late, the moping owl flies round,
Fear marks the flight and magnifies the sound;
The busy Priest, detained by weightier care,
Defers his duty till the day of prayer;
And waiting long, the crowd retire distrest,
To think a Poor Man's bones should lie unblest.

These "delineations of painful realities"[1] are interesting
if not pleasant reading. Crabbe's conviction that humble
lives are worth writing about reflects the changing spirit
of the time. Not less significant is his desire to avoid mere
prettiness, and to restore to poetry the "actuality of relation" and the "nudity of description" which seem to him
characteristic of Chaucer and Dryden and Pope. Before
long, Wordsworth (see page 406) will likewise challenge
the conventions in his *Lyrical Ballads* — turning to "humble and rustic life" for his themes, discarding the "phrases
and figures which have long been regarded as the common inheritance of poets," and insisting that the plain,
unadorned language of ordinary people is proper to
poetry.

[1] Other poems by Crabbe in the same mood are *The Parish Register* (1807),
The Borough (1810) and *Tales of the Hall* (1819).

It is rather as a forerunner of Wordsworth than as a poet in his own right, that Crabbe is worth remembering. His manner is harsh, his style often clumsy. He will find you the plain word for what he has to tell, but it will not often be the vivid, the "inspired" word, that transforms mere good descriptive or narrative verse into poetry. For that quality, we must turn to his contemporary, William Cowper (1731–1800).

Morbidly sensitive and shy, Cowper spent his early manhood in a vain effort to cope with the practical affairs of life. It was not until he established himself, in 1767, in the quiet village of Olney in Buckinghamshire, as an inmate of the household of Mrs. Unwin, that his poetic genius developed. Of his "Olney Hymns," at least two, *God moves in a mysterious way*, and *Oh, for a closer walk with God*, will be familiar to you. His merry ballad of John Gilpin's ride from London to Ware and back again is beloved by every reader young and old. His tragic tale of "The Castaway," and his touching poem "On the Receipt of My Mother's Picture" are reprinted in every anthology. But it is in the long meditative poem, "The Task" (1785), that he is at his best.

Developing out of a playful challenge to write a poem about a sofa, "The Task" rambles on from topic to topic to the extent of nearly five thousand lines of blank verse. Cowper's best thoughts — the thoughts of a sensitive, observant, wise, and high-minded man — are woven into it. In "The Task," the various elements of the romantic mood, which we have been tracing in this chapter, are happily blended — for example, distaste for the unrest of city life (it was Cowper who said,

God made the country, and man made the town),

and a quiet and contemplative affection for all the common
sights and sounds of the country —

> Scenes must be beautiful which, daily viewed,
> Please daily, and whose novelty survives
> Long knowledge and the scrutiny of years;
> Praise justly due to those that I describe.
>   Nor rural sights alone, but rural sounds,
> Exhilarate the spirit, and restore
> The tone of languid nature.   Mighty winds,
> That sweep the skirt of some far-spreading wood
> Of ancient growth, make music not unlike
> The dash of Ocean on his winding shore,
> And lull the spirit while they fill the mind;
> Unnumbered branches waving in the blast,
> And all their leaves fast flutt'ring, all at once.
> Nor less composure waits upon the roar
> Of distant floods, or on the softer voice
> Of neighb'ring fountain, or of rills that slip
> Through the cleft rock, and, chiming as they fall
> Upon loose pebbles, lose themselves at length
> In matted grass, that with a livelier green
> Betrays the secret of their silent course.

Equally characteristic is Cowper's "sensibility" —
whether it be in the freedom with which he lays bare his
own heart; in his tenderness toward all living things —

> I would not enter on my list of friends
> Though graced with polished manners and fine sense,
> Yet wanting sensibility, the man
> Who needlessly sets foot upon a worm, —

in his passionate championship of the negro slave —

>   My ear is pained,
> My soul is sick, with ev'ry day's report
> Of wrong and outrage with which earth is filled.

There is no flesh in man's obdurate heart,
It does not feel for man; the nat'ral bond
Of brotherhood is severed as the flax
That falls asunder at the touch of fire.
He finds his fellow guilty of a skin
Not coloured like his own, and, having pow'r
T' enforce the wrong, for such a worthy cause
Dooms and devotes him as his lawful prey.
Lands intersected by a narrow frith
Abhor each other.   Mountains interposed
Make enemies of nations who had else
Like kindred drops been mingled into one.
Thus man devotes his brother, and destroys;
And worse than all, and most to be deplored,
As human nature's broadest, foulest blot,
Chains him, and tasks him, and exacts his sweat
With stripes that Mercy, with a bleeding heart,
Weeps when she sees inflicted on a beast.
Then what is man?   And what man seeing this,
And having human feelings, does not blush
And hang his head, to think himself a man?
I would not have a slave to till my ground,
To carry me, to fan me while I sleep,
And tremble when I wake, for all the wealth
That sinews bought and sold have ever earned.
No: dear as freedom is, and in my heart's
Just estimation prized above all price,
I had much rather be myself the slave
And wear the bonds than fasten them on him, —

or in such passages as the following, in which his heart
goes out to the poor, enduring the rigors of a winter night.

Poor, yet industrious, modest, quiet, neat,
Such claim compassion in a night like this,
And have a friend in every feeling heart.

Warmed while it lasts, by labor, all day long
They brave the season, and yet find at eve,
Ill clad and fed but sparely, time to cool.
The frugal housewife trembles when she lights
Her scanty stock of brushwood, blazing clear,
But dying soon, like all terrestrial joys;
The few small embers left she nurses well.
And while her infant race with outspread hands
And crowded knees sit cowering o'er the sparks,
Retires, content to quake, so they be warmed.
The man feels least, as more inured than she
To winter, and the current in his veins
More briskly moved by his severer toil;
Yet he, too, finds his own distress in theirs.
The taper soon extinguished, which I saw
Dangled along at the cold finger's end
Just when the day declined, and the brown loaf
Lodged on the shelf, half-eaten, without sauce
Of sav'ry cheese, or butter costlier still,
Sleep seems their only refuge. For alas,
Where penury is felt the thought is chained,
And sweet colloquial pleasures are but few.
With all this thrift they thrive not. All the care
Ingenious parsimony takes, but just
Saves the small inventory, bed and stool,
Skillet and old carved chest, from public sale.
They live, and live without extorted alms
From grudging hands, but other boast have none
To soothe their honest pride that scorns to beg,
Nor comfort else, but in their mutual love.

With Cowper, we may fittingly end our survey of eighteenth-century poets. As you read the early nineteenth-century group, you will probably feel that these eighteenth-century romanticists suffer by comparison. We have not come upon any among them who could equal the noble simplicity and serene beauty which you will find in Wordsworth at his best; any, with the spell-casting imagination of Coleridge or the lyric energy of Byron; any, who could spin a romantic tale in rhyme with half the zest of Walter Scott; any, who could create such pure loveliness as Shelley and Keats. On this account, there has been a tendency, in recent times, to neglect them. That is a pity. For, quite aside from the fact that they are worth reading for their own sake, what the greater poets of the early nineteenth century did becomes more understandable and even more interesting, when we have seen how the eighteenth century paved the way.

Courtesy of National Gallery, London

Costumes, Latter Part of Eighteenth Century

The Beaumont Family. Painting by George Romney (about 1776)

405

XI

POETS OF THE EARLY NINETEENTH CENTURY

In 1798, two young men, William Wordsworth (1770–1850) and Samuel Taylor Coleridge (1772–1834) published (anonymously) a little volume of verse. It opened with Coleridge's "The Rime of the Ancient Mariner," a tale of enchantment in Antarctic seas, and closed with Wordsworth's "Lines Composed a Few Miles above Tintern Abbey," a meditation on the development of the poet's responsiveness to beauty. Between "The Ancient Mariner" and the Tintern Abbey "Lines" were a number of little tales in verse, so baldly simple, so nearly commonplace in subject matter and language, that the "gentle reader" of the year 1798 might very well doubt whether they could be called poetry at all. Wordsworth — for it was he who had written most of them — evidently feared that that was exactly what the gentle reader would think. "Readers of superior judgment," he wrote in the brief introductory note, "may disapprove of the style in which many of these pieces are executed. . . . It will perhaps appear to them that . . . the author has sometimes descended too low, and that many of his expressions are too familiar, and not of sufficient dignity."

There was, for example, the story of the little girl, too young to understand death, who tells her questioner about her six brothers and sisters —

"Seven are we;
And two of us at Conway dwell,
And two are gone to sea.

Two of us in the church-yard lie,
My sister and my brother;
And in the church-yard cottage I
Dwell near them with my mother."

"You say that two at Conway dwell
And two are gone to sea,
Yet you are seven; I pray you tell,
Sweet Maid, how this may be."

Then did the little Maid reply,
"Seven boys and girls are we
Two of us in the church-yard lie,
Beneath the church-yard tree . . .

The first that died was sister Jane
In bed she moaning lay,
Till God released her of her pain
And then she went away.

So in the church-yard she was laid;
And all the summer day,
Together round her grave we played,
My brother John and I.

And when the ground was white with snow,
And I could run and slide,
My brother John was forced to go
And he lies by her side."

"How many are you then," said I,
"If they two are in heaven?"
The little maiden did reply,
"O Master, we are seven."

"But they are dead; those two are dead!
Their spirits are in Heaven!"
'Twas throwing words away: for still
The little Maid would have her will,
And said, "Nay, we are seven!"

There was the story of Harry Gill who once upon a time
caught poor old shivering Goody Blake stealing firewood
from his hedge —

And fiercely by the arm he took her,
And by the arm he held her fast,
And fiercely by the arm he shook her,
And cried, "I've caught you then at last!"
Then Goody, who had nothing said,
Her bundle from her lap let fall;
And kneeling on the sticks, she prayed
To God that is the judge of all.

She prayed, her withered hand uprearing,
While Harry held her by the arm —
"God! who art never out of hearing
O may he never more be warm!"
The cold, cold moon above her head,
Thus on her knees did Goody pray.
Young Harry heard what she had said,
And icy cold he turned away.

He went complaining all the morrow
That he was cold and very chill:
His face was gloom, his heart was sorrow,
Alas! that day for Harry Gill!
That day he wore a riding-coat,
But not a whit the warmer he:
Another was on Thursday brought,
And ere the Sabbath he had three.

'Twas all in vain, a useless matter,
And blankets were about him pinned;
Yet still his jaws and teeth they clatter,
Like a loose casement in the wind.
And Harry's flesh it fell away;
And all who see him say, 'tis plain,
That live as long as live he may,
He never will be warm again.

No word to any man he utters,
A-bed or up, to young or old;
But ever to himself he mutters,
"Poor Harry Gill is very cold."
A-bed or up, by night or day;
His teeth they chatter, chatter still.
Now think, ye farmers all, I pray,
Of Goody Blake and Harry Gill.

There was the story of old Simon Lee, once the merry
huntsman of Ivor Hall, but now a weak and poor old man —

And he is lean and he is sick,
His little[1] body's half awry;
His ankles they are swoln and thick;
His legs are thin and dry.
When he was young he little knew
Of husbandry or tillage;
And now he's forced to work, though weak,
— The weakest in the village.

Old Simon is trying to chop out a stump of rotten wood.
The poet takes the mattock from his shaking hand and
severs the root at a single blow —

The tears into his eyes were brought,
And thanks and praises seemed to run
So fast out of his heart, I thought
They never would have done.

[1] Changed in later editions to "dwindled."

> — I've heard of hearts unkind, kind deeds
> With coldness still returning.
> Alas! the gratitude of men
> Has oftener left me mourning.

There was the long story of a mother's love for her idiot boy. It is night. A neighbor is sick. The boy is told to ride to a nearby town to fetch the doctor. The boy forgets his errand and wanders witlessly about. Finally the poor mother, after looking for him most of the night and becoming herself nearly crazed with anxiety, finds him where he has been for many hours contentedly gazing at the waterfall.

> Now Johnny all night long had heard
> The owls in tuneful concert strive;
> No doubt too he the moon had seen;
> For in the moonlight he had been
> From eight o'clock till five.
>
> And thus, to Betty's question, he
> Made answer, like a Traveller bold.
> (His very words I give to you,)
> "The cocks did crow to-whoo, to-whoo,
> And the sun did shine so cold."
> — Thus answered Johnny in his glory,
> And that was all his travel's story.

The puzzled readers of the little volume of 1798 came upon these plain and homely tales and various others, like them in manner and matter. They found, too, a pair of short poems, "Expostulation and Reply" and "The Tables Turned," recounting a conversation between "William" and "Matthew," in which the poet states his philosophy —

> Books! 'tis a dull and endless strife:
> Come, hear the woodland linnet,

How sweet his music! on my life
There's more of music in it.

And hark! how blithe the throstle sings!
And he is no mean preacher:
Come forth into the light of things,
Let Nature be your teacher.

She has a world of ready wealth,
Our minds and hearts to bless —
Spontaneous wisdom breathed by health,
Truth breathed by cheerfulness.

One impulse from a vernal wood
May teach you more of man,
Of moral evil and of good
Than all the sages can.

And then these readers of the 1798 volume, having
readjusted their minds from the nightmares and enchantments of "The Ancient Mariner" to the tales of little girls
who keep saying "we are seven," and lusty drovers who
maltreat old women and spend the rest of their lives with
their teeth chattering, and old huntsmen with legs that are
thin and dry, and worried mothers who love their idiot
offspring — these readers, having thus once adjusted
their bewildered minds, turned to the last poem in the little
volume and found — the grave and stately music of
the Tintern Abbey "Lines." In it Wordsworth tells of
how, as a boy, Nature

To me all was in all. — I cannot paint
What then I was.   The sounding cataract
Haunted me like a passion: the tall rock,
The mountain, and the deep and gloomy wood,

> Their colors and their forms, were then to me
> An appetite; a feeling and a love,
> That had no need of a remoter charm,
> By thought supplied, or any interest
> Unborrowed from the eye;

and of how, as he grew up, he had learned

> To look on Nature, not as in the hour
> Of thoughtless youth; but hearing oftentimes
> The still, sad music of humanity,
> Nor harsh nor grating, though of ample power
> To chasten and subdue.   And I have felt
> A presence that disturbs me with the joy
> Of elevated thoughts: a sense sublime
> Of something far more deeply interfused,
> Whose dwelling is the light of setting suns,
> And the round ocean and the living air,
> And the blue sky, and in the mind of man.

No wonder the few readers to whom the little volume found its way were bewildered. The Tintern Abbey "Lines" were clearly poetry of a high order; but probably to most readers, as to the reviewer in *The Monthly Review* of May, 1799, "the rustic delineations of low life" seemed mere "doggerel verses."   But Wordsworth was not dismayed. Enlarged to two volumes, the *Lyrical Ballads* appeared again in 1800 — this time, as "by W. Wordsworth."   The reprinted pieces were put into a new order, with "Expostulation" and "The Tables Turned" at the beginning, and Coleridge's "Ancient Mariner" next to the Tintern Abbey "Lines" at the end.   The new poems (in the second volume) were about equally divided between pieces in the plain style of "Goody Blake" and "The Idiot Boy," and delicate little lyrics as free from "lowness" as the Tintern Abbey "Lines."   And with the two volumes, Wordsworth published a long "Preface" (destined in due time to be recognized as one of the great landmarks of English literary history), in which he argued the case for the kind of poetry in which he believed. Burns had shown

> How Verse may build a princely throne
> On humble truth.

Other poets, too, were finding themes in the joys and sorrows of ordinary people — especially people who lived close to Nature. Could not this tendency be given shape, and more purposefully exemplified? Were not such people the very ones in whom "the great and simple affections of our nature" could be most easily traced? Do not these deeper feelings really "speak a plainer and more emphatic language" in them than in sophisticated city people? And if the old ballads, with their "naked and simple style" and their "artless metre" had given pleasure, why should not modern verse be written in somewhat the same fashion? Would it not be interesting to "ascertain how far the language — or, at least, a selection of the language — of conversation in the middle and lower classes of society" would do as the language of poetry? With such possibilities in his mind, Wordsworth had composed these plain and homely tales.

Again enlarged, and with the "Preface" considerably revised, the *Lyrical Ballads* went to new editions in 1802 and 1805. With the appearance in two volumes in 1807 of Wordsworth's collected poems, most of his best work was in print. That best was certainly not the "experiments" of the *Lyrical Ballads*. But the instinct and the powers which produced these "artless" narratives were the very things that made his best work possible. The two points that really stand out in his "Preface" are that he wanted to portray "the great and simple affections of our nature" and that the only way, as it seemed to him, in which any reasonable and honest poet could do this was "as far as possible to adopt the very language of men." Shorn of all the controversies that have raged round his famous "Preface," this means merely that he sought to get down beneath the veneer and the affectations and the sophistications to the realities of life — the deeper feelings that are in us all, whether we live in the Cumberland hills or in a big city. He sought to do this, and he knew that the only way in which these deeper feelings could be given the semblance of reality was by using a language that is at once accurately descriptive and perfectly natural. He wanted his poetry not only to be true but also to sound true.

He went at his problem bunglingly. He didn't seem to have the power to detach himself and see how the thing would look to somebody else. He composed "We Are Seven" during a ramble in the woods and then came home to recite it to his sister and Coleridge. Wordsworth had begun it —

> I met a little cottage girl:
> She was eight years old, she said.

He felt that a prefatory stanza was needed. The Wordsworths had a friend, James Tobin, familiarly known to them as "Jem." Coleridge jokingly suggested

> A simple child, dear brother Jem
> That lightly draws its breath,
> And feels its life in every limb,
> What should it know of death?

Wordsworth, vaguely aware that it might seem "ludicrous," nevertheless adopted this opening stanza, because

"we all enjoyed the joke of hitching in our friend's name."
And thus (with "Jem" changed to "Jim," for the sake of
the rhyme) the opening stanza remained through edition
after edition of Wordsworth's poems, until "dear brother
Jim" was at length bowled out by the derisive laughter of
his readers, and the opening stanza became

> A simple child
> That lightly draws its breath, etc.

Again, in a narrative poem called "The Thorn," in which
occur two lines as lovely as ever poet wrote —

> And she is known to every star,
> And every wind that blows —

Wordsworth could write as if he were drawing up a list of
specifications:

> And to the left, three yards beyond,
> You see a little muddy pond
> Of water never dry;
> I've measured it from side to side:
> 'Tis three feet long, and two feet wide.

Here, too, Wordsworth yielded after a while to the ridicule
of his readers, and changed the last lines of the stanza to —

> a little muddy pond
> Of water — never dry,
> Though but of compass small, and bare
> To thirsty suns and parching air.

Futile absurdities of this sort are scattered through the
poems. It does seem extraordinary that a poet who wanted
his "experiments" to be taken seriously, and who had the
potency of a flawless perfection in him, should have put
such unnecessary hindrances in his own way. Call it a

lack of a sense of humor, if you like — and, maybe, a touch of mulish obstinacy.

He went at his problem bunglingly. But even in his crudest narratives, there are moments of pure poetry which show what he was moving towards. That passion for truth, for reality, that virtue, to which Wordsworth lays claim in his "Preface," of endeavoring "at all times to look steadily at (his) subject" — these same qualities enabled him, when the mood was on him, to write with supreme beauty — the beauty which arises always from a perfect understanding of the thing described, and a perfectly chosen word with which to describe it. I know of no better way to convince you of this than to quote, without any comment whatsoever, a few of these perfect things —

> There was a Boy: ye knew him well, ye cliffs
> And islands of Winander! — many a time
> At evening, when the earliest stars began
> To move along the edges of the hills,
> Rising or setting, would he stand alone
> Beneath the trees or by the glimmering lake,
> And there, with fingers interwoven, both hands
> Pressed closely palm to palm, and to his mouth
> Uplifted, he, as through an instrument,
> Blew mimic hootings to the silent owls,
> That they might answer him; and they would shout
> Across the watery vale, and shout again,
> Responsive to his call, with quivering peals,
> And long halloos and screams, and echoes loud,
> Redoubled and redoubled, concourse wild
> Of jocund din; and, when a lengthened pause
> Of silence came and baffled his best skill,
> Then sometimes, in that silence while he hung
> Listening, a gentle shock of mild surprise
> Has carried far into his heart the voice

Of mountain torrents; or the visible scene
Would enter unawares into his mind,
With all its solemn imagery, its rocks,
Its woods, and that uncertain heaven, received
Into the bosom of the steady lake.

THE SOLITARY REAPER

Behold her, single in the field,
Yon solitary Highland Lass!
Reaping and singing by herself;
Stop here, or gently pass!
Alone she cuts and binds the grain,
And sings a melancholy strain;
O listen! for the Vale profound
Is overflowing with the sound.

No Nightingale did ever chant
So sweetly to reposing bands
Of Travellers in some shady haunt,
Among Arabian sands;
A voice so thrilling ne'er was heard
In spring-time from the Cuckoo-bird,
Breaking the silence of the seas
Among the farthest Hebrides.

Will no one tell me what she sings?
Perhaps the plaintive numbers flow
For old, unhappy, far-off things,
And battles long ago:
Or is it some more humble lay,
Familiar matter of to-day?
Some natural sorrow, loss, or pain,
That has been, and may be again!

Whate'er the theme, the Maiden sang
As if her song could have no ending;
I saw her singing at her work,
And o'er the sickle bending; —
I listened till I had my fill,
And when I mounted up the hill,
The music in my heart I bore,
Long after it was heard no more.

"She Was a Phantom of Delight."

She was a Phantom of delight
When first she gleamed upon my sight;
A lovely Apparition, sent
To be a moment's ornament;
Her eyes as stars of Twilight fair;
Like Twilight's, too, her dusky hair;
But all things else about her drawn
From May-time and the cheerful Dawn;
A dancing Shape, an Image gay,
To haunt, to startle, and waylay.

I saw her upon nearer view,
A Spirit, yet a Woman too!
Her household motions light and free,
And steps of virgin liberty;
A countenance in which did meet
Sweet records, promises as sweet;
A Creature not too bright or good
For human nature's daily food;
For transient sorrows, simple wiles,
Praise, blame, love, kisses, tears, and smiles.

And now I see with eye serene
The very pulse of the machine;
A Being breathing thoughtful breath,
A Traveller between life and death;

The reason firm, the temperate will,
Endurance, foresight, strength, and skill;
A perfect Woman, nobly planned,
To warn, to comfort, and command;
And yet a Spirit still, and bright
With something of angelic light.

ELEGIAC STANZAS

Suggested by a Picture of Peele Castle, in a Storm,
Painted by Sir George Beaumont

I was thy neighbour once, thou rugged Pile!
Four summer weeks I dwelt in sight of thee:
I saw thee every day; and all the while
Thy Form was sleeping on a glassy sea.

So pure the sky, so quiet was the air!
So like, so very like, was day to day!
Whene'er I looked, thy Image still was there;
It trembled, but it never passed away.

How perfect was the calm! it seemed no sleep;
No mood, which season takes away, or brings:
I could have fancied that the mighty Deep
Was even the gentlest of all gentle things.

Ah! then, if mine had been the Painter's hand,
To express what then I saw; and add the gleam,
The light that never was, on sea or land,
The consecration, and the Poet's dream;

I would have planted thee, thou hoary Pile,
Amid a world how different from this!
Beside a sea that could not cease to smile;
On tranquil land, beneath a sky of bliss.

A Picture had it been of lasting ease
Elysian quiet, without toil or strife;
No motion but the moving tide, a breeze,
Or merely silent Nature's breathing life . . .

COMPOSED UPON WESTMINSTER BRIDGE, SEPT. 3, 1803

Earth has not anything to show more fair;
Dull would he be of soul who could pass by
A sight so touching in its majesty;
This City now doth like a garment wear
The Beauty of the morning; silent, bare,
Ships, towers, domes, theatres, and temples lie
Open unto the fields, and to the sky;
All bright and glittering in the smokeless air.
Never did sun more beautifully steep
In his first splendour valley, rock, or hill,
Ne'er saw I, never felt, a calm so deep!
The river glideth at his own sweet will:
Dear God! the very houses seem asleep;
And all that mighty heart is lying still!

LONDON, 1802

Milton! thou shouldst be living at this hour:
England hath need of thee: she is a fen
Of stagnant waters: altar, sword, and pen,
Fireside, the heroic wealth of hall and bower,
Have forfeited their ancient English dower
Of inward happiness. We are selfish men;
Oh! raise us up, return to us again;
And give us manners, virtue, freedom, power.
Thy soul was like a Star, and dwelt apart:
Thou hadst a voice whose sound was like the sea:
Pure as the naked heavens, majestic, free,
So didst thou travel on life's common way,
In cheerful godliness; and yet thy heart
The lowliest duties on herself did lay.

It took Wordsworth's contemporaries some time to realize that he was a great poet. He expected ridicule. The readers of these pages, he had written in 1798, "will look around for poetry, and will be induced to inquire by what species of courtesy these attempts can be permitted to assume that title." Some people, he remarked in 1800, would like his poems, but "by those who should dislike them they would be read with more than common dislike." It was a good guess. "Infantine prattle," they called them; "the extreme simplicity and lowliness of tone which wavered so prettily, in the *Lyrical Ballads*, between silliness and pathos"; "all the world laughs at elegiac stanzas to a suckling pig — a hymn on washing-day — sonnets to one's grandmother — or pindarics on gooseberry pie; and yet, we are afraid, it will not be quite easy to convince Mr. Wordsworth that the same ridicule must infallibly attach to most of the pathetic pieces in these volumes"; "childish language, mean incidents, incongruous images";

> That mild apostate from poetic rule;
> The simple Wordsworth . . .
> Who, both by precept and example, shows
> That prose is verse, and verse is merely prose.

Then the tide began to turn. Wordsworth's best had gone into the two volumes of 1807. Gradually his greatness was realized. By the 1830's Coleridge's opinion that "in imaginative power Wordsworth stands nearest of all modern writers to Shakespeare and Milton" had become, with few dissenting voices, the opinion of the public at large. For a time after his death — he lived on, and wrote on, till 1850 — his fame seemed to be on the wane. New poets started new fashions. But in 1879 a poet and critic,

Matthew Arnold, who had grown up under Wordsworth's shadow, and much of whose poetry is in the Wordsworthian spirit, selected from the vast and uneven mass of Wordsworth's work a little volume of his best, and prefaced it with a critical essay. This essay and these selections served, if not to reinstate Wordsworth (for in any event his fame would have been sure), at least to recall those who had been led astray to a sense of Wordsworth's real significance. Arnold found him not merely "the pure and sage master of a small band of devoted followers," but also "one of the very chief glories of English Poetry." That is still the way in which all thoughtful lovers of poetry feel about Wordsworth to-day; and in the poetry of to-day — indeed, far more in the poetry of to-day than in the poetry of forty or fifty years ago — the hand of Wordsworth is visible.

But Wordsworth was not the only great poet of those opening years of the nineteenth century, nor was Wordsworth's kind of poetry the only kind, belonging to that period, that has influenced us. Poetry has a way of swinging pendulum-like from one extreme to another. Elizabethan poetry seems to us as we look back to it a thing of ecstasy, of intense emotions put into singing words, of Spenser's dream-shapes and fascinations, of Shakespeare's exquisite phrasings of passion and desire. Slowly, through the seventeenth century, we see the pendulum swinging away from all that, until, in the hands of Pope the pendulum reaches the other end of its arc, and poetry (in its prevalent form) becomes as edged and polished as a surgeon's scalpel, an instrument of dissection and analysis, an instrument wielded by men who wished above all things to be *reasonable* and *sane*, and to whom "enthusiasm," effervescence of emotion, seemed rather unsafe. Then the pendulum began once more to swing in the other direction. Emotion began to come to the surface again. The poet became less and less interested in playing the part of urbane philosopher and critic and more and more filled with the desire to unlock his own heart, to pour himself out in words. He began to look for excitement — finding it sometimes in the beauty or the wildness of nature, sometimes in strange or marvelous happenings, remote as possible from his everyday world.

Wordsworth stood a little aside from this current. He did not look for strangeness. "The human mind," he insisted in the Preface to the *Lyrical Ballads* "is capable of being excited without the application of gross and violent stimulants." He deplored "the deluges of extravagant stories in verse" then being published. But among these same *Lyrical Ballads* appeared "The Ancient Mariner," one of the strangest and eeriest, and (in subject matter though not in style) one of the most extravagant stories in verse, that poet ever invented. "The Ancient Mariner" is interesting not only in itself as a strange story wonderfully told, but also as a connecting link between what Wordsworth was doing and what a few great poets were about to do a few years later. There is a grave simplicity and directness and concreteness in the language that is wholly "Wordsworthian";[1] but in its glamour and mystery, in its varied and responsive music, in the effect aimed at and in every device employed to produce that effect, it is as far removed from the old ballads and from Wordsworth's "experiments,"

---

[1] Wordsworth himself, as it happened, suggested a few lines, here and there, notably the peculiarly characteristic ones —

> And listened like a three years' child:
> The Mariner hath his will;

but there is not a particle of difference in tone between these and the rest of the poem.

as a poem could possibly be. It is, in fact, the first really great achievement of that "romantic" spirit toward which the pendulum had been swinging since Pope's day.

"The Ancient Mariner" was born of a dream, related to Coleridge by a friend, of "a skeleton ship with figures in it." It was just the thing to set Coleridge going, for his head was already full of the tales of marvelous adventures on uncharted seas told by the old voyagers, and he had been setting down in his notebook, from them and from other sources, jottings of roaring alligators and glossy-black snakebirds and the "two mighty Bears" which "walk round and round the Pole," and notes of mutinies on the high seas and of a projected "wild poem on a Maniac" and of an "Image of Ice in the mountains of Cashmere" and of "beautiful colors of the hoarfrost on snow in sunshine — red, green and blue — in various angles," and of how "the sun paints rainbows on the vast waves during snowstorms in the Cape," and of numberless other things as strange.[1] And now came this dream — the very stuff to weave a story 'round. No less than an eye-witness must tell it, an old seafaring man who had in some way become involved with the skeleton ship and those fearsome figures, and had lived to tell the tale. Oddly enough, it was the sober Wordsworth who suggested the way to work out the story. He too had been reading the narratives of the old voyagers. A ship, southbound to round Cape Horn, was so beset with storm that the sailors had almost given up hope. A "disconsolate black Albatross" kept hovering overhead. Thinking it a creature of ill-omen, one of the sailors had shot the bird. "Why not," said Wordsworth

---

[1] One of the most delightful "books about books" ever written is *The Road to Xanadu* in which John Livingstone Lowes, with this notebook as a point of departure, traces Coleridge's reading and gleans the suggestions of incident and imagery which in due time became molded into *The Ancient Mariner*.

"represent *your* voyager as having killed one of these birds on entering the South Sea, and that the tutelary spirits of these regions take upon them to avenge the crime?"

> It is an ancient Mariner,
>   And he stoppeth one of three.
> "By thy long gray beard and glittering eye,
>   Now wherefore stopp'st thou me?
>
> The Bridegroom's doors are opened wide,
>   And I am next of kin;
> The guests are met, the feast is set:
>   May'st hear the merry din."
>
> He holds him with his skinny hand,
>   "There was a ship," quoth he.
> "Hold off! unhand me, gray-beard loon!"
>   Eftsoons his hand dropped he.
>
> He holds him with his glittering eye —
>   The Wedding-Guest stood still,
> And listens like a three years' child:
>   The Mariner hath his will.

His ship, said the Ancient Mariner, had been driven south by the storm-blast into a world empty of all life. With the ice-floes closing round them, they saw an albatross come out of the mist and hover over the ship. It seemed to bring them good luck, for the ice parted, the helmsman steered them through, the ship sped north with the bird still hovering overhead. But — and the Wedding-Guest starts back in horror at what is written in the old man's face —

> "God save thee, ancient Mariner!
>   From the fiends that plague thee thus. —

> Why look'st thou so?" — "With my crossbow
> I shot the Albatross."

At first his shipmates reproached him; but when the good south wind still blew behind,

> "'Twas right, said they, such birds to slay,
> That bring the fog and mist."

But the spirits were only biding their time. The wind died. Day after day the ship lay becalmed.

> "About, about, in reel and rout
> The death-fires danced at night;
> The water, like a witch's oils
> Burnt green and blue and white."

They were like to die of thirst, and knowing now that the spirits were punishing them for shooting the albatross, they cursed the Ancient Mariner and hung the dead bird about his neck. When for a weary time the ship had lain motionless, the Ancient Mariner saw a moving speck upon the western rim.

> "With throats unslaked, with black lips baked
> We could not laugh nor wail;
> Through utter drought all dumb we stood!
> I bit my arm, I sucked the blood,
> And cried, A sail! a sail!"

But as the ship drove in between them and the setting sun, her sails became as gossamers, her skeleton ribs flecked the face of the sun

> "As if through a dungeon-grate he peered . . .
>
> And is that Woman all her crew?
> Is that a Death? And are there two?
> Is Death that Woman's mate . . .

The naked hulk alongside came,
　　And the twain were casting dice;
'The game is done! I've won, I've won!'
　　Quoth she, and whistles thrice.

The sun's rim dips; the stars rush out:
　　At one stride comes the dark;
With far-heard whisper, o'er the sea,
　　Off shot the spectre-bark."

Then indeed the spell was upon them.　Round about
him the Ancient Mariner saw all his shipmates fall dead
upon the deck —

"The souls did from their bodies fly —
　　They fled to bliss or woe!
And every soul it passed me by,
　　Like the whizz of my cross-bow! . . .

The many men, so beautiful!
　　And they all dead did lie:
And a thousand, thousand slimy things
　　Lived on; and so did I."

At first, as he found himself alone on that wide, wide sea,
black despair and horror filled the Ancient Mariner's
heart — horror of death, horror of the sea-life all around
him, these slimy living things that seemed to mock the
dead.　But as the days passed, horror of them melted and
their beauty began to grow upon him —

"Beyond the shadow of the ship,
　　I watched the water-snakes:
They moved in tracks of shining white,
And when they reared, the elfish light
　　Fell off in hoary flakes.

> Within the shadow of the ship
> I watched their rich attire:
> Blue, glossy green, and velvet black,
> They coiled and swam; and every track
> Was a flash of golden fire."

They too were of God's making.

> "A spring of love gushed from my heart
> And I blessed them unaware! . . .
>
> The selfsame moment I could pray;
> And from my neck so free
> The Albatross fell off, and sank
> Like lead into the sea."

Refreshing sleep came to him and when he waked at night
it seemed that the dead men were moving about the ship
and sailing her northward.

> "It had been strange, even in a dream,
> To have seen those dead men rise."

But it was a troop of spirits blest, that moved in the bodies
of the dead. Till dawn they seemed to sail her, and when
they vanished, the ship still moved on, impelled by the
Spirit from the land of mist and snow. Then came a moment when the ship paused in her course, held spellbound
on some mysterious dividing line between the world of
that pursuing Spirit and the good world of living men.
The Mariner swooned and Voices came to him —

> "'Is it he?' quoth one, 'Is this the man?
> By him who died on cross,
> With his cruel bow he laid full low,
> The harmless Albatross.

> The spirit who bideth by himself
> In the land of mist and snow,
> He loved the bird that loved the man
> Who shot him with his bow.'
>
> The other was a softer voice,
> As soft as honey-dew:
> Quoth he, 'The man hath penance done,
> And penance more will do.'"

Once more the Mariner awoke. Once more, as night fell, the dead seemed to stand upon the deck and reproach him with their stony eyes. But now again the ship sped northward, and at length reached the harbor whence the Mariner had embarked so long before. And upon the bodies that lay once more inert upon the deck stood "seraph-men," voiceless, but with forgiveness in their waving hands. From the shore put out the pilot to meet the incoming ship and with him a Hermit of the wood. As the little boat approached, there came a dreadful sound and the ship with all its grim freight sank like a stone. The Mariner found himself lying in the little boat. The good Hermit shrived him of his sin.

But for the Ancient Mariner there is penance yet to do — the penance of telling again and yet again, as now to the Wedding-Guest, this tale of wrongdoing and expiation. Was there ever such a story? — "There was a ship." To the Ancient Mariner, possessed by what he had been through, penance-driven to tell it, nothing else mattered. "There was a ship." And from that moment we, like the Wedding-Guest, cannot choose but hear. Under the spell of the poet's magic, all too inadequately represented in the foregoing outline, there simply *is* no other world than that world of phantasms melting into one another, of mist and fog and white moonshine, of whispering keel and sails dripping deadly dew, of spectral shapes and unearthly voices. Coleridge was twenty-five years old when he wrote it. He was never again to do anything so perfect; but for that matter, no other poet has even once succeeded in weaving such magic as Coleridge has woven in "The Ancient Mariner."

Certainly that other story-telling poet, Walter Scott, had no such magic at his command. But he did know how to tell a spirited story. Born in Edinburgh and brought by the circumstances of his childhood into intimate contact with the Scotch peasantry, Scott had become a passionate lover of the old ballads — the stories of border warfare and of weird adventure, which the peasants still told about their firesides. From his childhood, his heart was in the past, the old wild days of his native Scotland. And like other "romantically" minded people of his time who were tired of sophisticated poetry, it seemed to him that these old days of border raids and bitter feuds between the clans, of knights who rode a-tilt or listened in hall to a minstrel-tale of brave adventure, were the only days that could furnish poetry with the glamor that it ought to have.

He had collected Border ballads, he had tried his hand at writing them — and then one day a tale began to grow in his mind too elaborate to be kept within the ballad form. It was to celebrate events in the history of his own clan, of which his friend and patron, Henry Scott, Duke of Buccleugh, was chief. The scene was to be the ancestral castle of the Dukes of Buccleugh, Branxholm, or as Scott calls it "Branksome Hall," on the upper reaches of the Teviot, not far north of the Border. There were to be both

black and white magic in it, and a Border raid, and a love-
story between the daughter of the house and a knight belonging to an enemy clan. The events take place in the
mid-sixteenth century, but Scott ingeniously links them
with a less remote past. In the days when "a stranger"
(William of Orange, 1688–1702) "filled the Stuarts' throne,"
an aged minstrel —

> The last of all the Bards was he
> Who sung of Border chivalry —

comes to Branksome Hall, and encouraged by the kindness of "the noble Duchess" and her attendants, tunes his
harp, and sings to them this tale

> Of the old warriors of Buccleugh.

The opening lines of the minstrel's story are full of the
vividness and raciness and energy which were to win for
Scott's poetry such instant popularity:

> The feast was over in Branksome tower,
> And the Ladye had gone to her secret bower;
> Her bower that was guarded by word and by spell,
> Deadly to hear, and deadly to tell —
> Jesu Maria, shield us well!
> No living wight, save the Ladye alone,
> Had dared to cross the threshold stone.
>
> The tables were drawn, it was idlesse all;
> Knight, and page, and household squire,
> Loitered through the lofty hall,
> Or crowded round the ample fire:
> The stag-hounds weary with the chase
> Lay stretched upon the rushy floor,
> And urged, in dreams, the forest race,
> From Teviot-stone to Eskdale-moor.

Nine and twenty knights of fame
Hung their shields in Branksome-Hall;
Nine and twenty squires of name
Brought them their steeds to bower from stall;
Nine and twenty yeomen tall
Waited duteous on them all:
They were all knights of metal true,
Kinsmen to the bold Buccleugh.

But after this, the story has rather hard going. The black magic was to be furnished by a goblin page, the Gilpin Horner of Scottish legend; and the white magic, as the opening stanza rather too portentously announces, by the "Ladye" herself.[1]

The Ladye is bent on preventing a marriage between her daughter, the Lady Margaret, and Lord Cranstoun, with whose clan the Scotts are at feud. Through her magic she hears spirit voices warning her that good fortune cannot come to her mansion "till pride be quelled and love be free." Disregarding this warning she sends one of her retainers to Melrose Abbey to secure a book of magic, buried there with the body of the old conjurer who had

---

[1] A friend of Scott's had recited to him part of an unpublished poem by Coleridge called "Christabel." Here is a bit of it:

Hush, beating heart of Christabel!
Jesu Maria, shield her well!
She folded her arms beneath her cloak,
And stole to the other side of the oak.
    What sees she there?
There she sees a damsel bright,
Drest in a silken robe of white,
That shadowy in the moonlight shone.

The rhythm of "Christabel" was beating in Scott's brain when he wrote the *Lay*, and the magic of "Christabel" had captured his imagination. But Coleridge had a genius for the uncanny. The spell that he could cast in a dozen opening words, and sustain indefinitely, was beyond Scott's power. Scott begins as if the whole thing were going to turn on that spell, "deadly to hear and deadly to tell"; but what comes of it is chiefly a border raid and some good hard fighting. Coleridge's magic was at the heart of his poetry. Scott's was pasted on the surface.

made the spells, by which she may prevent the match. On his way back with the book, her retainer, William of Deloraine, is wounded by Lord Cranstoun. Lord Cranstoun's goblin page finds the book on Deloraine's body, and by one peep into it learns a spell which enables him to transport the wounded Deloraine to the Ladye's Hall and to abduct the Ladye's little son. This child is found by the English, who march three thousand strong across the border, and surround Branksome Hall. They demand the surrender of Deloraine (who it seems has been raiding their lands) and the admission of an English garrison to Branksome. Failing this, they will hold the Ladye's son in captivity. But even to save her son, the Ladye will not yield. The English are about to besiege the castle; but hearing that the clans are rising, they agree to settle the quarrel by a duel between Deloraine and the English Musgrave whose lands Deloraine had raided. Deloraine still lies sorely wounded in the castle. It is apparently he who engages in the combat and conquers Musgrave. But when the conqueror lifts his visor he is seen to be Lord Cranstoun himself, who has been spirited into the castle by the magic of the goblin page. The English return the young heir of Branksome and retire from the field. The Ladye gives up her spells, and Lord Cranstoun marries Margaret.

It is evident that this sort of romantic stuff was precisely what Scott's generation was hungry for. The rapid verse, the verve of the story, caught them. The picturesque setting appealed to them. The description of Melrose Abbey —

> When the broken arches are black in night
> And each shafted oriel glimmers white;
> When the cold light's uncertain shower
> Streams on the ruined central tower —

was soon on every tongue. The poem had a tremendous sale and Scott was encouraged to spin another yarn. *Marmion* is a much better story than the *Lay*. The English king, Henry VIII, who has just entered upon a war with France, sends Lord Marmion to find out why the Scots are gathering their forces. On his way to Scotland, Marmion is joined by a mysterious holy palmer, who with his face concealed behind his cowl, guides Marmion to the Scottish camp. King James of Scotland tells Marmion that the Scots have sided with France and will make war upon the English. Marmion, under orders to remain in Scotland while there is still any hope of averting war, is directed to go to Tantallon Castle, the seat of the aged and haughty Douglas. Meanwhile it develops that Marmion is involved in a very complicated love affair. He had deserted a devoted mistress in order to win the hand of Lady Clara de Clare. Her betrothed, de Wilton, Marmion had falsely accused of treason to get rid of him. They had resorted to trial by combat and de Wilton had been left for dead upon the field. To escape Marmion's unwelcome attentions Clara had found asylum in a nunnery. The Abbess and the novice Clara have been captured by the Scots, and King James avails himself of Marmion's presence in Scotland to send the Abbess and the novice back to England under his escort. They accompany him to Tantallon. To Douglas, the master of the castle, the holy palmer discloses himself as de Wilton, miraculously recovered of his wounds, and Clara and de Wilton are reunited. Then at length comes the actual historical event which Scott has all the while been working up to. The Scottish forces meet the English on Flodden Field. Marmion and de Wilton take part in the battle. Marmion is slain and buried in a nameless grave. De Wilton survives and marries the Lady Clara.

It is a good story, but it is still not Scott at his best. The tangled skein of Marmion's love affair incommodes the story-teller. The various threads are not skillfully interwoven. Five of the six cantos are, in their way, good stories, but they are not *the* story. But after all, that sixth canto, where the Scotch and English meet and fight it out on Flodden Field, is what Scott himself has been waiting for. It redeems the poem. It may be doubted whether there is another battle-piece in the whole range of English poetry that can compare with it for dash and vividness.

And, structurally faulty as the poem is, how our ancestors loved it! They sang or recited the songs which Scott scattered through the story,— and one of these songs,

> Oh, young Lochinvar is come out of the west,

our ancestors' descendants have not yet given up reciting. And brave bits of that sixth canto —

> Burned Marmion's swarthy cheek like fire
> And shook his very frame for ire,
> And — "This to me!" he said . . .

and Douglas's

> Darest thou then
> To beard the lion in his den,
> The Douglas in his hall?

and Marmion's dying words

> Charge, Chester, charge! On, Stanley, on!

are still heard on school platforms of a Friday afternoon. And who of us of the older generation are there to whom the memory comes not back of fathers who quoted with unction —

> Oh! what a tangled web we weave
> When first we practise to deceive!

O Woman! in our hours of ease
Uncertain, coy, and hard to please,
And variable as the shade
By the light quivering aspen made;
When pain and anguish wring the brow,
A ministering angel thou!

Popular as the *Lay* and *Marmion* were, Scott had not yet hit upon a plot which would bring out his best. He found it, or rather the suggestion for it, in the career of the Scottish King James V, who had fallen heir to the throne in his infancy, when his father was killed on Flodden Field. During his childhood, James was under the control of Douglas, Earl of Angus. In his sixteenth year the king succeeded in getting the power into his own hands, and bitterly resenting the authority of the Douglases, exiled all the leading members of that house, including his former favorite, the gigantic Archibald Douglas of Kilspindie. This situation, and the practice in which the king frequently indulged, of slipping away from his palace and mingling in disguise with his subjects,[1] were all that were needed to launch Scott into the enthralling romance of *The Lady of the Lake*.

It must be a very dull fellow who does not feel the thrill of the stag-hunt with which the story begins. And when the headmost hunter, forced by the death of his gallant steed to give up the chase, climbs the precipice and looks down upon Loch Katrine, and sees the maiden bring her little skiff to shore, then, indeed, there is a story toward. In any properly constructed world of brave adventure, what else could possibly happen than that fair Ellen should

[1] Some of James's adventures while thus wandering about under the guise of "the Goodman of Ballengiech" are related by Scott in his *Tales of a Grandfather*.

be a daughter of the exiled Douglas; that this chance visitor
to her humble lodge, who calls himself the Knight of Snow-
doun, James Fitz-James, and who is ignorant of her parentage, should fall in love with her; that when he finds
that her heart is given to another, he should magnani-
mously give her a signet-ring with which, in her hour of
need, she may claim a boon from Scotland's king; that
Ellen's outlaw cousin, Roderick Dhu, should call his clan
to arms, and put James Fitz-James in peril of his life;
that to avert a war, the secretly-returned Douglas should
generously decide to go to Stirling to surrender himself;
that Ellen should go to Stirling to claim with the ring her
father's freedom; that James Fitz-James should turn out
to be none other than the king himself; that Douglas
should be taken back into favor; and that Ellen's lover,
most opportunely captured by the king, should be handed
over to her with the royal blessing. And what brave moments, what spirited climaxes! — Fitz-James's erstwhile
amiable guide suddenly signaling his five hundred fighting
men up from the bracken —

> These are Clan-Alpine's warriors true;
> And, Saxon, — I am Roderick Dhu!

And Fitz-James himself facing them undaunted —

> This rock shall fly
> From its firm base as soon as I.

And Fitz-James leading shy Ellen into the waiting throng
of lords and ladies —

> He stood in simple Lincoln green,
> The centre of the glittering ring, —
> And Snowdoun's Knight is Scotland's king!

Delightful stuff! Nobody with a spark of romance in his heart can help enjoying it. And yet, even in the full heat of it, we have a feeling that it is far from being great poetry. Does it really make the story poetic for the outlaw Roderick to begin what he calls his "blunt speech"? —

> Blasted be yon Pine,
> My father's ancient crest and mine,
> If from its shade in danger part
> The lineage of the Bleeding Heart.

Or for Scott to call Ellen's log cabin a "rustic bower," or to say that the Douglas's huge weapons "garnish the sylvan hall" or to describe Ellen's reception at Stirling in such terms as these? —

> For her use a menial train
> A rich collation spread in vain.

Does this "grand style" really contribute to the romantic atmosphere of the poem, as Scott meant that it should? Is it really desirable to tell the story, and to make these early sixteenth-century Scots talk in the mannered language of eighteenth-century poetry? Certainly our grandfathers found it to their taste, and when they themselves "took pen in hand," were all too ready to call waiters a menial train and a good dinner a rich collation. (This sort of "fine writing" has been slow a-dying, and, indeed, in modified forms, is with us yet.) But wouldn't Ellen's love story have been even more appealing, and the exploits of James Fitz-James and Roderick Dhu and Douglas have been more convincing, if Scott had told their story as simply and directly as the Ancient Mariner told his? And even though the Mariner's adventures are incredible, and most of *The Lady of the Lake* is entirely credible, do Ellen and Fitz-James and Roderick and Douglas seem as real to you as that possessed and conscience-driven old sailor of Coleridge's story?

Isn't Scott's story just a bit too dramatically *arranged?* Could Roderick's five hundred fighting men have invisibly attended him while he guided Fitz-James along narrow mountain paths and then at his whistle popped up as one man from the bracken? It need not detract from our enjoyment of a poem to read it with our eyes open. And if we can feel the difference between the passionate sincerity, the directness, the utter rightness of word, in the Mariner's story, and the not infrequent tinsel in *The Lady of the Lake,* we shall be in a better position to see the good and the bad in Byron and to appreciate the superlatively beautiful things that wait for us in Keats and Shelley.

Byron was a greater poet than Scott. Scott himself said that Byron was better "in the description of the strong passions, and in deep-seated knowledge of the human heart." That suggests the essential difference between the two men. Scott's was not a deeply emotional nature. His life was too well-ordered, his temperament too wholesomely balanced and sane, for him to plumb depths or scale heights, or experience the agonies and ecstasies, the expression of which can sometimes be great poetry. Scott had a lively imagination, and tremendous vigor; but he had not the spiritual intensity by which imagination is kindled into flame. In Byron's poetry, on the other hand, intensity, lyric fervor, are what gives it its chief claim to distinction. If ever a poet wrote himself completely into his poetry, it was Byron. He came of a family which had played a prominent part in English life ever since the Norman Conquest. There was a wildness in his blood, which had manifested itself in generation after generation of his forebears, and which was heightened in him by a peculiarly ill-conditioned and unhappy childhood. Boy and man, he was overweeningly proud and morbidly sensitive. He was vain, boastful, ostentatious. He was so impulsive, so fiery, so reckless of consequences in all that he did, that his life brought much misery to others as well as to himself. As he flung himself into life, so he flung himself into poetry, at times finding emotional relief in it, at times chafing at the impossibility of finding words intense enough. So in the description of the storm on Lake Leman —

> Could I embody and unbosom now
> That which is most within me, — could I wreak
> My thoughts upon expression, and thus throw
> Soul, heart, mind, passions, feelings, strong or weak,
> All that I would have sought, and all I seek,
> Bear, know, feel, and yet breathe — into *one* word,
> And that one word were Lightning, I would speak;
> But as it is, I live and die unheard,
> With a most voiceless thought, sheathing it as a sword.

At its best, Byron's work has a kind of splendor, a rush and sweep, as of a surging wind. But even in the best of it there is something lacking. Byron had the gift of making words sing themselves. His lyrics, and some of his perfervid descriptive passages, are sheer music. They carry you with them, and have a swing and vividness that imprint them upon the memory. But their music is melody rather than harmony. It has not the delicate interplay of tones which, in great poetry, so completely satisfies the ear and mind. And even at its best Byron's work does not have the finality of great poetry. You do not feel as you read it that the thought has been crystallized into the perfect word — the one word that the thought has been waiting for, the word from which it can never now be parted.

Here, for example, is Byron thinking of a palace once glittering with life, but now in ruins —

> But now, as if a thing unblest by Man,
> Thy fairy dwelling is as lone as thou!
> Here giant weeds a passage scarce allow
> To halls deserted, portals gaping wide:
> Fresh lessons to the thinking bosom, how
> Vain are the pleasaunces on earth supplied;
> Swept into wrecks anon by Time's ungentle tide!

And here is another poet, to whom the sculptured figures on an urn have likewise brought the thought of the passing of life —

> What little town by river or sea shore,
> Or mountain-built with peaceful citadel,
> Is emptied of this folk, this pious morn?
> And, little town, thy streets for evermore
> Will silent be; and not a soul to tell
> Why thou art desolate, can e'er return.

Once again, here is Byron, lifted now to one of those moments of ecstasy, in which the everyday world fades into utter insignificance and the awareness of beauty is all in all —

> All heaven and earth are still — though not in sleep,
> But breathless, as we grow when feeling most;
> And silent, as we stand in thoughts too deep: —
> All heaven and earth are still: From the high host
> Of stars, to the lulled lake and mountain-coast,
> All is concentered in a life intense,
> Where not a beam, nor air, nor leaf is lost,
> But hath a part of being and a sense
> Of that which is of all Creator and defence.

> Then stirs the feeling infinite, so felt
> In solitude, where we are *least* alone;
> A truth, which through our being then doth melt,
> And purifies from self: it is a tone,
> The soul and source of music, which makes known
> Eternal harmony, and sheds a charm
> Like to the fabled Cytherea's zone,
> Binding all things with beauty; — 'twould disarm
> The spectre Death, had he substantial power to harm.

And here is another poet, similarly rapt, when the stillness of the night is broken by the song of the nightingale —

> Darkling I listen; and for many a time
> I have been half in love with easeful Death,
> Called him soft names in many a mused rhyme,
> To take into the air my quiet breath;
> Now more than ever seems it rich to die,
> To cease upon the midnight with no pain,
> While thou art pouring forth thy soul abroad
>   In such an ecstasy!
> Still wouldst thou sing, and I have ears in vain —
> To thy high requiem become a sod.

Read the two paired passages — the first pair and the second pair — aloud to yourself. The two passages from Byron, especially the one beginning: "All heaven and earth are still," are beautiful. But aren't they at the same time a little rhetorical? And do you not feel, in the paired passages from Keats, a greater concreteness and sureness of word and phrase, a lovelier harmony, a supreme felicity that is not in Byron's lines?

But (though it is well for us to read him with our eyes open) there is much in Byron that is worth enjoying and worth remembering.[1] There is, for example, the moving story of Bonnivard, chained with his two brothers

> In Chillon's dungeons deep and old,

doomed to see them die beside him, and becoming at length so inured to those confining walls that his very chains and he grew friends —

> Lake Leman lies by Chillon's walls:
> A thousand feet in depth below
> Its massy waters meet and flow;
> Thus much the fathom-line was sent
> From Chillon's snow-white battlement,
>   Which round about the wave inthrals:
> A double dungeon wall and wave
> Have made — and like a living grave
> Below the surface of the lake
> The dark vault lies wherein we lay,
> We heard it ripple night and day;
>   Sounding o'er our heads it knocked;
> And I have felt the winter's spray
> Wash through the bars when winds were high
> And wanton in the happy sky;

---

[1] It is the *romantic* Byron, the Byron that left the most vivid impress upon his generation, that concerns us here. But it must not be forgotten that there was another side to his genius. As a satirist, he was second only to Pope. Byron's *English Bards and Scotch Reviewers* is an extraordinarily witty — and altogether merciless — attack upon the poets of his day. A part of his contemptuous reference to Wordsworth has already been quoted (p. 421). The plodding Southey, who had

> written much blank verse and blanker prose
> And more of both than any body knows,

and who had offended Byron by calling him and his imitators "the Satanic School," Byron pursued with peculiar vindictiveness. *The Vision of Judgment*, in which Byron imagines Southey attempting to read his poetry to the guard of angels at St. Peter's gate, and, "at the fifth line," getting knocked down and sent spinning by a blow from St. Peter's keys, is a masterpiece of witty absurdity. Even in *Don Juan* (of which more hereafter) Byron renews his attack on Southey, and takes a farewell fling at the other members of the "Lake School" — Wordsworth and his imitators.

And then the very rock hath rocked,
And I have felt it shake, unshocked,
Because I could have smiled to see
The death that would have set me free . . .
It might be months, or years, or days,
    I kept no count, I took no note,
I had no hope my eyes to raise,
    And clear them of their dreary mote;
At last men came to set me free;
    I asked not why, and recked not where;
It was at length the same to me,
Fettered or fetterless to be,
    I learned to love despair.
And thus when they appeared at last,
And all my bonds aside were cast,
These heavy walls to me had grown
A hermitage — and all my own!

There are such stories as *Mazeppa*, in which the verse itself
goes with the wild rush of the hero's steed —

" 'Bring forth the horse!' — the horse was brought;
    In truth, he was a noble steed,
    A Tartar of the Ukraine breed,
Who looked as though the speed of thought
Were in his limbs; but he was wild,
    Wild as the wild deer, and untaught,
With spur and bridle undefiled —
    'Twas but a day he had been caught;
And snorting, with erected mane,
And struggling fiercely, but in vain,
In the full foam of wrath and dread
To me the desert-born was led:
They bound me on, that menial throng;
Upon his back with many a thong;
Then loosed him with a sudden lash —

Away! — away! — and on we dash!
Torrents less rapid and less rash.

"Away! — away! My breath was gone,
I saw not where he hurried on:
'Twas scarcely yet the break of day,
And on he foamed — away! — away! . . .

"Away, away, my steed and I,
  Upon the pinions of the wind,
  All human dwellings left behind;
We sped like meteors through the sky,
When with its crackling sound the night
Is chequered with the northern light:
Town — village — none were on our track,
  But a wild plain of far extent,
And bounded by a forest black;
  And, save the scarce seen battlement
On distant heights of some strong hold,
Against the Tartars built of old,
No trace of man . . ."

There are such tales as *The Giaour* and *The Bride of Abydos*
and *The Corsair* in which Byron, profiting by the vogue
of the *Lay* and *Marmion* and *The Lady of the Lake*, gives
to the narrative poem of romantic adventure a glow and
intensity quite beyond Scott's reach. And best of all
there are those two wonderful blends of narration and
description and rhapsody and satire, *Childe Harold* and
Don Juan.

Childe Harold is a poem in the Spenserian stanza, with
occasional old words such as Spenser used. "Childe"
was a title given in the middle ages to youths of noble birth
who were candidates for knighthood. The hero (Byron
first thought of calling him "Childe Burun") is of course

Byron himself. Though the poem starts as if it were going to be a story of Harold's adventures, it soon resolves itself into a series of descriptions of spots of beauty and historic interest in southern Europe which Byron had visited. As these places in Spain and Portugal and Italy kindle his imagination, description gives place to lyrical outbursts concerning the great events and great men associated with them. Many passages are deservedly famous. The two that are perhaps best known are the description of the battle of Waterloo —

> There was a sound of revelry by night —

and the oft-quoted lines beginning

> Roll on, thou deep and dark blue Ocean — roll!
> Ten thousand fleets sweep over thee in vain;

but there are also many long passages of sustained magnificence such as the apostrophe to Italy —

> Italia! Oh Italia! thou who hast
> The fatal gift of beauty,

and the descriptions of Venice,

> Throned on her hundred isles,

and of Rome

> The Niobe of nations.

There are, too, many single stanzas of arresting power, such as the meditation on Napoleon —

> Conqueror and captive of the earth art thou,

and the lines on the Roman Pantheon —

> Simple, erect, severe, austere, sublime —
> Shrine of all saints and temple of all gods,
> From Jove to Jesus — spared and blest by time —

Continuously interwoven with these descriptive passages and lyrical outbursts is Byron's characteristic theme — his hatred of society, his love of solitude, of the gloomy grandeur of nature.

> I have not loved the world nor the world me.

His own pride, arrogance and folly had turned the world against him. Byron retaliated by turning against the world.

> Have I not —
> Hear me, my mother Earth! behold it, Heaven!
> Have I not had to wrestle with my lot?
> Have I not suffered things to be forgiven?
> Have I not had my brain seared, my heart riven,
> Hopes sapped, name blighted, Life's life lied away?
> And only not to desperation driven,
> Because not altogether of such clay
> As rots into the soul of those whom I survey? . . .
>
> I live not in myself, but I become
> Portion of that around me; and to me
> High mountains are a feeling, but the hum
> Of human cities torture . . .
>
> Where rose the mountains, there to him were friends;
> Where rolled the ocean, thereon was his home;
> Where a blue sky, and glowing clime, extends,
> He had the passion and the power to roam;
> The desert, forest, cavern, breaker's foam,
> Were unto him companionship.

Don Juan is rather more of a story than *Childe Harold*. Again the hero is Byron himself, now masking under the name of that personage of Spanish legend, whose not altogether respectable adventures had already furnished a theme for various novelists, dramatists and poets. Byron's

Don Juan is a series of episodes, some of which Byron coined out of his own wanderings, some of which are entirely imaginary. Among the best things in the poem are the vivid story of the shipwreck, culminating in the stanza —

> And first one universal shriek there rushed
> Louder than the loud ocean, like a crash
> Of echoing thunder; and then all was hushed,
> Save the wild wind and the remorseless dash
> Of billows; but at intervals there gushed,
> Accompanied with a convulsive splash,
> A solitary shriek, the bubbling cry
> Of some strong swimmer in his agony;

and the lovely idyl of Juan's meeting with the island maiden, Haidée —

> They were alone, but not alone as they
> Who shut in chambers think it loneliness;
> The silent ocean, and the starlight bay,
> The twilight glow, which momently grew less,
> The voiceless sands, and dropping caves, that lay
> Around them, made them to each other press,
> As if there were no life beneath the sky
> Save theirs, and that their life could never die

Scattered through the poem are songs, such as the one beginning

> The isles of Greece, the isles of Greece!
> Where burning Sappho loved and sung,

which have stirred the pulses of many generations of readers. But the mood of *Don Juan* is far less intense than the foregoing quotations would suggest. In the main, *Don Juan* is a jester's tale — the tale of a very flippant and scoffing jester, who, the moment you begin to take him seriously, lets you down with a thump.

'Tis sweet to hear the watch-dog's honest bark
Bay deep-mouth welcome as we draw near home;
'Tis sweet to know there is an eye will mark
Our coming, and look brighter when we come;
'Tis sweet to be awakened by the lark,
Or lulled by falling waters; sweet the hum
Of bees, the voice of girls, the song of birds,
The lisp of children, and their earliest words . . .

Sweet is a legacy, and passing sweet
The unexpected death of some old lady
Or gentleman of seventy years complete,
Who've made "us youth" wait too-too long already —

This flippant, cynical, and scoffing mood is partly in
keeping with the character of the traditional Don Juan;
but chiefly a reflection of Byron's chronic feeling that he
was at odds with society. The melancholy and solitude-
loving Byron of *Childe Harold* has put on the jester's mask.

The sad truth which hovers o'er my desk
Turns what was once romantic to burlesque.
And if I laugh at any mortal thing,
'Tis that I may not weep.

He filled *Don Juan* with flippancies and gibes and mockery; but though the Southeys of his generation were properly shocked, and accused him of "polluting" English
poetry, the public at large not only continued to read him
with delight, but also fell to imitating him. This unconventional Byron, who took a bitter pride in his aloofness,
became himself the creator of a convention, the maker of a
pattern. A host of melancholy little poets began to rave
in rhyme. Sundry fine gentlemen cultivated the Byronic
pose. Novelists made their heroes "grand, gloomy, and
peculiar," and provided them with a proper setting of
ancient abbeys and moldy ruins. In a contemporary

satire, *Nightmare Abbey*, by Thomas Love Peacock, this mood of the moment is delightfully hit off. Nightmare Abbey is "a venerable family mansion, in a highly picturesque state of semi-dilapidation." The owner, Mr. Glowry, uses the skull of one of his aristocratic ancestors as a drinking-cup, and always chooses his servants "by one of two criterions — long faces or a dismal name." His butler is named Raven; his steward, Crow, his grooms, Mattocks and Graves; his footman, Diggory Deathshead. Mr. Cypress (Byron) comes to bid Mr. Glowry and his friends adieu. "Mr. Cypress said he was on the point of leaving England, but could not think of doing so without a farewell look at Nightmare Abbey, and his respected friends, the moody Mr. Glowry and the mysterious Mr. Scythrop, the sublime Mr. Flosky and the pathetic Mr. Listless, to all of whom, and the morbid hospitality of the melancholy dwelling in which they were then assembled, he assured them he would always look back with as much affection as his lacerated spirit could feel for anything." They drink a farewell bumper together — "the only social habit," remarks Mr. Cypress, "that the disappointed spirit never unlearns." The parting — and the bumper — fill them with "a delightful melancholy," and Mr. Cypress sings them a song about lone dark souls and spectral memories and the fire that burns, blasts and consumes the heart. "Admirable!" says Mr. Glowry. "Let us all be unhappy together."

There was a good deal of pose in Byron himself, and of course nothing else but pose in "Byronism"; but time enough has passed since Byron's day for us to escape the dross and value the gold. The stirring music, the passionate intensity, the sheer power, the versatility, which so completely captivated his own generation have not dimmed in the century that has elapsed since his death. If we are disposed as we look back to rank Chaucer and Shakespeare and Milton and Wordsworth and Shelley and Keats higher than Byron, we still think of him as one of the great names of English poetry.

Byron died in 1824. During that first quarter of the nineteenth century, Wordsworth's reputation had been slowly mounting, but opinion was still divided as to whether he was a great poet or a great bore. Coleridge, after fulfilling the promise of "The Ancient Mariner" with two poems of extraordinary beauty, "Christabel" and "Kubla Khan," and producing a variety of others less deserving of mention, had subsided into a critic and lecturer on literature and philosophy. Scott, recognizing the superiority of Byron, had turned from poetry to novel-writing. Probably, at any time during the five years between 1816 (when three of the four cantos of *Childe Harold* were in print) and 1821 (when the first five cantos of *Don Juan* were finished), to the question, "Who is the greatest living English poet?" nine out of ten men would have confidently answered, "Byron." Byron was spectacular. He filled men's minds. But as *we* look back to those five years, all things else sink into insignificance beside the fact that within them Keats and Shelley did their work. The year 1816 saw the publication of Keats's sonnet on Chapman's Homer, and Shelley's "Alastor." By February of 1821 Keats was dead. By July of the next year Shelley's life was at an end.[1] Shelley

[1] Keats died of consumption in Rome. Shelley was drowned in the Mediterranean, while sailing in a small boat from Leghorn to Spezia. His body was found near Via Reggio with a volume of Keats's poems in his pocket. The body was cremated on the shore in the presence of Trelawney and Leigh Hunt, friends of Byron and Shelley. The ashes were buried in the Protestant Cemetery at Rome. Not far away is the grave of Keats. In *Adonais* (stanzas XLIX–L) Shelley describes that place of burial.

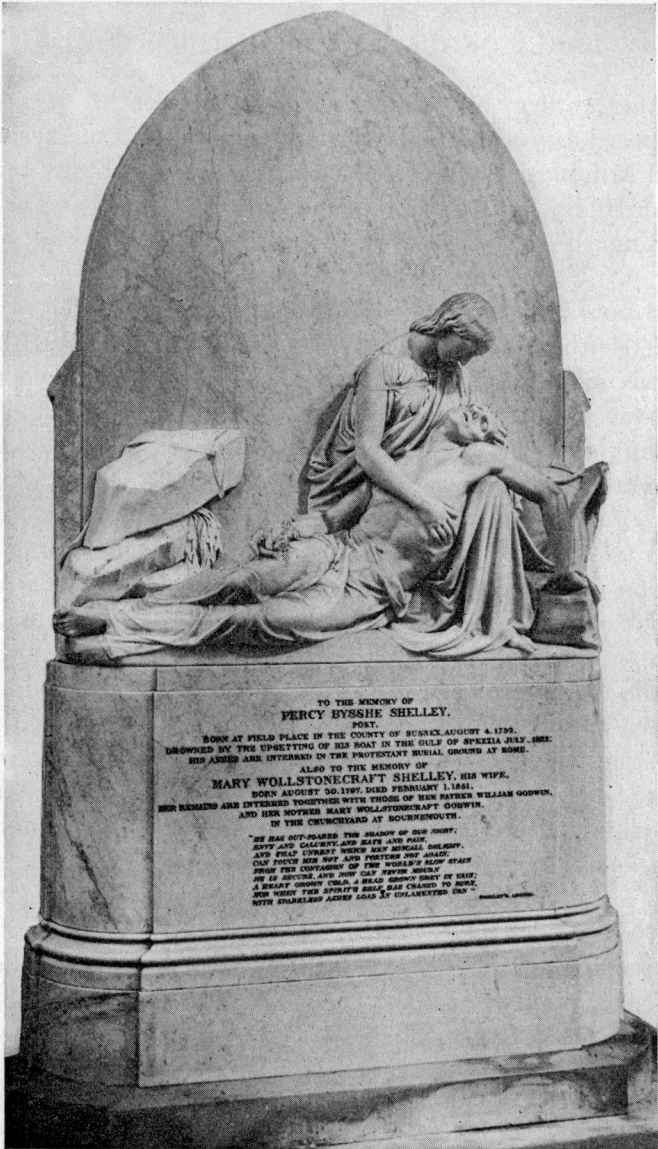

Photograph by Ewing Galloway, New York

MEMORIAL TO SHELLEY

This is in The Priory Church in Christ Church Village, in Hampshire,
on the Southern Coast of England

was thirty when he died, Keats only twenty-five.   But they left enough to place them in the first rank of English poets.

In some ways, Shelley was like Byron.   He was of aristocratic birth; he was intensely emotional and imaginative and romantic; he hated and violently rebelled against the conventions and commonly accepted beliefs of society. But the differences between the two men are greater than the resemblances.   Byron's energy defeated itself.   Byron could never escape from Byron.   But to Shelley, poetry was an almost selfless thing, a pure and complete realization of beauty.   Poetry, he wrote, "makes immortal all that is best and most beautiful in the world"; it "turns all things to loveliness; it exalts the beauty of that which is most beautiful, and it adds beauty to that which is most deformed; it marries exultation and horror, grief and pleasure, eternity and change; it subdues to union under its light yoke all irreconcilable things.   It transmutes all that it touches, and every form moving within the radiance of its presence is changed by wondrous sympathy to an incarnation of the spirit which it breathes."[1]

No poet is always at his best.   The moment of vision, the moment when words can be found for the vision, comes not for the asking.   "Poetry," said Shelley, "is not like reasoning, a power to be exerted according to the determination of the will.   A man cannot say, 'I will compose poetry.'   The greatest poet even cannot say it."

The beauty which he sought,

> An image of some bright Eternity
> A shadow of some golden dream —

that beauty which

> Floats though unseen amongst us, — visiting
> This various world with as unconstant wing

[1] From Shelley's *Defence of Poetry*.

As summer winds that creep from flower to flower,
Like moonbeams that behind some piny mountain shower,
It visits with inconstant glance
Each human heart and countenance;
Like hues and harmonies of evening, —
Like clouds in starlight widely spread, —
Like memory of music fled, —
Like aught that for its grace may be
Dear, and yet dearer for its mystery,

is too ethereal to be readily or often found. In "Alastor,"
in "Epipsychidion," and elsewhere, is recorded his unavailing search for it. The poems in which Shelley tried
thus to distill the essence of beauty and failed, or tried
and did not wholly succeed, need not concern us here.
But the poems in which he did succeed have a loveliness,
a kind of radiant loveliness, such as no other English
poetry possesses.

Sometimes he found it in a strain of nature's music.
Even to less imaginative souls, the moment when a skylark wings up from an English meadow and vanishes sky-
ward, pouring down the while its crystal stream of song,
is pure ecstasy. Shelley's magic makes it the perfect symbol
of the elusive spirit of beauty which he is always seeking.

Hail to thee, blithe spirit!
    Bird thou never wert,
That from heaven, or near it,
    Pourest thy full heart
In profuse strains of unpremeditated art.

Higher still and higher
    From the earth thou springest
Like a cloud of fire;
    The blue deep thou wingest,
And singing still dost soar, and soaring ever singest.

In the golden lightning
　　Of the sunken sun,
O'er which clouds are bright'ning,
　　Thou dost float and run;
Like an unbodied joy whose race is just begun.

The pale purple even
　　Melts around thy flight;
Like a star of heaven
　　In the broad day-light
Thou art unseen, but yet I hear thy shrill delight,

Keen as are the arrows
　　Of that silver sphere,
Whose intense lamp narrows
　　In the white dawn clear,
Until we hardly see, we feel that it is there.

All the earth and air
　　With thy voice is loud,
As, when night is bare,
　　From one lonely cloud
The moon rains out her beams, and heaven is overflowed.

What thou art we know not;
　　What is most like thee?
From rainbow clouds there flow not
　　Drops so bright to see
As from thy presence showers a rain of melody.

Like a poet hidden
　　In the light of thought,
Singing hymns unbidden,
　　Till the world is wrought
To sympathy with hopes and fears it heeded not . . .

Better than all measures
Of delightful sound —
Better than all treasures
That in books are found —
Thy skill to poet were, thou scorner of the ground!

Teach me half the gladness
That thy brain must know,
Such harmonious madness
From my lips would flow,
The world should listen then — as I am listening now.

Again this etherealized beauty may be revealed in the most fleeting and delicate moods of nature —

For the Sensitive Plant has no bright flower;
Radiance and odour are not its dower;
It loves, even like Love; its deep heart is full;
It desires what it has not, the beautiful!

The light winds which from unsustaining wings
Shed the music of many murmurings;
The beams which dart from many a star
Of the flowers whose hues they bear afar;

The plumèd insects swift and free,
Like golden boats on a sunny sea,
Laden with light and odour, which pass
Over the gleam of the living grass;

The unseen clouds of the dew, which lie
Like fire in the flowers till the sun rides high,
Then wander like spirits among the spheres,
Each cloud faint with the fragrance it bears;

The quivering vapours of dim noontide,
Which like a sea o'er the warm earth glide,

> In which every sound, and odour, and beam,
> Move, as reeds in a single stream.

Not only could Shelley sometimes capture, as no other poet has succeeded in capturing, these moments of pure and etherealized beauty; but he had also another gift in greater measure than most other poets. He could make words sing, he could create the most delicate and subtle music. At times, when his poetry breaks into song, the meaning of the words seems hardly to matter, so borne along are we by the music. Here, for example, is the song of one of the allegorical beings in *Prometheus Unbound:*

> My soul is an enchanted boat,
> Which, like a sleeping swan, doth float
> Upon the silver waves of thy sweet singing;
> And thine doth like an angel sit
> Beside a helm conducting it,
> Whilst all the winds with melody are ringing.
> It seems to float ever, forever,
> Upon that many-winding river,
> Between mountains, woods, abysses,
> A paradise of wildernesses!
> Till, like one in slumber bound,
> Borne to the ocean, I float down, around,
> Into a sea profound, of ever-spreading sound.

And here is a part of the "Hymn of Pan":

> From the forests and highlands
>   We come, we come;
> From the river-girt islands,
>   Where loud waves are dumb
>   Listening to my sweet pipings.
> The wind in the reeds and the rushes,
>   The bees on the bells of thyme,
> The birds on the myrtle bushes,
>   The cicale above in the lime,

> And the lizards below in the grass,
> Were as silent as ever old Tmolus was,
>   Listening to my sweet pipings.

Finally, when Shelley rises to his best, these qualities enter into wonderful combination; words which are themselves pure music capture for us thoughts and images of a most rare and delicate beauty. There are three poems especially of which this is true, poems which, after this taste of them, you will wish to read in their entirety. One is the "Ode to the West Wind."

> O, wild West Wind, thou breath of Autumn's being,
> Thou, from whose unseen presence the leaves dead
> Are driven, like ghosts from an enchanter fleeing,
>
> Yellow, and black, and pale, and hectic red,
> Pestilence-stricken multitudes: O, thou,
> Who chariotest to their dark wintry bed
>
> The wingèd seeds, where they lie cold and low,
> Each like a corpse within its grave, until
> Thine azure sister of the spring shall blow
>
> Her clarion o'er the dreaming earth, and fill
> (Driving sweet buds like flocks to feed in air)
> With living hues and odours plain and hill:
>
> Wild Spirit, which art moving everywhere;
> Destroyer and preserver; hear, O, hear! . . .
>
> Make me thy lyre, even as the forest is:
> What if my leaves are falling like its own!
> The tumult of thy mighty harmonies
>
> Will take from both a deep, autumnal tone,
> Sweet though in sadness. Be thou, Spirit fierce,
> My spirit! Be thou me, impetuous one!

Drive my dead thoughts over the universe
Like withered leaves to quicken a new birth!
And, by the incantation of this verse,

Scatter, as from an unextinguished hearth
Ashes and sparks, my words among mankind!
Be through my lips to unawakened earth

The trumpet of a prophecy!   O Wind,
If Winter comes, can Spring be far behind?

Another is "The Cloud":

I bring fresh showers for the thirsting flowers,
    From the seas and the streams;
I bear light shade for the leaves when laid
    In their noon-day dreams.
From my wings are shaken the dews that waken
    The sweet buds every one,
When rocked to rest on their mother's breast,
    As she dances about the sun.
I wield the flail of the lashing hail,
    And whiten the green plains under,
And then again I dissolve it in rain,
    And laugh as I pass in thunder . . . ;

That orbèd maiden with white fire laden,
    Whom mortals call the moon,
Glides glimmering o'er my fleece-like floor,
    By the midnight breezes strewn;
And wherever the beat of her unseen feet,
    Which only the angels hear,
May have broken the woof of my tent's thin roof,
    The stars peep behind her and peer;
And I laugh to see them whirl and flee,
    Like a swarm of golden bees,

When I widen the rent in my wind-built tent,
    Till the calm rivers, lakes, and seas,
Like strips of the sky fallen through me on high,
    Are each paved with the moon and these . . .

I am the daughter of earth and water,
    And the nursling of the sky;
I pass through the pores of the ocean and shores;
    I change, but I cannot die.
For after the rain when, with never a stain,
    The pavilion of heaven is bare,
And the winds and sunbeams with their convex gleams
    Build up the blue dome of air,
I silently laugh at my own cenotaph,
    And out of the caverns of rain,
Like a child from the womb, like a ghost from the tomb,
    I arise and unbuild it again.

The third is *Adonais*. Keats was dead — hounded to his death, Shelley thought, by certain brutal attacks on his poetry which had appeared in the critical reviews. Shelley's lament for him, like Milton's *Lycidas*, is modeled on the classical elegies — Bion's *Elegy on Adonis*, for example, of which the name, Adonais, is intended to be a reminder. In *Adonais*, Shelley is moved not only by his sorrow at the untimely death of Keats, but also — and perhaps more largely — by his feeling that Keats and he are alike — both thwarted wanderers in a world where beauty can be only imperfectly known. Shelley believed, with Plato, that in that world from which our spirits come, and to which, upon the release of death, they return, the ideal beauty, of which we catch only faint shadowings here, can be in some way realized. Despite his sorrow, it is chiefly in this mood that he thinks of Keats,— as one who has realized and become a part of that ideal beauty denied to mortal life, as one who has gained that for which he himself longs. In *Adonais*, there is no such lyric rush of words as in "The Cloud," but, appropriately, a grave and stately music. The poem is much too long to be quoted in full, and too closely knit to be adequately represented by extracts,[1] but these stanzas will perhaps give you a glimpse of its beauty:

> Peace, peace! he is not dead, he doth not sleep —
> He hath awakened from the dream of life . . .
>
> He is made one with Nature: there is heard
> His voice in all her music, from the moan
> Of thunder, to the song of night's sweet bird;
> He is a presence to be felt and known
> In darkness and in light, from herb and stone,
> Spreading itself where'er that Power may move
> Which has withdrawn his being to its own;
> Which wields the world with never-wearied love,
> Sustains it from beneath, and kindles it above.
>
> He is a portion of the loveliness
> Which once he made more lovely: he doth bear
> His part, while the one Spirit's plastic stress
> Sweeps through the dull dense world, compelling there
> All new successions to the forms they wear;
> Torturing th' unwilling dross that checks its flight
> To its own likeness, as each mass may bear;
> And bursting in its beauty and its might
> From trees and beasts and men into the Heaven's light . . .
>
> What Adonais is, why fear we to become?
>
> The One remains, the many change and pass;
> Heaven's light forever shines, Earth's shadows fly;

---

[1] "It is a highly wrought *piece of art*," said Shelley, "and perhaps better in point of composition than anything I have written."

Life, like a dome of many-coloured glass,
Stains the white radiance of Eternity,
Until Death tramples it to fragments. — Die,
If thou wouldst be with that which thou dost seek! . . .

The breath whose might I have invoked in song
Descends on me; my spirit's bark is driven,
Far from the shore, far from the trembling throng
Whose sails were never to the tempest given;
The massy earth and sphered skies are riven!
I am borne darkly, fearfully, afar:
Whilst burning through the inmost veil of Heaven,
The soul of Adonais, like a star,
Beacons from the abode where the Eternal are.

In its stately music, and its dream of an abstract beauty, *Adonais* is entirely characteristic of Shelley; but the "gentle child" for whom Shelley mourns, the defenseless being crushed by unfavorable criticism,[1] is not the real Keats. The real Keats had not only been a much sturdier person than Shelley implies, but had come much nearer to reaching the goal of his endeavor. He had, in fact, produced poetry which many critics are disposed to think greater than any other since Shakespeare. How he came to this, and how in the process he exposed himself both to the pity of his well-wishers and to the derision of unfriendly critics, are matters worth looking into.

His father, Thomas Keats, was head-ostler in a livery-

[1] Oh gentle child, beautiful as thou wert,
Why didst thou leave the trodden paths of men
Too soon, and with weak hands though mighty heart
Dare the unpastured dragon in his den?
Defenceless as thou wert, oh where was then
Wisdom the mirrored shield, or scorn the spear?
Or hadst thou waited the full cycle, when
Thy spirit should have filled its crescent sphere,
The monsters of life's waste had fled from thee like deer.

stable in Finsbury. His mother was the daughter of Thomas
Keats's employer. John Keats's formal education was
confined to five years in a school at Enfield. He was an
active boy, much more disposed, during the first four of
those five years, to fighting than to study. In his last
year he threw himself into reading. The books which
he cared for most were collections of classic myths — re-
tellings in English of the stories which the imaginative
Greeks had woven about their myriad gods and goddesses
and demigods. In his sixteenth year he was withdrawn
from school and apprenticed to an apothecary in Edmonton. While he was thus employed, a school-friend read
one of Spenser's shorter poems aloud to him. Keats borrowed the volume, took it home, and read *The Faerie
Queene*, going through it (said this friend), "as a young
horse would through a spring meadow — ramping."

The romantic adventures in *The Faerie Queene*, the
vagrant fancies, the rich imagery, the mellow music of

> Spenserian vowels that elope with ease
> And float along like birds on summer seas,

affected Keats's emotional nature like the sudden uncoil-
ing of a spring. He would write poetry. What would he
not do, if the gods would only grant him time!

> O for ten years, that I may overwhelm
> Myself in poesy; so I may do the deed
> That my own soul has to itself decreed.
> Then I will pass the countries that I see
> In long perspective, and continually
> Taste their pure fountains. First the realm I'll pass
> Of Flora, and old Pan: sleep in the grass,
> Feed upon apples red, and strawberries,
> And choose each pleasure that my fancy sees . . .

> And can I ever bid these joys farewell?
> Yes, I must pass them for a nobler life,
> Where I may find the agonies, the strife
> Of human hearts —

He was a mere boy, intensely emotional, with what he himself called "an exquisite sense of the luxurious." He had had little schooling and was unlessoned in self-criticism and self-discipline. He tended to lose himself in mere sensation, to luxuriate in beauty, to fill his poetry with dream-shapes over-richly and over-rapturously described; and (because he was saturated with Spenser,

> Fed too much with cloying melody)

he was altogether too prone to soften his describing words into sugary forms —"bloomy," "streamy," "paly," "lawny," "rushy," and the like — which give to much of the poetry of his earlier years an effeminate and languishing quality.

These defects (and very real defects they were) were what exposed him to the ridicule of the critics when he published his first long poem, "Endymion." The little Preface which Keats wrote to "Endymion" is an interesting document. He was not lacking in pride. He had faith that, given the ten years he prayed for, he would do great things. But he had not that pride of birth, that easy assurance, which enabled Byron, for example, to fling his juvenile poems in the face of the critics and, when they lashed at him, lash back at them. Keats is deprecating, uneasy, apologetic. The reader, says he, "must soon perceive great inexperience, immaturity, and every error denoting a feverish attempt, rather than a deed accomplished." The poem is not worth revising. "The foundations are too sandy. It is just that this youngster should die away: a sad thought for me, if I had not some hope that while it is dwindling I may be plotting, and fitting myself for verses fit to live." He expresses the hope that the critics will not deal harshly with him. "This is not written with the least atom of purpose to forestall criticisms of course, but from the desire I have to conciliate men who are competent to look, and who do look with a zealous eye, to the honour of English literature.

"The imagination of a boy is healthy, and the mature imagination of a man is healthy; but there is a space of life between, in which the soul is in a ferment, the character undecided, the way of life uncertain, the ambition thick-sighted: thence proceeds mawkishness, and all the thousand bitters which those men I speak of must necessarily taste in going over the following pages."

The boyishness of this might have disarmed criticism. The very opening lines of the poem might have shown the critics what possibilities were in him.

"A thing of beauty is a joy for ever:
  Its loveliness increases; it will never
  Pass into nothingness; but still will keep
  A bower quiet for us, and a sleep
  Full of sweet dreams, and health, and quiet breathing.
  Therefore, on every morrow, are we wreathing
  A flowery band to bind us to the earth,
  Spite of despondence, of the inhuman dearth
 Of noble natures, of the gloomy days,
  Of all the unhealthy and o'er-darkened ways
  Made for our searching: yes, in spite of all,
  Some shape of beauty moves away the pall
  From our dark spirits.   Such the sun, the moon,
  Trees old and young, sprouting a shady boon
  For simple sheep; and such are daffodils
  With the green world they live in; and clear rills

That for themselves a cooling covert make
'Gainst the hot season; the mid-forest brake,
Rich with a sprinkling of fair musk-rose blooms:
And such too is the grandeur of the dooms
We have imagined for the mighty dead;
All lovely tales that we have heard or read:
An endless fountain of immortal drink,
Pouring unto us from the heaven's brink."

But most of the critics confined themselves to gross ridicule, and made of his poetry a byword. "The most incongruous ideas in the most uncouth language"; "gratuitous nonsense"; "we almost doubt that any man in his senses would put his real name to such a rhapsody"; "we venture to make one small prophecy, that his bookseller will not a second time venture £50 upon anything he can write. It is a better and wiser thing to be a starved apothecary than a starved poet; so back to the shop, Mr. John, back to 'plasters, pills, and ointment boxes!'"

Keats was hurt, as any sensitive man would have been, by such vulgar ridicule; but his faith in himself was not shaken. "I begin to get a little acquainted with my own strength and weakness," he wrote to a friend. "Praise or blame has but a momentary effect on the man whose love of beauty in the abstract makes him a severe critic on his own works. . . . I have written independently *without Judgment*. I may write independently, and *with Judgment* hereafter."

But even before "Endymion" there had been moments when he had written "with judgment." Spenser had aroused him, stimulated him; it is doubtful whether Spenser had been altogether good for him. But another kind of poetry contended with Spenser's in influencing his taste and molding his art. At about the time of his twenty-first birthday, not long after he had been released from his apprenticeship to become a medical student in a London hospital, the same school-friend who had introduced him to Spenser read aloud for all one night the translation of Homer made by the Elizabethan poet, George Chapman. What that experience meant to Keats must be told in his own words, set down as the morning dawned.

> Much have I travelled in the realms of gold,
> And many goodly states and kingdoms seen;
> Round many western islands have I been
> Which bards in fealty to Apollo hold.
> Oft of one wide expanse had I been told
> That deep browed Homer ruled as his demesne:
> Yet did I never breathe its pure serene [1]
> Till I heard Chapman speak out loud and bold:
> Then felt I like some watcher of the skies
> When a new planet swims into his ken;
> Or like stout Cortez when with eagle eyes
> He stared at the Pacific — and all his men
> Looked at each other with a wild surmise —
> Silent, upon a peak in Darien.

It would be an undue simplification of the process to say that the "pure serene" of the Homeric story and the masculine vigor and concreteness of Chapman's English were what rescued Keats from mawkishness. As a matter of fact, after writing the sonnet "On First Looking into Chapman's Homer," he went on with the

> Gentle tale of love and languishment

[1] In the first draft this line reads: "Yet could I never judge what men could mean" — a dull line, transformed by a prompt and happy inspiration into one of the most beautiful in the poem. Many of the revisions in Keats's other poems are equally happy.

which exposed him to the ridicule of the critics. But in
that inspired moment when the sun dawned on a night of
Chapman, he set a mark for himself. This youngster had
written a sonnet which in its contained strength, in its
exquisitely chosen words, in its stately music, in its flow
and ebb of sound —

> swelling loudly
> Up to its climax, and then dying proudly —

is one of the most perfect in the language. It stood as a
mark to shoot at, when he should have got "Endymion"
out of his system.

That time was not long in coming. It was a brief time,
for the ten years which he had prayed for in 1816 were cut
to five, and during his last year he was too ill to write; but
it was enough to produce a few poems which rank among
the masterpieces of English poetry.

One of these poems is the "Ode to the Nightingale."
With Shelley's lines "To the Skylark" fresh in your mind,
you will be inclined to think of the two side by side. You
will feel that many of the differences rise naturally out of
the difference of subject — that the quick, short-line
measure of Shelley's verse, the delicate music of the light
vowels, the rapid succession of images, each caught in a
golden glow, are as appropriate to the "unbodied joy" of
the skylark's song, as the slower movement of the *Ode*, the
deeper and richer tones, and the pensive musings are to the
"full-throated ease" of the nightingale's song heard amid
the shadows. You will feel that the two poems are both
exquisitely appropriate and exquisitely beautiful, and that
it would be futile to argue as to which is the greater. And
yet I think that the "Ode to the Nightingale" will appeal
to you more; that you will find yourself admiring Shelley's

poem as a work of art, a wonderful feat of word-magic; but, with Keats's poem, not so much admiring as yielding — feeling what he felt, thinking what he thought. That is what poetry as sincere, as intense, and as concrete as Keats's does for us. It does not let us stand off and analyze.

My heart aches, and a drowsy numbness pains
　My sense, as though of hemlock I had drunk,
Or emptied some dull opiate to the drains
　One minute past, and Lethe-wards had sunk:
'T is not through envy of thy happy lot,
　But being too happy in thine happiness, —
　　That thou, light-wingèd Dryad of the trees,
　　　In some melodious plot
Of beechen green, and shadows numberless,
　　Singest of summer in full-throated ease . . .

I cannot see what flowers are at my feet,
　Nor what soft incense hangs upon the boughs,
But, in embalmèd darkness, guess each sweet
　Wherewith the seasonable month endows
The grass, the thicket, and the fruit-tree wild;
　White hawthorn, and the pastoral eglantine;
　　Fast fading violets covered up in leaves;
　　　And mid-May's eldest child,
The coming musk-rose, full of dewy wine,
　　The murmurous haunt of flies on summer eves.

Darkling I listen; and, for many a time
　I have been half in love with easeful Death,
Call'd him soft names in many a musèd rhyme,
　To take into the air my quiet breath;
Now more than ever seems it rich to die,
　To cease upon the midnight with no pain,
　　While thou art pouring forth thy soul abroad
　　　In such an ecstasy!

Still wouldst thou sing, and I have ears in vain —
To thy high requiem become a sod.

Thou wast not born for death, immortal Bird!
No hungry generations tread thee down;
The voice I hear this passing night was heard
In ancient days by emperor and clown:
Perhaps the self-same song that found a path
Through the sad heart of Ruth, when, sick for home,
She stood in tears amid the alien corn;
The same that oft-times hath
Charmed magic casements, opening on the foam
Of perilous seas, in faery lands forlorn.

Forlorn! the very word is like a bell
To toll me back from thee to my sole self!
Adieu! the fancy cannot cheat so well
As she is famed to do, deceiving elf.
Adieu! Adieu! thy plaintive anthem fades
Past the near meadows, over the still stream,
Up the hill-side; and now 't is buried deep
In the next valley-glades:
Was it a vision, or a waking dream?
Fled is that music: — do I wake or sleep?

With the "Ode to the Nightingale" you will wish to read
another Ode of almost equal richness and beauty, the lines
"To Autumn"— a little poem full of the precise and vivid
picture-words that Keats loved, and of a mellow music
which no extract would do justice to. So, without quotation from that, let us go on to the narratives in verse.

It was to be expected that Keats with his devotion to
Spenser, would try his hand again and again at story-poems.
"Endymion," as we have seen, did not come off very well.
But the romantic richness which at first Keats did not
know how to control, served him well when he learned to

write with clear vigor and a due sense of proportion.   He
is at his best in "The Eve of St. Agnes."

It is a tale of olden times — of two lovers who have
been kept apart because there is strife between the families
to which they belong.   On a midwinter night[1] of snow and
sleet, the castle which is Madeline's home is thronged
with revelers,

> With plume, tiara, and all rich array,
> Numerous as shadows haunting fairily
> The brain, new-stuffed, in youth, with triumphs gay
> Of old romance.

But Madeline moves indifferently among them.   Her
thoughts are bent on the legend that if a maiden goes fasting to sleep on St. Agnes' Eve, at midnight she will dream
that she sees a man standing beside her bed, and that man
she will marry.   So Madeline slips away early; and meanwhile Porphyro comes across the moors, and waits muffled
at the entrance to the great hall, in peril of his life, to catch
a glimpse of Madeline.   Here the friendly old waiting-
woman, Angela, finds him and tells him of Madeline's faith
in the legend.   Porphyro persuades Angela to lead him to
Madeline's room.

> Then by the bed-side, where the faded moon
> Made a dim, silver twilight, soft he set
> A table, and, half anguished, threw thereon
> A cloth of woven crimson, gold, and jet: —
> O for some drowsy Morphean amulet!
> The boisterous, midnight, festive clarion,
> The kettle-drum, and far-heard clarionet,
> Affray his ears, though but in dying tone: —
> The hall-door shuts again, and all the noise is gone.

[1] "St. Agnes' Eve" is January 20th.

And still she slept an azure-lidded sleep,
In blanchèd linen, smooth, and lavendered,
While he from forth the closet brought a heap
Of candied apple, quince, and plum, and gourd;
With jellies soother than the creamy curd,
And lucent syrops, tinct with cinnamon;
Manna and dates, in argosy transferr'd
From Fez; and spicèd dainties, every one,
From silken Samarcand to cedared Lebanon.

These delicates he heaped with glowing hand
On golden dishes and in baskets bright
Of wreathèd silver: sumptuous they stand
In the retired quiet of the night,
Filling the chilly room with perfume light. —
"And now, my love, my seraph fair, awake!
Thou art my heaven, and I thine eremite:
Open thine eyes, for meek St. Agnes' sake,
Or I shall drowse beside thee, so my soul doth ache." . . .

Awakening up, he took her hollow lute, —
Tumultuous, — and, in chords that tenderest be,
He played an ancient ditty, long since mute,
In Provence call'd "La belle dame sans merci:"
Close to her ear touching the melody; —
Wherewith disturbed, she uttered a soft moan:
He ceased — she panted quick — and suddenly
Her blue affrayèd eyes wide open shone:
Upon his knees he sank, pale as smooth-sculptured stone.

Her eyes were open, but she still beheld,
Now wide awake, the vision of her sleep:
There was a painful change, that nigh expelled
The blisses of her dream so pure and deep
At which fair Madeline began to weep,
And moan forth witless words with many a sigh;

While still her gaze on Porphyro would keep;
Who knelt, with joinèd hands and piteous eye,
Fearing to move or speak, she looked so dreamingly . . .

      Meantime the frost-wind blows
Like Love's alarum pattering the sharp sleet
Against the window-panes; St. Agnes' moon hath set . . .

"Hark! 't is an elfin storm from faery land,
Of haggard seeming, but a boon indeed:
Arise — arise! the morning is at hand: —
The bloated wassailers will never heed: —
Let us away, my love, with happy speed;
There are no ears to hear, or eyes to see, —
Drowned all in Rhenish and the sleepy mead:
Awake! arise! my love, and fearless be,
For o'er the southern moors I have a home for thee."

She hurried at his words, beset with fears,
For there were sleeping dragons all around,
At glaring watch, perhaps, with ready spears —
Down the wide stairs a darkling way they found. —
In all the house was heard no human sound.
A chain-drooped lamp was flickering by each door;
The arras, rich with horseman, hawk, and hound,
Fluttered in the besieging wind's uproar;
And the long carpets rose along the gusty floor.

They glide, like phantoms, into the wide hall;
Like phantoms to the iron porch they glide,
Where lay the Porter, in uneasy sprawl,
With a huge empty flagon by his side:
The wakeful bloodhound rose, and shook his hide,
But his sagacious eye an inmate owns:
By one, and one, the bolts full easy slide: —
The chains lie silent on the footworn stones; —
The key turns, and the door upon its hinges groans.

And they are gone: aye, ages long ago
These lovers fled away into the storm.
That night the Baron dreamt of many a woe,
And all his warrior-guests, with shade and form
Of witch, and demon, and large coffin-worm,
Were long be-nightmared. Angela the old
Died palsy-twitched, with meagre face deform;
The Beadsman, after thousand aves told,
For aye unsought-for slept among his ashes cold.

These are of course only stanzas selected here and there from the latter part of the poem. You will wish to read it all, and with it the other romantic story-poems, "Isabella, or the Pot of Basil," and "Lamia" and the fragmentary "Eve of St. Mark." From these you will wish to turn on to a poem in a wholly different mood, the great twice-tried experiment, "Hyperion." Keats had been steeping himself in Milton, as earlier he had steeped himself in Spenser. "Hyperion," in blank verse as grave and stately as Milton's own, tells a story of the elder gods of Greek and Roman mythology — the Titans, whom, according to the classic myth, the younger gods, led by Zeus, dethroned and destroyed. The central figures are Saturn, already deprived of power, and the elder sun-god, "blazing Hyperion," soon himself to be supplanted by Apollo. Keats did not complete the story, and tried it once again in "Hyperion: a Vision," and again was unable to complete it; but it is clear that what he had in mind was a symbolic presentation of the slow betterment of man — the passing of the elder world in which brute force was law, the coming of a time when brute force has yielded to beauty and truth. In the words of Oceanus:

As Heaven and Earth are fairer, fairer far
Than Chaos and blank Darkness, though once chiefs;

And as we show beyond that Heaven and Earth
In form and shape compact and beautiful,
In will, in action free, companionship,
And thousand other signs of purer life;
So on our heels a fresh perfection treads,
A power more strong in beauty, born of us,
And fated to excel us, as we pass
In glory that old Darkness —

The "Ode on a Grecian Urn" (because it seems to me the most flawlessly perfect poem that I know, and because I should like you to have it as your final impression of Keats) I have left to the last. Keats had been haunting the British Museum, looking and ever again returning to look at the sculptured figures on the Parthenon frieze.[1] There he saw depicted in continuous sequence the festive procession winding up the hill toward the temple — youths on horseback, warriors in chariots, girls carrying baskets, young men leading heifers and rams for the sacrifice, long-robed musicians playing on lute or lyre — all wrought with such skill that every figure seems instinct with life, and the whole scene one of pressing, eager, joyful movement. Blending with this scene in Keats's mind were painted figures on Greek vases (urns) of Bacchic dances —

What mad pursuit? What struggle to escape?
What pipes and timbrels? What wild ecstasy?

And out of these blended impressions sprang, as if at a single breath of inspired creation, the five perfect stanzas of the *Ode.* It is a moment of vivid life, caught by the sculptor, recaptured by the poet. But the poem is more

[1] These sculptures, which adorned the Parthenon, or temple of Pallas Athene on the Acropolis at Athens, were purchased by Lord Elgin, and had just been installed in the British Museum when Keats first saw them. The profound impression which they made upon him is recorded in his sonnet "On Seeing the Elgin Marbles."

than a picture. It is an impassioned expression of the poet's mood — a mood that culminates in the declaration that "beauty is truth, truth beauty." Critics have often accused Keats of marring an otherwise perfect poem by patching on to it a theory that the creation of beauty is the only "truth." But that is not what Keats means; nor, in the sense in which Keats means the words, are they an afterthought, or a "tag." Keats finds himself living over again that moment imperishably wrought on the urn, and sharing that wild ecstasy. The moment of beauty and ecstasy is communicable to the poet, as it will be to other lovers of beauty, "when old age shall this generation waste." But the men and maidens are dust long ago. What does it mean — that human beings whose capacity for joy seems so boundless and inextinguishable should vanish into nothingness? The truth about that is beyond our understanding. But at least beauty endures. That is something real, a truth to hold to. And as the poet clings to the one thing that seems to him real, amid so much that is inexplicable, it is as if that scene of ecstasy, captured for all time by the sculptor's art, were saying to him:

> That is all
> Ye know on earth, and all ye need to know.

Thou still unravished bride of quietness,
　Thou foster-child of Silence and slow Time,
Sylvan historian, who canst thus express
　A flowery tale more sweetly than our rhyme:
What leaf-fringed legend haunts about thy shape
　Of deities or mortals, or of both.
　　In Tempe or the dales of Arcady?
What men or gods are these? what maidens loth?
What mad pursuit? What struggle to escape?
　What pipes and timbrels? What wild ecstasy?

Heard melodies are sweet, but those unheard
  Are sweeter; therefore, ye soft pipes, play on;
Not to the sensual ear, but, more endeared
  Pipe to the spirit ditties of no tone:
Fair youth, beneath the trees, thou canst not leave
  Thy song, nor ever can those trees be bare;
    Bold Lover, never, never canst thou kiss,
Though winning near the goal — yet, do not grieve;
    She cannot fade, though thou hast not thy bliss,
  For ever wilt thou love, and she be fair!

Ah, happy, happy boughs! that cannot shed
  Your leaves, nor ever bid the Spring adieu;
And, happy melodist, unwearièd,
  For ever piping songs for ever new;
More happy love! more happy, happy love!
  For ever warm and still to be enjoyed,
    For ever panting, and for ever young;
All breathing human passion far above,
  That leaves a heart high-sorrowful and cloyed,
    A burning forehead, and a parching tongue.

Who are these coming to the sacrifice?
  . To what green altar, O mysterious priest,
Lead'st thou that heifer lowing at the skies,
  And all her silken flanks with garlands drest?
What little town by river or sea shore,
  Or mountain-built with peaceful citadel,
    Is emptied of this folk, this pious morn?
And, little town, thy streets for evermore
  Will silent be; and not a soul to tell
    Why thou art desolate, can e'er return.

O Attic shape! Fair attitude! with brede
  Of marble men and maidens overwrought,
With forest branches and the trodden weed;

Thou, silent form, dost tease us out of thought
As doth eternity: Cold Pastoral!
When old age shall this generation waste,
  Thou shalt remain, in midst of other woe
Than ours, a friend to man, to whom thou say'st,
"Beauty is truth, truth beauty," — that is all
  Ye know on earth, and all ye need to know.

Keats's reputation was of slow growth. In the years immediately following his death, his friends continued to sing his praises, but outside of this small circle there was little talk about him. In 1825 a fourteen-year-old boy, Robert Browning, chanced upon a volume of Shelley on a bookstall, was led by Shelley to Keats, and, stirred by the beauty which they opened to him, dedicated himself to poetry. At about the same time another youth, Alfred Tennyson, discovered Keats, found that there was "something magic and of the innermost soul of poetry in almost everything which he wrote," and learned from him lessons of imaginative richness and tonal beauty which were to have a profound effect upon his own poetic art. These were chance discoveries. To the reading public at large Keats remained unknown. But along toward 1835, when a younger generation (who had not, like their parents, been swept off their feet by Scott and Byron) were growing up and beginning to think for themselves, a change of taste began to manifest itself, a tendency toward a general revaluation. The novelist Thackeray, in *The Newcomes*,[1] gives us a passing glimpse of it. Young Clive Newcome and his companions are discussing "the merits of our present poets and writers." Clive's father, the Colonel,

---

[1] *The Newcomes* was published in 1855; but in this passage, Thackeray is turning back to a period twenty years earlier, when Colonel Newcome's son, Clive, was first tasting the independence of young manhood.

who is a gentleman of the old school, "heard opinions that amazed and bewildered him: he heard that Byron was no great poet, though a very clever man; . . . that young Keats was a genius to be estimated in future days with young Raphael; and that a young gentleman of Cambridge who had published two volumes of verses, might take rank with the greatest poets of all . . . Lord Byron not one of the greatest poets of the world! Sir Walter a poet of the second order! . . . Mr. Keats and this young Mr. Tennyson of Cambridge, the chief of modern poetic literature! What were these new dicta, which Mr. Warrington delivered with a puff of tobacco smoke; to which Mr. Honeyman blandly assented, and Clive listened with pleasure? Such opinions were not of the Colonel's time. . . . And that reverence for Mr. Wordsworth, what did it mean? Had he not . . . been turned into deserved ridicule by all the reviews?"

The new generation were beginning to think for themselves, and, along with Wordsworth, Keats was coming into his own. In the late 40's and 50's a group of painters and poets styling themselves the "Pre-Raphaelites" attempted to get back to a directness and simplicity and unconventionality which they found in the art of painting before Raphael and tried to give their poetry an equal directness and simplicity and unconventionality and to make it as pictorial as their paintings. The fact that Keats had these qualities, blended with the romantic imagination which was to them the soul of poetry, attracted them to him as to no other modern poet. He was to them "the one true heir of Shakespeare," his work "the final achievement" of English poetry.[1] They used incidents in his story-poems as subjects for their paintings, they imitated him in their

[1] These are the words of Dante Gabriel Rossetti, the leader of the group.

own poems; and while they did not themselves at any time rise to his level in power or fundamental sincerity or felicity of phrase, they did pave the way to a wider appreciation of him. But it remained for Matthew Arnold to do for Keats's reputation what, as we have already seen, he did for Wordsworth's. "No one else in English poetry, save Shakespeare," Arnold wrote in 1880, "has in expression quite the fascinating felicity of Keats, his perfection of loveliness;" and "in one of the two great modes by which poetry interprets, in the faculty of naturalistic interpretation, in what we call natural magic, he ranks with Shakespeare."

Between that year of 1880 and the present moment, the interest in Keats has been very great. In 1921, the centenary of Keats's death, *The John Keats Memorial Volume* was issued, containing tributes in prose and verse not only from English and American poets and critics, but also from admirers of Keats in many other countries,— France, Germany, Belgium, Spain, Italy, Norway, Sweden, Serbia, and (in a picturesque variety of strange tongues and odd alphabets) from Oriental lands. Of late there have been in English a number of careful editions of his works and several scholarly biographies. The most recent is by an American, Amy Lowell, who up to her death a short time ago, had been herself opening new fields of poetic beauty. It is appropriate that the most extensive biography of Keats should have come from her pen; for, while her poetry and that of her fellow-experimenters has pursued new ways and found new rhythms, the essential spirit of it — its search for the vivid image and the exact pictorial word, its movement toward a goal "at once realistic and romantic"— is the spirit of Keats renewing itself in poetry.

XII

THE HEYDAY OF THE NOVEL

The adventure-story keeps us wondering what's going to happen next. The novel does that too. If it does not, it is likely to find few readers. But that is not enough. The characters must become more real, more intimately known to us, from page to page; and the relation between these characters, their effect upon one another's lives, becomes the really absorbing thing. The novelist does not have to depend upon startling events, or upon bringing in kings and princes or fabulously rich or terrifically villainous characters, to make his story interesting. Real life and ordinary people — those are interesting enough if only the novelist can see into their hearts and minds better than we can. If he cannot, he is wasting his time and ours.

The novel in this sense of the word is comparatively modern. It began to come into its own in the eighteenth century with Defoe, Richardson, Fielding, and Smollett groping for a method, working out a technique. But it was still hardly more than a poor relation in the aristocracy of letters. Writers turned to prose-fiction as a by-product, a chance venture. Defoe, trying his hand at various kinds of lively journalism, caught his public with *Robinson Crusoe*. Richardson's *Pamela* was the unpremeditated outcome of a plan to weave a collection of model letters into the semblance of a story. Fielding started *Joseph Andrews* with no other intention than to make fun of Richardson. Smollett pinned his hope of fame not to *Roderick Random* or *Humphrey Clinker*, but to his — now forgotten — *History of England*. Not until the early years of the nineteenth century when Walter Scott set the pace with the brilliant success of the "Waverley Series," did the novel come into its heyday. Since then, every generation has had its share of professional novelists, and novels have grown on every bush. Many — in some generations, most — of the most genuinely creative minds have devoted themselves to this form of composition; and a host of lesser writers with a facility which would have been the envy and despair of Richardson and Fielding, produce novels which are the talk of the town for a month and are forgotten in a year.

Some starts toward this modern kind of novel we noticed in the chapter on Elizabethan Prose. In the seventeenth century Bunyan (see page 250) showed how much homely touches could do in making fictitious characters seem real. We may have noticed in reading Addison's sketches of Sir Roger de Coverley that that eccentric and lovable old knight just barely fell short of being the hero of a novel. Certainly we get to know him well enough. If Sir Roger's friends had been a little more in the picture, and if his devotion to the widow had been developed into a story; or if Addison had begun with him as a gay young blade in the days of Charles II (it was then perhaps that he met his first rebuff from the widow), and had followed him through — staunch, crotchety, kindly Sir Roger, clinging to his old ways and his old cloak as times and manners changed — if Addison had chosen thus to tell Sir Roger's story, involving him with other characters and setting him against the changing background of the times, why, then, with the great Mr. Addison showing the way, the eighteenth century rather than the nineteenth might have been the Era of the Novel. More than a century later Thackeray took Sir Roger's period as the setting for *Henry Esmond* (see page 518) and caught Addison's manner to a marvel; but what a delightful story and what a precious document it would have been if only Addison himself had thought to do it!

Addison, characterizing in a series of detached sketches, was moving toward the novel from one direction; Daniel Defoe with his fictitious biographies was moving toward it from another. Born in 1660, Defoe had been a writer of political pamphlets for many years before he tried his hand at story-writing. His writing career began as early as 1687 when he attacked James II for the "Act of Indulgence" which repealed all penal laws against Roman Catholics. Defoe supported William of Orange and was rewarded with minor political offices during William's reign. William's death put an end to Defoe's office-holding. Himself a Dissenter, Defoe wrote a mocking pamphlet, *The Shortest Way with Dissenters*, purporting to be an argument by a churchman that all Dissenters should be hanged. The author was imprisoned and put in the pillory. With characteristic audacity he wrote a *Hymn to the Pillory*, describing the persons who really deserved to be where he was. When he was released, he began a periodical, *The Review*, consisting in part of political essays, in part of social gossip and witty comment on life and manners. In *The Review* Defoe supported the Tories. When the Tory ministry went out of office on the death of Queen Anne, Defoe gave up *The Review* and wrote for other papers on behalf of the Whigs. Meanwhile he busied himself with what modern journalism would call "feature articles." All was grist that came to his mill. A few grains of fact would suffice; his ready imagination would supply the

rest. He interviewed famous criminals in Newgate and
"wrote them up." He heard of strange events in foreign
lands and described them as an eyewitness. He became
a "master of the art of forging a story and imposing it
on the world for truth."

His masterpiece in this kind is *Robinson Crusoe* (1719).
The grain of truth was the actual marooning of Alexander
Selkirk upon the island of Juan Fernandez. The few avail-
able details of Selkirk's experience were all that was needed
to set Defoe going. What would a man do, alone on a
desert island, with a few tools saved from the wreck, but
with no practical experience or knowledge of woodcraft?
And what would he think about the while? It is because
every reader, young and old, finds himself in Robinson
Crusoe, sharing his bungling failures and hard-won successes,
his elations and despairs, that *Robinson Crusoe* has been
everyman's book during all the generations since it came
from the press. Should not we ourselves blunder just as
Crusoe did when he was making his boat?

I felled a cedar-tree. I question much whether Solomon ever
had such a one for the building of the Temple at Jerusalem. It
was five foot ten inches diameter at the lower part next the stump,
and four foot eleven inches diameter at the end of twenty-two
foot, after which it lessened for a while, and then parted into
branches. It was not without infinite labour that I felled this
tree. I was twenty days hacking and hewing at it at the bottom.
I was fourteen more getting the branches and limbs, and the vast
spreading head of it cut off, which I hacked and hewed through
with axe and hatchet, and inexpressible labour. After this, it
cost me a month to shape it and dub it to a proportion, and to
something like the bottom of a boat, that it might swim upright
as it ought to do. It cost me near three months more to clear
the inside, and work it so as to make an exact boat of it. This I
did indeed without fire, by mere mallet and chisel, and by the dint

of hard labour, till I had brought it to be a very handsome *periagua* and big enough to have carried six and twenty men, and consequently big enough to have carried me and all my cargo.

When I had gone through this work, I was extremely delighted with it. The boat was really much bigger than I ever saw a canoe, or *periagua*, that was made of one tree, in my life. Many a weary stroke it had cost, you may be sure; and there remained nothing but to get it into the water; and had I gotten it into the water, I make no question but I should have begun the maddest voyage, and the most unlikely to be performed, that ever was undertaken.

But all my devices to get it into the water failed me; tho' they cost me infinite labour too. It lay about one hundred yards from the water, and not more. But the first inconvenience was, it was uphill towards the creek; well, to take away this discouragement, I resolved to dig into the surface of the earth, and so make a declivity. This I begun, and it cost me a prodigious deal of pains; but who grudges pains, that have their deliverance in view? But when this was worked through, and this difficulty managed, it was still much at one; for I could no more stir the canoe than I could the other boat.

Then I measured the distance of ground, and resolved to cut a dock, or canal, to bring the water up to the canoe, seeing I could not bring the canoe down to the water. Well, I began this work; and when I began to enter into it, and calculate how deep it was to be dug, how broad, how the stuff to be thrown out, I found, that by the number of hands I had, being none but my own, it must have been ten or twelve years before I should have gone through with it; for the shore lay high, so that at the upper end, it must have been at least twenty·foot deep; so at length, tho' with great reluctancy, I gave this attempt over also.

This grieved me heartily, and now I saw, tho' too late, the folly of beginning a work before we count the cost; and before we judge rightly of our own strength to go through with it.

And Crusoe's thrill becomes our thrill when he sees Friday's footsteps on the sand.

It happened one day, about noon, going toward my boat, I was exceedingly surprised with the print of a man's naked foot on the shore, which was very plain to be seen in the sand. I stood like one thunderstruck, or as if I had seen an apparition; I listened, I looked round me, I could hear nothing, nor see anything; I went up to a rising ground to look farther; I went up the shore and down the shore, but it was all one, I could see no other impression but that one. I went to it again to see if there were any more, and to observe if it might not be my fancy; but there was no room for that, for there was exactly the very print of a foot, toes, heel, and every part of a foot; how it came thither I knew not, nor could in the least imagine. But after innumerable fluttering thoughts, like a man perfectly confused and out of myself, I came home to my fortification, not feeling, as we say, the ground I went on, but terrified to the last degree, looking behind me at every two or three steps, mistaking every bush and tree, and fancying every stump at a distance to be a man; nor is it possible to describe how many various shapes affrighted imagination represented things to me in, how many wild ideas were found every moment in my fancy, and what strange, unaccountable whimsies came into my thoughts by the way.

When I came to my castle, for so I think I called it ever after this, I fled into it like one pursued; whether I went over by the ladder as first contrived, or went in at the hole in the rock, which I called a door, I cannot remember; no, nor could I remember the next morning; for never frighted hare fled to cover, or fox to earth, with more terror of mind than I to this retreat.

I slept none that night; the farther I was from the occasion of my fright, the greater my apprehensions were, which is something contrary to the nature of such things, and especially to the usual practice of all creatures in fear. But I was so embarrassed with my own frightful ideas of the thing, that I formed nothing but dismal imaginations to myself, even tho' I was now a great way off of it. Sometimes I fancied it must be the Devil; and reason joined in with me upon this supposition. For how should any other thing in human shape come into the place? Where was the vessel that brought them? What marks were there of any other footsteps? And how was it possible a man should come there? But then to think that Satan should take human shape upon him in such a place where there could be no manner of occasion for it, but to leave the print of his foot behind him, and that even for no purpose too, for he could not be sure I should see it; this was an amusement the other way. I considered that the Devil might have found out abundance of other ways to have terrified me than this of the single print of a foot. That as I lived quite on the other side of the island, he would never have been so simple to leave a mark in a place where 'twas ten thousand to one whether I should ever see it or not, and in the sand too, which the first surge of the sea, upon a high wind, would have defaced entirely. All this seemed inconsistent with the thing itself, and with all the notions we usually entertain of the subtilty of the Devil.

Abundance of such things as these assisted to argue me out of all apprehensions of its being the Devil. And I presently concluded then, that it must be some more dangerous creature, *viz.* that it must be some of the savages of the mainland over against me, who had wandered out to sea in their canoes, and either driven by the currents, or by contrary winds, had made the island; and had been on shore, but were gone away again to sea, being as loath, perhaps, to have stayed in this desolate island, as I would have been to have had them.

Robinson Crusoe is not a novel in the sense in which we have used that word. It is a fictitious biography, imagined with a minuteness of detail and a completeness of understanding that make it a remarkable book. Encouraged by the success of *Robinson Crusoe*, Defoe wrote several other fictitious biographies. One of these, *Moll Flanders*, anticipates a kind of fiction which is very popular to-day. It is a "psychological" story, a study of a woman's mind in the successive stages of her downfall. It is cumbered with needless detail, it is needlessly gross, and occasionally artificial; but there are moments in which Defoe's analysis is extraordinarily penetrating. One of these is the description of Moll's first yielding to the temptation to pilfer. Her struggle to resist, her yielding under the stress of poverty, the gradual hardening of her conscience until she becomes first a professional thief and then the organizer of a gang of thieves, is one of Defoe's most masterly pieces of work.

Eighteen years intervened between Defoe's *Moll Flanders* and Richardson's *Pamela* (1740). Richardson was a printer who had passed his fiftieth year comfortably jog-trotting in that trade, when the suggestion was made to him to write "a book of familiar letters on the useful concerns in modern life." Pamela is a poor girl, daughter of respectable parents, who becomes a servant in a county family. Her letters to her parents describe the unwelcome attentions of the unscrupulous son of her employers, his gradual realization that her character is above reproach, his proposal of marriage, her acceptance, and her efforts to live up to the social plane to which her marriage has lifted her. Richardson's professed purpose was to turn his readers away from "the pomp and parade of romance writing" by laying before them a tale which would "promote the cause of religion and virtue." What he actually accomplished was to make the experiences and heart-searchings of a girl without social "class" so interesting that "the pomp and parade of romance" palled in comparison.

The popularity of *Pamela* encouraged Richardson to try again. *Clarissa Harlowe* (1748–1749) is the story of a pure and high-minded young woman who, in her effort to escape from an unhappy home, is entrapped and persecuted by a man whom she had mistakenly trusted. The plot is unfolded in letters written by Clarissa to her confidante and by the unscrupulous and cynical Lovelace to his confederate. The death of Clarissa, the repentance and death of Lovelace, form the climax. The story is inordinately long. Dr. Johnson, who preferred to gulp a book, said that you would hang yourself before you finished it. But for all its length, and the repetitions inevitable in a story told through letters, the plot presses forward with an effect of rapid movement to its tragic close. Richardson knew what he was about. In these hundreds of letters, some of them many pages in length, there is singularly little waste. Trifles, minor peculiarities of mind and heart, accumulate until character stands revealed. Even the modern reader, separated by nearly two centuries from Richardson's world, feels that these people really lived, that they were no mere inventions of the novelist. As for Richardson's own generation who followed the story chapter by chapter as the successive parts came from the press, Clarissa was so real to them that they flooded Richardson with appeals to save her: "After you have brought the divine Clarissa to the very brink of destruction, let me entreat, nay, insist upon, a turn that will make your almost despairing readers half mad with joy. . . . Only suppose all the good-natured, compassionate and distressed on their knees at your feet, can you let them beg in vain?"

Richardson refused to rescue Clarissa. As a matter of fact, he knew his readers better than they knew themselves. The mood of the time was changing; as we have already noticed (see pp. 387 ff.) cynicism and restraint were ceasing to be fashionable. *I think* was giving way to *I feel.* Richardson's compassionate and distressed readers wept — and enjoyed it. He left no trick untried to harrow their feelings. In her last hours Clarissa orders her coffin, has it placed where she can see it from her bed, and reads to her sorrowing friends a moving memorial inscription of her own devising. *Clarissa Harlowe* was the first of a long succession of "sentimental" novels — novels which played upon the emotions and asked no better reward than to reduce their readers to a flood of tears.

Richardson's rival, Henry Fielding, scorned these sentimentalizing and moralizing ways. Fielding peoples his pages with honest, hearty, impulsive, and often blundering people, in whom his soul delights, and with hypocritical "goody-goodies" whom he unsparingly ridicules.

Fielding had already made a reputation with his satirical comedies before he tried his hand at a burlesque of Richardson's *Pamela*. In *Joseph Andrews* (1742) Fielding introduces Joseph as "brother to the illustrious Pamela whose virtue is at present so famous." A servant in the household of Lady Booby, Joseph rejects her advances with a solemn piety which burlesques Pamela's attitude toward the "Mr. B.——" of Richardson's novel. Dismissed from Lady Booby's London establishment, Joseph sets out afoot to seek his sweetheart, Fanny, who is a servant in Lady Booby's country-house. When he finds her he discovers that the humble Fanny (stolen, it appears, by gypsies in her infancy) is a sister of the illustrious Pamela; and that he himself, instead of being, as he had always supposed, Pamela's brother, was likewise "mislaid" in his infancy, and is the son of Mr. Wilson, a gentleman living near Lady Booby's country-estate. Pamela, now "up in the world" as the wife of Mr. B.——, accepts her new-found sister with proper condescension; and Joseph, now duly raised to the rank of gentlefolk, marries Fanny.

Thus outlined, *Joseph Andrews* will probably seem no

more than a clever skit, a farce-comedy disguised as prose-fiction. Perhaps that is all that Fielding, the erstwhile writer of farce-comedies, meant to make of it. But with Joseph once launched on his penniless journey from London to Lady Booby's country-house, Fielding's true genius suddenly finds itself. The story becomes a veritable epic of the road. Parson Adams, Lady Booby's country-curate, meets Joseph on the way and turns back to travel home with him. Together they encounter the varied society of the road — innkeepers, highwaymen, parsons good and bad, kind travelers and selfish travelers, amiable gentlemen and supercilious gentlemen. Together Joseph and Parson Adams listen to the strange life-histories of chance-made friends — among them that very Mr. Wilson who is later discovered to be the father of Joseph. And page by page, as the story progresses, Parson Adams emerges as one of the greatest creations of the novelist's art — simple, kindly, impractical, unworldly, absent-minded Parson Adams, who starts to London to sell his sermons, and finds that he has left them behind; whose simplicity is always getting him into the most ridiculous scrapes, and whose transparent honesty is always getting him nobly out of them.

Joseph Andrews suffers from the fact that it starts as a burlesque, develops into a novel, and then in the last few pages becomes a burlesque again. In *Tom Jones* (1749), Fielding writes the story for its own sake. It is a rollicking tale of Tom, the foundling, who is taken into the household of the rich and good-natured Squire Allworthy; grows up to fall in love with Sophia, the daughter of a neighboring squire; incurs Allworthy's wrath and is driven from home; goes afoot to London, meeting all sorts of people and getting into all sorts of scrapes on the way; meets Sophia there, repents his misdeeds and wins her forgiveness; and is discovered to be the nephew of Squire Allworthy, who blesses his union with Sophia and makes him his heir.

Fielding is at his best in *Tom Jones*. The plot is managed with great skill. Tom's character — his honesty, his happy-go-lucky ways, his absolutely natural boyishness — grows upon us with every page. As his love for Sophia develops and as we get better acquainted with her, we are struck by the contrast between Fielding's kind of heroine and Richardson's. Sophia is the sort of girl whom we may find in many a modern novel — healthy, vigorous, taking life as she finds it, not stopping to moralize about it very much, but thoroughly decent and square. Tom, the foundling, is socially far beneath her; but when driven from Squire Allworthy's home, he sets out for London to enlist, Sophia defies the conventions and takes the road to London in search of him. On the way they come near to finding each other time and time again, but never meet. Tom's foolish, and often worse than foolish, acts come to her ears, and put her to shame. Will the two ever meet and become reconciled, Fielding keeps one wondering. And is Tom, will he be, good enough for her? Fielding's answer is characteristic. Defoe, Richardson, any other story-writer of the time, would have transformed his repentant hero into a perfect man, spending the rest of his life in the odor of sanctity. But Fielding scorned to make his characters to order. He was, he declared, a "historian of human nature." Tom repents but no novelist's miracle happens to him. He makes his exit much the same happy-go-lucky, honest, well-meaning but thoughtless fellow that he has been all the while. If anybody can cure him of his follies, it will be Sophia; but Fielding does not commit himself.

There is the enduring worth, the real greatness of Fielding as a novelist. We find much that is repulsive in *Tom Jones*. Life was more frankly coarse in the eighteenth century than it is now. Fielding took life as he found it; but the essentials of human nature change very little from age to age. It is because Fielding represented the essentials of human nature so truthfully, and because he brought to that representation such sympathy with honesty and kindness, and such hearty scorn of meanness and pretentiousness and hypocrisy, that *Tom Jones* is numbered among the great novels.

Richardson, of course, is historically important. He was a master of the intricacies of the heart and conscience. He reprehends immorality, and Fielding takes it in his stride as a part of the life of his time. But with all that, I think that we find Fielding more wholesome reading than Richardson.

No other novelist of the eighteenth century approached Fielding in power or skill. As a realist — if by that term we understand one who shows life as it is, without any of the rose-color of romance — Tobias Smollett probably ranks next to him. Smollett's first novel, *The Adventures of Roderick Random*, appeared as early as 1748; his last, *Humphrey Clinker*, as late as 1771, the year of Smollett's death. He had no gift for organizing and developing a plot. In most of his novels the hero makes friends, falls in love, becomes a vicious ne'er-do-well, reforms and marries. This is mere machinery to enable the novelist to describe the sordid life of London, or conditions in the navy (where Smollett was once a surgeon), or to satirize society in London or Bath. Here and there his caustic realism is relieved by a racy humor. We enjoy his account, in *Peregrine Pickle*, of the devices of the retired old sea-dog,

Commodore Hawser Trunnion, and his servants, Hatchway and Pipes, to lead a nautical life on land, and of how he is maneuvered into matrimony. Smollett's close observation and minuteness of detail give his novels historical value. He has significance, too, as the literary ancestor of Charles Dickens who, both in his realism and in his love of eccentric characters, was indebted to Smollett. But most readers to-day find Smollett's novels, with one exception, both unpleasant and dull.

That exception, *Humphrey Clinker*, is even more devoid of plot than the others. Old Matthew Bramble suffering from a variety of diseases, imaginary and real, is advised by his doctor to go on a coaching trip to several English health resorts. His old maid sister, Tabitha, with her maid, Winifred Jenkins, accompanies him. He employs young Humphrey Clinker as his coachman. How Tabitha finds a husband and Humphrey falls in love with Winifred make up the semblance of a plot. The real delight of the story is in the revelation of character in the letters which each member of the party writes about their experiences on the road. Hypochondriacal Matthew, husband-hunting Tabitha, and Methodistical Winifred with her genius for misspelling and misusing words, are as amusing characters as one could find in many a day.

One other of the group of novelists who center about the midpoint of the century is worth mentioning. Laurence Sterne made his contribution to prose-fiction (one hesitates to call it a novel) in 1760, when he was forty-seven years old. A clergyman, brilliant, erratic, and in morals not above reproach, Sterne had done much out-of-the-way reading. His tastes ran to humorous characterization — to the grotesque humor of Rabelais; to the delicate irony, the characterization through rambling, desultory talk, of *Don Quixote*. *The Life and Opinions of Tristram Shandy* is a collection of the literary oddments with which Sterne's mind was stored and of his opinions about life in general, scattered with whimsical irrelevance through an account of the sayings and doings of the Shandy family and their circle. Tristram is not born till well on in the story. There is no "life" of him or of anybody else. There is no plot, in the ordinary sense of the word. Walter Shandy, Tristram's father, talks with Mrs. Shandy and with Dr. Slop who has been called in to assist at Tristram's birth. Uncle Toby, the invalided war veteran, and his servant, Corporal Trim, talk. Uncle Toby, lured by the widow Wadman to extract an imaginary mote from her eye, falls in love with her and they talk. The talk jumps from topic to topic, quotes incredible absurdities from long-forgotten books (Walter Shandy's, this); turns to a moving tale of a dying soldier, or flies off a million miles into the solar system. Turn over to the next page of the book, and as likely as not that page will be a blank. Fill it in to suit yourself, says Sterne. Something must be left to the imagination of the reader. But underneath all this whimsicality and trickery there is a definite artistic purpose. Our knowledge of human nature, our gradually accumulated understanding of one another comes, Sterne would remind us, just that way. Through just such desultory, quick-jumping, wide-ranging talk, character emerges. It certainly does in the pages of *Tristram Shandy*. Crotchety Walter Shandy with his store of strange learning; Uncle Toby, chronic sufferer from an old wound, always fighting his old campaigns over again, and so tender-hearted that he would not hurt a fly; devoted Corporal Trim, shielding him, helping him, managing him with infinite tact; the widow Wadman who, despite all that Corporal Trim can do, lures

Uncle Toby to gaze into the pellucid depth of her eye, and *has* him from that moment — these are extraordinarily vivid characterizations.

Sterne, like Richardson, belongs among the sentimentalists, the writers who were always "playing up" the emotions. But the mood differs. Richardson took himself very seriously. His compassionate and despairing readers wept with Clarissa, and the story moved solemnly on. Sterne's touch is lighter. His sympathy is genuine enough while it lasts, his tears flow easily; but there is always a whimsical smile, a grin even, lurking just round the corner.

One of the best examples is Tristram's encounter with the ass, at the entrance to a narrow lane in the French town of Lyons (How Tristram happened to be wandering in France is beyond my ability to explain. Only a few pages before, Father and Mother Shandy were debating whether to put him into breeches):

'Twas by a poor ass, who had just turned in with a couple of large panniers upon his back, to collect eleemosynary turnip-tops and cabbage leaves; and stood dubious, with his two fore-feet on the inside of the threshold, and with his two hinder-feet towards the street, as not knowing very well whether he was to go in or no.

Now, 'tis an animal (be in what hurry I may) I cannot bear to strike: — there is a patient endurance of sufferings, wrote so unaffectedly in his looks and carriage, which pleads so mightily for him, that it always disarms me; and to that degree, that I do not like to speak unkindly to him: on the contrary, meet him where I will, whether in town or country, — in cart, or under panniers, — whether in liberty or bondage, — I have ever something civil to say to him on my part; and as one word begets another (if he has as little to do as I) — I generally fall into conversation with him; and surely never is my imagination so busy as in framing his responses from the etchings of his countenance, and where those carry me not deep enough, — in flying from my own heart into his, and seeing what is natural for an ass to think, — as well as a man, upon the occasion. In truth, it is the only creature of all the classes of beings below me, with whom I can do this; — for parrots, jackdaws, &c. I never exchange a word with them, — nor with apes, &c. for pretty near the same reason; they act by rote, as the others speak by it, and equally make me silent: nay, my dog and my cat, though I value them both — (and for my dog, he would speak if he could) — yet, somehow or other, they neither of them possess the talents for conversation; — I can make nothing of a discourse with them beyond the proposition, the reply, and rejoinder, which terminated my father's and my mother's conversation in his beds of justice; — and those utter'd, — there's an end of the dialogue.

— But with an ass, I can commune for ever.

— Come, Honesty! said I, — seeing it was impracticable to pass betwixt him and the gate, — art thou for coming in or going out?

— The ass twisted his head round, to look up the street.

— Well, replied I, we'll wait a minute for thy driver. — He turned his head thoughtful about, and looked wistfully the opposite way.

I understand thee perfectly, answered I: — if thou takest a wrong step in this affair, he will cudgel thee to death. — Well, a minute is but a minute, and, if it saves a fellow-creature a drubbing, it shall not be set down as ill spent.

He was eating the stem of an artichoke as this discourse went on, and, in the little peevish contentions of nature betwixt hunger and unsavoriness, had dropt it out of his mouth half a dozen times, and pick'd it up again. — God help thee, Jack! said I, thou hast a bitter breakfast on't, — and many a bitter day's labor, — and many a bitter blow, I fear, for its wages! — 'tis all — all bitterness to thee, whatever life is to others! — And now, thy mouth, if one knew the truth of it, is as bitter, I dare say, as soot — (for he had cast aside the stem) and thou hast not a friend, perhaps, in all this world, that will give thee a macaroon. — In saying this, I pull'd out a paper of 'em, which I had just purchased, and gave him one, — and, at this moment that I am telling it, my heart smites

me, that there was more of pleasantry in the conceit of seeing how
an ass would eat a macaroon, — than of benevolence in giving
him one, which presided in the act.

When the ass had eaten his macaroon, I press'd him to come in;
— the poor beast was heavy loaded, — his legs seemed to tremble
under him, — he hung rather backwards; and, as I pull'd at his
halter, it broke short in my hand. — He look'd up pensive in my
face — "Don't thrash me with it; — but, if you will, you may."
— "If I do," said I, "I'll be d — d."

Sterne stands apart from the orderly development of the
novel. There were a few who tried to write like him; but
his whimsical, eccentric genius defied imitation.

Of the novels that fall between *Tristram Shandy* and the
end of the century, by far the most delightful is Goldsmith's
The Vicar of Wakefield (1766). We have met Goldsmith
before, as Dr. Johnson's friend, and as the author of *The
Deserted Village* (see page 392). The manuscript of the
Vicar had remained in Goldsmith's hands for five years when
Johnson rescued him from financial straits by recommend-
ing it to a publisher. It became immediately popular. It
has remained so ever since. That it should have become
so firmly established as a classic is the more remarkable
when one considers the slightness and the absurdities of
the plot. Suddenly reduced to poverty, the Reverend Mr.
Primrose moves to a little country living. With his simple
ways he could be content there, like the parson in *The
Deserted Village* passing rich on forty pounds a year. But
foolish Mrs. Primrose and a family of irresponsible sons
and vain and ambitious daughters make life a problem.
Blows fall thick and fast upon the Vicar's head. The supposed Squire Thornhill, whom the family had set their
caps for, turns out to be a complete villain and abducts
one of the daughters. A son is arrested. The Vicar's

house burns down, the Vicar's landlord presses him for debt. Before long the whole family is in prison. And then, with startling abruptness, everything comes right again. The poor neighbor, whom the ambitious Primrose family had despised, having revealed himself as the real Squire Thornhill, himself marries one of the daughters and coerces the villain into repentance, reformation, and marriage with the other. The son is exonerated and released from prison, and the Vicar's fortune is miraculously restored. If a good plot is one that makes things happen as they do in real life, the plot of *The Vicar of Wakefield* must be reckoned one of the worst, one of the most naïve and incredible, in the whole range of English fiction. But nobody minds. The characterization is the thing. No one who has read the story can ever forget the Vicar, with his love of theological controversy, his mixture of vanity and humility, his simple faith and natural goodness, his efforts to guide and discipline his impossible family, his own blunders. Be it remembered that it is the Vicar himself who tells the story. There is no finer art than this of unconscious self-revelation as we have it in *The Vicar of Wakefield*.

Between this mid-century group — Richardson, Fielding, Smollett, Sterne, Goldsmith — and the appearance of Scott's *Waverley* in 1814, there are only two novelists who must be mentioned. One of them, a young girl named Fanny Burney, did what was really a new thing in fiction. Her *Evelina* (1778) is a "novel of manners." On a visit to London the heroine, who is a well-bred, intelligent girl, finds herself thrown among a group of social "climbers." Their fine airs and efforts to get into good society; Evelina's acquaintance with a gentleman of high position; the embarrassments which she suffers among these "climbers" while her acquaintanceship is ripening into love, make up the story. Richardson, we remember, had been interested in manners as in everything which helped his minute delineations of character; but his picture of life was always moralized, molded to "promote the cause of religion and virtue." Fanny Burney was chiefly interested in making the picture.

The other novelist of this period whom it is important to bear in mind is Mrs. Radcliffe. In the chapter on Romantic Poets (see pp. 357–8) we noticed that one of the products of the Gothic revival was a novel by Horace Walpole called *The Castle of Otranto.* Ancient castles with mysterious subterranean passages and vaults were the obvious place for thrills and shivers. Walpole supplied them because they "went with" the castle. Romantic readers of the second half of the eighteenth century thrilled and shivered with equal gusto amid the charnels of a graveyard or the glooms of a moonlit ruin. The revival of a superstitious era made superstition a fad. Writers of prose-fiction fed this appetite with stories of mystery and terror which were in many cases merely crudely sensational. In *The Mysteries of Udolpho* (1795) and a number of other only slightly less successful novels, Mrs. Radcliffe handled such themes with a finer art. Other novelists of "mystery and terror" (the term became standardized) seemed to be bent only on giving the reader a scare. The reader gets scares aplenty in the castle in the Apennines in which Mrs. Radcliffe lays her plot; but in the end the apparently supernatural finds a rational explanation and becomes — what every good novel must be — convincing.

It is interesting to think of these "Gothic," terror-manufacturing novelists as leading up to the novels of Walter Scott. His greater genius, too, found its themes in the past. To him, as to them, life was more exciting, more "romantic," as it was lived a while ago, or long ago, than in the everyday world of his own time. The long ago of his native Scotland had absorbed his mind since childhood. From the lips of old peasant women he had listened to ballads of war and adventure passed down through centuries of oral transmission. He had collected these ballads and published his *Minstrelsy of the Scottish Border* (1802–1803). He had stored his mind with the history of his native country and had found his way into the histories of other countries — attracted always by tales of warfare and heroic adventure and by the human element, the little personal things that transform mere historical figures into real people. That is what history meant to him — not political or constitutional or economic processes such as most historians devote themselves to, but an opportunity for his imagination to reconstruct life and personality. He did this in the narrative poems based on Scottish history which we considered in the preceding chapter. He continued to do it, with greater freedom and amplitude of detail, when he turned from poetry to prose and published *Waverley*. In finding life in the past more exciting, more thrilling than life in the present, he has, as we have noticed, something in common with the "Gothic" novelists; but he did what not one of them could do. He made his people real.

When we call Scott the first great "historical" novelist, we mean that history furnished him with plots and an enlivening background for the re-creation of character. We call his novels romances. The mood of heroic adventure and the thread of love-story woven through the historical material are certainly romantic enough. Scott himself used to jest about his "big bow-wow strain." But the common folk with whom he surrounded his historical figures and romantic lovers, he drew with just such homely detail and relish for idiosyncrasies of speech and manner as we find in the most thoroughgoing realist.

Waverley (1814) was an experiment. Scott felt that as a poet he had shot his bolt. Some years before while in the full swing of his poems, he had started a prose-story and left it unfinished. He finished it now with characteristic speed, and published it anonymously, leaving it to take its chance without the advantage of his name. *Waverley* is a tale of Scotland in 1745, centering in the Highland uprising which attempted to replace the Stuarts in the person of Charles Edward, the "Young Pretender," upon the throne. The battles of Prestonpans and Culloden give the historical setting. But Scott's real object, he confessed, was to introduce the natives of Scotland "to those of the sister-kingdom in a more favorable light than they had been placed hitherto, and to secure sympathy for their virtues and indulgence for their foibles." He makes his hero an Englishman in order that English readers may see Scotland through English eyes; and before young Captain Waverley becomes involved in the battles of Prestonpans and Culloden, he sees much of the Lowlanders and Highlanders. Baron Bradwardine and his family and dependents and friends are drawn with great vividness and with no lack of insight into their foibles as well as their virtues. In the beautiful Flora MacIvor and the wild Highland plotters who surround her, Scott gives his romantic imagination full rein — but they are very real people for all that.

The immediate and enormous success of *Waverley* urged Scott to go on, and to write under his own name. In his seventeen years as a novelist Scott produced twenty-six novels — sixteen of them pictures of various periods of Scottish history; six, of English; and four laid outside the British Isles. Of these the group of Scottish novels, written in the first flush of his vigor, are among his best. Two of them, certainly, *Old Mortality* (1816) and *The Heart of Midlothian* (1818), in the splendid energy and constructive skill of their plots and in vividness of characterization, deserve to be numbered among the great novels of the world. Of the English novels, *Ivanhoe* (1819) and *Kenilworth* (1821) are the best. Of those laid beyond the bounds of the British Isles, *The Talisman* (1825) contains a few scenes endeared to the heart of every reader; but for sustained power, *Quentin Durward* (1823), with its vivid picture of the times of Louis XI of France, is most worth reading.

Scott's leisureliness in developing his plot is sometimes a little exasperating to the modern reader; but there are few novelists whose work is so rewarding. Dominie Sampson in *Guy Mannering*, Baillie Nicol Jarvie in *Rob Roy*, the faithful and dauntless Jeanie Deans (perhaps the finest of all Scott's creations) in *The Heart of Midlothian*, Robin Hood and Friar Tuck in *Ivanhoe*, Caleb Balderstone in *The Bride of Lammermoor*, and a host of others will come to be not mere characters in novels, but old friends. And let the critics say what they will about Scott's inaccuracies, there is no better way to read history. He makes it alive.

Scott's novels make a huge shelfful. Jane Austen produced only six novels, the quietest little tales imaginable, in which amiable and sensible people mingle unexcitingly with crabbed and silly people and in which no heroic deeds are performed and nobody gets killed. It is characteristic of the range and diversity of the novel that these contemporaries, Scott and Jane Austen, so different in every particular, should rank among the greatest of English novelists.

Jane Austen lived quietly in a country rectory and wrote of the life that she saw around her. "Three or four families in a country village is the very best thing to work on," she declared. "I could not sit seriously down to write a serious romance under any other motive than to save my life; and if it were indispensable for me to keep it up, and never relax into laughing at myself or other people, I am sure I should be hung before I had finished the first chapter."

If you belong to the "something-doing-every-minute" school of readers, you will not enjoy Jane Austen; but if your interest in people goes beyond what they do to what they are, if you have any curiosity about your next-door neighbor, even though he may never have flown an airplane or won a championship or done anything more unconventional than falling in love and getting married, you will find Jane Austen interesting. She will lead you so quietly into intimacy with her "three or four families in a country village," the process of getting acquainted with them will seem so natural and easy and *unplanned*, that the fact that you do know them through and through will come to you after a while as a sort of private discovery of your own. "This isn't Jane's doing," you will feel. "I have just heard them talk and put two and two together — and there you are!"

And then you will look around for somebody with whom to share your discovery. There is a war-time story of Rudyard Kipling's called "The Janeites." A private tells of three officers who whenever they got together would return to the same topic. At first Humberstall thinks that "Jane" is some kind of password, but before long he learns better. "Real! Jane? Why she was a little old maid 'oo'd written 'alf a dozen books about a 'undred years ago. 'Twasn't as if there was anythin' *to* 'em either. *I* know. I 'ad to read 'em. They weren't adventurous, nor smutty, nor what you'd call even interestin'— all about girls o' seventeen (they begun young then, I tell you) not certain 'oom they'd like to marry; an' their dances an' card-parties an' picnics." Humberstall decides that the way into his officers' hearts is to become a Janeite himself. "But as I was sayin', what beat me was there was nothin' *to* 'em nor *in* 'em. Nothin' at all, believe me."

"You seem good an' full of 'em, any'ow," said Anthony.

"I mean that 'er characters was no *use!* They was only just like people you run across any day. One of 'em was a curate — the Reverend Collins — always on the make an' lookin' to marry money. Well, when I was a Boy Scout, 'im or 'is twin brother was our Troop-leader. An' there was an upstandin' 'ard-mouthed Duchess or a Baronet's wife that didn't give a curse for any one 'oo wouldn't do what she told 'em to; the Lady — Lady Catherine (I'll get it in a minute) De Bugg. Before Ma bought the 'airdressin' business in London I used to know of an 'olesale grocer's wife near Leicester (I'm Leicestershire myself) that might 'ave been 'er duplicate. And — oh yes — there was a Miss Bates; just an old maid runnin' about like a 'en with 'er 'ead cut off, an' 'er tongue loose at both ends. I've got an aunt like 'er. Good as gold — but, *you* know."

· Humberstall gets shell-shocked and is sent back to where a hospital-train is filling up. One of the Sisters corners him, tells him there's no room for him on the train, and then nearly talks him to death. "Then a woman with a nose an' teeth on 'er marched up. 'What's all this?' she says. 'What do you want?' 'Nothin', I says, 'only make Miss

Bates, there, stop talkin' or I'll die.' 'Miss Bates?' she says. 'What in 'Eaven's name makes you call 'er that?' 'Because she is,' I says. 'D'you know what you're sayin'?' she says, an' slings her bony arm round me to get me off the ground. 'Course I do,' I says, 'an' if you knew Jane, you'd know too.' 'That's enough,' says she. 'You're comin' on this train if I have to kill a Brigadier for you.'"

Miss Bates, "a great talker upon little matters," who says everything in her mind in one gush and stops only when she is out of breath, is one of the characters in Jane Austen's *Emma*. The Reverend Mr. Collins and Lady Catherine de Bourgh are in *Pride and Prejudice*. Perhaps *Pride and Prejudice* will serve as well as any to illustrate the sort of story which Jane Austen liked to tell and the sort of people whom she liked to portray. Elizabeth Bennett is a sensible and spirited girl. Her mother, a "climber," is one of the most convincingly silly women that ever stepped out of real life into the pages of a novel. Darcy, a rich and aristocratic young man, who is even more of a prig than Jane Austen meant him to be, falls in love with Elizabeth; but the vulgar rattle-brained talk of Elizabeth's mother and Elizabeth's younger sisters makes the family-connection seem impossible to him. Mr. Collins, a conceited, empty-headed, toadying parson, after proposing in vain to Elizabeth, finds a young lady in the neighborhood who would rather have even a Mr. Collins than no husband at all. He is appointed to a living, by Darcy's aunt, the haughty Lady Catherine de Bourgh, who patronizes and bullies Mr. Collins to her — and his — heart's content. Meanwhile Darcy finds that his love for Elizabeth is stronger than his pride. Her pride too has been aroused and at first she will have none of him; but his devotion, and his serviceableness in saving one of Elizabeth's foolish sisters from the consequences of her folly, bring about a reconciliation, and Elizabeth and Darcy are married amid Mrs. Bennett's voluble rejoicings. And when you have read *Pride and Prejudice* for yourself and found there just what Humberstall found, if you too do not become a "Janeite," I shall be very much surprised.

Midway of the nineteenth century stand another pair of novelists who, like Richardson and Fielding, and Scott and Jane Austen, pursued diverse ways to greatness. Thackeray wrote somewhat in the tradition of Fielding. Dickens, while he was perhaps more influenced by Smollett than by any other of his predecessors, does not really belong in any tradition. He started one for himself.

It was a book of sketches rather than a novel that first revealed Dickens's genius. An artist had undertaken to produce a series of drawings of the misadventures of a group of Londoners trying to be sportsmen. Dickens (whose *Sketches by Boz*, contributed to a daily paper, had already attracted some attention) was invited to write humorous sketches to go with the pictures. The sudden death of the artist who was to have drawn the pictures left the development of the theme in Dickens's hands. The result was *The Pickwick Papers,* wherein are described the wanderings of the benevolent Mr. Pickwick and three fellow-members of the Pickwick Club, the too susceptible Tupman, the poetic Snodgrass, and the sporting Winkle, in quest of anything which shall make for "the advancement of knowledge and the diffusion of learning." How Mr. Pickwick employs Sam Weller as his body-servant and finds him always "in the right, although his mode of expressing his opinion is somewhat homely and occasionally incomprehensible"; how Mr. Pickwick meets Sam's father, the coachman, and is advised by the "old 'un' to beware of widders"; how Mr. Pickwick's landlady, Mrs. Bardell, misinterprets a chance remark and sues him for breach of promise; how Mr. Pickwick and his companions get into various difficulties and wriggle out of them — these, and a host of other things, are duly set forth in the four stout volumes of *The Pickwick Papers*. There is no plot, in the strict sense of the word; but in the course of Mr. Pickwick's varied mishaps, Dickens gathers into his dragnet an extraordinary collection of odd characters. They are not real people in the way that Jane Austen's/people are real. Hers, though they are often foolish and occasionally disagreeable, are entirely normal and sane. When you turn from Jane Austen to Dickens, you find yourself wondering how it has come about that somewhere between 1813 and 1837 everybody in the world has gone a little mad.

If this were true only of *The Pickwick Papers*, it would not be hard to justify. The "playing up" of eccentrics, the humor of exaggeration, happened to be in fashion at just the time when Dickens was writing — and, in any event,/*The Pickwick Papers* grew out of the idea of writing around a series of humorous drawings — caricatures. It was part of the game to make the characters all rather absurd. But when Dickens passed from these humorous sketches to full-fledged novels, and undertook to show life as it really is, the readiness to intensify, to "play up" some physical peculiarity or mental twist, just as a caricaturist draws an impossibly long nose in a funny picture, had become a habit with him. This kind of character-drawing is effective in its way. The sheer energy, the persistent iteration with which Dickens "plays up" the peculiarities of his characters makes you remember them. And a little of that sort of thing is immensely entertaining. But I think that you get to resent it after a while and to feel that the world is not quite so hectic a place as Dickens makes it out to be.

From *Oliver Twist,* which was his first, to *The Mystery of Edwin Drood,* which he left unfinished at his death, Dickens wrote many novels, with a great variety of plot and incident and an amazing number of spiritedly drawn characters. Two out of these many novels will suffice as illustrations. *Oliver Twist* is a rather lurid story of the underworld of London. *David Copperfield* is a tale of everyday middle-class people in which Dickens wove a thread of autobiography.

It was Dickens's own experience as a penniless boy in the London slums that gave him his material for *Oliver Twist.* One of the most popular novels of the day was Harrison Ainsworth's *Rookwood,* a romantic tale of the adventures of the eighteenth-century highwayman, Dick Turpin. In contrast to this false glitter of crime, these "canterings on moonlit heaths," Dickens undertakes to tell "the stern and plain truth." The central figure of *Oliver Twist* is old Fagin, the Jew, who gathers the homeless waifs of London about him, sends them out to pick pockets, and hoards their takings in his filthy den. To Fagin's, too, come the grown-up thieves, among them the brutal Bill Sikes, whose murder of his sweetheart Nancy and whose leap to death when the hue and cry are closing in upon him are the most lurid episodes in the book. Through these sordid scenes runs the story of little Oliver, the poor-house waif, who is tossed back and forth like a shuttlecock between vice and respectability — now in Fagin's clutches and forced to take part in petty theft, now adopted by wealthy people, and surrounded by comfort and kindness. There is some

of Dickens's best and much of his worst in *Oliver Twist.*
The sordid life of the underworld is vividly, and in all
likelihood, truthfully pictured. The story of Bill Sikes's
last hours as a fugitive from justice with the eyes of the
murdered Nancy haunting him, the swift closing-in of the
mob, his leap from the roof, is told with a terrific energy,
a pitiless piling-up of gruesome detail that stamps the
scene upon one's mind and makes it haunt one's dreams.
If it is not great art (and when you reread it coolly you
begin to suspect Dickens of "piling it on," of straining
after theatrical effect) — if it is not great art, it is at least
an extraordinary manifestation of power. But in the
thread of plot on which these underworld pictures are
hung, Dickens is at his worst — and that worst is pretty
bad. A nameless poor-house waif, little Oliver falls into
Fagin's clutches, is taken out to help pick pockets by
Fagin's crew, and stands wonderingly by to get caught by
the police while the guilty boys escape. The benevolent
old gentleman whose pocket has been picked secures his
release and adopts him. Oliver is recaptured by Fagin's
crew, forced by Bill Sikes to creep into a window of a country house in order to admit the thieves, is caught, and is
now duly adopted by the benevolent lady whose house is
broken into. The benevolent old gentleman (the first
adopter) observes Oliver's resemblance to a picture hanging upon the wall, and thus becomes the one person in
London (out of the million or so with pockets equally
pickable that day) who is in a position to trace Oliver's
parentage. Oliver's father, it ultimately appears, was the
benevolent old gentleman's dearest friend. As for the
benevolent lady (the second adopter), whose country
house was one of a thousand or so which Bill Sikes might
have hit upon, she has an adopted daughter, also a found-

ling, who, when at length *her* parentage is traced, is discovered to be little Oliver's aunt! Of such coincidences is the kingdom of the "movies"; but in reputable novels the arm of coincidence is seldom quite so long. Through this tangled skein of threatening disasters and providential coincidences moves a typical "heavy villain" of melodrama — a dark mysterious "Monks," whose one object in life is to prevent Oliver's parentage from being discovered, and who turns out to be Oliver's half-brother, the heir to a fortune which rightly belongs to Oliver himself. And clinging to the fringes of the pattern are Dickens's characteristic eccentrics with their characteristic names — old Mr. Grimwig, who is always threatening to eat his head, Mr. Fang, the bullying magistrate, Mr. Bumble, the pompous beadle, and half a dozen more.

Not all of Dickens's plots are as bad as the plot of *Oliver Twist*, but his habit of caricature and his disposition to collect the oddest specimens of human nature became even more marked as he went on. In *David Copperfield*, he has less opportunity for lurid melodrama (though there is a fair share of that too), but more for his miscellany of oddities. David's unhappy home life at the mercy of his stepfather Mr. Murdstone and the incredibly metallic Miss Murdstone; David's equally unhappy school-life under the heavy thumb of Mr. Creakle; the friends of David's youth, including his great-aunt and protectress, Miss Betsy Trotwood, his schoolmate, the fascinating Steerforth, the clumsy, kindly fisherman, Ham Peggoty, and Ham's sweetheart, little Em'ly; David's experience as a journalist in London, where he meets the "'umble" Uriah Heep, and the indomitably hopeful Wilkins Micawber; David's "child-wife" Dora, her death, and David's marriage to Agnes Wickfield — these are the elements of the story. Woven into the tale of David's ups and downs is the dark thread of Steerforth's life — his easy superiority and mastery over David at school, his meeting with little Em'ly, his luring of her into wrongdoing, his drowning in the storm. And here again Dickens is at his old trick of melodramatic coincidence, for it is Ham Peggoty, little Em'ly's simple and honest lover, who, without knowing whom he is rescuing, swims out to the ship, and gives his life in vain to save the man who has injured him.

But after all, in Dickens it is not the story that matters. For one person who remembers what happens in this, or any other, of Dickens's novels, there are a thousand to whom his characters, the people whom you meet on the way through his plots, will remain lastingly vivid. It is perfectly true that there was never anybody as smirkingly "'umble" as Uriah Heep; it may be doubted whether anybody ever concealed as good a heart under as excitable and erratic and "notiony" a manner as Miss Betsy Trotwood; it may be doubted whether there was ever anybody who could be at one and the same time so oratorical and so complacent and so incompetent and so incurably optimistic as Mr. Micawber; it is certainly true that nobody in real life was ever as raspingly metallic as Miss Murdstone, or as quick and sharp and needle-like as Steerforth's cousin, Miss Rosa Dartle. And yet, even though our sense of the novelist's obligation to present life as it really is is continually offended by a world of one-track minds and eccentric behavior and catch-words, we do, for some reason, enjoy and continue to enjoy Dickens. I think that it is because most of us never entirely grow up, never altogether outgrow the child-mood in which we like to see the world played with as Dickens plays with it. "Come now," says Dickens, "would you like to see the most hard-hearted

and stingy miser that ever was, changed by one wave of
the magic wand into a generous old gentleman? *I'll* do
it in *The Christmas Carol,* whether it can be done or not.
Do you pity poor little Oliver Twist and do you hate Fagin
for having treated him so badly? Then every time Oliver
gets projected into a theft, we'll see that it lands him in
the one place in a thousand where he'll find protectors and
friends — *and* relatives. And when Oliver is properly disposed of, we'll put Fagin in a cell and make his last moments so harrowing — with little Oliver standing by to
witness them! — that the account will be perfectly squared.
Have you taken a liking for Mr. Micawber with his genial
ways and his swelling phrases and his complete inability to
make a success of anything? Then we'll send him to
Australia and suddenly transform him into a competent
business man. There *are* smirking hypocrites in the world,
aren't there? Then in Uriah Heep I'll give you the 'um-
blest and the meanest going, with a red head and a pale
face and hardly any eyebrows and no eyelashes and stealth-
ily staring eyes and a long, lank, skeleton, clammy hand,
and a mother who is likewise a very 'umble person and a
father who, having 'umbly died as an 'umble sexton, is now
a partaker of glory. And after Uriah has schemed and
lied and very nearly succeeded in involving David's best
friends in disgrace and ruin, I'll put Uriah in a cell and
for good measure put Mr. Creakle, whom we had very
nearly forgotten, in charge of him."

It isn't life, and in our moments of critical intelligence
we feel that we are being played with; but it is all extraordinarily vivid and rememberable; and as we go on
from *Oliver Twist* and *David Copperfield* to Dickens's other
novels, we accumulate such a gallery of portraits, such a
collection of types, that we find ourselves classifying the

actual world in terms of them. If the people whom we know are not like that, at least they too have their dominant peculiarities, their ruling passions, their characteristic ways and turns of phrase — and we tag them with Dickens's well-remembered names.

Dickens's world — the people whom he was most interested in and drew most vividly — consisted chiefly of the lower classes, the common folk. Among these, with their unguarded speech and informal ways, he could more readily find the eccentrics whom he loved, and could have freer scope in heightening their oddities. Thackeray's world, on the other hand, was the upper middle-class society of his time, with a sprinkling of titled folk, Sir This and Lord That — the "toffs," as Dickens's Sam Wellers and Uriahs called them. And what most interested Thackeray in these people was the social striving that was always going on among them — the efforts to "get into Society," and the actual stupidity and sordidness and meanness and selfishness of the so-called "high society" which the climbers were trying to get into. This is the theme of his first great novel *Vanity Fair*, and in a measure also (though the story is conceived in a very different mood) of the other novel of his which is most worth reading, *Henry Esmond*.

The story of *Vanity Fair* is "dated" by the battle of Waterloo (1815), around which the threads of the plot are woven. The central character is Becky Sharp, whom we discover as an articled pupil and teacher of French at Miss Pinkerton's school. She gets very little consideration there, does Becky; for Miss Pinkerton, being a born snob, is interested only in rich pupils, and Becky, a penniless orphan of not too respectable parentage, has no position and no prospects. But Becky is shrewd and clever and witty and quite capable of doing her own climbing. How she climbs, and what people she meets on the rungs of the social ladder, and the involvements of their lives, make the story of *Vanity Fair*.

One of these rich pupils, Amelia Sedley, takes Becky home with her for a visit. Here Becky meets Amelia's brother, Jos, rich, unmarried, fat, awkward and shy. Becky sets to work at once. "'This is my friend, Miss Sharp,' says Amelia, 'whom you have heard me mention.'

'No, never, upon my word,' said the head under the neckcloth, shaking very much, — 'that is, yes, — what abominably cold weather, Miss;' — and herewith he fell to poking the fire with all his might although it was in the middle of June.

'He's very handsome,' whispered Rebecca to Amelia, rather loud.

'Do you think so?' said the latter. 'I'll tell him.'

'Darling! not for worlds,' said Miss Sharp, starting back as timid as a fawn. She had previously made a respectful, virgin-like curtsey to the gentleman, and her modest eyes gazed so perseveringly on the carpet that it was a wonder how she should have found an opportunity to see him."

It is in this tone of playful irony, of pretending that all his characters are the best and sincerest and most virtuous people in the world, while he is actually exposing their pretenses and schemings, that Thackeray satirizes the dwellers in *Vanity Fair*.

Becky just misses snaring the awkward Jos; and after her visit to the Sedleys is concluded, and she has secured a position as governess in the household of Sir Pitt Crawley, she goes after bigger game. Sir Pitt is not an agreeable person. He is dirty, foul-mouthed, drunken, without manners or decency;[1] but after all he is a baronet, and a baronet is "Society." Lady Crawley falls conveniently ill; but before Sir Pitt is free to take a second wife, his son, Captain Rawdon Crawley, returns on leave from his regiment and Becky captures him. And then, just a little too late, Lady Crawley dies —

" 'Say yes, Becky,' Sir Pitt continued. 'I'm an old man, but a good'n. I'm good for twenty years. I'll make you happy, zee if I don't. You shall do what you like; spend what you like; and 'av it all your own way. I'll make you a zettlement. I'll do everything reg'lar. Look year!' and the old man fell down on his knees and leered at her like a satyr.

Rebecca started back, a picture of consternation. In the course of this history we have never seen her lose her presence of mind; but she did now, and wept some of the most genuine tears that ever fell from her eyes.

'O Sir Pitt!' she said. 'O sir — I — I'm *married already*.' "

Rawdon Crawley is a gambler, who ekes out his slender income with his winnings at cards. Husband and wife coöperate; but the calling of the troops for Waterloo spoils the game. Captain Rawdon, and the gentle Amelia Sedley's newly-wedded husband, Captain Osborne, and all England's thousands are in the field; and at Brussels, Becky and sundry others whose lives have become involved with hers await the issue of the battle. Thackeray's picture of Waterloo is one of the supreme masterpieces of literature — not a description of the actual battle, the massing of troops upon the field, but rather a vision of it seen through the eyes of the civilians who are waiting at Brussels, — in the rumors that fly thick and fast, in the

---

[1] When Thackeray's readers protested that Sir Pitt was "overdrawn"; that it was "impossible to find such coarseness in his rank of life," Thackeray replied: "That character is almost the only exact portrait in the whole book."

baring of souls torn with anxiety, the panic and cowardice and selfishness of most, the courage and unselfishness of some, the shrewd, cool, profiteering of the indomitable little Becky, the wild shivering panic of poor Jos Sedley,— I know of nothing in English fiction that can match for sheer power and vividness the thirtieth, thirty-first and thirty-second chapters of *Vanity Fair*.

Captain Osborne is killed at Waterloo. The fortunes of the Sedley family decline. Amelia is reduced to poverty. Her hand is finally won by Captain Dobbin, the clumsy kindly Dobbin, the grocer's son, who had served and loved Amelia, unselfishly and devotedly, for many years. "I dislike everybody in the book except Dob. and poor Amelia," wrote Thackeray, and he called Amelia the heroine of the story; but it is Becky who really interested him and interests us. Becky continues her climbing. With Rawdon's winnings at cards and Becky's skill in getting credit and standing off creditors, they set up an establishment and live precariously but fashionably. Rawdon grows ever prouder of his able little helpmate — until one day he finds her accepting gifts and attentions from Lord Steyne. That great nobleman, that topmost pinnacle and perfectest achievement of high society, is incontinently knocked down and ejected by the disillusioned Rawdon. Becky disappears, taking with her all the money she can lay her hands on. Long afterward, when Amelia and Dobbin and Jos are traveling on the continent they come upon Becky, staking — and losing — her last florin at *roulette*. Amelia befriends her. Jos becomes her devoted slave and obliges her as best he can (for his fortune is spent) by insuring himself for her benefit and promptly dying. With the money Becky establishes herself in the respectable society of Bath, where she conducts herself with perfect discretion; is always ready to take charge of a stall at a Fancy Fair for the benefit of the Destitute Orange-girl, the Neglected Washerwoman and the Distressed Muffinman; and gathers about her "a very strong party of excellent people who consider her to be a most injured woman."

It is not a pretty story.   It leaves a bad taste in the mouth, which not even the gentle Amelia and the unselfish Dobbin can sweeten.   But you would have to look a long time to find a story more unflaggingly interesting or one which has such a wealth of characters so vividly and so convincingly drawn.   And two of them certainly are great creations.   One of course is Becky herself.   The other is neither the amiable Amelia nor the faithful Dobbin, but that clumsy dragoon and unscrupulous gambler, Captain Rawdon Crawley.   To find the good in him, to make him capable of an unselfish devotion, to give him a final touch of tragic dignity by making him lavish that devotion upon the calculating and selfish and wholly indifferent Becky, was a stroke of genius.

In *Vanity Fair*, the characters are of Thackeray's own day.   In *Henry Esmond*, the clock is turned back to the late seventeenth and early eighteenth centuries, and many of the characters are actual personages of that time.   The historical novel had degenerated after Scott died.   Thackeray reinvigorated it, and changed the method.   In place of Scott's romanticism and "big bow-wow" style, Thackeray tells his story simply, naturally, realistically.   In this respect, and in its perfection of form, and truth and consistency of atmosphere, *Henry Esmond* set a new standard for historical fiction.

The tale is told by Henry Esmond himself, in the form of reminiscences of his boyhood and young manhood.   As the illegitimate son of the old Lord Castlewood he is taken into the household of the new Lord, and though the ignominy of his birth is not forgotten, is kindly treated by the young and beautiful Lady Castlewood and her children, Frank and Beatrix. Henry Esmond grows up in an atmosphere of plots, for the Castlewoods are Stuart sympathizers, and schemes are afoot to oust King William and place James Stuart,[1] son of King James II, on the throne. As Henry Esmond grows to manhood, his heart is divided between his devotion to his kind patroness, Lady Castlewood, and his love for the brilliant and beautiful Beatrix. Upon the death of Lord Castlewood in a duel with the unscrupulous gambler, Lord Mohun, Henry Esmond, who has acted as his patron's second, leaves England to take part in the war with France. He has learned from the lips of his dying patron that his birth was legitimate and that he himself is heir to the title; but he keeps silent, unwilling to deprive his beloved lady of her inheritance. When he returns from France, it is to find Beatrix in the flower of womanhood, and far too ambitious to consider marriage with one who is supposed to have a stain upon his name. From this point on, the story centers in the career of the beautiful Beatrix. It is the "climber" once more, as in the story of Becky Sharp in *Vanity Fair*. Like Becky, Beatrix is calculating, selfish, bent only on making a great marriage; but Becky was a nameless little adventuress, dependent upon her wits; Beatrix has beauty and breeding and social position. Only the highest will do for her — and at length she captures the great Duke of Hamilton. The tragic climax of the story, when, on the very eve of marriage,

---

[1] Known to history as "the Pretender." Scott's *Rob Roy* is likewise concerned with a Jacobite plot to place James Stuart on the throne. Scott's *Waverley* and *Redgauntlet* have to do with plots to place James Stuart's son, Charles Edward ("the Young Pretender"), upon the throne. If you will read any one of these novels side by side with *Henry Esmond*, you will see how sharply Thackeray's use of historical background differs from Scott's.

Beatrix's dreams are shattered by the sudden death of
the Duke, in a duel at the hands of Lord Mohun,[1] is one of
the great scenes of fiction:

As Esmond and the Dean walked away from Kensington dis-
coursing of this tragedy, and how fatal it was to the cause which
they both had at heart, the street criers were already out with
their broadsides, shouting through the town the full, true and
horrible account of the death of Lord Mohun and Duke Hamilton
in a duel. A fellow had got to Kensington and was crying it in
the square there at very early morning, when Mr. Esmond happened to pass by. He drove the man from under Beatrix's very
window, whereof the casement had been set open. The sun was
shining though 'twas November: he had seen the market-carts
rolling into London, the guard relieved at the palace, the laborers
trudging to their work in the gardens between Kensington and the
City — the wandering merchants and hawkers filling the air
with their cries. The world was going to its business again,
although dukes lay dead and ladies mourned for them; and
Kings, very likely, lost their chances. So night and day pass
away, and tomorrow comes, and our place knows us not. Esmond
thought of the courier, now galloping on the North road to in-
form him who was Earl of Arran yesterday, that he was Duke of
Hamilton today, and of a thousand great schemes, hopes, ambi-
tions, that were alive in the gallant heart, beating a few hours
since, and now a little dust quiescent.

The death of the Duke is the turning point of Beatrix's
life. Her disappointment hardens her and makes her reckless. It is her recklessness that spoils the great plot in
which the Castlewood family now engage. Henry Esmond
goes to France, secretly brings back the Stuart prince, and
houses him in the London house of the Castlewoods. The
reigning sovereign, Queen Anne, is on her deathbed. Her-

[1] The actual duel between James Douglas, fourth Duke of Hamilton, and
Lord Mohun occurred in 1712.

self a daughter of James II, it is thought that she will wish
a Stuart to succeed her. The plotters bring the prince into
her presence and she seems to favor him. It is planned
that on a certain day, a group of influential Stuart sympathizers shall secretly assemble, escort the prince to the
presence of the Queen, and have her formally announce
him as her successor. The day comes, the leaders assemble
— but the prince is missing. Beatrix, once more under the
spell of a great name, has lured him away to Castlewood.
When at length Esmond finds him and brings him back to
London, it is too late. The Queen is dead and George I
is King. The thwarted prince, the thwarted Beatrix, go
their separate ways. Esmond, cured of his infatuation for
Beatrix, wins the hand of Lady Castlewood; and Frank,
by Esmond's grace the heir, turns over to them the Castlewood estates in Virginia where Esmond and his beloved
lady spend their remaining years.[1]

It is a great story, far more compact than *Vanity Fair*,
more unified, even more breathlessly interesting. It is,
with respect to Beatrix, a great piece of characterization.
Her beauty, her fascination (which becomes as real to the
reader as ever it was to Esmond), her pride and overweening
ambition, the tragedy of her thwarted hopes — and with
it all, something almost approaching greatness of soul in
her, the nullifying of which is indeed the real tragedy —
these are the things that we remember, the qualities that
go to make up what has been described as the most completely portrayed woman in English fiction.

And how apt is the style in which the story is told!
Turn over the pages of the *Spectator* to some of Addison's
graver essays — that on Westminster Abbey, for example,

---

[1] Thackeray continues his account of the fortunes of the Castlewood family
in *The Virginians*.

or "The Vision of Mirza," and see how perfectly Thackeray has attuned his style to the best prose of the day in which the plot is laid. And when the story rises to its great moments, the style rises with it — not, as in Dickens, by a palpable straining after effects, an *air* of the dramatic — but by a spontaneous rhythm, a grave and restrained music. Try upon your ear the brief paragraph quoted a few pages back from the description of the death of the Duke of Hamilton. Something has been lost from English prose since Thackeray's pen was stilled.

But plot and characterization and style are not the only things which make *Henry Esmond* interesting to us. The men whom Esmond gets to know in the course of his adventurous life — Addison, Steele, Dean Swift (it is Swift who brings the news of the Duke's death) the foolish and depraved Pretender, Mohun and Hamilton, Marlborough and General Webb, come to life under Thackeray's touch. As one turns the last page of *Esmond*, one finds oneself wishing, not merely that there were more such historical novels, but that the writing of history itself might be more after this fashion — with the historian's full and precise knowledge lightened and vivified by the novelist's creative imagination.

Dickens, whose last novel appeared in 1870, Thackeray, whose last novel appeared in 1867, were the "giants before the flood"— the flood of modern fiction. In the enormous output that has marked the last quarter of the nineteenth and the first quarter of the twentieth century, no novelist has risen to the unquestioned preëminence which these two enjoyed. To dwell upon typical works of the later novelists as we have dwelt upon a few of Dickens's and Thackeray's would be to lengthen this book unduly — and even to enumerate them would but involve us in a confusion of names. But it will be possible to note briefly a few of the more important figures, and a few recent trends.

It is in her simplest and least ambitious novels, *Adam Bede, The Mill on the Floss*, and *Silas Marner*, that George Eliot, (1819–1880) is at her best. In these she drew upon the life that she had known as a girl in Warwickshire — the life that still remained the most vivid thing in her experience, when as a middle-aged woman in London, she turned aside from the writing of philosophical essays to try her hand at fiction. One does not need to be told that Adam Bede and Dinah Morris and Mrs. Poyser in *Adam Bede;* and the impulsive tender-hearted little Maggie and her delightfully absurd aunts in *The Mill on the Floss;* and the quaint villagers in *Silas Marner* are such as George Eliot had lived among. They could not ring so true if she had not watched them from day to day and stored their sayings and then allowed her memories to guide her pen. "I aspire," she says in *Adam Bede,* "to give no more than a faithful account of men and things as they have mirrored themselves in my mind. The mirror is doubtless defective; and the outlines will be sometimes distorted; the reflection faint and confused; but I feel as much bound to tell you as precisely as I can what that reflection is as if I were in the witness box narrating my experience on oath." Every one knows (to take that novel of hers which is at once the simplest and the best) how spontaneously and truthfully the tale of Silas Marner emerges from the well-filled storehouse of George Eliot's mind. The ignorant credulity of the dull weavers of Lantern Yard; the way in which poor Silas Marner's faith in God and in human nature is shattered when his dearest friend accuses him falsely and the casting of the lots confirms the accusation; the suspicions and superstitious fears of the villagers when Silas comes to Raveloe, the naturalness with which his empty and lonely soul turns to the hoarding of the gold coins which his weaving brings to him, the utter confusion and despair to which he is reduced when his hoard is stolen; the coming of the little golden-haired girl to waken his mind from its dull lethargy to a human love — these things take us beneath the surface of life to its very essence. No romantic plot, no brave adventure, is required to make *Silas Marner* interesting. "Depend upon it," wrote George Eliot at the outset of her career as a novelist, "you would gain unspeakably if you would learn with me to see some of the poetry and the pathos, the tragedy and the comedy, lying in the experience of a human soul that looks out through dull grey eyes, and that speaks in a voice of quite ordinary tones."

George Eliot's work would have been better if she had been content in all of her novels to do just that. But she was by instinct and experience a philosopher rather than a creative artist. She had trained her mind to analyze, to explain, to ask the why of things, and to attempt to find some sort of logic in the rather illogical thing that we call life. To a certain extent in her early novels and increasingly as she continued, this habit of looking at life as a scientific observer, as a psychologist, as a philosopher, got in her way. A psychologist is a person who takes human clocks to pieces to see what makes the wheels go round, and who is persuaded that if he can take enough of them to pieces, he will be able to put them together again and make them run better. The artist in George Eliot "aspired to give no more than a faithful account of men and things as they mirrored themselves in her mind." The psychologist in her was bent on explaining every step of the progress by which a temptation took shape, all the feelings, all the inward struggles, that led up to and bore fruit in a given act. The philosopher in her was bent on demonstrating just how the yielding to that impulse, the doing of that deed, must inevitably set going a whole train of such impulses, and so gradually mold, or re-mold, the yielder's character. It is true, of course, that life works more or less in that way. A picture of life, a portrayal of character, which fails to take that into account is an incomplete picture. But the great artist is content to let life speak for itself. He prefers to leave it to us to do the analyzing; and whatever theories there may be in the back of his mind, he will not appear to be demonstrating anything. "Here," says he, "are people doing things. I have nothing to prove. I have not arranged anything. I am simply telling you about them. The moral (and if my picture is true, there is likely to be one) you can draw for yourself." It was because George Eliot could not be content to let life take its course and be its own comment, but had always to be dissecting it and logically ordering it, that her more ambitious novels fall short of being great novels. You catch a glimpse of this habit of hers even in as fine and simple a tale as *Silas Marner*. It is more marked in another one of her early novels, *The Mill on the Floss*, because that novel is conceived on a larger scale than *Silas Marner*. And if you will read some of her later novels, such as *Romola* and *Middlemarch*, you will see it carried to an extreme.

This does not mean that George Eliot's later work is dull. *Middlemarch*, for example, is full of vivid touches, of moments of effective character portrayal. It is interesting, too, for this reason: George Eliot is the first modern "psychological" novelist; and in our own day the "psychological novel" has borne some queer fruit. There is a tendency just now to throw overboard the very thing which we have always thought of as most fundamental to a novel, namely, the plot itself; and to turn the novel into a sort of picture of the conscious and what is called the subconscious mind. Imagine what Shakespeare's *Hamlet* would be like if the "action" were cut out, if our interest were not kept on edge by Hamlet's long struggle with Claudius in pursuit of his revenge, and if Hamlet's soliloquies and asides, the ebb and flow of his thoughts, the emotions aroused by chance contacts, were so elaborated as to fill the whole five acts of the play. That is the sort of thing with which a number of present-day novelists are experimenting. It is worth watching because there will probably be a good deal more of it before it runs its course. Possibly out of these incoherent jumbles of moods and impressions which we are still calling novels for lack of a better name, some good may come; but I think that if you should happen to sample one of them, you will feel that however truthfully our mental jumble is pictured in them, it is not the kind of truth which gets anywhere or is worth knowing; and that, as in life, so in the novel, it is what we *do* and how we face the consequences of our acts, that reveals character. And that after all is what we mean by the plot of a novel. It is something more than a mere frame-work for characterization. It is the author's selection, out of the multitude of things that did happen or might have happened to a group of people, of only the most testing and revealing things. It is the story of these people doing these things, good people and bad people, working for or against one another. I am inclined to think that this will be the material of the great novels of the future as it has been of the great novels of the past.

During these late years, there have been many other experiments in fiction. Two of the boldest experimenters have been George Meredith and Thomas Hardy. The most characteristic of Meredith's novels is *The Egoist*. The central character is a rich young gentleman, Sir Willoughby Patterne, just come of age, and ready — if he can find her — to take to himself a wife worthy of his dignity. His meetings with and courtship of a succession of more or less eligible young ladies forms the story. *The Egoist* is like a play, with extraordinarily witty conversation largely taking the place of narrative. As we read on from scene to scene, from courtship to courtship, we gradually penetrate beneath Sir Willoughby's polished manners and elegant sentimentality to the real Sir Willoughby — the egoist, with his ingrained habit of thinking and talking about himself, his feeling that everything in his world must be arranged for his special benefit. The eligible young ladies ultimately see through him too. That is why there is a succession of them. When Meredith gets through with him, the soul of the thrice-jilted Sir Willoughby is pretty thoroughly laid bare.

You will find it an interesting study in methods of satire to read Jane Austen's *Pride and Prejudice* and Thackeray's *Vanity Fair* and Meredith's *The Egoist* side by side. Thackeray's range is the widest. He gathers a great variety of people into his dragnet. But, in *Vanity Fair* they are all there for one purpose. His playful irony only thinly veils a passionate hatred of the sham, the hypocrisy, the pretense of what passes for good society. He does not distort. He sticks to the truth.. But it is the kind of truth that hurts. *Pride and Prejudice* and *The Egoist* are narrower in their scope — a few people in the drawing-room. Jane Austen is interested, not in any one person particu-

larly, but in the group.   In *The Egoist*, though there are
vivid incidental portraits, Meredith concentrates absolutely
on the one character.   Sir Willoughby is never for a moment "off-stage."   Jane Austen is mildly amused at human folly, and there are very few characters in *Pride and
Prejudice* that have not laughable foibles — foibles that
get pretty thoroughly exposed by the time the book is
finished.   But they are average people, in most of whom
virtues and weaknesses are not unevenly mixed.   It is a
complete portrait that Jane Austen is after.   *The Egoist*
too is a complete portrait; but it is a portrait of a kind of
person who fortunately is not "average"— a portrait in
which Egoism is so specialized that it is elevated into a
fine art.   But it is in Meredith's approach that he differs
most from his predecessors.   "Comedy," says Meredith,
"throws no infamous reflection upon life."   *The Egoist* is
pure comedy — not the raw stuff that stirs uproarious
laughter, but things to smile at and meditate upon — the
delicately manifested follies of the world.   The mischievous
little imps of the Comic Spirit are always watching their
chance.   Walk as circumspectly as you may, they will
catch you in an unguarded moment.   There is a priceless
scene in *The Egoist*, in which Sir Willoughly, finding that
his fiancée is beginning to see through him, and anxious
not to be humiliated by another jilting, secretly offers his
hand to a young lady, a mere tenant on his estate, who,
he thinks, has always adored him.   To his astonishment
she refuses him; and next morning, he tries once more to
save his face by persuading his fiancée of his unswerving
devotion to her.   But a little boy, who has been asleep
under a sofa in the drawing-room, has overheard the secret
proposal, and has told.   Sir Willoughly tries again to save
his face by pretending that he was proposing not for him-

self but on behalf of a friend. The gossips gather. All talk at once and at cross-purposes; and Sir Willoughby's precious Ego fights its last battle of wits and wiles. You may find *The Egoist* a little too fine-spun and elusive for reading straight through at a first trial; but if you will read this part of it (chapters XL–XLIII), you will see that it is almost a staged comedy rather than a novel that Meredith is giving us; and you will hear the tinkling laughter of the imps of the Comic Spirit, as they maneuver poor Sir Willoughby into a situation where the very elements seem to have conspired against him.

Hardy affords a striking contrast to Meredith. In Hardy's novels there is no "society," and there is no personal satire, no effort on the novelist's part to ridicule human folly. His are stories of the plain people of a single locality, that area of southwestern England including the counties of Somerset, Dorset, and Devon, which is called Wessex. These simple folk, at the time when he was writing novels about them (1870–1895), mixed little with the rest of the world. Humanly speaking, Wessex gives the impression of being the oldest part of England. Celt and Roman had lived out their time there and left their mark, before ever Saxon and Norman had begun to struggle for a foothold. The people of Hardy's novels are continuators of a tradition that began long before recorded history began. The sense of these innumerable lives lived out — one knows not why or for what — upon the unchanging face of nature, wrought strongly upon Hardy's imagination and imparted to his novels a rather grim philosophy of life. "It was at present," he writes of the desolate upland country which he calls Egdon heath, "a place perfectly accordant with man's nature — neither ghastly, hateful nor ugly; neither commonplace, unmeaning, nor tame; but, like man, slighted and enduring; and withal singularly colossal and mysterious in its swarthy monotony. As with some persons who have long lived apart, solitude seemed to look out of its countenance. It had a lonely face suggesting tragical possibilities." In Hardy's novels, physical nature, in some mysterious way wrapping itself around the souls of the human beings who live out their little lives upon its surface, becomes the outward manifestation of what appears to him to be the blind Force that moves the world. Human nature wants its own way, wants to plan and shape its own life. But often things do not come out right; and indeed they often come out so very wrong that it would almost seem as if the Force were not blind after all, but were maliciously or ironically thwarting human endeavor. That is not a very comfortable philosophy; but it inspired Hardy to do what no other creative writer in the field of English literature has done. If you will read a number of Shakespeare's plays, for example, you will find in them many real people very vividly portrayed. You will find accident or mischance sometimes playing a part in their lives; but, by and large, you will find them shaping their own destinies and paying the price. What they do, and the direct and immediate consequences of what they do makes the play. There seems to be no Force, benevolent or malevolent or blind, to shape them. It is as if they were moving in a vacuum. Since Shakespeare's day, creative literature, whether drama or fiction, has largely followed his lead. But Hardy tries not only to represent life but to find a meaning, a compulsion, in it.

In *The Return of the Native*, for example, Egdon heath itself is in a sense the central "character" of the story. It broods over the furze-cutters and the few families of better class who live on or near it. Clym Yeobright who has been away in Paris and has come back to start a school for the ignorant furze-cutters, loves its vast quietude and austere beauty and becomes as much a part of its spirit as if he had never been away. The heath-dwellers live out their simple lives upon it, carrying on unwittingly, in their Christmas mummings, their Maypole dances, their bonfires, the traditions of an immemorial past. "It was," writes Hardy of one of these midnight bonfires on the heath, "as if these men and boys had suddenly dived into past ages, and fetched therefrom an hour and deed which have before been familiar with this spot. The ashes of the original British pyre which blazed from that summit lay fresh and undisturbed in the barrow beneath their tread. The flames from funeral piles long ago kindled there had shone down upon the lowlands as these were shining now."

But among these people whose lives are a part of Egdon, there is one alien spirit. Eustacia Vye has been brought from the outside world to live in this quiet spot. She hates it, rebels against its stern simplicity, its wholesome plainness. Through her come the misunderstandings, the tragic mischances, of the story.

It is a tragic story, and yet, in spite of Hardy's feeling that life is so largely a matter of misfits and mischances, it is not depressing. If Hardy's were a railing spirit, it might be so. But there is something in his calm undismayed acceptance of life, in his freedom from harsh judgments, in his large sympathy and understanding, in the simplicity and restraint with which he tells the story, that saves this and most of his other novels from bitterness.

It has often been said that there is a Shakespearian quality in Hardy's minor characterizations, his portrayal of the Wessex peasants whose doings and sayings make the background of his stories. If you will turn to Shakespeare's

Love's Labour's Lost and read the scenes in which Costard and Jaquenetta appear; or to *A Midsummer Night's Dream* and watch Bottom and his fellow artizans rehearsing for their play; or to *Much Ado about Nothing*, where those prudent constables, Dogberry and Verges, are engaged in keeping the peace; or listen to the talk of Audrey in *As You Like It*, or foregather with the musicians in *Romeo and Juliet* — and then make the acquaintance of Grandfer Cantle and the Christmas mummers in Hardy's *The Return of the Native*, or read that part of *The Trumpet Major* in which Festus hears that the French are coming; or, perhaps best of all, if you will read the grave-digger scene in *Hamlet* and the twenty-sixth chapter of *A Pair of Blue Eyes* side by side, you will see what is meant by saying that Hardy's peasants are "Shakespearian." Hardy dramatizes his peasants and makes them extraordinarily vivid. But in Hardy these humorously sympathetic studies are not incidental as they are in Shakespeare. They become not merely a background for his plots but also (taking his novels all together) a remarkably complete picture of the life of a peculiar people. Hardy "caught" his Wessex peasantry while they were still largely unaffected by the outside world, still expressing in their lives the customs and credulities of their remotest forefathers, still interlarding their speech with proverbs and turns of phrase as old as the race. It was almost the last possible moment before the expansion of railway transportation and the development of the motor car began to break down boundaries and blur individualities.

There is a sturdiness, a vigor, an originality in Hardy's work which are likely to make his novels last for a long time. They will last, too, because of the fidelity, the completeness and the vividness with which he pictured the little isolated bit of the world which he knew so intimately and loved so understandingly. For in accomplishing this, he accomplished a bigger thing. It may be that, as Wordsworth felt, "the essential passions of the heart are less under restraint and speak a plainer and more emphatic language" in humble and rustic life than in the complexities of a highly developed society. At any rate it was a language to which Hardy's ear was peculiarly attuned. Because he knew his own people so well and presented them so truly, and because it was the essential passions of the heart rather than the outward show that interested him, he has turned his picture of Wessex into a pretty complete picture of human nature and human life.

Hardy's last novel was written in 1895.[1] Since that time, prose-fiction has followed many paths. One of these, the experiment of turning the novel into a mere record of conscious and subconscious impressions and impulses, has already been noted. The good old story of romantic adventure continues to thrive. In that field, Robert Louis Stevenson is the acknowledged master among the moderns. Every one has read *Treasure Island*. One could not ask a better proof of the fact that it is not mere ability to spin a yarn that makes a good story. It is because that ingenious and lucky youngster, Jim Hawkins, and the cool and courageous Dr. Livesey, and the rash and impulsive squire and the plausible rascal, Long John Silver, are such real people, and act so characteristically in the ex-

---

[1] Between 1895 and his death in 1928, Hardy gave himself to the writing of poetry. With the exception of an epic drama, *The Dynasts*, a mystic vision of human life with the Napoleonic war as its central theme, his verse has been largely a record of moods and impressions of the life immediately around him. Like his novels, his poetry is remarkably vigorous and independent. There is a thoughtfulness in it, and a curious sort of rough strength, which catch and hold the attention of the reader; and, as in Samson's riddle, out of the strong comes forth sweetness.

traordinary adventures in which they take part, that *Treasure Island* is perennially interesting. There is nothing new about searches for treasure. Stevenson took an old pattern and transformed it by his genius. You can find adventures as startling in any penny-dreadful. But it is only when the people who take part in them cease to be mere pegs to hang the adventures on and become so real that you are with them — or "down on them" — every step of the way, that such a story is worth reading and rereading. *Treasure Island* is the kind of story to read first for the sheer zest of adventure, and then to come back to after a while when you are in a mood to read it critically, and discover the skill in weaving, the ingenuity in leading up to dramatic moments, the "bringing off" of the climaxes, the shrewd touches of characterization — the technique, in short, which underlies the apparently artless and effortless ease of the story. Of his other novels, *Kidnapped* comes nearest to *Treasure Island* in excellence. The romantic and boastful Alan Breck is a great creation. You will wish to compare him with Fergus MacIvor in Scott's *Waverley*, and with Rob Roy in Scott's novel of that name; and you will find it even more interesting to put Alan Breck beside another study in that particular temperament — Owen Glendower in Shakespeare's *Henry IV, Part I*. But with all the vividness of Stevenson's other novels, there is a touch of self-consciousness in them, a flavor as of a dancing-master showing his tricks, that becomes a bit irritating after a while. As with George Eliot, it is the shortest and most elementary of his stories that is likely to live the longest.

In such stories as Stevenson's, characterization, however vivid in itself, is not the chief object. The novelist has an exciting tale to tell, and must make his characters as life-like as possible. But since Stevenson's day, in the hands of Joseph Conrad, the tale of romantic adventure has been put to a new use. Conrad, who had been for many years a sailor and sea-rover, and whose wanderings had taken him to the strangest of strange strands, had a wealth of out-of-the-way stories to tell. *The Nigger of the Narcissus, Lord Jim, Nostromo,* and *Victory* are the ones which you will perhaps enjoy most. Adventure crowds upon adventure in them. But you will see as you read them that the adventures are not there primarily for their own sake. A human soul — not mere mannerisms or externalities of character, but something deeper that is the very essence of the man — is to be revealed. Struggles with natives on a wild Malayan coast, or shipwreck, or the long musings that come when a ship is becalmed on a tropic sea, or schemings for wealth and power in some lawless South American republic — whatever it may be, there comes, out of what seems for a time to be mere chaotic confusion, an extraordinarily vivid revelation of a human soul. Read *Lord Jim,* for example, and see how the exciting adventures are molded into a study of one of the basic elements of character. Self-confidence, faith in oneself, is the theme of the story. It tells of the effect which the loss of that faith in self had upon a human soul, and of how, at once tragically and nobly, that faith was regained. And whatever novels of Conrad's you chance upon, you will find yourself caught and held by the beauty of his prose. No other writer of our day[1] has such magic at his command, no other prose such rhythm, such exaltation, such splendor.

Of contemporary English novelists, the three best known

[1] Joseph Conrad died February 17, 1930.

are H. G. Wells, John Galsworthy and Arnold Bennett.[1]   All these reflect, in their several ways, the scientific turn of mind which is so largely coloring all our thought and writing to-day.   Of the three, Wells has made the biggest splash, and will be, almost certainly, the soonest forgotten. Were it not for the bigness of the splash, indeed, it is doubtful if he should be included here, for fiction with him is not an end in itself, but a means to an end.   "In the books which I have written," he says, "it is always about life being altered I write, or about people developing schemes for altering life.   And I have never once 'presented life.' My apparently most objective books are criticisms and incitements to change."   Fiction is a jealous god.   Theories or sermons or soap-box exhortations to the man in the street — however cleverly they may be disguised — are not like to give the theorist or the exhorter an enduring reputation as a novelist.   Whether Mr. Wells will live as a reformer and prophet only time can tell.   He has published in the guise of novels a series of guesses about how modern inventions (machines) may change our way of living.   He has written a whole series of sociological treatises, exemplifications in story form of how the organization of society, the legalized relations of man to man, may be changed for the better.   He has of late years turned his attention to man's idea of God.   If Mr. Wells lives long enough, there will be few ologies or isms that will have escaped his exposition.   He is widely read to-day because ologies and isms are more entertaining when you can see them being tried out by characters in a story.   It saves mental effort on the part of the reader, and deludes him into thinking that what is represented as happening to an imaginary John Smith and James Jones (who are after all only pawns on

[1] Arnold Bennett died March 27, 1931.

Mr. Wells's chessboard) must be true. If Mr. Wells is remembered at all two or three generations hence, it will be,
not as a creative artist, but as a recorder of the infinite
variety of notions and speculations about life with which
our restless generation is occupied.

Galsworthy and Bennett, too, are scientifically minded.
They are much more genuine artists than Mr. Wells. They
do what Wells boasts that he never does: they "present
life." They have a sense of form, and write with a grace,
a finish, which is either denied to Mr. Wells, or which he
has not thought it worth his while to cultivate. It is perhaps only indirectly that they reflect the scientific tendency of the age — in a sort of dogged determination, not
merely to present life, but to make a scientifically thorough
exposition of the age we live in. If you will read Bennett's
The Old Wives' Tale, a minutely careful study of the psy-
chology of a group of rather commonplace small-town
tradespeople, who have been doing business as their fathers
did before them, and who are struggling to adapt themselves to the new ways and changed standards of the present day, you will see something of the exhaustive thor-
oughness with which Bennett studies his characters. And
if you will go on from this to the other novels in which
Bennett studies his "Five Towns" (a cluster of intercom-
municating towns in the pottery-district of central England), you will no doubt feel when you get through that
certain aspects of life and certain kinds of people have
been "presented" as thoroughly as it is possible to present
them. And yet, unless I am very much mistaken, your
final feeling will be that what you have been reading is a
remarkable "document" rather than a series of great
novels. And you will have the same feeling, I think, when
you turn from Bennett's "Five Towns" to Galsworthy's

The Forsyte Saga. *The Forsyte Saga* is a putting together of a number of Galsworthy's novels having to do with five successive generations of the Forsyte family — prosperous London business people. It is an amazingly thorough study of the changes in mental attitude, in industrial methods, in social and moral standards, that have been going on between the 1880's and the 1920's. Galsworthy makes his people very real to us. There are in *The Forsyte Saga* a subtleness, a sensitiveness to the fine shadings of character, a dramatic power, that surpass anything that Bennett accomplished. And yet I think that you will feel that *The Forsyte Saga* too is rather a great document than a great novel. If, after reading Bennett's studies of human nature in the "Five Towns," you will turn back to Hardy's portrayal of human nature in Wessex; and if after reading Galsworthy's satirical study of five generations of Forsytes, you will turn back to Thackeray's *Vanity Fair*, you will understand why such novels as Hardy's and Thackeray's impress us as great novels, and such novels as Bennett's and Galsworthy's impress us as being somehow a little less than great. For after all, it is neither closeness of observation, nor mastery of technique that turns the scale. What does turn the scale, what does give us the sense of enduring greatness in a novel, is not easily put into words. But, whether the book is approved by time or was born yesterday, if you feel as you read it, a sense of driving power behind it; if there comes to you a realization of the largeness of sympathy and breadth of understanding of the man who wrote it; if its pages seem to you to be suffused with a kind of glow, as if the writer had not only thought it but wholly and intensely lived it, then you may be fairly sure that you have your hands on a great novel.

XIII

ESSAYISTS, CRITICS, SAGES

Through most of the eighteenth century the essay kept
the pattern which Steele and Addison had given it. Essayists continued to write anonymously or under a pen-name.
They continued (the words are Steele's) "to expose the
false arts of life, to pull off the disguises of cunning vanity
and affectation, and to recommend a general simplicity
in dress, discourse, and behaviour." They endeavored in
Addison's manner, "to enliven morality with wit, and to
temper wit with morality." They cultivated the tone of
light irony which had been elevated to a fine art in the
pages of the *Tatler* and the *Spectator*. Not one of them
equaled and few of them even approached Addison and
Steele; but Goldsmith who did so many things so well,
came nearest.

Goldsmith's essays appeared in his own short-lived
periodical, *The Bee*, in Smollett's *British Magazine*, and
in Newbery's *Public Ledger*. Goldsmith's contributions
to the *Ledger*, purporting to be the comments of a Chinese
visitor on English manners, were reprinted in 1762 as *The
Citizen of the World*. The following paragraphs are a fair
example of Goldsmith's quality as an essayist:

As I am one of that sauntering tribe of mortals who spend the
greatest part of their time in taverns, coffee-houses, and other
places of public resort, I have thereby an opportunity of observing
an infinite variety of characters, which to a person of a contemplative turn is a much higher entertainment than a view of all
the curiosities of art or nature. In one of these my late rambles, I

accidentally fell into a company of half a dozen gentlemen, who were engaged in a warm dispute about some political affair, the decision of which, as they were equally divided in their sentiments, they thought proper to refer to me, which naturally drew me in for a share of the conversation.

Amongst a multiplicity of other topics, we took occasion to talk of the different characters of the several nations of Europe; when one of the gentlemen, cocking his hat, and assuming such an air of importance as if he had possessed all the merit of the English nation in his own person, declared that the Dutch were a parcel of avaricious wretches; the French a set of flattering sycophants; that the Germans were drunken sots, and beastly gluttons; and the Spaniards proud, haughty, and surly tyrants; but that in bravery, generosity, clemency, and in every other virtue, the English excelled all the world.

This very learned and judicious remark was received with a general smile of approbation by all the company — all, I mean, but your humble servant, who, endeavoring to keep my gravity as well as I could, and reclining my head upon my arm, continued for some time in a posture of affected thoughtfulness, as if I had been musing on something else, and did not seem to attend to the subject of conversation; hoping by this means to avoid the disagreeable necessity of explaining myself, and thereby depriving the gentleman of his imaginary happiness.

But my pseudo-patriot had no mind to let me escape so easily. Not satisfied that his opinion should pass without contradiction, he was determined to have it ratified by the suffrage of every one in the company; for which purpose, addressing himself to me with an air of inexpressible confidence, he asked me if I was not of the same way of thinking. As I am never forward in giving my opinion, especially when I have reason to believe that it will not be agreeable; so, when I am obliged to give it, I always hold it for a maxim to speak my real sentiments. I therefore told him that, for my own part, I should not have ventured to talk in such a peremptory strain unless I had made the tour of Europe, and examined the manners of these several nations with great care and accuracy: that perhaps a more impartial judge would not scruple to affirm, that the Dutch were more frugal and industrious, the French more temperate and polite, the Germans more hardy and patient of labour and fatigue, and the Spaniards more staid and sedate than the English; who, though undoubtedly brave and generous, were at the same time rash, headstrong, and impetuous; too apt to be elated with prosperity and to despond in adversity.

I could easily perceive that all the company began to regard me with a jealous eye before I had finished my answer, which I had no sooner done, than the patriotic gentleman observed, with a contemptuous sneer, that he was greatly surprised how some people could have the conscience to live in a country which they did not love, and to enjoy the protection of a government to which in their hearts they were inveterate enemies. Finding that by this modest declaration of my sentiments I had forfeited the good opinion of my companions, and given them occasion to call my political principles in question, and well knowing that it was in vain to argue with men who were so very full of themselves, I threw down my reckoning and retired to my own lodgings, reflecting on the absurd and ridiculous nature of national prejudice and prepossession.

. . . .

Is it not very possible that I may love my own country, without hating the natives of other countries? that I may exert the most heroic bravery, the most undaunted resolution, in defending its laws and liberty, without despising all the rest of the world as cowards and poltroons? Most certainly it is; and if it were not — But why need I suppose what is absolutely impossible? — But if it were not, I must own I should prefer the title of the ancient philosopher, viz., a citizen of the world, to that of an Englishman, a Frenchman, an European, or to any other appellation whatever.

These periodical essays were a product of the coffee-house phase of London life and in a degree depended on it. While that phase lasted it was possible to "live as a spectator of mankind" as in no time before or since. Delightful as the periodical essays still are, we miss half the fun of them. The "well-regulated families" who, as Addison advised, "looked upon the paper as part of their tea-equipage," were the readers who really savored them — seeing again through Mr. Spectator's twinkling eyes what they themselves had seen, but missed the humor of, the day before. As the coffee-house phase passed, the Spectator type of essay gradually lost its spontaneity and degenerated into a mere literary exercise.

The writers of these papers were all "spectators." Their business was observation and criticism. Except as a means to this end, they generally kept themselves out of the picture. It rested with Charles Lamb (1775–1834) to restore to the essay the quality which it had started with in the hands of Montaigne (see page 192). "My wish," Montaigne had written, "is to be seen simply in my own fashion, natural and ordinary, unstudied and without artifice: for it is myself that I am painting." And again: "I have nothing to teach. I simply ramble on about this or that." Lamb was still sufficiently in the Addison tradition to affect a pen-name. In the South Sea House he had known a fellow-clerk named Elia, long since dead. Lamb signed that name to his contributions to the *London Magazine* (1820–22), and in "Elia's" reminiscences and confessions of likes and dislikes painted himself. *The Essays of Elia* run the gamut from the sheer fun of the "Dissertation on Roast Pig" to the sheer poetry of "Dream Children." In "Dream Children" and a few others of like quality Lamb creates a type. He puts the essay to the use to which the poet puts the lyric — the evocation of a mood — self-revelation that is intimate without being either mawkish or sentimental.

Lamb was unmarried. "Dream Children" is a dream of the children who would have been his had he married the sweetheart of his youth. He amuses these imaginary children with recollections of his boyhood —

"What a tall, upright graceful person their great-grand-mother Field once was; and how in her youth she was esteemed the best dancer — here Alice's little right foot played an involuntary movement;" and of how great-grand-mother Field used to sleep by herself in a lone chamber of the great house and how she

believed that an apparition of two infants was to be seen at mid-night gliding up and down the great staircase. . . . Here John ex-panded all his eyebrows and tried to look courageous. . . . Then I told how for seven long years, in hope sometimes, sometimes in despair, yet persisting ever, I courted the fair Alice W—n; and, as much as children could understand, I explained to them what coyness, and difficulty, and denial meant in maidens — when suddenly, turning to Alice, the soul of the first Alice looked out of her eyes with such a reality of re-presentment, that I became in doubt which of them stood there before me, or whose that bright hair was; and while I stood gazing, both the children gradually grew fainter to my view, receding, and still receding till nothing at last but two mournful features were seen in the uttermost distance, which, without speech, strangely impressed upon me the effects of speech: "We are not of Alice, nor of thee, nor are we children at all. The children of Alice call Bartrum father. We are nothing; less than nothing, and dreams. We are only what might have been, and must wait upon the tedious shores of Lethe, millions of ages before we have existence, and a name"— and immediately awaking, I found myself quietly seated in my bachelor arm-chair where I had fallen asleep.

Lamb's essays have the spontaneity, the sudden shifts of fireside talk. One of the most characteristic and delight-ful of them, "Old China," begins with a consideration of the quaint figures, so innocent of perspective, on old china tea-cups.

Here is a young and courtly mandarin, handing tea to a lady from a salver — two miles off. See how distance seems to set off respect! And here the same lady or another — for likeness is identity on tea-cups — is stepping into a little fairy boat, moored on the hither side of this calm garden river, with a dainty mincing foot, which in a right angle of incidence (as angles go in our world) must infallibly land her in the midst of a flowery mead — a furlong off on the other side of this strange stream!

Farther on — if far or near can be predicated of their world — see horses, trees, pagodas, dancing the hays.

Here — a cow and rabbit couchant, and co-extensive — so objects show, seen through the lucid atmosphere of fine Cathay.

Then swiftly, but with the deftest of transitions, the theme changes. Elia and "Cousin Bridget" have just bought this set of old blue china — without feeling the expense. Time was when every penny had to be considered, when the *for* and *against* had to be debated for days before even the smallest luxury could be ventured. We are back in the days of Elia's eager youth, sharing the joys of poverty, doing without a new suit to buy a folio Beaumont and Fletcher; squeezing out our shillings to sit three or four times in a season in the one-shilling gallery — "What mattered it where we were sitting when our thoughts were with Rosalind in Arden, or with Viola at the court of Illyria?"— saving to buy a dish of strawberries and savoring every spoonful —"A thing was worth buying then when we felt the money that we paid for it."

Lamb wrote of others as delightfully as he wrote of himself. Many of his most charming essays, such as "Christ's Hospital" and "The Old Benchers of the Inner Temple" are full of vivid little pen-pictures, half fact, half fancy — sketches of the men of law whom he had seen during his childhood days in the Inner Temple, of boys whom he had known at school, of fellow-clerks in his days at South Sea House. He loved books and wrote about them with zest and whimsicality. His "Detached Thoughts on Books and Reading" is pure joy. Books and the spectacle of human nature were all his world. Poetical raptures about the beauties of nature left him cold.

Let them talk of lakes and mountains and romantic dales — all that is fantastic stuff: give me a ramble by night — in the winter nights in London — the lamps lit, the pavements of the motley Strand crowded with to and fro passengers, the shops all brilliant and stuffed with obliging customers and obliging tradesmen; give me the old book-stalls, a walk in the bright piazzas of Covent Garden. I defy a man to be dull in such places — perfect Mahometan paradises upon earth! I have lent out my heart with usury, to such scenes from my childhood up, and have cried with fulness of joy at the multitudinous scenes of life in the crowded streets of ever dear London.

The Latin poet-critic, Horace, commends the *ars celare artem*, the art of concealing art. Lamb was a master at telling a story with such simplicity that the story seems to tell itself. "Barbara S——" is of this sort. How sympathetically Lamb tells it, and yet with what complete freedom from sentimentality! How easily it might have become the kind of "Sunday-school story" to which our fathers were subjected in their youth!

. . . At the desk of the then treasurer of the old Bath theatre — not Diamond's — presented herself the little Barbara S——.

The parents of Barbara had been in reputable circumstances. The father had practised, I believe, as an apothecary in the town. But his practice, from causes which I feel my own infirmity too sensibly that way to arraign — or perhaps from that pure infelicity which accompanies some people in their walk through life, and which it is impossible to lay at the door of imprudence — was now reduced to nothing. They were, in fact, in the very teeth of starvation, when the manager who knew and respected them in better days, took the little Barbara into his company.

At the period I commenced with, her slender earnings were the sole support of the family, including two younger sisters. I must throw a veil over some mortifying circumstances. Enough to say that her Saturday's pittance was the only chance of a Sunday's (generally their only) meal of meat.

One thing I will only mention, that in some child's part, where in her theatrical character she was to sup off a roast fowl (O joy to Barbara!) some comic actor, who was for the night caterer for this dainty — in the misguided humour of his part, threw over the dish such a quantity of salt (O grief and pain of heart to Barbara!) that when she crammed a portion of it into her mouth, she was obliged sputteringly to reject it; and what with shame of her ill-acted part, and pain of her real appetite at missing such a dainty, her little heart sobbed almost to breaking, till a flood of tears, which the well-fed spectators were totally unable to comprehend, mercifully relieved her.

This was the little starved, meritorious maid who stood before old Ravenscroft, the treasurer, for her Saturday's payment.

Ravenscroft was a man, I have heard many old theatrical people besides herself say, of all men least calculated for a treasurer. He had no head for accounts, paid away at random, kept scarce any books, and summing up at the week's end, if he found himself a pound or so deficient, blest himself that it was no worse.

Now Barbara's weekly stipend was a bare half-guinea. By mistake he popped into her hand — a whole one.

Barbara tripped away.

She was entirely unconscious at first of the mistake: God knows Ravenscroft would never have discovered it.

But when she got down to the first of those uncouth landing-places, she became sensible of an unusual weight of metal pressing her little hand.

Now mark the dilemma.

She was by nature a good child. From her parents and those about her she had imbibed no contrary influence. But then they had taught her nothing. Poor men's smoky cabins are not always porticoes of moral philosophy. This little maid had no instinct to evil, but then she might be said to have no fixed principle. She had heard honesty commended, but never dreamed of its application to herself. She thought of it as something which concerned grown-up people, men and women. She had never known temptation, or thought of preparing resistance against it.

Her first impulse was to go back to the old treasurer, and explain to him his blunder. He was already so confused with age, besides a natural want of punctuality, that she would have had some difficulty in making him understand it. She saw *that* in an instant. And then it was such a bit of money! and then the image of a larger allowance of butcher's meat on their table next day came across her, till her little eyes glistened, and her mouth moistened. But then Mr. Ravenscroft had always been so good-natured, had stood her friend behind the scenes, and even recommended her promotion to some of her little parts. But again the old man was reputed to be worth a world of money. He was supposed to have fifty pounds a year clear of the theatre. And then came staring upon her the figures of her little stockingless and shoeless sisters. And when she looked at her own neat white cotton stockings, which her situation at the theatre had made it indispensable for her mother to provide for her, with hard straining and pinching from the family stock, and thought how glad she should be to cover their poor feet with the same — and how then they could accompany her to rehearsals, which they had hitherto been precluded from doing, by reason of their unfashionable attire — in these thoughts she reached the second landing-place — the second, I mean, from the top — for there was still another left to traverse.

Now virtue support Barbara!

And that never-failing friend did step in — for at that moment a strength not her own, I have heard her say, was revealed to her

— a reason above reasoning — and without her own agency, as it seemed (for she never felt her feet to move), she found herself transported back to the individual desk she had just quitted, and her hand in the old hand of Ravenscroft, who in silence took back the refunded treasure, and who had been sitting (good man) insensible to the lapse of minutes, which to her were anxious ages, and from that moment a deep peace fell upon her heart, and she knew the quality of honesty.

A year or two's unrepining application to her profession brightened up the feet, and the prospects, of her little sisters, set the whole family upon their legs again, and released her from the difficulty of discussing moral dogmas upon a landing-place.

I have heard her say that it was a surprise, not much short of mortification to her, to see the coolness with which the old man pocketed the difference, which had caused her such mortal throes.

Not less-perfect examples of the story-teller's art are the *Tales from Shakespeare*, written by Lamb and his sister Mary (the "Bridget Elia" of the Essays). These story-versions of the plays were intended as an introduction to Shakespeare for young readers. They are useful in that way; but you will enjoy them and profit by them even more, if you will read the play first, make your own story of the plot; and then compare it point for point with Lamb's. The comparison may cost you a pang or two; you may never succeed in making your own version as graceful; but to try to make it as simple, as unaffected, and as well-proportioned, is about the best practice there is.

Lamb's friend, William Hazlitt (1778–1830), must also be ranked among the masters of the essay. He has not Lamb's geniality and gentleness; in comparison, Hazlitt seems a veritable bundle of violent antipathies and of no less violent enthusiasms. It is indeed this zest and energy in all that he writes, this "gusto" as he himself liked to call it, that makes Hazlitt's essays such stimulating reading. He writes with equal gusto about books and about life. It would be hard to find another collection of critical essays as enlivening as his *Characters of Shakespeare's Plays* (1817) and *Lectures on the English Comic Writers* (1819). Here is no elaborate balancing of *pros* and *cons*, no disinterested "judicial" criticism. Hazlitt's heart is in it. "This is my experience with this character or that book. This is how I have come to feel, and this is the way it happened." His "critical" essays are as personal as his personal essays — and as full of color and warmth and play of fancy. Consider this comment on some old friends of ours, from the essay "On the Periodical Essayists," in *English Comic Writers:*

The characters of Will Wimble and Will Honeycomb are not a whit behind their friend, Sir Roger, in delicacy and felicity. The delightful simplicity and good-humored officiousness in the one are set off by the graceful affectation and courtly pretension in the other. How long since I first became acquainted with these two characters in the *Spectator!* What old-fashioned friends they seem, and yet I am not tired of them, like so many other friends, nor they of me! How airy these abstractions of the poet's pen stream over the dawn of our acquaintance with human life! how pure they remain in it to the last, like the rainbow in the evening cloud, which the rude hand of time can neither soil nor dissipate! What a pity that we cannot find the reality, and yet if we did the dream would be over. I once thought I knew a Will Wimble and a Will Honeycomb, but they turned out but indifferently: the originals in the *Spectator* still read, word for word, the same that they always did. We have only to turn to the page and find them where we left them!

Hazlitt's hates are as enlivening as his loves, especially when, instead of a book-character, it is some actual per-

sonage of his own time who has incurred his animosity.
His "Essay on William Gifford" [1] in *The Spirit of the Age*
is as fine a piece of energetic hating as we shall come upon
in many a day. Not elsewhere in English prose, surely, can
there be a more diabolical piece of impertinence, a more
comprehensive damnation compressed into fewer words
than the opening paragraph of Hazlitt's essay:

Mr. Gifford was originally bred to some handicraft; he afterwards contrived to learn Latin, and was for some time an usher
in a school, till he became a tutor in a nobleman's family. The
low-bred, self-taught man, the pedant, and the dependant on the
great, contribute to form the Editor of the *Quarterly Review*. He
is admirably qualified for this situation, which he has held for
some years, by a happy combination of defects, natural and acquired; and in the event of his death, it will be difficult to provide
him a suitable successor.

Hazlitt's general essays are to be found in *Table Talk*
(1822), *The Spirit of the Age* (1825), and in *Winterslow* and
in *Sketches and Essays,* published nine years after his
death. The following passages from his essay "On Going
on a Journey" in *Table Talk*, reflect the zest with which
he entered into every kind of experience:

In general, a good thing spoils out-of-door prospects: it should
be reserved for Table-talk. Lamb is for this reason, I take it, the
worst company in the world out of doors; because he is the best
within. I grant there is one subject on which it is pleasant to
talk on a journey, and that is, what one shall have for supper and
when we get to our inn at night. The open air improves this sort
of conversation or friendly altercation, by setting a keener edge on
appetite. Every mile of the road heightens the flavour of the
viands we expect at the end of it. How fine it is to enter some old
town, walled and turretted, just at approach of nightfall, or to come

[1] Editor of the *Quarterly Review* (see page 553 n.).

to some straggling village, with the lights streaming through the surrounding gloom; and then, after enquiring for the best entertainment that the place affords, to "take one's ease at one's inn!" These eventful moments in our lives' history are too precious, too full of solid, heartfelt happiness to be frittered and dribbled away in imperfect sympathy. I would have them all to myself, and drain them to the last drop: they will do to talk of or to write about afterwards. What a delicate speculation it is, after drinking whole goblets of tea —

"The cups that cheer, but not inebriate —"

and letting the fumes ascend into the brain, to sit considering what we shall have for supper — eggs and a rasher, a rabbit smothered in onions, or an excellent veal cutlet! . . .

The incognito of an inn is one of its striking privileges — "lord of one's self, uncumbered with a name." Oh! it is great to shake off the trammels of the world and of public opinion — to lose our importunate, tormenting, everlasting personal identity in the elements of nature, and become the creature of the moment, clear of all ties — to hold to the universe only by a dish of sweetbreads, and to owe nothing but the score of the evening — and no longer seeking for applause and meeting with contempt, to be known by no other title than *the Gentleman in the parlour!* One may take one's choice of all characters in this romantic state of uncertainty as to one's real pretensions, and become indefinitely respectable and negatively right-worshipful. We baffle prejudice and disappoint conjecture; and from being so to others, begin to be objects of curiosity and wonder even to ourselves. We are no more those hackneyed commonplaces that we appear in the world; an inn restores us to the level of nature, and quits scores with society! I have certainly spent some enviable hours at inns. . . . It was on the 10th of April 1798 that I sat down to a volume of the *New Eloise*, at the inn at Llangollen, over a bottle of sherry and a cold chicken. The letter I chose was that in which St. Preux describes his feelings as he first caught a glimpse from the heights of the Jura of the Pays de Vaud, which I had brought down with

me as a *bonne bouche* to crown the evening with.   It was my birthday, and I had for the first time come from a place in the neighborhood to visit this delightful spot.   The road to Llangollen turns
off between Chirk and Wrexham; and on passing a certain point
you come all at once upon the valley, which opens like an amphi-
theatre, broad, barren hills rising in majestic state on either side,
with "green upland swells that echo to the bleat of flocks" below,
and the river Dee babbling over its stony bed in the midst of them.
The valley at this time "glittered green with sunny showers,"
and a budding ash tree dipped its tender branches in the chiding
stream.   How proud, how glad I was to walk along the high road
that overlooks the delicious prospect, repeating the lines which
I have just quoted from Mr. Coleridge's poems!   But besides the
prospect which opened beneath my feet, another also opened to
my inward sight, a heavenly vision, on which were written, in
letters large as Hope could make them, these four words, LIBERTY,
GENIUS, LOVE, VIRTUE; which have since faded into the light of
common day, or mock my idle gaze.

"The beautiful is vanished, and returns not."

Still I would return some time or other to this enchanted spot;
but I would return to it alone.   What other self could I find to
share that influx of thoughts, of regrets and delight, the fragments
of which I could hardly conjure up to myself, so much have they
been broken and defaced.   I could stand on some tall rock, and
overlook the precipice of years that separates me from what I
then was.   I was at that time going shortly to visit the poet whom
I have above named.   Where is he now?   Not only I myself have
changed; the world, which was then new to me, has become old
and incorrigible.   Yet will I turn to thee in thought, O sylvan Dee,
in joy, in youth and gladness as thou then wert; and thou shalt
always be to me the river of Paradise, where I will drink of the
waters of life freely!

The Spirit of the Age had just issued from the press,
and Elia's whimsical meditations were appearing in the

London Magazine, when *The Edinburgh Review*[1] published a remarkable essay on Milton. This essay was by Thomas Babington Macaulay (1800–1859), a young man fresh out of Cambridge. The publication of a prose work of Milton's not previously printed furnished the occasion. In the characteristic *Edinburgh* manner, the essayist proceeded from a brief comment on the new work and the editing, to a detailed and authoritative consideration of Milton himself. The learning displayed by the young reviewer, the minute knowledge of the literature and life of Milton's time, were remarkable enough; but even more remarkable was the style. The seasoned editor of the *Edinburgh* was amazed: "The more I think the less I can conceive where you picked up that style." Macaulay was as finished a stylist at twenty-five when he wrote his first essay for the *Edinburgh* as he was thirty years later when he astonished the world with a *History of England* that was more interesting and had a bigger sale than any novel.

At first acquaintance Macaulay's style surprises the modern reader as much as it did the editor of the *Edinburgh*. From arresting topic-sentence to dramatic climax each paragraph moves with race-horse speed. The short, nervous, crowding sentences reflect an inexhaustible energy. Contrasting ideas, hit off in tellingly balanced phrases, hold and continuously excite the attention. "If the Puritans were unacquainted with the works of philosophers and poets, they were deeply read in the oracles of God.

[1] *The Edinburgh Review*, first of the great English quarterlies, had been started in 1802. *The Edinburgh* and its rival, *The Quarterly Review*, founded in 1809, were intended for long and substantial articles dealing with literature and politics. Rivals in politics, each of the quarterlies sought to dictate public opinion. Their editors, Jeffrey of the *Edinburgh* and Gifford of the *Quarterly*, were autocrats. Jeffrey, for example, opened his review of Wordsworth's *Excursion* with the words: "This will never do." Contributors took the editorial tone, became omniscient *ex officio*, as spokesmen for the magazine.

If their names were not found in the registry of heralds, they were recorded in the book of life." "The Puritan hated bear-baiting, not because it gave pain to the bear, but because it gave pleasure to the spectators." "Byron had a head which sculptors loved to copy, and a foot at which beggars laughed in the street."

Macaulay's memory was phenomenal. He had read everything and forgotten nothing. His mind effervesced with illustrative detail. If it is to be said, for example, that in late eighteenth-century London every clique and faction had its coffee-house, Macaulay will dramatize it thus: "There were Puritan coffee-houses where no oath was heard, and where lank-haired men discussed election and reprobation through their noses; Jew coffee-houses where dark-eyed money-changers from Venice and from Amsterdam greeted each other; and Popish coffee-houses where, as good Protestants believed, Jesuits planned, over their cups, another great fire, and cast silver bullets to shoot the king."

Macaulay's essays deal with a great variety of topics. Whatever he writes about — literature, philosophy, history, politics — springs to life and sparkles under his touch. Here, for example, is a part of his account of Ignatius Loyola, founder of the order of Jesuits. How effective the contrasts, how vivid the concrete details, with what breathless speed it moves!

Poor, obscure, without a patron, without recommendations, Loyola entered the city where now two princely temples, rich with painting and many-coloured marble, commemorate his great services to the Church;. where his form stands sculptured in massive silver, where his bones, enshrined, are placed beneath the altar of God. His activity and zeal bore down all opposition, and under his rule the order of Jesuits began to exist, and grew rapidly to the full measure of his gigantic powers. With what vehemence, with what policy, with what exact discipline, with what dauntless courage, with what self-denial, with what forgetfulness of the dearest private ties, with what intense and stubborn devotion to a single end, with what unscrupulous laxity and versatility in the choice of means, the Jesuits fought the battle of their church, is written in every page of the annals of Europe during several generations. In the order of Jesus was concentrated the quintessence of the Catholic spirit; and the history of the order of Jesus is the history of the great Catholic reaction. That order possessed itself at once of all the strongholds which command the public mind, of the press, of the confessional, of the academies. Wherever the Jesuit preached, the church was too small for the audience. The name of Jesuit on a title-page secured the circulation of a book. It was in the ears of the Jesuit that the powerful, the noble and the beautiful, breathed the secret history of their lives. It was at the feet of the Jesuit that the youth of the higher and middle classes were brought up from childhood to manhood, from the first rudiments to the courses of rhetoric and philosophy. Literature and science, lately associated with infidelity or with heresy, now became the allies of orthodoxy. Dominant in the South of Europe, the great order soon went forth conquering and to conquer. In spite of oceans and deserts, of hunger and pestilence, of spies and penal laws, of dungeons and racks, of gibbets and quartering blocks, Jesuits were to be found under every disguise, and in every country; scholars, physicians, merchants, serving-men; in the hostile court of Sweden, in the old manorhouse of Cheshire, among the hovels of Connaught; arguing, instructing, consoling, stealing away the hearts of the young, animating the courage of the timid, holding up the crucifix before the eyes of the dying.

No one can read that passage, or a hundred other such, from the *Essays* or the *History*, without a stirring of the pulses. If vigor, vivacity, vividness, mastery of dramatic effects were all that mattered, we might well reckon

Macaulay the greatest, as we must reckon him the most brilliant, of nineteenth-century prose-writers. Of authors concerned with serious matters, no other captivates us so promptly or carries us with him for a while so easily. And yet he does not wear well. His efficiency defeats itself. Nothing is left to the imagination. The mind grows restive under this unremitting flow of clever contrasts and arranged effects. What first seemed so spontaneously vivid becomes at length a kind of posturing. The reader grows suspicious, and discovers that many of the sharp contrasts and vivid dramatizations are achieved at the expense of truth. Were most of the Puritans who remained stanch after the Restoration "lank-haired men who discussed election and reprobation through their noses"? Did the Puritans really "hate bear-baiting not because it gave pain to the bear but because it gave pleasure to the spectators"? Gradually, too, as you read other accounts of the periods of history which Macaulay describes, you realize that he was extraordinarily one-sided, that his Whig prejudices colored and distorted a great part of what he wrote. You will end by distrusting Macaulay as a guide, and, for pleasure, preferring him in homeopathic doses; but even so you will find the doses extraordinarily enlivening; and for sheer brilliance, you will find no other writer of the century to match him.

Between Macaulay and his contemporary, Thomas Carlyle,[1] the contrast is striking. Macaulay was a man

[1] Carlyle outlived Macaulay by many years. To one who can remember the profound impression made upon the whole reading world by the death of the old sage in 1881, it is curious to think of Carlyle and Macaulay as contemporaries; but Carlyle was five years older than Macaulay, and Carlyle's best work — *Sartor Resartus* (1833–1834), *The French Revolution* (1837), *Heroes and Hero-Worship* (1841), *Past and Present* (1843), the *Life of Sterling* (1851)— was done while Macaulay was alive.

of his time, sharing the prejudices, speaking the language of the world about him. He stood out from his contemporaries, not because he was spiritually greater, or had anything new to say, but because his mind was better stocked and more adroit. Macaulay had his powers at his fingertips. Carlyle seems always stumblingly great, as if struggling with thoughts not easily to be put into words. He never seems to belong to his world, to be at one with it. Rather he speaks to it — sometimes *at* it — as if from some separated vantage-point, some cloudy mountain top, of his own. Carlyle is not easy to read. To put a chapter of his *French Revolution* or *History of Frederick the Great* beside a chapter of Macaulay's *History of England*, or to put one of his essays beside one of Macaulay's, is to get a renewed impression of Macaulay's skill and vividness: but to read the two extensively side by side is to realize the inferiority of mere intellectual brilliance such as Macaulay's to Carlyle's "rude greatness of soul."

Carlyle was born of peasant parents in the little Scotch village of Ecclefechan. During his student days at the University of Edinburgh he steeped himself in the writings of Goethe and other German philosophers and men of letters just beginning to be known in Great Britain. The rough vigor of his peasant father's way of talking, and the involutions of the German idiom are both reflected in Carlyle's style. He discusses the peculiarities of it with humorous frankness in the opening of *Sartor Resartus* — for the "Professor Teufelsdröckh" of *Sartor* is of course Carlyle himself:

In respect of style our Author manifests the same genial capability, marred too often by the same rudeness, inequality, and apparent want of intercourse with the higher classes. Occasionally, as above hinted, we find consummate vigour, a true inspiration; his burning Thoughts step forth in fit burning Words, like so many full-formed Minervas, issuing amid flame and splendour from Jove's head; a rich, idiomatic diction, picturesque allusions, fiery poetic emphasis, or quaint tricksy turns; all the graces and terrors of a wild Imagination, wedded to the clearest Intellect, alternate in beautiful vicissitude. Were it not that sheer sleeping and soporific passages, circumlocutions, repetitions, touches even of pure doting jargon so often intervene! On the whole Professor Teufelsdröckh is not a cultivated writer. Of his sentences not more than nine tenths stand straight on their legs: the remainder are in quite angular attitudes, buttressed-up by props (of parentheses and dashes) and ever with this or the other tagrag hanging from them; a few even sprawl out helplessly on all sides, quite broken-backed and dismembered. Nevertheless, in almost his very worst moods, there lies in him a singular attraction. A wild tone pervades the whole utterance of the man, like its keynote and regulator; now screwing itself aloft as into the Song of Spirits, or else the shrill mockery of Fiends; now sinking in cadences, not without melodious heartiness, though sometimes abrupt enough, into the common pitch, when we hear it only as a monotonous hum; of which hum the true character is extremely difficult to fix. Up to this hour, we have never fully satisfied ourselves whether it is a tone and hum of real Humour, which we reckon among the very highest qualities of genius, or some echo of mere Insanity and Inanity, which doubtless ranks below the very lowest.

Sartor Resartus is Carlyle's attempt to explain the meaning of life. "Herr Teufelsdröckh," the German professor whose scattered manuscript-notes Carlyle pretends to be putting together and commenting upon, passes through just such a period of pessimism and despair as Carlyle himself had experienced, and emerges with a solution, a definite belief. "Meditation," as Carlyle says elsewhere,[1] "has taught all men in all ages, that this world is after all

---

[1] *Hero and Hero-Worship.*

profonde

but a show, — a phenomenon or appearance, no real thing.
All deep souls see into that, — the Hindoo Mythologist, the
German Philosopher, — the Shakespeare, the earnest Thinker,
wherever he may be: *étoffe, matière*

> We are such stuff as Dreams are made of."

The things which meet our eye and seem at first glance
real to us, are only the clothes, the coverings, the conventions made by human beings through the thousands of years
during which they have been trying to adjust themselves
to one another. As cynical Jonathan Swift had said in
A Tale of a Tub, "What is man himself but a micro-coat,
or rather a complete suit of clothes with all its trimmings?
As to his body, there can be no dispute: but examine even
the acquirements of his mind, you will find them all contribute in their order towards furnishing out an exact
dress: to instance no more; is not religion a cloak; honesty
a pair of shoes worn out in the dirt; self-love a surtout;
vanity a shirt; and conscience a pair of breeches?"[1]

"Clothes," as Carlyle puts it, "gave us individuality,
distinctions, social polity; clothes have made men of us;
they are threatening to make clothes-screens of us." And
so Carlyle gives to this book, which attempts to penetrate
beneath the clothes to the reality, the title of *Sartor Resartus* — the *tailor retailored*. *Tailleur*

And the reality? Perhaps of all the deceptive garments
of life, the most deceptive is the notion that we have a
right to be happy, that the world owes us happiness or *dever*
pleasure: "What is this that ever since earliest years,
thou hast been fretting and fuming, and lamenting and
self-tormenting, on account of? Say it in a word: is it not
because thou art not HAPPY? Because the Thou (sweet

---

[1] Carlyle does not quote Swift, but the parallel is worth noting.

gentleman) is not sufficiently honoured, nourished, soft-bedded, and lovingly cared for? Foolish soul! What Act of Legislature was there that *thou* shouldst be Happy? A little while ago thou hadst no right to *be* at all. What if thou wert born and predestined not to be Happy, but to be Unhappy! Art thou nothing other than a Vulture, then, that fliest through the universe seeking after somewhat to *eat;* and shrieking dolefully because carrion enough is not given then? Close thy *Byron;* open thy *Goethe.*"

For the reality is not happiness, but work — the privilege of doing. "The Ideal is in thyself: thy Condition is but the stuff thou art to shape that same Ideal out of: what matters whether such stuff be of this sort or that, so the Form thou give it be heroic, be poetic? . . . Produce! Produce! Were it but the pitifullest infinitesimal fraction of a Product, produce it, in God's name! 'Tis the utmost thou hast in thee: out with it, then. Up, up! Whatsoever thy hand findeth to do, do it with thy whole might. Work while it is called To-day; for the Night cometh, wherein no man can work."

Two other books of Carlyle's are especially worth reading — *The French Revolution* and *Heroes and Hero-Worship.* In a previous chapter (see page 390), something has been said of the growth of radical ideas in the eighteenth century culminating in the bloody upheaval of the French Revolution. The overthrow of the French monarchy, the explosion of human passions, the Reign of Terror, the abrupt rise and fall of leader after leader, the effort to wipe out every tradition and remake the world, constitutes in itself the most dramatic story which history affords. In Carlyle's hands it becomes a dramatic prose-poem.[1] The

---

[1] "It is part of my creed," Carlyle wrote to Emerson, "that the only Poetry is History, could we tell it right."

passionate intensity, the "fiery poetic emphasis," the occasional wildness characteristic of Carlyle's style find here an appropriate theme. The individuals round whom the Revolution centered — Robespierre, Danton, Mirabeau, Charlotte Corday, Marat, and the rest — cease to be mere historical names and become living, thinking, passionately feeling human beings. See with what intensity Carlyle dramatizes Charlotte Corday's assassination of Marat:

About eight on the Saturday morning, she purchases a large sheath-knife in the Palais Royal; then straightway, in the Place des Victoires, takes a hackney-coach: "To the Rue de l'Ecole de Médecine, No. 44." It is the residence of Citoyen Marat! — The Citoyen Marat is ill, and cannot be seen; which seems to disappoint her much. Her business is with Marat, then? Hapless beautiful Charlotte; hapless squalid Marat! From Caen in the utmost West, from Neuchâtel in the utmost East, they two are drawing nigh each other; they two have, very strangely, business together. — Charlotte, returning to her Inn, dispatches a short Note to Marat; signifying that she is from Caen, the seat of rebellion; that she desires earnestly to see him, and "will put it in his power to do France a great service." No answer. Charlotte writes another Note, still more pressing; sets out with it by coach, about seven in the evening, herself. Tired day-labourers have again finished their Week; huge Paris is circling and simmering, manifold, according to its vague wont: this one fair Figure has decision in it; drives straight, — towards a purpose.

It is yellow July evening, we say, the thirteenth of the month; eve of the Bastille day, — when "M. Marat," four years ago, in the crowd of the Pont Neuf, shrewdly required of that Besenval Hussar-party, which had such friendly dispositions, "to dismount, and give up their arms, then;" and became notable among Patriot men. Four years: what a road he has travelled; — and sits now, about half-past seven of the clock, stewing in slipper-bath; sore afflicted; ill of Revolution Fever, — of what other malady this History had rather not name. Excessively sick and worn, poor man: with precisely eleven-pence-halfpenny of ready money, in paper; with slipper-bath; strong three-footed stool for writing on, the while; and a squalid — Washerwoman, one may call her: this is his civic establishment in Medical-School Street; thither and not elsewhither has his road led him. Not to the reign of Brotherhood and Perfect Felicity; yet surely on the way towards that? — Hark, a rap again! A musical woman's voice, refusing to be rejected: it is a Citoyenne who would do France a service. Marat, recognizing from within, cries, "Admit her." Charlotte Corday is admitted.

"Citoyen Marat, I am from Caen, the seat of rebellion, and wished to speak with you." "— Be seated, *mon enfant*. Now what are the Traitors doing at Caen? What Deputies are at Caen?" — Charlotte names some Deputies. "Their heads shall fall within a fortnight," croaks the eager People's-friend, clutching his tablets to write: *Barbaroux, Pétion*, writes he with bare shrunk arm, turning aside in the bath: *Pétion* and *Louvet*, and — Charlotte has drawn her knife from the sheath; plunges it, with one sure stroke, into the writer's heart. "*A moi, chère amie*, Help, dear!" no more could the Death-choked say or shriek. The helpful Washerwoman running in, there is no Friend of the People, or Friend of the Washerwoman left; but his life with a groan gushes out, indignant, to the shades below.

In *Heroes and Hero-Worship* Carlyle exemplifies and expands the method of writing history which he had experimented with in *The French Revolution*. "As I take it," he says in his introduction to *Heroes*, "Universal History, the history of what man has accomplished in this world, is at bottom the History of the Great Men who have worked here. They were the leaders of men, these great ones; the modellers, patterns, and in a wide sense creators, of whatsoever the general mass of men contrived to do or to attain; all things that we see standing accomplished in the world are properly the outer material result, the practical realization and embodiment, of Thoughts that dwelt in the Great Men sent into the world: the soul of the whole world's history, it may justly be considered, were the history of these."

Caryle's "Heroes" are a strangely assorted group. Thor, Mohammed, Luther, Dante, Cromwell, Napoleon, Rousseau rub shoulders. If you should draw up a complete list of Carlyle's "Heroes" and read a brief sketch of the life of each such as you will find in the *Encyclopædia Britannica*, you will wonder why he brought them together. But Carlyle has his answer ready. The common quality, his touchstone of true leadership, is Sincerity.

Matthew Arnold (1822–1888) too had something to say. He began his literary career as a poet. His admiration for Greek literature is reflected in the clearness, the precision of phrase, and the austerity of his poetry. You will enjoy most the tale, written in stately blank verse, of "Sohrab and Rustum," and the meditative beauty of "The Scholar Gipsy." To his collected *Poems* of 1853, he prefixed an essay on *The Choice of Subjects in Poetry* which prepares the way for the criticisms of the literature and of the ideals of his time to which he was to devote the rest of his life. To Arnold the romantic mood which had prevailed for so long in English poetry was mere confused emotion, lacking clearness and form and unity and dignity. "Poems seem to exist merely for the sake of single lines and passages; not for the sake of producing any total impression." And the very aim of such poetry is false. Poets are told that "a true allegory of the state of one's own mind is the highest thing that one can attempt in the way of poetry. . . . An allegory of the state of one's own mind, the highest problem of an art which imitates actions! No, assuredly, it is not, it never can be so: no great poetical work has ever been produced with such an aim." It is, Arnold insists, by the greatness of the theme, the nobility of the action, that the worth of poetry must be measured. "This the Greeks understood far more clearly than we do. The radical difference between their poetical theory and ours consists, as it appears to me, in this: that with them the poetical character of the action in itself, and the conduct of it, was the first consideration; with us, attention is fixed mainly on the value of the separate thoughts and images which occur in the treatment of an action. They regarded the whole; we regard the parts." Arnold does not mean that style, beauty of expression, was unimportant to the Greeks. They were "the unapproached masters of the *grand style:* but their expression is so excellent because it is so admirably kept in its right degree of prominence: because it is so simple and so well subordinated; because it draws its force directly from the pregnancy of the matter which it conveys."

You will find this criticism of Arnold's well worth thinking over, not only as you read the romantic poetry of the early nineteenth century which he referred to, but also as you read the poetry of to-day.

It is this Greek conception of a beauty inseparable from nobility of mind which determined all of Arnold's subsequent criticism of the literature and of the ideals of his day. It is expressed in his *Essays in Criticism, First Series* and *Second Series,* and in the book which he calls *Culture and Anarchy* (1869). Criticism, to Arnold, was no mere process of interpreting a book or picking it to pieces. It was "a disinterested endeavour to learn and propagate the best that is known and thought in the world." It meant, as far as literature was concerned, a broadening of standards, an appeal to other literatures for comparison of values. It meant, as far as ideals of living were concerned, a challenge to the sordidness, the money-mindedness, the absorption in the mere machinery of life, which Arnold thought characteristic of his generation — and which is surely no less characteristic of ours. A challenge and an appeal, instead, for that kind of culture, that ideal of perfection which should consist "in becoming something rather than in having something, in an inward condition of the mind and spirit, not in an outward set of circumstances. . . . The pursuit of perfection, is the pursuit of sweetness and light. . . . He who works for sweetness and light united, works to make reason and the will of God prevail. He who works for machinery, he who works for hatred, works only for confusion. Culture looks beyond machinery, culture hates hatred; culture has one great passion, the passion for sweetness and light. Yes, it has one greater! — the passion for making them *prevail*. . . Culture does not try to teach down to the level of inferior classes; it does not try to win them for this or that sect of its own, with ready-made judgments and watchwords. It seeks to do away with classes; to make all men live in an atmosphere of sweetness and light, and use ideas, as it uses them itself, freely, — to be nourished, and not bound by them. This is the social idea; and the men of culture are the true apostles of equality."

Arnold had no illusions about his gospel of Culture. The preachers of it, he admitted, "are likely to have a hard time of it and will much oftener be regarded, for a long time to come, as elegant or spurious Jeremiahs than as friends and benefactors." Certainly a good many of his contemporaries regarded Arnold in that way. He does seem a little supercilious sometimes. But that need not prevent us from recognizing the value of his ideal of "becoming something rather than having something," and honoring him for the steadfastness of purpose and clearness of vision with which he worked for it.

As a critic of literature Arnold had his share of prejudices. Some of his opinions are discounted; but many of his judgments profoundly influenced the thought of his time, and remain substantially unchallenged to-day. His condemnation of the excess of romanticism; the effect (noted elsewhere; see pages 421–2 and 480) upon the public mind of his essays on Wordsworth and Keats, are instances in point. His sensitiveness to beauty, his steadfast application of high standards of theme and treatment, his "Hellenic" taste, make him one of the most salutary of English critics.

Like Arnold, John Ruskin (1819–1900) was an idealist with a passion for making his ideas prevail. Arnold's gospel sprang from his criticism of literature; Ruskin's, in the first half of his curiously divided life, from his studies of painting and architecture. At King's College, London, and at Christ Church, Oxford, he studied drawing and painting. Upon taking his degree, he threw himself with characteristic intensity into a defense of J. M. W. Turner whom, against the general opinion of his day, he believed to be the greatest of landscape painters. The effort to justify Turner led him into a critical examination of the whole field of pictorial art. The result was the series entitled *Modern Painters*, the first volume of which appeared in 1843, the fifth and last in 1860. From painting Ruskin turned to architecture, *The Seven Lamps of Architecture* appearing in 1849, *The Stones of Venice* in 1851–1853.

These writings of Ruskin's are remarkable for three things — his theory of the moral or ethical significance of

The National Gallery of British Art, Millbank

"FOLKSTONE FROM THE SEA"

One of the most successful of the series of drawings by Turner entitled *The Rivers and Ports of England.*

art; the vividness and the lyrical intensity of his appreciation of beauty in art and nature; the richness and the occasional golden eloquence of his style.

"Whatever may be the means, or whatever the more immediate end of any kind of art," Ruskin insisted, "all of it that is good agrees in this, that it is the expression of one soul talking to another, and is precious according to the greatness of the soul that utters it." A painting of Nature must be more than photographically true. It must *interpret* Nature — and only to those who approach her with sincerity, with utter reverence for the truth, does she reveal herself. In like manner architecture reveals the character of the people who create it. So sharply does Ruskin distinguish here that he finds in Venetian Gothic the expression of "a state of pure national faith and of domestic virtue," and in Venetian architecture of the Renaissance, the expression of "a state of concealed national infidelity and of domestic corruption."

Ruskin pushed his theories too far. His effort to interpret art ethically, to relate it in this precise way to the moral character of the artist, has been largely discounted. His theories are interesting to us rather because in exemplifying the spiritual fineness and reverence for truth which must underlie great art, he was led into describing the beauty of Nature as the artist should see it. His own eye for color and form was amazingly exact. His vocabulary (developed largely, as he believed, from the systematic reading of the Bible in his childhood — "the one essential part of my education," he called it) was extraordinarily rich.

The noonday sun came slanting down the rocky slopes of La Riccia, and their masses of entangled and tall foliage, whose autumnal tints were mixed with the wet verdure of a thousand evergreens, were penetrated with it as with rain. I cannot call it colour; it was conflagration.   Purple, and crimson, and scarlet, like the curtains of God's tabernacle, the rejoicing trees sank into the valley in showers of light, every separate leaf quivering with buoyant and burning life; each, as it turned to reflect or to transmit the sunbeam, first a torch and then an emerald.   Far up into the recesses of the valley, the green vistas arched like the hollows of mighty waves of some crystalline sea, with the arbutus flowers dashed along their flanks for foam, and silver flakes of orange spray tossed into the air around them, breaking over the grey wall of rock into a thousand separate stars, fading and kindling alternately as the weak wind lifted and let them fall.   Every glade of grass burned like the golden floor of heaven, opening in sudden gleams as the foliage broke and closed above it, as sheet-lightning opens in a cloud at sunset; the motionless masses of dark rock — dark though flushed with scarlet lichen, casting their quiet shadows across its restless radiance, the fountain underneath them filling its marble hollow with blue mist and fitful sound, and over all, — the multitudinous bars of amber and rose, the sacred clouds that have no darkness, and only exist to illumine, were seen in fathomless intervals between the solemn and orbed repose of the stone pines, passing to lose themselves in the last, white blinding lustre of the measureless line where the Campagna melted into the blaze of the sea. . . . Not in his most daring and dazzling efforts could Turner himself come near it; but you could not at the time have thought of or remembered the work of any other man as having the remotest hue or resemblance of what you saw.

Not less gorgeous are some of his descriptions in *The Stones of Venice* — notably that of the exterior adornment of the church of St. Mark — culminating in such a burst of word-music as has no parallel in English prose:

In the broad archivolts, a continuous chain of language and of life — angels, and the signs of heaven, and the labours of men, each in its appointed season upon the earth; and above these another range of glittering pinnacles, mixed with white arches edged with scarlet flowers, — a confusion of delight, amidst which the breasts of the Greek horses are seen blazing in their breadth of golden strength, and the St. Mark's Lion, lifted on a blue field covered with stars, until at last, as if in ecstasy, the crests of the arches break into a marble foam, and toss themselves far into the blue sky in flashes and wreaths of sculptured spray, as if the breakers on the Lido shore had been frost-bound before they fell, and the sea-nymphs had inlaid them with coral and amethyst.

The later years of Ruskin's life, beginning with the publication of *Unto This Last* (1872) were devoted to a series of essays and letters addressed chiefly to English workingmen. In Ruskin's mind there was no actual break between the period of *Modern Painters* and *The Stones of Venice* and these efforts of his to change the whole social and economic scheme of English life. "*The Stones of Venice*," he said, "taught the laws of constructive art, and the dependence of all human work on the happy life of the workman." The workers, Ruskin insisted in these later books, could be happy only if they lived as people had lived in the Middle Ages, making everything that they needed with their own hands, taking pride in their work, and fulfilling the natural human instinct for beauty.[1] To make this possible, Ruskin would abolish machines and machine-made products, and purge the landscape of the reeking railway trains which were destroying the integrity and pride of villages. Life would become simple and natural once more, and every man, seeing clearly the purpose and end of all that he made and did, would be happy in the making and doing. Each man would be rewarded according to his labor, and the state would prevent any man from

[1] Carlyle had preached the same doctrine in *Past and Present* (1843). Ruskin was a disciple of Carlyle.

accumulating wealth at his neighbor's expense. In "St. George's Guild" Ruskin attempted to put his theories into practice, but though he contributed a tenth of his own fortune to start his communistic colony, it soon collapsed. Ruskin's was a futile — it may seem to you a foolish — effort to withstand the trend of the times. He stood on the threshold of an age more mechanical than even he could foresee. He is remembered now rather for his mastery of English prose than for his theories. But the criticisms of such men as Ruskin and Carlyle and Arnold are not to be lightly dismissed. They speak to us no less than to their own generation; and whatever we may think of the remedies which they proposed, we can learn from them to test life by other and better standards than material progress and "volume of production."

TENNYSON, BROWNING AND SOME RECENT POETS

In 1830 — nine years after Keats's death — appeared a little volume of *Poems, Chiefly Lyrical,* by Alfred Tennyson (1809–1892). They were hardly more than poetical exercises, musical echoes, such as any talented youth, steeped in the poetry of Keats, might have produced. But here and there, in *Oriana,* for example, was a very delicate and lovely word-music, a touch of the enchanter's wand. Two years later appeared *The Lady of Shalott and Other Poems.* The word-music was richer and more complex, the poet's fancy had ripened, Tennyson the artist stood revealed. "The Palace of Art," "A Dream of Fair Women" and "The Lady of Shalott" made this volume memorable. The third volume, which appeared in 1842, contained, among new poems, "Ulysses," "The Two Voices," "Locksley Hall," "The Vision of Sin," "Morte d'Arthur," "Sir Galahad," "Sir Launcelot and Queen Guinevere," and, in addition, selections reprinted from the earlier volumes, with revisions which showed how careful was Tennyson's artistry. Eight years later "In Memoriam" was published. The most notable production after that was the completed group of blank-verse narratives, based on the Arthurian legends, called *The Idylls of the King* (1885). From 1850 (the date of "In Memoriam") till his death in 1892, Tennyson's "sovereignty" in the realm of English poetry was uncontested.

There are two ways in which it will be worth our while to think of Tennyson — as an artist, and as an interpreter of the thought of his time.

One of the most musical and delicately imagined of his early poems is "The Lady of Shalott"— an experiment with the Arthurian legend. Bowered in her island home the Lady

> weaves by night and day
> A magic web with colors gay.
> She has heard a whisper say,
> A curse is on her if she stay
>   To look down to Camelot.
> She knows not what the curse may be,
> And so she weaveth steadily,
> And little other care hath she,
>   The Lady of Shalott.
>
> And moving thro' a mirror clear
> That hangs before her all the year,
> Shadows of the world appear.
> There she sees the highway near
>   Winding down to Camelot.

In her mirror she sees Sir Lancelot riding past. Forgetting the curse, she turns from web and mirror to look. The curse is upon her; her heart breaks for love of him. Robing for death, she commits herself to a little boat, which carries her dead body down past Camelot. The poem is sheer music, the lines flow with a sparkling ripple like clear swift water on a sunny day — and then, with the coming of sorrow, the music changes —

> In the stormy east wind straining
> The pale yellow woods were waning,
> The broad stream in his banks complaining,
> Heavily the low sky raining
>   Over towered Camelot.

But the technical perfection of the poem, the smoothness, the grace, came only through the most persistent reworking. Tennyson hated the hisses of a series of *s*'s (try those last six words on your own affronted ear!), and he spared no pains, as he said, to "kick the geese out of the boat."

> A pale, pale corpse she floated by,

one line read in the 1833 edition. Tennyson changed it to

> A gleaming shape she floated by.

And here again the geese were hissing —

> Willows whiten, aspens shiver,
> The sunbeam-showers break and quiver
> In the stream that runneth ever.

He changed it to

> Willows whiten, aspens quiver
> Little breezes dusk and shiver
> Through the wave that runs for ever.

And here, in addition to the forced accents, and a kind of silliness in the rhymes, the movement is a hop instead of a flow —

> The yellow-leavéd waterlily
> The green-sheathéd daffodilly,
> Tremble in the water chilly
>   Round about Shalott.

Tennyson changed it to

> And up and down the people go,
> Gazing where the lilies blow
> Round an island there below,
>   The island of Shalott.

It is, however, in the last stanza that Tennyson most improved the poem. Here the problem was of sense rather

than sound.   The dwellers in Camelot are watching the
little boat floating down the river —

> They crossed themselves, their stars they blest,
> Knight, minstrel, abbot, squire, and guest.
> There lay a parchment on her breast,
> That puzzled more than all the rest,
>   The well-fed wits of Camelot.
> *"The web was woven curiously,*
> *The charm is broken utterly,*
> *Draw near and fear not — this is I,*
>   *The Lady of Shalott."*

So, as Tennyson printed it in 1833, the poem ends.

There are obviously several things wrong with this
stanza.   I doubt if the Lady would have thus placarded
herself.   I doubt if the possibility of anybody's being
afraid to approach her would have occurred to her stricken
spirit.   I fear there is no doubt at all that Tennyson, with
the third line already in mind when he began to compose
the stanza, had rather a laborious time making the first
and second and fourth lines, and allowed the rhyme to
dictate the thought of each of these lines.   And the picture
of knight, minstrel, abbot, squire, and guest, all peering
down at the parchment and with one voice exclaiming
"Bless my stars!" is perhaps not so poetical as Tennyson
meant it to be.   The stanza is amusingly bad, but it is not
quoted here for the sake of having fun with it.   It is quoted
because, when you put beside it the words which took its
place in the 1842 edition of the poems, you will not only
see what Tennyson could accomplish by his patient artistry, but you will have before you one of the best examples
that I know of the difference between bad poetry and good
poetry.   For in this rewritten stanza there are no rhymes
which you feel have engendered the thought of the line

to which they belong. The thoughts move so naturally and simply and rightly that you are not even conscious that there *are* rhymes. The music of the rhymes is all in the back of your head where it belongs. And there is nothing artificial, nothing arranged, about the stanza. You know that those simple words are just what Sir Lancelot really said.

As in the discarded stanza, the dwellers in Camelot are watching the little boat floating down the river —

> Who is this? and what is here?
> And in the lighted palace near
> Died the sound of royal cheer;
> And they crossed themselves for fear,
>   All the knights at Camelot:
> But Lancelot mused a little space;
> He said, "She has a lovely face;
> God in his mercy lend her grace,
>   The Lady of Shalott!"

"The Lady of Shalott" gives us a glimpse of Tennyson in his workshop, when his technical skill and taste were just maturing. It will be interesting to see him once more in his workshop, not now molding lyric rhythms and clustering rhymes, but engaged in the far more exacting task of making blank verse. It is in that part of the Arthur legends describing the last earthly hours of the wounded king — that part which Tennyson printed in 1842, and which was too right to need any revision when he incorporated it into the *Idylls*. He had gone back to Sir Thomas Malory's prose for his materials:

Therefore, said Arthur, take thou Excalibur, my good sword, and go with it to yonder water side, and when thou comest there, I charge thee throw my sword in that water, and come again, and tell me what thou there seest. My lord, said Bedivere, your commandment shall be done, and lightly bring you word again. So

Sir Bedivere departed, and by the way he beheld that noble sword, that the pommel and haft were all of precious stones, and then he said to himself, If I throw this rich sword in the water, thereof shall never come good, but harm and loss. And then Sir Bedivere hid Excalibur under a tree. And as soon as he might he came again unto the king, and said he had been at the water, and had thrown the sword into the water. What sawest thou there? said the king. Sir, he said, I saw nothing but waves and winds. That is untruly said of thee, said the king; therefore go thou lightly again, and do my command as thou art to me lief and dear, spare not, but throw it in. Then Sir Bedivere returned again, and took the sword in his hand; and then him thought sin and shame to throw away that noble sword; and so eft he hid the sword, and returned again, and told to the king that he had been at the water, and done his commandment. What saw thou there? said the king. Sir, he said, I saw nothing but the waters wap and the waves wan. Ah traitor, untrue, said king Arthur, now hast thou betrayed me twice. Who would have wend that thou that hast been to me so lief and dear, and thou art named a noble knight, and would betray me for the riches of the sword. But now go again lightly, for thy long tarrying putteth me in great jeopardy of my life, for I have taken cold. And but if thou do not as I bid thee, if ever I may see thee, I shall slay thee with mine own hands, for thou wouldest for my rich sword see me dead. Then Sir Bedivere departed, and went to the sword, and lightly took it up, and went to the water side, and there he bound the girdle about the hilts, and then he threw the sword as far into the water as he might, and there came an arm and an hand above the water, and met it, and caught it, and so shook it thrice and brandished, and then vanished away the hand with the sword in the water. So Sir Bedivere came again to the king, and told him what he saw. Alas, said the king, help me hence, for I dread me I have tarried over long.

This is beautiful prose. As you read the blank verse into which Tennyson turned it, see how unerringly Tennyson

picked every vivid picture-word, every well-flavored word,
to enrich his story.   And see with what sure skill and
with what deft reordering he transformed Malory's rhythmic phrases into the other harmony of blank verse. Take
this, for example: "What saw thou there? said the king.
Sir, he said, I saw nothing but the waters wap and the
waves wan. Ah traitor, untrue, said king Arthur."

> "What is it thou hast seen, or what hast heard?"
>   And answer made the bold Sir Bedivere:
> "I heard the water lapping on the crag
> And the long ripple washing in the reeds."
>   To whom replied King Arthur, much in wrath:
> "Ah, miserable and unkind, untrue,
> Unknightly, traitor-hearted!"

And see, on the other hand, how Tennyson has taken
Malory's picture-words and elaborated upon them, made
the plain words gorgeous: "He beheld that noble sword,
that the pommel and haft were all of precious stones"—

> For all the haft twinkled with diamond sparks,
> Myriads of topaz-lights, and jacinth-work
> Of subtlest jewellery.

And once more: "There came an arm and an hand above
the water, and met it, and caught it, and so shook it thrice
and brandished, and then vanished away the hand with the
sword into the water"—

> But ere he dipt the surface, rose an arm
> Clothed in white samite, mystic, wonderful,
> And caught him by the hilt, and brandished him
> Three times, and drew him under in the mere.

But these are only one or two of the things worth looking
for. Judge now the entire passage —

"Thou therefore take my brand Excalibur,
Which was my pride; for thou rememberest how
In those old days, one summer noon, an arm
Rose up from out the bosom of the lake,
Clothed in white samite, mystic, wonderful,
Holding the sword — and how I rowed across
And took it, and have worn it, like a king;
And, wheresoever I am sung or told
In aftertime, this also shall be known.
But now delay not; take Excalibur,
And fling him far into the middle mere;
Watch what thou seest, and lightly bring me word."
    To him replied the bold Sir Bedivere:
"It is not meet, Sir King, to leave thee thus,
Aidless, alone, and smitten thro' the helm.
A little thing may harm a wounded man.
Yet I thy hest will all perform at full,
Watch what I see, and lightly bring thee word!"
    So saying, from the ruined shrine he stept
And in the moon athwart the place of tombs,
Where lay the mighty bones of ancient men,
Old knights, and over them the sea-wind sang
Shrill, chill, with flakes of foam.   He, stepping down
By zigzag paths and juts of pointed rock,
Came on the shining levels of the lake.
    There drew he forth the brand Excalibur,
And o'er him, drawing it, the winter moon,
Brightening the skirts of a long cloud, ran forth
And sparkled keen with frost against the hilt;
For all the haft twinkled with diamond sparks,
Myriads of topaz-lights, and jacinth-work
Of subtlest jewellery.   He gazed so long
That both his eyes were dazzled, as he stood,
This way and that dividing the swift mind,
In act to throw; but at the last it seemed
Better to leave Excalibur concealed

There in the many-knotted water-flags,
That whistled stiff and dry about the marge.
So strode he back slow to the wounded king.
    Then spake King Arthur to Sir Bedivere:
"Hast thou performed my mission which I gave?
What is it thou hast seen, or what hast heard?"
    And answer made the bold Sir Bedivere:
"I heard the ripple washing in the reeds,
And the wild water lapping on the crag."
    To whom replied King Arthur, faint and pale:
"Thou hast betrayed thy nature and thy name,
Not rendering true answer, as beseemed
Thy fealty, nor like a noble knight;
For surer sign had followed, either hand,
Or voice, or else a motion of the mere.
This is a shameful thing for men to lie.
Yet now, I charge thee, quickly go again
As thou art lief and dear, and do the thing
I bade thee, watch, and lightly bring me word."
    Then went Sir Bedivere the second time
Across the ridge, and paced beside the mere,
Counting the dewy pebbles, fixed in thought;
But when he saw the wonder of the hilt,
How curiously and strangely chased, he smote
His palms together, and he cried aloud:
    "And if indeed I cast the brand away,
Surely a precious thing, one worthy note,
Should thus be lost forever from the earth,
Which might have pleased the eyes of many men.
What good should follow this, if this were done?
What harm, undone? deep harm to disobey,
Seeing obedience is the bond of rule.
Were it well to obey then, if a king demand
An act unprofitable, against himself?
The king is sick, and knows not what he does.
What record, or what relic of my lord

Should be to aftertime, but empty breath
And rumors of a doubt? but were this kept,
Stored in some treasure-house of mighty kings,
Some one might show it at a joust of arms,
Saying, 'King Arthur's sword, Excalibur,
Wrought by the lonely maiden of the lake;
Nine years she wrought it, sitting in the deeps
Upon the hidden bases of the hills.'
So might some old man speak in the aftertime
To all the people, winning reverence;
But now much honor and much fame were lost."

So spake he, clouded with his own conceit,
And hid Excalibur the second time,
And so strode back slow to the wounded king.

Then spoke King Arthur, breathing heavily:
"What is it thou hast seen, or what hast heard?"

And answer made the bold Sir Bedivere:
"I heard the water lapping on the crag,
And the long ripple washing in the reeds."

To whom replied King Arthur, much in wrath:
"Ah, miserable and unkind, untrue,
Unknightly, traitor-hearted! Woe is me!
Authority forgets a dying king,
Laid widowed of the power in his eye
That bowed the will.   I see thee what thou art,
For thou, the latest-left of all my knights,
In whom should meet the offices of all,
Thou wouldst betray me for the precious hilt;
Either from lust of gold, or like a girl
Valuing the giddy pleasure of the eyes.
Yet, for a man may fail in duty twice,
And the third time may prosper, get thee hence;
But, if thou spare to fling Excalibur,
I will arise and slay thee with my hands."

Then quickly rose Sir Bedivere, and ran,
And, leaping down the ridges lightly, plunged

Among the bulrush-beds, and clutched the sword,
And strongly wheeled and threw it. The great brand
Made lightnings in the splendor of the moon,
And flashing round and round, and whirled in an arch,
Shot like a streamer of the northern morn,
Seen where the moving isles of winter shock
By night, with noises of the northern sea.
So flashed and fell the brand Excalibur;
But ere he dipt the surface, rose an arm
Clothed in white samite, mystic, wonderful,
And caught him by the hilt, and brandished him
Three times, and drew him under in the mere.
And lightly went the other to the king.

These will serve as examples of Tennyson's artistry.
Even in the later years, when the easy adulation of his
readers might have tempted him to relax, his passion for
perfection was unabated. His tribute to Virgil, written in
1881, "at the request of the Mantuans for the nineteenth
centenary of Virgil's death," reveals him as a "lord of
language" second only to that master in whose footsteps
he had trod.

Landscape-lover, lord of language more than he that
     sang the "Works and Days,"
All the chosen coin of fancy flashing out from
     many a golden phrase;

Thou that singest wheat and woodland, tilth and
     vineyard, hive and horse and herd;
All the charm of all the Muses often flowering
     in a lonely wood . . .

I salute thee, Mantovano, I that loved thee since
     my day began,
Wielder of the stateliest measure ever moulded by
     the lips of man.

Meanwhile, Tennyson became, more completely than any other poet had ever been, the Voice of England. The English landscape lives in his pages —

> Deep-meadowed, happy, fair with orchard lawns;

the lanes, "white with May"; fields whence

> Drowned in yonder living blue
> The lark becomes a sightless song;

forests where

> In deeps unseen
> The topmost elm-tree gathered green
> From draughts of balmy air;

the varied streams of a well-watered land,

> The slow broad stream
> That, stirred with languid pulses of the oar
> Waves all its lazy lilies, and creeps on,
> Barge-laden, to three arches of a bridge
> Crowned with the minster-towers,

or the brook that

> sparkles out among the fern
> To bicker down the valley . . .
> By twenty thorpes, a little town
> And half a hundred bridges;

the villager's cottage

> Neat and nest-like, half-way up
> The narrow street that clambered toward the mill;

or

> an English home — gray twilight poured
> On dewy pastures, dewy trees
> Softer than sleep — all things in order stored,
> A haunt of ancient Peace.

Equally vivid are his pictures of the surrounding sea —

> With all
> Its stormy crests that smote the skies;

or

> As the foam bow brightens
> When the wind blows the foam;

or where the angry waves, beating upon an iron coast,

> Climb and fall
> And roar, rock-thwarted, under bellowing caves —
> Beneath the windy wall;

or when there is

> Calm on the seas and silver sleep
> And waves that sway themselves in rest;

or when

> The long day wanes; the slow moon climbs; the deep
> Moans round with many voices.

And as with the English landscape and seascape, so with the English people. You will find them all in the "Idylls of the Hearth" (as he thought of calling the *Enoch Arden* volume) —"the sailor, the farmer, the parson, the city lawyer, the squire, the country maiden, and the old woman who dreams of her life in a restful old age."

While he was picturing the England of his own day, he was concerning himself also with her legendary past. The more or less mythical King Arthur,[1] whom the imagination of medieval story-tellers had surrounded with a glittering court, and a Round Table of knights dedicated to chivalrous and noble deeds, had come to seem, if not actually historical, at least more real than any of the authentic kings whose reigns are briefly and dryly recorded in the

[1] See page 17.

early chronicles. The importance of the theme was established by a great tradition. In the fifteenth century Sir
Thomas Malory had gathered the stories of King Arthur
and his knights into his book, *Le Morte Darthur*, and the
first of English printers, William Caxton, had prefaced his
imprinting of it with the injunction that "King Arthur
ought most to be remembered amongst us English tofore
all other Christian kings." The sixteenth-century poet,
Edmund Spenser, having as his purpose in *The Faerie
Queene* "to fashion a gentleman or noble person in virtuous
and gentle discipline . . . chose the history of King Arthur,
as most fit for the excellency of his person, being made
famous by many men's former works." Milton, casting
about for a subject for his projected epic, planned to "recall in song the kings of my native land and Arthur who
carried war even into fairyland," and to "tell of those
great-hearted champions bound in the society of the Round
Table." The story of Arthur and his knights was the most
English of themes. Tennyson gathered up the threads —
the story of Arthur's coming, of his wars and of his departure to Avalon, the stories of Gareth and Lynette, of Ge-
raint and Enid, of Balin and Balan, of Merlin and Vivien,
of Lancelot and Elaine, of the search for the Holy Grail, of
Pelleas and Ettarre, of "The Last Tournament," and of
Arthur's queen, Guinevere — gathered up the threads,
and retold the stories after his own fashion — and with
such success that to nine out of ten readers to-day the
Knights of the Round Table are not the figures of medieval
legend but the personages whom Tennyson's imagination
recreated and reinterpreted.

While Tennyson was thus retelling his country's legends
and celebrating her beauties of landscape and sea, he was
concerning himself also with her spiritual problems. Even

before Charles Darwin published his *Origin of Species*
(1859) and *Descent of Man* (1871), there had been much
debate about the theory that all life has evolved from a
primitive organism and that man himself has thus evolved,
with some form of ape as his immediate ancestor. It was
not easy to reconcile this theory with the belief that man,
unlike the brute creation, has an immortal soul, and that
God, according to the words of the book of Genesis, "created
man in his own image." The death of Tennyson's friend
Arthur Hallam, for whom he had a love and admiration
amounting to reverence, set Tennyson to thinking about
this. The result of his thinking is the long poem called
"In Memoriam." In "In Memoriam," Tennyson virtually
accepts the scientific theory but finds it possible to reconcile
it with faith — a faith (in the words of one of Tennyson's
friends) "in the growing purpose of the sum of life, and in
the noble destiny of the individual man as he offers himself
for the fulfilment of his little part." It is a faith

> That men may rise on stepping-stones
> Of their dead selves to higher things;

a belief, emerging through hopes and fears, that evolution
is still going on toward

> the crowning race

> Of those that, eye to eye, shall look
> On knowledge; under whose command
> Is Earth and Earth's, and in their hand
> Is Nature like an open book;

> No longer half-akin to brute,
> For all we thought and loved and did,
> And hoped and suffered, is but seed
> Of what in them is flower and fruit;

Whereof the man that with me trod
This planet was a noble type
Appearing ere the times were ripe,
That friend of mine who lives in God,

That God, which ever lives and loves,
One God, one law, one element,
And one far-off divine event,
To which the whole creation moves.

"In Memoriam" appeared in 1850. Probably no other poem of meditation on the problem of life and death has been so widely read. It contains passages of great beauty; but its real hold is that it deals very simply and feelingly and sincerely, and at times very eloquently, with matters which every one tries, with whatever help he can get, to think out for himself.

In the year in which "In Memoriam" appeared, Tennyson succeeded Wordsworth as poet laureate.[1] While the laureateship had previously been looked upon as a rather empty honor, Tennyson gave it a peculiar significance. He had already shown a keen interest in public affairs. He had a gift for putting into glowing words every phase of national feeling. That eight-line exposition of their theory of government with which he provided his countrymen in 1833 could hardly be bettered —

It is the land that freemen till,
That sober-suited Freedom chose,
The land where, girt with friends or foes
A man may speak the thing he will;

A land of settled government,
A land of just and old renown,
Where Freedom slowly broadens down
From precedent to precedent.

[1] See pages 266–7.

As the years passed and his reputation grew, he became the acknowledged poet-spokesman of the nation. It fell to his lot at times to speak words of warning or exhortation;[1] but it was to moments of intense patriotic feeling that he best responded — in the stirring rhythm of "The Charge of the Light Brigade" and in that voice of an Empire's lamentation, the "Ode on the Death of the Duke of Wellington," with its marvelously varied music, the tolling of the bell, the solemn funeral march, the swift rush of battle, the mounting fervor as the poem draws toward its close, the sudden beautiful quietness of the last four lines —

> Speak no more of his renown,
> Lay your earthly fancies down,
> And in the vast cathedral leave him,
> God accept him, Christ receive him!

It is needful to bear these things in mind, needful to realize how completely Tennyson had become the Voice of England, if we are to understand the feeling that his public had about him. He had fitted so completely into the world which our fathers knew and had gathered so many threads of it into his poetry. He had written of so many vital things and had written of them all so brilliantly. To our fathers it seemed that the absoluteness of his supremacy and the lastingness of his fame were beyond question.

After his death, came a reaction. To a new school of poets, who prefer the sharply precise and rugged word to the musical word, who seek to suggest rather than to elaborate, and who are disposed to find their themes in the strangeness, the mischances, the irony of life, rather than its more gracious aspects, Tennyson is merely "conventional" and "ornate." That attitude, too, is passing. The

---

[1] Read for example *The Third of February, 1852, The Fleet, Hands all round* (the first version), and *Riflemen, form.*

truth lies between. He had not the substantial greatness of Chaucer or Shakespeare or Milton or Wordsworth. There are a few poems of Keats's which attain to a purer beauty than anything Tennyson ever wrote. But, next to these, he ranks secure.

Fame came more slowly to Robert Browning (1812–1889) than to Tennyson; but toward the end of Browning's career, their names were linked as the two great poets of the age. The fact that they were both poets dedicate, giving their lives to their art, and that over the same great period — from the early 1830's to a time within living memory — they were continuously productive, serves to emphasize their unlikeness in style and in interests. When, after steeping yourself in Tennyson's smooth harmonies, you turn to Browning, your ear will be jarred with all sorts of roughnesses. He had a way of hewing through words to the core of thought — and sometimes leaving some very awkward chips by the way. And his rhymes! In his lighter verse, those hard-pushed dissyllabic and trisyllabic and quadrisyllabic rhymes are amusing and enlivening. In "The Pied Piper of Hamelyn," for instance, you enjoy them —

> Great rats, small rats, lean rats, brawny rats,
> Brown rats, black rats, gray rats, tawny rats —

or

> And it seemed as if a voice
> (Sweeter far than by harp or by psaltery
> Is breathed) called out, "Oh rats, rejoice!
> The world is grown to one vast drysaltery!"

But even in his most serious poems, Browning could not resist the temptation. In "A Grammarian's Funeral" (see page 596), for example, with all its reverence and high idealism, you will find such rhymes as

> Image the whole, then execute the parts —
>   Fancy the fabric,
> Quite, ere you build, ere steel strike fire from quartz,
>   Ere mortar dab brick.

Except in his lighter poems, we shall have to admit that this jingle-trickery does mar Browning's work. The roughnesses, the discords of his style, on the other hand, most of us easily get used to, and rather come to enjoy. They breathe a more tonic air than Tennyson's unfailing smoothness. They are natural to Browning's vigor, his splendid energy.

Browning and Tennyson are no less sharply contrasted in their subject matter, in the things that interested them. Tennyson was wholly English, insularly English. Browning spent much of his time in Italy, and found most of his themes there. Unlike Tennyson, whose bent was mainly descriptive and lyrical, and who generally looked at life with a picture-maker's eye, Browning was preëminently an interpreter of character. To lift from the vast range of his reading some personage in whom were possibilities of vividness or unusualness; to recreate him imaginatively in the setting of his time; to recreate him, not by description, but dramatically — in other words to place him before us at some revealing moment of his life, to let him speak for himself, and to leave it to us to draw our own conclusions about him, just as we might if he were a character in a play — that was Browning's way.

One of the best of his "dramatic monologues" is "My Last Duchess." Imagine the period as toward the middle of the sixteenth century. The Duke of Ferrara is speak-

ing.   Lover of beauty, patron of painters and poets, he is
at the same time the ruthless and self-centered ruler of his
petty kingdom.   The marvel of the poem is not only the
Duke's unconscious self-characterization, but even more
the picture which emerges from that cynical narrative of
the Duchess herself — so young and so inexperienced, with
a heart

> too soon made glad,
> Too easily impressed.

That's my last Duchess painted on the wall,
Looking as if she were alive.   I call
That piece a wonder, now: Frà Pandolf's hands
Worked busily a day, and there she stands.
Will 't please you sit and look at her?   I said
"Frà Pandolf" by design, for never read
Strangers like you that pictured countenance,
The depth and passion of its earnest glance,
But to myself they turned (since none puts by
The curtain I have drawn for you, but I)
And seemed as they would ask me, if they durst,
How such a glance came there; so, not the first
Are you to turn and ask thus.   Sir, 'twas not
Her husband's presence only, called that spot
Of joy into the Duchess' cheek: perhaps
Frà Pandolf chanced to say, "Her mantle laps
Over my lady's wrist too much," or "Paint
Must never hope to reproduce the faint
Half-flush that dies along her throat:" such stuff
Was courtesy, she thought, and cause enough
For calling up that spot of joy.   She had
A heart — how shall I say? — too soon made glad,
Too easily impressed: she liked whate'er
She looked on, and her looks went everywhere.
Sir, 'twas all one!   My favor at her breast,

The dropping of the daylight in the West,
The bough of cherries some officious fool
Broke in the orchard for her, the white mule
She rode with round the terrace — all and each
Would draw from her alike the approving speech,
Or blush, at least. She thanked men, — good! but thanked
Somehow — I know not how — as if she ranked
My gift of a nine-hundred-years-old name
With anybody's gift. Who'd stoop to blame
This sort of trifling? Even had you skill
In speech — (which I have not) — to make your will
Quite clear to such an one, and say, "Just this
Or that in you disgusts me; here you miss,
Or there exceed the mark" — and if she let
Herself be lessoned so, nor plainly set
Her wits to yours, forsooth, and made excuse,
— E'en then would be some stooping; and I choose
Never to stoop. Oh, sir, she smiled, no doubt,
Whene'er I passed her; but who passed without
Much the same smile? This grew; I gave commands;
Then all smiles stopped together. There she stands
As if alive. Will 't please you rise? We'll meet
The company below, then. I repeat,
The Count your master's known munificence
Is ample warrant that no just pretence
Of mine for dowry will be disallowed;
Though his fair daughter's self, as I avowed
At starting, is my object. Nay, we'll go
Together down, sir. Notice Neptune, though,
Taming a sea-horse, thought a rarity,
Which Claus of Innsbruck cast in bronze for me!

Interested above everything in this art of characterization by dramatic monologue, Browning found a mine of
unexampled richness in Italian history and legend. Aristo-
crats, ecclesiastics, painters, musicians and charlatans come

to life under his touch.   One of his most perfect realizations of the Renaissance spirit, with its worldliness and egoism and passion for beauty, is "The Bishop Orders His Tomb at Saint Praxed's Church."   Again it is sixteenth-century Italy.   As the bishop lies in the statechamber dying by degrees, stately Scripture phrases mingle on his lips with memories of the hated rival who had intrigued against him for so many years, and, dying, had thwarted him once again.   Thoughts of a tomb which shall surpass Gandolf's fill the dying bishop's mind.

"Do I live, am I dead?" Peace, peace seems all.
Saint Praxed's ever was the church for peace;
And so, about this tomb of mine.   I fought
With tooth and nail to save my niche, ye know:
— Old Gandolf cozened me, despite my care;
Shrewd was that snatch from out the corner South
He graced his carrion with, God curse the same!
Yet still my niche is not so cramped but thence
One sees the pulpit o' the epistle-side,
And somewhat of the choir, those silent seats,
And up into the aery dome where live
The angels, and a sunbeam's sure to lurk:
And I shall fill my slab of basalt there,
And 'neath my tabernacle take my rest,
With those nine columns round me, two and two,
The odd one at my feet where Anselm stands:
Peach-blossom marble all, the rare, the ripe
As fresh-poured red wine of a mighty pulse.
— Old Gandolf with his paltry onion-stone,
Put me where I may look at him!   True peach,
Rosy and flawless: how I earned the prize!
Draw close: that conflagration of my church
— What then? So much was saved if aught were missed!
My sons, ye would not be my death?   Go dig

The white-grape vineyard where the oil-press stood,
Drop water gently till the surface sink,
And if ye find . . . Ah God, I know not, I! . . .
Bedded in store of rotten fig-leaves soft,
And corded up in a tight olive-frail,
Some lump, ah God, of *lapis lazuli*,
Big as a Jew's head cut off at the nape,
Blue as a vein o'er the Madonna's breast . . .
Sons, all have I bequeathed you, villas, all,
That brave Frascati villa with its bath,
So, let the blue lump poise between my knees,
Like God the Father's globe on both his hands
Ye worship in the Jesu Church so gay,
For Gandolf shall not choose but see and burst!
Swift as a weaver's shuttle fleet our years:
Man goeth to the grave, and where is he?
Did I say basalt for my slab, sons? Black —
'Twas ever antique-black I meant! How else
Shall ye contrast my frieze to come beneath?
The bas-relief in bronze ye promised me,
Those Pans and Nymphs ye wot of, and perchance
Some tripod, thyrsus, with a vase or so,
The Saviour at his sermon on the mount,
Saint Praxed in a glory, and one Pan
Ready to twitch the Nymph's last garment off,
And Moses with the tables . . .
Well, go! I bless ye.   Fewer tapers there,
But in a row: and, going, turn your backs
— Ay, like departing altar-ministrants,
And leave me in my church, the church for peace,
That I may watch at leisure if he leers —
Old Gandolf — at me, from his onion-stone.

Among the best of Browning's poems of this sort are
his characterizations of painters and musicians. There is
"Fra Lippo Lippi," for example — that street-waif, whom

the monks had rescued and brought up as one of themselves, but who is too eager for life to be content with their shut-in quietness. He is artist born, is Brother Lippo; covers the gray walls of his cell with paintings; religious paintings, to be sure; but he is too vividly alive to content himself with stiff, conventional, symbolic figures; his must be real human beings, faces that he has seen, speaking faces; his fellow-monks look and wonder and shake their heads.

There is Andrea del Sarto, the "faultless painter." The fire that burned in Fra Lippo burns not in him. He can draw as no fellow-painter can. His technique is perfect. He can see, he could so easily correct, the mistakes those others make. But —

> There burns a truer light of God in them,
> In their vexed beating stuffed and stopped up brain,
> Heart, or whate'er else, than goes on to prompt
> This low-pulsed forthright craftsman's hand of mine,
> Their work drops groundward, but themselves, I know
> Reach many a time a heaven that's shut to me . . .
> Ah, but a man's reach should exceed his grasp,
> Or what's a heaven for?   All is silver-gray,
> Placid and perfect with my art.

So he sits meditating, in the presence of his mute Lucrezia — his Lucrezia whose perfect face he had depicted in painting after painting, and whose soulless perfection had held him bound —

> You don't understand
> Nor care to understand about my art . . .
> — All the play, the insight and the stretch —
> Out of me, out of me! And wherefore out?
> Had you enjoined them on me, given me soul,
> We might have risen to Rafael, I and you!

There is "Abt Vogler," whose musician's soul is rapt to ecstasy, as, with the organ of his invention, he builds his palace of sound —

> Painter and poet are proud in the artist-list enrolled:

> But here is the finger of God, a flash of the will that can,
> Existent behind all laws, that made them and, lo, they are!
> And I know not if, save in this, such gift be allowed to
>   man,
> That out of three sounds he frame, not a fourth sound,
>   but a star,
> Consider it well: each tone of our scale in itself is naught;
> It is everywhere in the world — loud, soft, and all is said,
> Give it to me to use!   I mix it with two in my thought:
> And there!   Ye have heard and seen: consider and bow
>   the head!

There is "Saul" (based on the incident described in 1 Samuel xvi), in which we hear from David's lips the story of how he was called to heal the King with his music, and stood before that tragically inert figure and played and sang — the shepherds' and the reapers' tunes and the pæan of manhood and courage and high endeavor and of what Saul had been and what Saul should be — until at length the great King emerged from his dark seizure and laid his hand upon David's brow — and David, lifted by his human love for Saul into a prophetic awareness of the Christ-love that was to be, made his way homeward through the night

> . . . . witnesses, cohorts about me to left and to right,
> Angels, powers, the unuttered, unseen, the alive, the
>   aware . . .
> And the stars of night beat with emotion, and tingled
>   and shot

> Out in fire the strong pain of pent knowledge: but I
>   fainted not,
> For the Hand still impelled me at once and supported,
>   suppressed,
> All the tumult, and quenched it with quiet, and holy
>   behest,
> Till the rapture was shut in itself, and the earth
>   sank to rest.
> Anon at the dawn, all that trouble had withered from
>   earth . . .
> And the little brooks witnessing murmured, persistent
>   and low,
> With their obstinate, all but hushed voices — "E'en
>   so, it is so!"

No other of Browning's monologues has such lyrical quality, no other approaches "Saul" in sustained music. It would be unfair to compare "Saul" to the others to their disadvantage. Such poems as "My Last Duchess" are essentially dramatizations — compressed dramas — characterization reduced to its barest essentials. "Saul" is the realization of a dramatic moment but it is not a characterization either of David or the King. It is a narra-tive-lyric, rising by successive gradations of emotional intensity to a height worthy of the noblest rhythms. Browning was not by habit a music-maker — but he had great music at his command.

But perhaps you will care most — as I confess I do — for "A Grammarian's Funeral." Not for poetic quality —"Saul" is much nobler poetry — but because of what it symbolizes, because it dramatizes and makes real a great moment in the history of the world. Something has been said in an earlier chapter (see page 72), of the devotion to learning in the early Renaissance — the feeling among

scholars that those Greek manuscripts which, at long last,
were beginning to drift into Italy, would effect a veritable
enfranchisement of the spirit, and that to regain an exact
knowledge of the Greek language down to the minutest
points of grammar and so to elucidate the precious thoughts
which they contained was the noblest of tasks. The Grammarian of Browning's poem had spent his life "grinding
at grammar."

> "Time to taste life," another would have said,
>   "Up with the curtain!"
> This man said rather, "Actual life comes next?
>   Patience a moment!
> Grant I have mastered learning's crabbed text,
>   Still there's the comment.
> Let me know all! Prate not of most or least,
>   Painful or easy!
> Even to the crumbs I'd fain eat up the feast,
>   Ay, nor feel queasy."
> Oh, such a life as he resolved to live,
>   When he had learned it,
> When he had gathered all books had to give!
>   Sooner, he spurned it.

But old age crept upon the Grammarian while yet he was
grinding at grammar — and now his disciples are carrying
his body to the mountain-top, the words of his story coming
from the lips of one of these disciples in a sort of rhythmic
chant, in unison with their upward march —

> Leave we the unlettered plain its herd and crop;
>   Seek we sepulture
> On a tall mountain, citied to the top,
>   Crowded with culture!
> All the peaks soar, but one the rest excels;
>   Clouds overcome it;

No! yonder sparkle is the citadel's
    Circling its summit.
Thither our path lies; wind we up the heights:
    Wait ye the warning?
Our low life was the level's and the night's;
    He's for the morning.
Step to a tune, square chests, erect each head,
    'Ware the beholders!
This is our master, famous, calm, and dead,
    Borne on our shoulders.

And from the disciple's words emerges Browning's characteristic philosophy — to do the day's work, to aim high, and to leave the rest to God, confident that even thwarted impulses and desires unachieved will weigh with Him —

That low man seeks a little thing to do,
    Sees it and does it:
This high man, with a great thing to pursue,
    Dies ere he knows it.
That low man goes on adding one to one,
    His hundred's soon hit:
This high man, aiming at a million,
    Misses an unit.
That, has the world here — should he need the next,
    Let the world mind him!
This, throws himself on God, and unperplexed,
    Seeking shall find him.

You will find that philosophy again in "Rabbi ben Ezra —"

Grow old along with me!
The best is yet to be,
The last of life, for which the first was made:
Our times are in his hand
Who saith, "A whole I planned,
Youth shows but half; trust God; see all, nor be
    afraid! . . . "

All the world's coarse thumb
And finger failed to plumb,
So passed in making up the main account:
All instincts immature,
All purposes unsure,
That weighed not as his work, yet swelled the man's
   amount:

Thoughts hardly to be packed
Into a narrow act,
Fancies that broke through language and escaped;
All I could never be,
All men ignored in me,
This, I was worth to God, whose wheel the pitcher
   shaped.

You will find it in "Apparent Failure," one of the most
moving poems Browning wrote — in which the bodies
waiting identification in the Paris Morgue, each with its
untold story of failure and despair and suicide, move him
to say —

My own hope is, a sun will pierce
The thickest cloud earth ever stretched:
That after Last, returns the First,
Though a wide compass round be fetched;
That what began best, can't end worst,
Nor what God blessed once, prove accurst.

You will find it once more in the resonant challenge of
Browning's farewell poem — the "Epilogue to Asolando —"

One who never turned his back but marched breast
   forward,
Never doubted clouds would break,
Never dreamed, though right were worsted, wrong
   would triumph,
Held we fall to rise, are baffled to fight better,
Sleep to wake.

No, at noonday in the bustle of man's work time
Greet the unseen with a cheer!
Bid him forward, breast and back as either should be,
"Strive and thrive!" cry "Speed, — fight on, fare ever
There as here!"

Browning's genius was at its best in the monologues.
In these he was free to focus upon a single motive or a
single trait or a single dramatic moment. His full-length
plays — of which the best are *Colombe's Birthday* and *A
Blot in the 'Scutcheon* — did not succeed upon the stage.
They move a little too slowly, are too much disposed to
elaborate character at the expense of plot-development.
More, perhaps, than these formally constructed dramas,
you will enjoy "Pippa Passes," which consists of a series
of scenes rather than a continuously developed plot. Pippa,
a working-girl in the silk-mills, celebrates her one day of
holiday by wandering about, singing as she goes.

The year's at the spring
And day's at the morn;
Morning's at seven;
The hillside's dew-pearled;
The lark's on the wing;
The snail's on the thorn:
God's in his heaven —
All's right with the world!

As Pippa wanders, this song and other songs of hers, no
less full of innocent happiness, reach the ears of those who
are at some parting of the ways, some crisis of their lives,
some irrevocable choice between right and wrong; and
Pippa, as the sun sets and her one day of freedom ends,
never knows that the great ones whom she wonders about
have been saved from wrongdoing by her songs.

In addition to the monologues and the plays, there is another side of Browning's work which will particularly interest you. As a story-teller, he is unsurpassed. Here the zest and energy of his style and his sense for the dramatic phrase stand him in good stead.

"The Pied Piper of Hamelyn" was written offhand to amuse a child — but it is incomparably well done. "An Incident of the French Camp" and "How They Brought the Good News from Ghent to Aix" are masterpieces of compact and vivid narrative. English literature possesses no more stirring battle-ballad than "Hervé Riel." This story-telling power Browning put to its severest test in the most remarkable of his poems, *The Ring and the Book.* From an "old yellow book" containing the materials of a seventeenth-century murder-case, which he picked up on a second-hand bookstall in Florence, he built his story. The bare outline requires few words. The gentle and innocent girl, Pompilia, marries Count Guido Franceschini. His cruelty drives her to flight. A priest, Caponsacchi, who loves her with a pure devotion, aids her escape. Guido pursues them, kills Pompilia, and is put on trial for the murder. In Browning's hands, the story is told and retold from many angles, from many points of view — the actual participants, the advocates on either side, the Pope himself who is to judge — even the gossiping onlookers, facile in opinion.

Gradually, as you read on through the ten long monologues, and live in the mind of one character after another, the massive scheme of the poem begins to justify itself. Not only the cynically heartless Guido, and Pompilia, "perfect in whiteness," and the devoted Caponsacchi, but also the subsidiary figures become extraordinarily real. Here are things that happened in a far, and to most of us a strange, country; but you find yourself sharing the emotions of these people, feeling with them or against them, as if you too were involved in this web of tragic circumstance three hundred years ago.

Was Browning a great poet?   A distinguished novelist of the present day said not long ago, after listening to the recitation of one of Browning's dramatic monologues: "The language of the poem, though it has fine qualities, is not in my opinion beautiful, shining, splendid.   And in my poetry I demand these qualities, and if I do not get them I refuse the name of poetry to the composition and call it verse.   For me poetry is an affair primarily of emotional words, not of thought."   That is a very common point of view, though in this instance expressed with somewhat more than usual downrightness.   Only rarely is Browning's poetry "shining."   It is evident that Mr. Arnold Bennett and those who agree with him would number among the true poets only those in whom the chosen coin of fancy flashes out from many a golden phrase.   But if rhythmic energy, and vision, and the power to lift us out of ourselves count, I think that we must number Browning among the great poets.   Not, certainly, among the greatest.   But next to Chaucer and Shakespeare and Milton and Wordsworth and Keats, we may, not unconfidently, number him among a second group which would include, with their infinite diversity, Spenser and Pope and Shelley and Tennyson.

Browning died in 1889; Tennyson in 1892.   This brings us very near our own time.   The nearer we get, the harder it is to decide which poets we should read, which we can afford to disregard.   The oblivion of time simplifies for us the problem of the past.   The innumerable forgotten poets of former generations are generally well forgotten.   Among the comparatively few whose works survive, it is not difficult to find our way. But our own day — though we sometimes accuse it of being exclusively absorbed in machinery and money-getting — is as prolific as any in the past. There is a bewildering number of minor poets, expert craftsmen, as like as peas in a pod. Are there any major ones? If vivid individuality, command of vigorous and stirring rhythms, and almost universal popularity count, Rudyard Kipling (1865–   ) must be considered.

Born in Bombay, India, of British parents, Kipling was sent to school in England, and returned to India to do newspaper work. His first volume of verse, *Departmental Ditties*, appeared in 1886, his first volume of short stories, *Plain Tales from the Hills*, in 1887. Since then he has produced many volumes of short stories; a vivid study of native Indian life, strung on a thread of narrative (*Kim*); one (less successful) novel (*The Light That Failed*); a series of fascinating animal stories (*The Jungle Book* and *The Second Jungle Book*); a group of stories of old times in England, which the good fairy, Puck, tells to two modern children (*Puck of Pook's Hill*);[1] and many volumes of verse.

The most popular of modern short-story writers, Kipling is also the most popular of modern poets. The qualities that made for his first success in the one field made no less for his first success in the other. Sharp eyes and a good memory, the habit formed in his journalist days of mixing, comrade-wise, with all sorts of people and turning them into "copy"; a talent for getting to the heart of a matter with a remarkable economy of words; a style that is plain

---

[1] These stories, done with extraordinary vividness and charm, are the finest sort of introduction to English history. It is a pity that more history has not been written as Kipling writes it in *Puck of Pook's Hill*.

and concrete and at the same time extraordinarily racy —
add to these a lively imagination and a command of swinging, pulse-stirring rhythms, and Kipling the short-story
writer becomes Kipling the poet. Life in India, now with
the native, now with the officers and their families, now
with the British "Tommy" at army-posts and on campaigns, gave him his opportunity. The color of the East,
the glories of Empire, the songs, the follies and the (altogether unsentimental) heroisms of the British soldier
were his themes. It was an unworked field and his poems
ran like wildfire through the English-reading world. Twenty
years ago everybody was reading and almost everybody
was reciting *Departmental Ditties* and the *Barrack Room
Ballads* —"Gunga Din," and the "Ballad of East and
West," and "Mandalay"—

> For the wind is in the palm-trees, and the temple
>   bells they say
> "Come you back, you British soldier, come you back to
>   Mandalay."

Since his return to England, Kipling has become the interpreter in verse of the marvels of modern invention.
No one can read "McAndrew's Hymn" without sharing
the old Scotch engineer's feeling that the steamship with
its throbbing engines and purring dynamos is a living and
sentient thing —

> Fra' skylight lift to furnace-bars, backed, bolted,
>   braced and stayed,
> An' singin' like the Mornin' Stars for joy that they
>   were made.

And as if to prove that with the passing of the years, he
has lost none of his pristine vigor, Kipling has only recently

(September 6th, 1929) published the "Hymn of the Triumphant Airman" ("Flying East to West at over 1000
m.p.h.") —

> Oh, long had we paltered
> With bridle and girth
> Ere those horses were haltered
> That gave us the Earth.
>
> Ere the Flame and the Fountain,
> The Spark and the wheel,
> Sank Ocean and Mountain
> Alike 'neath our keel.
>
> But the Wind in her blowing
> The bird on the wind,
> Made naught of our going,
> And left us behind.
>
> Till the gale was outdriven,
> The gull overflown,
> And there matched us in Heaven
> The Sun God alone.

Now and again, he has turned to graver themes. Of all
his poems, the one which will probably live longest is the
note of warning which he sounded on the occasion of Queen
Victoria's second jubilee in 1897, — a plea for humility in
a moment of national triumph —

> God of our fathers, known of old,
> Lord of our far-flung battle-line,
> Beneath whose awful hand we hold
> Dominion over palm and pine,
> Lord God of Hosts, be with us yet,
> Lest we forget, lest we forget!

> The tumult and the shouting dies,
> The captains and the Kings depart,
> Still stands thine ancient sacrifice,
> An humble and a contrite heart,
> Lord God of Hosts, be with us yet,
> Lest we forget, lest we forget!

But it is not often that Kipling rises above inspired journalism to the subtleties and exaltations of great poetry.

Like Kipling, John Masefield[1] (1875–   ) has touched life at many points and interpreted it with tremendous zest.   Born in England, he ran away to sea as a youth, had a brief experience on sailing ships, and then "took to the road" in America, earning a living by odd jobs.   He loved poetry, and, as he could, bought cheap editions of the poets to read on Sunday.   Chancing in this way upon a volume of Chaucer, he was so delighted that he began, as he has said, to read with "passion and system."   In turn, he read and tried to imitate Keats, Shelley, Milton and Shakespeare.   In 1897 the self-educated young poet returned to England and began to coin his varied experiences into verse.   His *Salt-Water Ballads* (1902) attracted some attention.   He tried his hand at prose stories and dramas.   In 1911 he achieved his first great success with a long narrative poem, *The Everlasting Mercy*, and followed it with other narrative poems, of which the best are *The Widow in the Bye Street*, *Dauber*, and *Reynard the Fox*.

Though Kipling is the most widely read of contemporary poets, it is possible that Masefield's work will have the longer life.   *The Everlasting Mercy*, *The Widow in the Bye Street* and *The Daffodil Fields* are starkly realistic narratives of the lives of lowly, and generally quite unlovely, people.   · Masefield never sentimentalizes over them; but

[1] Masefield was appointed poet laureate, May 10th, 1930.

his sympathetic understanding, his ability to perceive and reveal the spark of divinity that may be hidden within the filthiest human shell, lift these stories from drabness into beauty. And what splendid vigor there is in these, and in his later narrative verse!

Of late Masefield has turned to other themes. *Reynard the Fox* pictures the fox-hunt; *Right Royal,* the point-to-point steeplechase; *King Cole,* the circus travelers of the road. Of these you will enjoy *Reynard* most. It will go down to history as the classic of that most picturesque of sports — the color and zest of the human side, and the fox who pits his skill against the skill of man and horse and hound — and wins!

You will enjoy too some of his stirring lyrics, especially "Sea-Fever" and "Cargoes."

I have left to the end of this group a poet who, if chronology determined our order, would have been named before Kipling and Masefield, and might have been listed with Tennyson and Browning; but Thomas Hardy (1840–1928), though he began writing verse as early as 1860, has been recognized as a great poet only within recent years. I place him here, because, of the poets of this modern group, he seems to me most likely to be numbered among the immortals.

Hardy was born near Dorchester in that southwestern section of England known as Wessex. He studied architecture in London, but, abandoning that profession, returned to his native soil, to write. Fame came to him first as a novelist. The eleven novels which he produced between 1871 and 1895 are about his own people — the Wessex villagers and peasants and gentry among whom he spent his life.[1]

[1] See page 529 ff.

Hardy's are not "happy" novels. They are too full of the mischances and tragedies of life. Nor are Hardy's poems generally "happy." There is not a trace of hardness or callousness or cynicism in them. They are full of the tenderest sympathy. But they are the honest expressions of a mind which is incapable of accepting the belief which more optimistic people hold, that this is a well-ordered universe, and that suffering in this world is part of a divine plan which involves compensation in the next. Hardy was an "agnostic," in that while he did not deny, he frankly admitted that he did not know; and the beauty of many of his noblest poems — noble in their utter sincerity — springs from his pity for the futility of life in a universe whose purpose he cannot understand.

"Is it," even the fields and flocks and trees seem to ask,

> Is it that some high Plan betides,
> As yet not understood,
> Of Evil stormed by Good . . .
>
> Thus things around. No answerer I . . .
> Meanwhile the winds and rains,
> And Earth's old glooms and pains
> Are still the same, and gladdest Life Death neighbours nigh.

Again and again this mood finds poignant expression. Here are stanzas from "The Darkling Thrush," written in the dying moments of the nineteenth century.

> I leant upon a coppice gate
> When Frost was spectre-gray,
> And Winter's dregs made desolate
> The weakening eye of day . . .
>
> At once a voice outburst among
> The bleak twigs overhead

In a full-hearted evensong
Of joy illimited;
An aged thrush, frail, gaunt and small,
In blast-beruffled plume,
Had chosen thus to fling his soul
Upon the growing gloom.

So little cause for carollings
Of such ecstatic sound
Was written in terrestrial things
Afar or nigh around,
That I could think there trembled through
His happy good-night air
Some blessed Hope, whereof he knew
And I was unaware.

One hears it again in the wistfulness of "The Oxen":

Christmas Eve, and twelve of the clock,
"Now they are all on their knees,"
An elder said as we sat in a flock
By the embers in hearthside ease.

We pictured the meek, mild creatures where
They dwelt in their strawy pen,
Nor did it occur to one of us there
To doubt they were kneeling then.

So fair a fancy few would weave
In these years! Yet, I feel,
If someone said on Christmas Eve,
"Come, see the oxen kneel

"In the lonely barton by yonder coomb
Our childhood used to know,"
I should go with him in the gloom,
Hoping it might be so.

His pity and tenderness for human suffering, to him so purposeless, find expression again and again — as in these last two stanzas of the "Lines to an Unborn Pauper Child":

> Fain would I, dear, find some shut plot
> Of earth's wide wold for thee, where not
> One tear, one qualm
> Should break the calm.
> But I am weak as thou and bare;
> No man can change the common lot to rare.
>
> Must come and bide.   And such are we —
> Unreasoning, sanguine, visionary —
> That I can hope
> Health, love, friends, scope,
> In full for thee; can dream thou'lt find
> Joys seldom yet attained by human kind!

In reading the poems just quoted, you will have noticed how plain, simple, and direct is the style. It is almost a homely simplicity, with something of the downrightness of the Wessex peasant speech which Hardy reproduced with such fidelity in his novels. There is no decoration, no apparent effort to produce word-music, no avoidance of homely, "unpoetic" words. It is curiously monosyllabic. When non-Saxon, polysyllabic words, words that by contrast we may call "learned" — when such words do find their way into his poems, they have an effect of strangeness in that homespun company —

> Must come and bide.   And such are we —
> Unreasoning, sanguine, visionary —

There is no apparent effort to produce word-music; the effect is of mere thinking aloud, in natural speech; and the measures are as simple, as short, as free from intricacies of structure, as in the old folk-ballads; and yet I do not

Voices from Things Growing in a Churchyard

These flowers are I, poor Fanny Hurd,
        Sir or Madam,
A little girl here sepultured.
Once I flit-fluttered like a bird
Above the grass, as now I wave
In daisy shapes above my grave,
      All day cheerily,
      All night eerily! . . .

The Lady Gertrude, proud, high-bred,
        Sir or Madam,
Am I — this laurel that shades your head;
Into its veins I have stilly sped,
And made them of me; and my leaves now shine,
As did my satins superfine,
      All day cheerily,
      All night eerily! . . .

I'm old Squire Audeley Grey, who grew,
        Sir or Madam,
A-weary of life, and in scorn withdrew;
Till anon I clambered up anew
As ivy-green, when my ache was stayed,
And in that attire I have longtime gayed
      All day cheerily,
      All night eerily!

And so they breathe, these masks, to each
        Sir or Madam
Who lingers there, and their lively speech
Affords an interpreter much to teach,
As their murmurous accents seem to come
Thence hitheraround in a radiant hum,
      All day cheerily,
      All night eerily!

know of any other lyrics of modern times that can ﹖
the heart and hold the soul in thrall as these plain t﹖
Hardy's —

WAITING BOTH

A star looks down at me,
And says: "Here I and you
Stand each in our degree:
What do you mean to do —
Mean to do?"

I say: "For all I know,
Wait, and let Time go by,
Till my change come," — "Just so."
The star says: "So mean I: —
So mean I."

PAYING CALLS

I went by footpath and by stile
Beyond where bustle ends,
Strayed here a mile and there a mile,
And called upon some friends.

On certain ones I had not seen
For years past did I call,
And then on others, who had been
The oldest friends of all.

It was the time of midsummer
When they had used to roam;
But now, though tempting was the air,
I found them all at home.

I spoke to one and other of them
By mound and stone and tree
Of things we had done ere days were dim,
But they spoke not to me.

But not all of Hardy's lyrics are about sad things. Here is a cheerier note to end on:

> This is the weather the cuckoo likes,
>   And so do I;
> When showers betumble the chestnut spikes,
> And nestlings fly:
> And the little brown nightingale bills his best,
> And they sit outside at "The Travellers' Rest,"
> And maids come forth sprig-muslin drest,
> And citizens dream of the south and west,
>   And so do I.
>
> This is the weather the shepherd shuns,
>   And so do I;
> When beeches drip in browns and duns
> And thresh, and ply;
> And hill-hid tides throb, throe on throe,
> And meadow rivulets overflow,
> And drops on gate-bars hang in a row,
> And rooks in families homeward go,
>   And so do I.

The "Shakespearean" quality of Hardy's delineation of his peasants, in the novels, has often been pointed out; this little song seems to have stepped out of the pages of *As You Like It.*

The most comprehensive collections of Hardy's lyrics are the *Collected Poems* of 1920 and the *Late Lyrics and Earlier* of 1922. His most notable longer work in verse is *The Dynasts* (1904–1908), a sort of apocalyptic vision of human life, couched in dramatic form, and focused upon the Napoleonic Wars. When Hardy died in 1928, his ashes were buried in the "Poet's Corner" of Westminster Abbey. Few English poets have had a better right to burial there.

There are other modern British poets whose work you will wish to read — among them Robert Bridges (1844–1930), who, like Hardy, came late into his own as a poet,[1] and who has written many poems of a delicate and subtle beauty; A. E. Housman (1859–   ) whose *Shropshire Lad* (1896) and *Last Poems* (1922) contain a little sheaf ballad-like in their simplicity but most exquisitely wrought; W. B. Yeats (born in Ireland, 1865) whose *Lake Isle of Innisfree* is one of the loveliest of modern lyrics and in whom the Celtic imagination finds its best interpreter; and Walter de la Mare (1873–   ), who is master of a most delicate fancy; but, to start with, the reading of Kipling, Masefield and Hardy will afford you a very fair sample of some of the most significant and interesting things in modern English poetry.

---

[1] Bridges preceded Masefield as poet laureate.

INDEX

INDEX